S0-AFB-400

LETTERS OF C. S. LEWIS

BOOKS BY C. S. LEWIS

A Grief Observed
George MacDonald: An Anthology
Mere Christianity
Miracles
The Abolition of Man
The Great Divorce
The Problem of Pain
The Screwtape Letters (with "Screwtape Proposes a Toast")
The Weight of Glory
The Four Loves
Till We Have Faces
Surprised by Joy: The Shape of My Early Life
Reflections on the Psalms
Letters to Malcolm, Chiefly on Prayer
The Personal Heresy
The World's Last Night: And Other Essays
Poems
The Dark Tower: And Other Stories
Of Other Worlds: Essays and Stories
Narrative Poems
A Mind Awake: An Anthology of C. S. Lewis
All My Road Before Me
The Business of Heaven: Daily Readings from C. S. Lewis
Present Concerns: Journalistic Essays
Spirits in Bondage: A Cycle of Lyrics
On Stories: And Other Essays on Literature

ALSO AVAILABLE FROM HarperCollins

The Chronicles of Narnia
The Magician's Nephew
The Lion, the Witch and the Wardrobe
The Horse and His Boy
Prince Caspian
The Voyage of the Dawn Treader
The Silver Chair
The Last Battle

LETTERS OF
C. S. LEWIS

<small>EDITED AND WITH A MEMOIR BY W. H. LEWIS
REVISED AND ENLARGED EDITION
EDITED BY WALTER HOOPER</small>

HarperOne
An Imprint of HarperCollinsPublishers

LETTERS OF C. S. LEWIS. Copyright © 1966 by C. S. Lewis Pte. Ltd. and
W. H. Lewis. Copyright © 1988 by C. S. Lewis Pte. Ltd. All rights
reserved. Printed in the United States of America. No part of this book
may be used or reproduced in any manner whatsoever without written
permission except in the case of brief quotations embodied in critical
articles and reviews. For information, address HarperCollins Publishers,
195 Broadway, New York, NY 10007.

HarperCollins books may be purchased for educational, business, or
sales promotional use. For information, please email the Special Markets
Department at SPsales@harpercollins.com.

Originally published in 1966 by Harcourt. Revised Harvest edition
printed in 1993.

FIRST EDITION

Library of Congress Cataloging-in-Publication Data

Names: Lewis, C. S. (Clive Staples), 1898-1963, author. | Lewis, W. H.
   (Warren Hamilton), 1895-1973, editor. | Hooper, Walter, editor.
Title: Letters of C. S. Lewis / C. S. Lewis ; edited and with a memoir by
   W. H. Lewis ; revised and enlarged edition edited by Walter Hooper.
Description: First edition. | San Francisco : HarperOne, 2017. | Includes
   index.
Identifiers: LCCN 2016030642 | ISBN 9780062643568 (paperback) |
   ISBN 9780062565556 (e-book)
Subjects: LCSH: Lewis, C. S. (Clive Staples), 1898-1963. Correspondence.
   | Authors, English—20th century—Correspondence. | Christian
   converts—Great Britain—Correspondence. | BISAC: LITERARY
   COLLECTIONS / Letters. | RELIGION / Christianity / Literature
   & the Arts. | RELIGION / Christianity / General.
Classification: LCC PR6023.E926 Z48 2017 | DDC 823/.912 [B]—dc23
   LC record available at https://lccn.loc.gov/2016030642

17 18 19 20 21   LSC   10 9 8 7 6 5 4 3 2 1

To
All Those Overseas Friends Who
Helped Him in the Lean Years

CONTENTS

INTRODUCTION

This revision of the *Letters of C. S. Lewis* differs in many small ways from the first edition of 1966. And, paradoxically, it is as close to being a restoration of W. H. Lewis's original book as I am able to make it. The small differences and the attempt at restoration came about in this way.

For years the Estate of C. S. Lewis have been gathering Lewis's letters together for publication as his Collected Letters. As he corresponded with so many people the letters could run to, perhaps, half a dozen volumes. Such an undertaking as that cannot be hurried, because the Estate want to be sure they have found as many as they can before publication begins.

Meanwhile, such is the interest in Lewis's letters that Collins Publishers decided to observe the twenty-fifth anniversary of his death by reprinting the most interesting and diverse selection of his letters there is. The Estate were pleased with this way of celebrating the anniversary and, remembering that I had given 'Warnie' Lewis some assistance with the book, they instructed me to correct whatever errors it might contain. None of us had any idea what a surprise we were in for.

But at this point a story connected with the book is called for. Shortly after it was published, a good many of those who had lent their letters to Warnie Lewis felt that there should be a collection of C. S. Lewis's letters in his own city and university—The Bodleian Library in Oxford. I did not, however, move fast enough for the nun Jack Lewis referred to in one of these letters as 'his elder sister in the Faith'. This was Sister Penelope of the Community of St Mary the Virgin, in Wantage. When Professor Clyde S. Kilby asked if she would give her letters from C. S. Lewis to a collection he was making for Wheaton College in the United States she responded by telling me that I was dragging my feet over a *British* collection of C. S. Lewis's letters and papers. She propelled me into action by giving the fifty-six letters she had from Lewis to the Bodleian. That was in September 1967, and Sister Penelope's generous gift was followed by so many others that in February 1968 I published an announcement of the Bodleian collection of Lewis manuscripts in *The Times Literary Supplement*. Other notices about the collection have appeared since then, and Sister Penelope's gift is now one of a great many literary treasures which may be read in the Bodleian's magnificent 'Duke Humfrey Library', a description of which is found in Lewis's letter to his father of 25th February 1928. The collection in Wheaton College has flourished as well and, happily, in 1968 an arrangement was agreed upon which has resulted in the two libraries sending one another copies of the letters each collects.

One result of this is that many of those writing about C. S. Lewis are able to see either the originals or copies of the letters. And those who have glanced through this book will have noticed what a large number of the ones published here were written to Jack's father and brother. Most of these come from a single source. Mr Albert Lewis, Warnie and

Jack's father, preserved nearly every letter he received. When he died the family papers were brought to Oxford. Over a period of years Warnie typed the whole lot, including other documents such as his brother's diary. The pages were bound into eleven volumes and given the title *Lewis Papers: Memoirs of the Lewis Family 1850–1930*. The original of this typed work is in Wheaton College and there is a copy in the Bodleian. Once when I borrowed them from Warnie he said, in a letter of 1 April 1967, that he hoped I would take the greatest care of them 'for there is only this one copy in existence, and the originals from which all material was drawn were burnt by Jack in 1936'. Without the originals, it was the *Lewis Papers* which Warnie himself had to turn to for many of the letters contained in this volume.

It was the *Lewis Papers* which the Lewis brothers' friend, George Sayer, had to turn to while writing his notable and delightful biography *Jack: C. S. Lewis and His Times* (1988). Much careful research went into that book, and when reading it in proof I was struck by his discovery that Warnie's transcription of a passage from Jack's diary was quite different from what is found in the *Lewis Papers*. Later, when instructed to correct whatever errors there might be in this book, I remembered Mr Sayer's discovery. It was this which caused me to suspect that preparing this book for Collins might require as long as a week. If Warnie had made a mistake in transcribing one passage, might there be others?

I began this work by comparing the published letters with the originals and I was very surprised to discover what a free hand Warnie had taken in editing them. There were several hundred minor alterations in the first dozen pages — so many that I sent a xerox of the corrected pages to Collins and the Estate. Both felt that it would be dishonest to advertise as Lewis's letters anything other that what he actually wrote, and that this 'Anniversary Edition' must not contain anything which would have to be contradicted in the Collected Letters. Collins decided that it was worth while resetting the whole book.

I had been working on these letters for four months when I reached the inauspicious day of Friday, 13 November 1987. The realization of just how many changes I was having to make caused me to imagine Warnie looming behind me, much annoyed. I felt so uncomfortable about what I was doing that I wrote to George Sayer, asking for advice. What helped as much as anything was a conversation I had that evening with Father John Tolkien. He, too, had known Jack and Warnie well, and over dinner I explained what was causing me such uneasiness. 'Oh, I'm not surprised about the errors,' he said. 'Warnie was very *Victorian*. They didn't think the way a modern editor would.' On another occasion, when he saw I still felt as if I were betraying Warnie, he said, 'Remember that the same thing happened with Queen Victoria's diary. Of course the Queen put down what she wanted to say, but after her death her daughter changed it to what she thought her mother *should* have said. So it was practised in the highest circles!'

While it is necessary for me to account for what I have done, it is, to my mind, just as necessary to point out that Warnie did nothing that a sane man would call *wrong* in the way he went about his job. In nearly every instance he believed that he was correcting or improving his brother's letters, doing for Jack what Jack might have done for himself had he been the editor. Most of the corrections I've made will be invisible to all except those who sit down with both editions and search for them.

Even so, there are a good many instances in which words have been changed for what I believe was meant as improvement. In the letter of 20 June 1918 Jack describes how, coming back from the War, he goes down to visit his old tutor, Mr Kirkpatrick: 'I opened the gate of Kirk's garden almost with stealth and went on past the house, to the vegetable garden . . . And there among the cabbages, in his shirt and "Sunday" trousers, there sure enough was the old man, still digging and smoking his villainous pipe.' I am unable to see why Warnie, such a discriminating lover of words, thought he could enhance Jack's picture of the 'Great Knock' by giving him a 'horrible' pipe instead of a 'villainous' one. Mr Kirkpatrick would have been the first to point out the different meanings.

Nearly always it was the family letters which got 'improved' the most. I laughed out loud when I came to the end of Jack's letter to Warnie of Christmas Day 1931. The brothers were just becoming familiar with Russian literature and, after telling Warnie that he'd started reading *The Brothers Karamazov*, Jack went on to say that he had not forgotten Warnie's beginning for a Russian novel: 'Alexey Poldorovna lived on a hill. He cried a great deal.' I'm sure Warnie was only trying to make it more entertaining when he substituted for this a different story: 'Olga Opitubitch lived on a hill. She had two cows and eleven hens and a wart on one finger and cried a great deal.'

Those who own the edition of 1966 will not find that I have got rid of poor Olga. She was never in the book, having been deleted along with much else by the publishers. And this brings me to the second difference between this book and the first edition. Mr Sayer, in a letter of 18 November 1987, urged me to correct all the errors I found. He suggested as well that the letters 'be annotated a little'. It was this suggestion which led me to do what I could in restoring some of the features of the original book.

I suspect that from the time Warnie agreed to write a biography of his brother for Jocelyn ('Jock') Gibb of Geoffrey Bles Ltd, each had a different kind of book in mind. Two years later, when the book Warnie called 'C. S. Lewis: A Biography' was published as the *Letters of C. S. Lewis*, he was furious. A list of his grievances can be found in his diary for 16 April 1966. This is reproduced in those selections from it edited by the late Professor Clyde S. Kilby and Mrs Marjorie Lamp Mead and published as *Brothers and Friends: Diaries of Major Warren Hamilton Lewis* (San Francisco, 1982). In their Introduction to the book the editors say: 'While the supreme tragedy of his life was certainly the premature loss of Jack, Warren Lewis also struggled mightily with the disease of alcoholism. He was to battle this agony for over forty years. A man of integrity, and of strength even in his weakness, he knew that his occasional though intense fits of depression left him sadly ill-fitted to cope with the attractions of alcohol.'

Mrs Mead knows much more about how Warnie viewed his own problems with alcohol than I. And there are possibly others who know more about his editing of these letters than I do. Even so, because Warnie's grievances about this book have been made public, I believe I should do what I can to make things clearer than they are. I saw a great deal of Warnie from being with him most of the time he was working on the book, and I know how all but impossible it was for his publisher to discuss it with him. Besides the alcoholism Professor Kilby and Mrs Mead have written about, Warnie seemed to me to live in constant fear of bankruptcy. When Jack died, he believed that he couldn't afford to go on living at The Kilns, where they had been since 1930, and he bought a small, semi-detached house nearby in 51 Ringwood Road. When I came to know him in January 1964 he had already advertised for letters from his brother and was copying them on his typewriter at The Kilns. I had my own typewriter there and was helping him. After only three weeks he began drinking, and set off for Ireland and Our Lady of Lourdes Hospital in Drogheda. He had made a number of visits there since 1947 because, even though he drank during the day, the nuns of the Medical Missionaries of Mary looked after him with wonderful kindness. Prompted by Lady Dunbar of Hempriggs, and my own worries about the biography, I wrote asking if he wanted assistance in getting home. His reply of 8 February 1964 reveals that even then he had in mind something very different from what Jock Gibb expected: 'I am my old self once again, and hope to get home under my own steam about the 18th. When I get back I intend to see what sort of a hand I make at a "Life and Letters" of dear Jack. Not exactly an L. & L. in the usual sense, for of course I shall not use anything he has himself told us in *Surprised by Joy*. It will be more what the French

17th Cent. writers used to call *Mémoires pour Servir* etc. ...'
That is, Memories in order to help the understanding of a
man, or a period. I am told that a good example of this kind
of thing is Voltaire's posthumous *Mémoires pour servir à
l'histoire de M. de Voltaire,* ed. Louis Chaudon (1786).

When he returned to The Kilns I spent a good many
hours every day copying letters while Warnie wrote the
early chapters of his 'Life and Letters', combining reminiscences about Jack's childhood with a good many family letters. Unlike Jack, he composed all his books on a typewriter,
including this one, which he worked on at breakneck speed.
Although I kept the names and addresses of those whose letters I copied and returned, I regret terribly that Warnie did
not preserve any information about most of the people he
corresponded with. I still do not know who some of them
were. Everything went well until 19 May when, with most
of the furniture and books still at The Kilns, he spent his
first night at Ringwood Road. After a short while he began
drinking and returned to Drogheda. He'd been there six
weeks when I went over on 21 July, hoping I could persuade
him to come home. He made it clear that his only reason for
returning to Oxford was to 'finish the biography of Jack'.

When we got back on 27 July I moved into 51 Ringwood
Road with him. He disliked the house so much that, while
we slept there at night, he spent his days at The Kilns. The
book was finished to his satisfaction the second week in
October and, leaving me to get a copy typed for the pub-
lisher and help his housekeeper move everything out of The
Kilns, he slipped off to Ireland where he remained until 29
October. This was the time when Jock Gibb most needed

to talk with him about the book. However, I see from my diary that Warnie and I set off for yet another trip to Ireland on 14 November. It was during this visit to Drogheda that Warnie dictated a letter to his literary agent giving his publisher 'rights *carte blanche* to do whatever he wants' with the book. This may have been just as well because his problems with alcohol were worse in 1965 than in 1964. In May of 1965 I had to move into Oxford upon being appointed Chaplain of Wadham College, and this meant I could not see him every day.

I mention these peregrinations to illustrate how difficult it was for Warnie to settle to the book. But even if we had stayed put at The Kilns I'm not convinced that this would have made any great difference. Warnie was not interested in writing what most of us would think a standard kind of biography. As he said, his was meant to be of the sort the French called *Mémoires pour servir* etc. In fact, a work very like the *Lewis Papers* in which letters and diary entries are broken here and there with helpful notes and recollections by the editor. This explains, too, why he included entries from his brother's diary in this book. Of the approximately 230,000 words which made up the original 'Biography' only about 23,300 words were narration, and most of that came in the early chapters. It was a book which I liked very much in its original form, but he would probably have just as much trouble getting a publisher interested in it today as he did nearly twenty-five years ago.

I suspect that a suggestion made by Jack in 1962 could have played some part in the kind of letters he chose for this book. On his desk Warnie kept a letter written by his brother during that summer, when Jack was in the Acland Nursing Home and Warnie was in Drogheda. Jack was afraid that his death might leave his brother penniless, and in the letter he urged Warnie to try to keep the wolf from the door by collecting his *lettres spirituelles* and 'making a book of them'. The pastoral letters are the ones which Warnie cared for most anyway.

When the book was published Warnie learned that Jock Gibb had hired Christopher Derrick, a writer and former pupil of Jack's, to turn the 'Biography' into a volume of letters. In his diary entry of 16 April 1966 he says that Mr Derrick's 'worst outrage' was including Jack's philosophical letters to Owen Barfield about 'some withering discourse on the nothingness of the utterness or some similar topic!' It was Jock Gibb who chose to include the letters to Mr Barfield. Sometimes, however, Warnie failed to include letters to other close friends because he never bothered to ask them. For instance, when I suggested that he ask Professor Tolkien for his letters from Jack he said, 'Oh, *he* wouldn't have any. They talked to one another all the time!' I mentioned this to Professor Tolkien when I was at his house one day. '*Of course* I've got some letters from Jack!' he said. 'But Warnie will have to *ask* me for them.' When I mentioned this to Warnie, he said, 'You must have misunderstood him. Tollers couldn't have any letters from Jack!' As with some other letters Warnie didn't believe in, those to Professor Tolkien will appear in the Collected Letters.

Warnie and I did not know that the 'Biography' was being transformed into a volume of letters until I heard from Jock Gibb on 11 January 1966. He sent me a list of people to whom Jack had written, asking if I could persuade Warnie to supply their full names. I could certainly sympathize with him as he had no way of knowing who the recipient of a letter beginning, say, 'Dear Joan' might be. I sent the list to Warnie, suggesting that I try to stop Jock changing his book. Warnie wrote on 12 January saying: 'Here is such information as I have been able to collect. . . . It has been a very tiresome job for an old sick man, and if only I'd known when I thought I was writing a straightforward account of Jack what I was letting myself in for, I'd never have tackled it. In fact I'm turning over in my mind consulting Barfield to see if I can withdraw and burn the MS and be rid of the torment which it is putting me to. Naturally I cannot at this length of time remember who all these correspondents were, but I've done my best—and I'm doing no more. I never want to see or hear of that book again, and in fact have long since ceased to regard it as *my* book at all. I wouldn't write that "sharp letter" to Jock if I were you; it will lay you open to the retort that it is none of your business—and anyway I don't give a d**n when the thing appears. It has by now assumed the aspect of one of those films which, from the titles, seem to have about twenty-five authors!'

There are two main differences between the 'Biography' and the *Letters*. Jock Gibb was afraid to publish such a large book, and the number of letters was cut by about half. The other difference is that only about one half of Warnie's excellent narrative was brought together into the 'Memoir'. That I regret more than anything because Warnie was a very good writer. However, having decided what cuts must be made, Jock Gibb hired Christopher Derrick as editor.

I have since come to know and respect Mr Derrick very much, and he has kindly supplied me with this account, dated 16 November 1987, about his editing of the book: 'Here's how I see the question. Over the years, I have done a good many jobs of editorial carpentry for various publishers, ranging from petty correcting to full ghosting. This was one such job among many. Jock Gibb asked me to do it, on lines specified by himself: I did it to the best of my ability and to his satisfaction: I feel neither pride nor shame at the outcome, apart from the general satisfaction of pleasing a friend and *ad hoc* employer. . . . Do tell this aspect of the story exactly as you see fit, with or without any mention of my name. I don't suppose you'll want to cast me for the villain of the piece! In so far as there is any villain, it is doubtlessly the drink, as then making it impossible for Warnie to do a proper job or even supervise it. . . . Some further blame attaches, I suppose, to that very understandable error of judgement on Jock's part—his fear that a hot property would die on him, and his consequent reluctance to invest a lot of money in it. The vast present scale of the CSL-industry shows how wrong he was! But he wasn't making an *idiotic* mistake, recognizable as such at the time.'

Such then is the story of this book in so far as I am able to reconstruct it. If Warnie were still alive I believe he would consider all my corrections as pedantic, not really necessary but not wrong either. I think he would be more cheerful about my attempts at restoration, a job he incidently helped with by giving me the original typescript of his book. A number of female correspondents were willing to lend their letters to him on condition that he kept their identities secret.

He did this by giving them fictitious names. I passed these made-up names on to his publisher who decided instead that the letters to these different women should all be designated 'To A Lady'. The problem with this is that many have supposed there to be only *one* lady. My solution has been to reinstate the fictitious names but using inverted commas so that the reader will know that 'Mrs Arnold', 'Mrs Ashton' and the others between inverted commas are not real names.

The biggest difference between the edition of 1966 and this one is the 'thickening' which I felt was needed. It suited the kind of book Warnie was writing to quote only short excerpts from most letters. He rarely quoted a complete letter. Because this book is meant to be a selection of his brother's letters, and not a biography, I have extended some of the excerpts. For instance, it seemed to me a pity that Warnie gave only three sentences of the letter of 20 July 1940 about the conception of *The Screwtape Letters,* and I have quoted all he says about that book. In some places, where he gave most of a letter, I have given all of it. This edition is also more substantial for having in it a few complete letters which Warnie may not have known about. One of these is the letter of Dr Warfield Firor of 15 October 1949 in which Jack discusses Old Age. There are many more superb letters to Dr Firor, all of which will go into the Collected Letters.

Readers will discover that I took very seriously Mr Sayer's suggestion about the letters being 'annotated a little'. My annotations do not, however, include any of those bits and pieces of Warnie's narrative that were left out of the 'Memoir'. It would have been as impossible to make anything out of them as to put Humpty Dumpty together again.

Instead, I have supplied footnotes where I thought they were called for, as well as short notes providing such biographical information as was needed to make the letters clearer.

My task would have been even harder had it not been for all those friends whose advice helped so much. I am particularly grateful to Owen Barfield, Father John Tolkien, George Sayer, Christopher Derrick, Father Paul King, Ben Sykes and Madame Eliane Tixier.

One thing remains to be told. After all the heart-ache of remembering Warnie's initial disappointment over what happened to this book, it was surely appropriate that the last editorial problem to be faced was as delightful as Jack Lewis himself. He loathed having to date letters, and when he did the dates could be off by months, or even years. The penultimate letter in this book is dated 25 October 1963. Dear old Jock Gibb had wanted the book to end with a particular letter in which Jack expresses his regret that old age, like Autumn, doesn't last. The problem for him was that Warnie had given it the date '30 September'. To make it the last letter in the book Jock changed the date to '27 October'. When I looked at a copy of the original I found written in Jack's own hand — 31 September 1963. Nothing could persuade me to insert an ugly little '[*sic.*]' beside that date.

Walter Hooper
Holy Saturday 1988
Oxford

MEMOIR OF C. S. LEWIS

My brother was born in one of the inner suburbs of Belfast on 29 November 1898, when I was nearly three-and-a-half years old. I first remember him, dimly, as a vociferous disturber of my domestic peace and a rival claimant to my mother's attention: few detailed and particular memories remain of our first years together, though during these first years—up to our move to the new house in the spring of 1905—we laid the foundations of an intimate friendship that was the greatest happiness of my life and lasted unbroken until his death fifty-eight years later.

Looking back now upon the pattern of his life and work, I feel that one particular and even trivial circumstance in our early life together needs some emphasis. I refer to the wetness of Irish weather, and the nervousness of the parents of that time about damp and exposure. By the standards of present-day childhood in England, we spent an extraordinary amount of our time shut up indoors. We would gaze out of our nursery window at the slanting rain and the grey skies, and there, beyond a mile or so of sodden meadow, we would see the dim high line of the Castlereagh Hills—our world's limit, a distant land, strange and unattainable. But we always had pencils, paper, chalk, and paintboxes, and this recurring imprisonment gave us occasion and stimulus to develop the habit of creative imagination. We learnt to draw:

my brother made his first attempts at writing: together we devised the imaginary country of 'Boxen', which proliferated hugely and became our solace and joy for many years to come. And so, in circumstances that might have been merely dull and depressing, my brother's gifts began to develop; and it may not be fanciful to see, in that childhood staring out to unattainable hills, some first beginnings of a vision and viewpoint that ran through the work of his maturity.

The highlight of our year was the annual seaside holiday. Children of today, accustomed as they are to be driven casually to the coast on any fine Sunday afternoon, can hardly imagine the excitement, the bustle and glory of preparation that these holidays entailed, the unique moment of arrival. Of many such holidays, two pictures remain in my memory. The first is of my father's gloomy detachment. He would sometimes come down for the week-end, but he never stayed with his wife and children throughout this summer holiday. Urgent business was his excuse—he was a solicitor—and he may also have felt that eleven months of our company every year was more than enough. It may have gone deeper than that. I never met a man more wedded to a dull routine, or less capable of extracting enjoyment from life. A night spent out of his house was a penance to him: a holiday he loathed, having not the faintest conception of how to amuse himself. I can still see him on his occasional visits to the seaside, walking moodily up and down the beach, hands in trouser pockets, eyes on the ground, every now and then giving a heartrending yawn and pulling out his watch.

Then, in the course of one holiday, my brother made the momentous decision to change his name. Disliking 'Clive', and feeling his various baby-names to be beneath his dignity, he marched up to my mother, put a forefinger on his chest, and announced 'He is Jacksie'. He stuck to this next day and thereafter, refusing to answer to any other name: Jacksie it had to be, a name contracted to Jacks and then to Jack. So to his family and his intimate friends, he was Jack for life: and Jack he will be for the rest of this book.

Looking back in later years on our childhood, he once remarked to me that for one thing, and one thing only, he envied the modern child. In 1904 the rain kept us indoors, whether at home or in cramped seaside lodgings: the child of today splashes about outside, in gumboots and oilskins and sou'wester. Otherwise, not for a king's ransom did Jack wish to be a modern child, facing the stress and anxiety of today's world. This was no blind nostalgia, no mere regret for vanished class privilege and financial security: what he sighed for was the lost simplicity of country pleasures, the empty sky, the unspoilt hills, the white silent roads on which you could hear the rattle of a farm cart half a mile away.

The pleasures—all but unattainable to the modern child—were ours, and more especially after our move in 1905. Our new house, 'Little Lea', was on the borderline—suburb one way, open hilly farmland the other. We both had bicycles, and in these golden years before school, Jack developed a passionate and lifelong devotion to County Down. And the new house itself was a child's delight, by reason of its atrociously uneconomical design: on the top floor, cupboard-like doors opened into huge, dark, wasted spaces under the roof, tunnel-like passages through which children could crawl from one space into another, with here and there a rectangular pit, floored with the ceiling of a bedroom—space which the architect had despaired of putting to use. Best of all, we had our own day-room in the attic, instead of a day-nursery and bedroom combined, as in the old house: in this glorious privacy, never invaded by officiously tidying maids, 'Boxen' and the rest of our secret life flourished wonderfully. These were golden days, even after they became for Jack mere interludes in the horror of school: we remember them with delight to the end.

But 1908 was a year of death, and the happy times ended. During that year my father lost his own father, then his wife, then his brother. If I gave any account of my mother's lingering illness and death, it would only be a poor paraphrase of what Jack wrote in *Surprised by Joy*. She died on my father's birthday, 23 August: there was a Shakespearean calendar hanging on the wall of the room where she died, and my father preserved for the rest of his life the leaf for that day, with its quotation: 'Men must endure their going hence.'

In the Christmas term of that year, Jack followed me at the school referred to in *Surprised by Joy* as 'Belsen'. As he has made very clear, he hated the place, but he escaped its worse brutalities: he amused the headmaster, who even made something of a pet of him, so far as was possible for such a man.

Jack's letter and diaries of the time convey little of the full depressing story of this school and its headmaster. In 1901 a boy had been treated so brutally that his father brought a High Court action: this was settled out of court, but it confirmed local suspicions, and the school went downhill rapidly. In 1910 the headmaster wrote to my father that he was 'giving up school work', which meant deliverance for

Jack: in fact the school collapsed, the house was sold, and its proprietor retired to a country living. There, his behaviour towards his choir and churchwardens was such that he was put under restraint and certified insane: he died in 1912, soon afterwards. With his uncanny flair for making the wrong decision, my father had given us helpless children into the hands of a madman.

In the spring term of 1911, after a brief spell at Campbell College, Belfast, Jack came with me to Malvern—not to the College, of course, but to the preparatory school, which he calls 'Chartres'. Two years later, he entered for the scholarship examination to the College: when the day came, he was in bed with a high temperature, and I am inclined to rate his winning of a scholarship under these circumstances as the greatest academic triumph of his career. And so, in September 1913, he started his first term at Malvern.

There, as readers of *Surprised by Joy* will have gathered, he was something of a square peg in a round hole. By this time I had left the College and was reading for Sandhurst with W. T. Kirkpatrick, my father's old headmaster: that autumn, I visited Malvern to attend a House Supper, a noisy and cheerful function, of which I can remember only one thing—Jack's gloom and boredom, unaltered all through the evening, glaringly obvious to all, not calculated to increase his popularity with the House. He was no kind of failure academically—within a few weeks of arriving, still at the age of fourteen, he attracted the headmaster's attention with a brilliant translation from Horace—but Malvern was the wrong place for him: and in March 1914 he wrote home, imploring his father to take him away.

Much to my surprise, my father reacted to this letter by making an immediate and sensible decision: Jack was to leave Malvern at the end of the school year to become Kirkpatrick's pupil at Great Bookham in Surrey, reading for an Oxford scholarship. This meant one more term at the College, a burden that Jack carried bravely: then at the end of July 1914, he left Malvern for ever with profound relief.

Here I feel it my duty to make some comment upon his criticisms of the school, as expressed in his letters of the time as well as in *Surprised by Joy*. 'I would not', as Boswell says somewhere, 'war offensively with the dead', and least of all with my brother: and yet I find it very difficult to believe in the Malvern that he portrays. In July 1913 I had been on more or less close terms with all the brutes of prefects whom he describes, and I found them (with one exception) very pleasant fellows. How did they come to change their characters entirely during the summer holidays of that year? As regards his lurid descriptions of the immorality of Malvern, I am far from denying that there was immorality; but when I got to Sandhurst and could compare notes with boys from every public school in the country, I found that there was little to choose between them in this respect. And it must be remembered that a boy in his first year at a public school knows very little of what goes on: he lives by scandal and rumour, and tends therefore to see immorality in every sentimental association between an older boy and a younger. Such associations—inevitable under a system which keeps a youth of eighteen isolated from feminine company for two-thirds of the year—are certainly silly and undesirable: but they are very often physically innocent, a fact that Jack seemed reluctant to see or admit.

When I first read *Surprised by Joy* I pointed this out to him, and drew his attention to his absurd statement that 'there was only one topic of conversation' in the house. I could well remember many others—theatrical, sartorial, sporting, and so forth. I record the incident with pride, because on that occasion, and then only, I persuaded Jack to admit that he had been wrong.

The fact is that he should never have been sent to a public school at all. Already, at fourteen, his intelligence was such that he would have fitted in better among undergraduates than among schoolboys; and by his temperament he was bound to be a misfit, a heretic, an object of suspicion within the collective-minded and standardizing Public School system. He was, indeed, lucky to leave Malvern before the power of this system had done him any lasting damage.

Of his days under Kirkpatrick's tutorship at Great Bookham, he has left a full and lyrical record in *Surprised by Joy*. The stimulation of a sharp and vigorous mind, the romantic beauty which the Surrey countryside then possessed, the ordered security of Jack's life, his freedom to read widely and gratuitously—these factors combined to develop his particular gifts and determine his future. 'He was born with the literary temperament,' Kirkpatrick wrote to my father, 'and we have to face that fact with all that it implies.' And later: 'Outside a life of literary study, life has no meaning or attraction for him . . . he is adapted for nothing else. You may make up your mind to that.' There is a note here of warning and limitation, but for Jack these days were paradisal without qualification, his letters of the time being charged with the intoxication of literary discovery.

From time to time I would come home on leave from France, taking Jack with me to visit our father whenever I could; but already there were difficulties and reluctances in this respect, life at 'Little Lea' having certain irksome and frustrating aspects. I mention this subject with reluctance: nevertheless, some awareness of my father's smothering tendency to dominate the life and especially the conversation of his household is necessary to an understanding of Jack's mind and life. This tendency had borne curious fruit in early days. Ever since the days of the old house, which we left in 1905, Jack had been trying to write: after his death, we found among his papers any number of childish but ambitious beginnings of histories, stories, poems, nearly all of them dealing with our private fantasy world of Animal-Land or Boxen. Then, in 1912, he had produced a complete novel, a creditable performance for a boy not yet thirteen; and the interesting thing to note is that this novel, like the sequel to it that followed soon after, revolved entirely around politics.

To anyone who recalls Jack's adult contempt for politics and politicians this will seem extraordinary: but this first predilection and his subsequent revulsion from the whole subject stemmed from the same root. In the upper-middle-class society of our Belfast childhood, politics and money were the chief, almost the only, subjects of grown-up conversation: and since no visitors came to our house who did not hold precisely the same political views as my father, what we heard was not discussion and the lively clash of minds, but rather an endless and one-sided torrent of grumble and vituperation. Any ordinary parent would have sent us boys off to amuse ourselves, but not my father: we had to sit in silence and endure it. The immediate result, in Jack's case, was to convince him that grown-up conversation and politics were one and the same thing, and that everything he wrote must therefore be given a political framework: the long-term result was to fill him with a disgust and revulsion from the very idea of politics before he was out of his 'teens.

Now, during his happy days at Great Bookham, Jack's mind was developing and flowering on lines as unpolitical as can be imagined. His letters of the time are full of landscape and romance: they record his discovery of George Macdonald—a turning-point in his life—and his first and characteristic delight in Chaucer, Scott, Malory, the Brontës, William Morris, Coleridge, de Quincey, Spenser, Swinburne, Keats. In his friend Arthur Greeves he had found a kindred spirit, with whom he could share and celebrate these discoveries: they corresponded regularly, went on holiday together, and Jack enjoyed the hospitality of Arthur's home at Belfast. Here again, my father's temperament was a limiting and dampening influence. Jack would have liked to return Arthur's hospitality: had this been arranged, my father would certainly have welcomed his son's friend very cordially, but not for a moment would it have occurred to him that the two boys might want to talk together, alone. No: he would have joined them, inescapably, for a good talk about books, doing nine-tenths of the talking himself, eulogizing his own favourites without regard to their interests. Two bored and frustrated youths would have been subjected to long readings from Macaulay's essays, Burke's speeches, and the like, and my father would have gone to bed satisfied that he had given them a literary evening far more interesting than they could have contrived for themselves.

That Arthur's visit would have this character was something all too obvious to Jack: he hinted delicately at the 'obstacle' of his father's temperament, and the visit never took place.

In December 1916 Jack went to Oxford to sit for a classical scholarship: passed over by New College, he was elected to an open scholarship by University. The full list of awards, published in *The Times* a few days later, included the names of Alfred C. Harwood and Arthur Owen Barfield: these two, elected to classical scholarships at Christ Church and Wadham respectively, were to be for the rest of Jack's life among his most intimate personal friends.

The prospects offered by war-time Oxford were, of course, limited and determined by the imminence of military service for most undergraduates: there were few men in residence, and arrangements were flexible. It was proposed that Jack should take Responsions in March and come up for the Trinity Term, joining the Oxford O.T.C.: this, it was suggested, offered him the best chance of a commission. And so, after further coaching at Bookham and a visit home, Jack matriculated, signed his name in the College book, and began his University career on 28 April 1917.

It is noteworthy that in the circumstances of the time he was allowed to come into residence, having in the event failed the Responsions examination that Easter: one of his first concerns at Oxford was to find a coach and work harder at the elements of mathematics, with a view to another attempt. In fact, he never did pass the examination, being exempted from it later on by virtue of his military service. In this he was fortunate, for I do not believe that at any stage in his career he could have passed an examination of any kind in elementary mathematics: a view with which he himself agreed, when I put it to him many years later.

Before one full term was out, his papers came through, and Jack found himself a soldier, having crammed into those first few weeks at Oxford not only his unsuccessful work for Responsions and his O.T.C. training but also a good deal of miscellaneous reading, most of this (as recorded in his pocket-book) being characteristically a matter of poetry and romance. Joining the army was less of a break for him than for some others, since the cadet battalion to which he was drafted was billeted in Keble: he was able to keep in touch with his friends and even (for a time) to spend his week-ends in his own college.

Towards army life in war-time, his final attitude—as expressed in *Surprised by Joy*—was notably positive; and in these first days of initial training, his letters home conveyed more exhilaration than distress. It was during this period that a relationship first began that had a huge and determining effect upon the pattern of his subsequent life. Among the cadets at Keble, he found a few who were congenial company: one of them was E. F. C. ('Paddy') Moore, with whom he shared a room by alphabetic accident. In August, he had a couple of days' leave at home, and I had the misfortune to miss him by a few days: the next weekend he spent with Moore and his mother. On 25 September, Jack was commissioned in the 3rd Battalion of the Somerset Light Infantry and given a month's leave: he chose the same society for the first part of this leave, not coming home until 12 October.

My father's pocket-book contains a wry note of this order of priorities: the situation did not reach full development until much later, but its character may have been apparent already.

I do not wish to dwell upon the barriers that existed between Jack and my father, nor to exaggerate their importance in connection with Jack's subsequent involvement with Mrs Moore and her affairs. These barriers were not only of a purely personal kind: between Ireland and England there stood in those days a kind of iron curtain of misunderstanding. There was no conscription in Ireland, no rationing, no shortages (as far as I could see) of any kind: the war was a very remote thing, merely a topic of conversation unless one had relatives fighting in France. I never went on leave without getting an eerie feeling that I had somehow or other been jolted back into 1913. Into this remote atmosphere, Jack despatched on 15 November a telegram—one that would have made it clear to anyone in England that he was on the eve of embarkation for overseas service. My father simply wired back that he could not understand the telegram, and asked for leisured explanations: he made no attempt to keep the rendezvous in Bristol—proposed clearly enough by Jack— for what might well have been a last meeting, and Jack had to sail for France and the war without seeing him again.

This must have been felt as a rebuff, though it was probably due to a genuine misunderstanding, a failure in 'communication'. But the same thing happened again much more seriously, seven months later. Jack reached the front line on his nineteenth birthday, 29 November 1917: after an initial spell in the trenches and a short illness, he was among those who faced in March the final German attack on the Western

Front, and in April he was wounded. I was able to visit him at once in hospital, and I still recall my overwhelming relief when I found him sitting up in bed and greeting me with a cheerful 'Hullo, I didn't know you A.S.C. people got as far up the line as this!'

His wounds were not serious, but he was sent home to recuperate in London, having heard a little earlier that Mrs Moore's son was missing and believed dead; and from the hospital in Endsleigh Gardens he wrote home, cheerfully but with his first frank expression of homesickness, begging his father to come and visit him.

One would have thought it impossible for any father to resist an appeal of this kind, coming at such a moment. But my father was a very peculiar man in some respects: in none more than in an almost pathological hatred of taking any step which involved a break in the dull routine of his daily existence. Jack remained unvisited, and was deeply hurt at a neglect which he considered inexcusable. Feeling himself to have been rebuffed by his father, he turned to Mrs Moore as to a mother, seeking there the affection which was apparently denied him at home.

There was no breach between Jack and his father: things remained, outwardly, as they had been. But after this, 'Little Lea' lost its importance to Jack, and soon he was to write in his diary of 'coming home' in reference to the journey from his father's house to Oxford.

Before he was fit for any further service in France, the war was over; and after a certain amount of shifting around from one army camp to another, he was demobilized earlier than we had expected. I was at home on leave myself, not expecting to see him, when on 27 December 1918 he unexpectedly arrived, fit and free: in spite of all the stresses and tensions just mentioned it was a joyful reunion on all sides, a recovery of old days, the first occasion moreover on which I had champagne at home.

Within a month he was back at Oxford, and had embarked there upon a pattern of life that was to remain in many respects unaltered for the rest of his days. As such things are reckoned he had 'a successful career'; and in his progress from undergraduate brilliance through a double first to a fellowship and finally a professor's chair, in his world-wide celebrity as a writer on literary and religious subjects alike, there might appear to be an inevitable, even an effortless working-out of the destiny foreseen by Kirkpatrick.

My own contribution to the world's understanding of my brother must be limited: I do not propose in this memoir to give any full account of his work, and still less any evaluation of it. I offer only my own memories of Jack, as man, friend, and brother: and if these memories are to be useful to those who hope to understand his mind and his work, there must be no concealment of the difficulties under which he worked, the patterns of stress and tension that determined many aspects of his life.

There was, indeed, something natural and effortless about his strictly academic and literary work: Jack was one of those rare and fortunate people whose idea of recreation overlaps and even coincides with their necessary work. It was no matter of surprise that he should take a First in Honour Mods (1920), a First in Greats (1922), and a First in English (1923), or that he should win the Chancellor's Prize for an English

Essay. But even for a scholar of his ability and achievement, it was then no swift and easy matter to embark successfully upon an academic career. Immediately after taking Greats, he sat for a Fellowship by Examination at Magdalen: before this, he had looked into the possibility of a classical lectureship at Reading: later on, he applied for Fellowships at Trinity and St John's. For all these posts, Jack saw other men chosen; and there were times during this period of uncertainty when he tended towards despair of any academic or literary success.

For the fact that he persevered, some credit must be given to the support—both moral and material—given by his own College and by his father. The authorities at Univ. had faith in him, and extended his original scholarship for a fourth year, spent very congenially in reading for the English School: his early reading gave him a flying start here, and academic affairs were then tending in a direction that made a double First of this particular pattern a very formidable qualification indeed. And in the end it was his own College that first offered him a post—a very minor post, certainly, but still a beginning: it was with considerable relief that Jack polished up his Greats reading and began his tutorial work in October 1924.

This was strictly a temporary post, covering a single year's absence in America of one of the Fellows. Next Spring, it was announced that Magdalen proposed to make an election to a Fellowship in English. The competition seemed likely to be severe, and Jack applied listlessly, with little hope of success. The College elected him, nominally for five years: in fact, this appointment filled the bulk of his working life, from June 1925 until in 1954 he left Oxford to take up a professor's chair at Cambridge.

And so, after a long and discouraging struggle, Jack managed to fight his way into the apparently impregnable fortress which he had once described as 'the real Oxford'. Almost his first action was to write to his father in deep gratitude for six years of generous support. As I have hinted already, there was some degree of estrangement between them—though never any frank ill-feeling—and a certain amount of gloom and stress attended Jack's visits to 'Little Lea': nevertheless, my father had kept his promise made in 1923 of three years' further support for Jack at Oxford, even though he knew that there was some risk of failure, and that it would then be no easy matter for Jack to launch himself in some totally new career at the age of 28 or so.

The stress occasioned by this limited family estrangement was only intermittent. But there was a further source of stress and difficulty in Jack's life, continuous, long-lasting, and to some degree self-inflicted. I have already indicated how during the war Jack started to display a marked preference for Mrs Moore's company, rather than his father's: afterwards at Oxford this relationship developed much more strongly. Mrs Moore had lost her son; Jack had many years earlier lost his mother and now his father too seemed to have failed him emotionally. He may have felt also some sense of responsibility, a duty perhaps of keeping some wartime promise made to Paddy Moore. Be that as it may, Jack now embarked upon a relationship with Mrs Moore which was almost of son and mother; and as soon as his first year as an undergraduate was over, instead of moving from college into lodgings, he set up a joint ménage with her and her daughter Maureen. Having once embarked on this relationship with Mrs Moore, it was not in Jack's nature later to abandon her, and the ménage in fact continued in existence until her death in 1951; during this period Jack commonly referred to Mrs Moore as 'my mother'—not always with any explicit indication that the relationship was conventional and adoptive.

The thing most puzzling to myself and to Jack's friends was Mrs Moore's extreme unsuitability as a companion for him. She was a woman of very limited mind, and notably domineering and possessive by temperament. She cut down to a minimum his visits to his father, interfered constantly with his work, and imposed upon him a heavy burden of minor domestic tasks. In twenty years I never saw a book in her hands; her conversation was chiefly about herself, and was otherwise a matter of ill-informed dogmatism: her mind was of a type that he found barely tolerable elsewhere. The whole business had to be concealed from my father of course, which widened the rift between him and Jack; and since an allowance calculated to suit a bachelor living in college was by no means enough for a householder, Jack found himself miserably poor. Nevertheless he continued in this restrictive and distracting servitude for many of his most fruitful years, suffering the worries and expense of repeated moves, until in 1930 we all settled at The Kilns, Headington Quarry.

I dwell on this rather unhappy business with some regret, but it was one of the central and determining circumstances in Jack's life. He hinted at it, darkly, in *Surprised by Joy,* and it is reflected with painful clarity in various passages in his books; the stress and gloom that it often caused him must not be played down.

On the other hand, it would be wildly misleading to suggest that my brother lived the life of a solitary and embittered recluse. The case was quite otherwise. As all his friends will bear witness, he was a man with an outstanding gift for pastime with good company, for laughter and the love of friends—a gift which found full scope in any number of holidays and walking tours, the joyous character of his response to these being well conveyed in his letters. He had, indeed, a remarkable talent for friendship, particularly for friendship of an uproarious kind, masculine and argumentative but never quarrelsome.

In this connection I must say something of the Inklings, a famous and heroic gathering, one that has already passed into literary legend. Properly speaking it was neither a club nor a literary society, though it partook of the nature of both. There were no rules, officers, agendas, or formal elections—unless one counts it as a rule that we met in Jack's rooms at Magdalen every Thursday evening after dinner. Proceedings neither began nor terminated at any fixed hour, though there was a tacit agreement that ten-thirty was as late as one could decently arrive. From time to time we added to our original number, but without formalities: someone would suggest that Jones be asked to come in of a Thursday, and there could be either general agreement, or else a perceptible lack of enthusiasm and a dropping of the matter. Usually there was agreement, since we all knew the type of man we wanted or did not want.

The ritual of an Inklings was unvarying. When half a dozen or so had arrived, tea would be produced, and then when pipes were well alight Jack would say, 'Well, has nobody got anything to read us?' Out would come a manuscript, and we would settle down to sit in judgement upon it—real unbiased judgement, too, since we were no mutual admiration society: praise for good work was unstinted, but censure for bad work—or even not-so-good work—was often brutally frank. To read to the Inklings was a formidable ordeal, and I can still remember the fear with which I offered the first chapter of my first book—and my delight, too, at its reception.

To indicate the content of those evenings, let me look forward to 1946, a vintage year. At most of the meetings during that year we had a chapter from Tolkien's 'new Hobbit', as we called it—the great work later published as *The Lord of the Rings*. My diary records in October of that year 'a long argument on the ethics of cannibalism'; in November, that 'Roy Campbell read us his translations of a couple of Spanish poems', and 'John Wain won an outstanding bet by reading a chapter of *Irene Iddlesleigh* without a smile'; and of the next meeting, that 'David (Cecil) read a chapter of his forthcoming book on Gray'. In February 1949 we talked of red-brick universities; from where the talk drifted by channels which I have forgotten, to 'torture, Tertullian, bores, the contractual theory of mediaeval kingship, and odd place-names'.

Sometimes, though not often, it would happen that no one had anything to read to us. On these occasions the fun would be riotous, with Jack at the top of his form and enjoying every minute—'no sound delights me more', he once said, 'than male laughter'. At the Inklings his talk was an outpouring of wit, nonsense, whimsy, dialectical swordplay, and pungent judgement such as I have rarely heard equalled—no mere show put on for the occasion, either, since it was often quite as brilliant when he and I were alone together.

During the war years, and the even harder years after 1945, the routine would sometimes be varied slightly and Jack would give us all a cold supper in his rooms—a thing made possible by the great generosity of his many American admirers, whose tributes to him included many noble parcels of food. And there was also another ritual gathering, subsidiary to the Inklings proper: the same company used to meet for an hour or so before lunch every Tuesday at the Eagle and Child in St Giles', better known as the Bird and Baby. These gatherings must have attained a certain notoriety, for in a detective novel of the period a character is made to say 'It must be Tuesday—there's Lewis going into the Bird'.

In his Preface to *Essays Presented to Charles Williams*, Jack gave a lively and moving account of what this circle meant to him, with particular reference to one of the richest and most fruitful friendships of his life. For me to say anything further of Charles Williams in this context would be an unnecessary impertinence.

Through all these years, from 1925 onwards, Jack was bearing the exacting and sometimes tedious burdens of a college tutor and a University lecturer. He would take two or three pairs of pupils for tuition in his own rooms in College every morning, and then go to Headington for lunch; in the afternoon, if he was in luck, he would be allowed to take a walk, returning for tea, and then he would return to College for the rest of the day and for the night. He had, therefore, a precarious freedom from domestic drudgery: later on, however, he took to sleeping at home instead of in College, at some loss to this freedom.

His rooms at Magdalen were magnificent: a big sitting-room on the first floor of New Buildings, looking out on to the Grove, and another and smaller sitting-room and a bed-room, looking across to the Cloisters and the Tower. But he had to furnish these rooms himself at his own expense, and did so in perfunctory and notably economical style: the effect, described by Mr Betjeman as 'arid', continued long after Jack could have afforded new furniture, better chosen and more comfortable. My father suggested, plausibly, that Jack chose this furniture as he chose his clothes—by a hurried acceptance of the first thing offered to him by the shop-keeper. This was part of his general impatience with the mechanical business of living: to get his hair cut, to go to the bank, to go shopping—all such activities were a penance and a burden. His own clothes were a matter of complete indifference to him: he had an extraordinary knack of making a new suit look shabby the second time he wore it. One of his garments has passed into legend. It is said that Jack once took a guest for an early-morning walk round Addison's Walk, after a very wet night. Presently the guest brought his attention to a curious lump of cloth hanging on a bush. 'That looks like my hat!' said Jack; then, joyfully, 'It *is* my hat!' and clapping the sodden mass on to his head, he continued the walk.

This fine indifference was not extended to food: in that matter his requirements were simple but strongly felt. Plain domestic cookery was what he wanted, with the proviso that if the food was hot the plates should be hot as well.

What he really disliked was 'messed-up food', by which he meant any sort of elaborately dressed dish: he could never be persuaded to experiment with new foods. Normally, he drank nothing at table: on special occasions, he liked to share a bottle of Burgundy or Hock, and in College he usually drank a glass of port after dinner. One oddly feminine trait was the immense importance which he attached to afternoon tea. When we were off on a walking tour together, or out on my motor-cycle with Jack in the sidecar, the whole day had to be planned around the necessity of finding ourselves at four o'clock in some place where afternoon tea would be available. The only time I ever saw him really disgruntled in any matter of eating or drinking came in Ireland: we were motoring with a friend, and found no tea in a place where we had counted on it. The friend and I naturally dived into the nearest pub for whisky and soda: Jack refused even this consolation.

These various holidays and tours were a great feature of his life and mine: they were inspired by a joy in landscape that developed out of the Boxonian visions of our childhood and was—together with books—the most enduring element in cementing our friendship. Until 1939 our annual walking tour was a regular fixture: on these long days, and during the pleasant evening hours when we took our ease in an inn, Jack was always at his most exuberant, his most whimsical, his most perceptive—the overworked cabhorse released from the shafts and kicking his heels.

Over-worked he certainly was: not only by the burden of his routine work as tutor and lecturer, not only by the domestic tasks laid on him by Mrs Moore ('He is as good as an extra maid in the house', she would say complacently to visitors), but also by the extent and depth of his own reading, the creative effort of original work both scholarly and religious, and (as the years passed) the increasing volume of his correspondence, much of it from total strangers. In view of all this, visitors to his rooms were often struck by the modest size of his personal library. In his younger days he was something of a bibliophile, but in the middle and later life he very seldom bought a book if he could consult it in the Bodleian: long years of poverty, self-inflicted but grinding, had made this economical habit second nature to him—a factor that contributed, no doubt, to the extraordinarily retentive character of his memory.

For all their arid furnishings and their few books, those rooms in Magdalen came by habit and long association to seem cosy and home-like. When I left the army I made them my own headquarters, and was able to give Jack some help of secretarial and similar kinds: and it was in these rooms that many generations of students enjoyed and suffered the stimulation of his erudite and dialectical mind. Since his death, a number of tributes and reminiscences from former pupils have come into my hands: from these I would like to summarise one, provided by Mr H. M. Blamires, who began to read English with Jack in 1936, and who has managed to convey admirably the particular flavour of those tutorial hours.

He was personally interested in his pupils and permanently concerned about those who became his friends. Though he was a most courteous and considerate person his frankness could, when he wanted, cut through the ordinary fabric of reticences with a shock of sudden warmth or sudden devastation, indeed of both at once. No one knew better how to nourish a pupil with encouragement and how to press just criticism when it was needed, without causing resentment. He did not think of himself as taking pupils through a course; rather he saw his pupils as having two years or so under his guidance, during which they could start on a process which would occupy the responsive ones for the rest of their lives. The literature stood waiting on the shelves; the pupil's appetite was to be whetted and fed. It would be wrong to give the impression that he encouraged indiscriminate reading. Once I went to a tutorial proudly nursing a substantial and, as I thought, admirably comprehensive essay on Abraham Cowley. Half-way through I undertook a critical survey of Cowley's historical epic, the *Davideis*. Well launched upon my reading of this survey, I was suddenly conscious of Lewis rocking in suppressed amusement. Eventually he interrupted me gently. 'But you don't mean to say you've actually *read* the thing?' The tone was of mock horror. 'Every word,' I said. 'I'm terribly sorry,' he said gravely, as though nothing could atone for the suffering he had unwittingly brought upon me. Then he brightened, having found the crumb of consolation. 'But think of it. You must be the only man in the country, perhaps the only man alive, to have read every word of Cowley's *Davideis*.' He expected you to share his life-long companionship with his favourite authors. There was never a fit point in life for saying

'Yes, I've *read* Malory or Spenser or Milton'. It would be like saying, 'Yes, I've *eaten* bacon and eggs'. There was a good deal of fun about tutorials. Lewis sat there on his vast Chesterfield, smoking a pipe and cigarettes alternately, periodically beaming and bouncing with good humour in a hugely expansive way. He looked big, sitting down opposite one, with his great fist bulging round a pipe bowl, eyes wide open and eyebrows raised behind a cloud of smoke. As a lecturer he was the biggest 'draw' the English School had in the nineteen-thirties. He could fill the largest lecture rooms. He was popular because his lectures were meaty. He purveyed what was wanted in a palatable form. Proportion and direction were always preserved, but without forcing. Points were clearly enumerated; arguments beautifully articulated; illustrations richly chosen. The physical images of the Lewis of the 'thirties that stay with me are symbols rather than clearly defined pictures. One remembers his shapeless hat and ill-fitting overcoat seen to peculiar disadvantage from the top of a bus . . . the rich, chanting voice at one of his Thursday 'Beer and Beowulf' evenings, the big red face bulging out of the graceless clothes, and alive with a zest and intensity which won and warmed you in defiance of aesthetic considerations. It is not easy to carry together in the mind the picture Lewis presented in a relaxed mood and the realization of the vast amount of work he did. His liking for beer and bawdy late-night talk might together have misled the unobservant with a completely false picture. His hospitality, like his help, generously but unforcingly offered, was easy to accept, easy to decline.

His 'churchmanship' could not be labelled. It was never the meaningful things or the important things that displeased him from the 'Catholic' side; it was excessive ritualistic concern over inessentials, or the exaggeration of trivialities.

It would be quite wrong to imagine that Lewis's deep and unfailing charity left him incapable of being decisive and frank about defect in others. He would not gossip. He would not sustain a malicious conversation. But he would not conspire to veil a person's deficiency if it might be harmful to veil it. He did his best to be scrupulously fair in his judgements. Praise and criticism were always absolutely honest. He had a near-fanatical devotion to Charles Williams, but when Williams wrote a bad book Lewis readily described it as 'bloody awful'.

It was, of course, during these years at Magdalen that Jack underwent his re-conversion to Christianity, and also developed into a best-selling author of international reputation. A certain reticence in the one matter, and in the other a conviction that writers more scholarly than myself will be studying my brother's literary work for many years to come, lead me to pass over these subjects briefly.

I well remember that day in 1931 when we made a visit to Whipsnade Zoo, Jack riding in my sidecar: as recorded in *Surprised by Joy,* it was during that outing that he made his decision to rejoin the Church. This seemed to me no sudden plunge into a new life, but rather a slow, steady convalescence from a deep-seated spiritual illness of long standing—an illness that had its origins in our childhood, in the dry husks of religion offered by the semi-political church-going of Ulster, in the similar dull emptiness of compulsory church during our schooldays. With this background, we both found the difficulty of the Christian life to lie in public worship, rather than in one's private devotions. In Jack's case, this difficulty was overcome slowly: he had been a practising Christian again for some time when he said to me, of Communion: 'I think that to communicate once a month strikes the right balance between enthusiasm and Laodiceanism.' In later years he saw that 'right balance' differently, and never failed to communicate weekly and on the major feast days as well.

I offer no gloss or comment upon his own experience and understanding of the Christian religion itself: to the profit of many thousands, he has himself told all that words can carry. So far as his outward life was concerned, his conversion had various consequences: it was the occasion of a notable literary development, of wide popularity coupled with hostility in some quarters, and of certain war-time lecturing engagements with the RAF and the BBC. It was in connection with his religious rather than his scholarly writing that his name became a household word in the 'forties and 'fifties, and the same emphasis may be behind the two honorary degrees conferred upon him—the Doctorate of Divinity (1946) by St Andrews, and the Doctorate of Literature (1952) by Laval University, Quebec. (A further honour, the C.B.E., was offered by the Prime Minister in 1951, but Jack felt obliged to refuse this: his appearance in a Conservative Honours List might, he felt, strengthen the ill-founded case of those who identified religious writing with anti-leftist propaganda.)

The remarkable thing about his literary career is that it never occurred to him until a relatively late date that his great achievement would be in prose. *Spirits in Bondage* appeared in 1919, a collection of poems, some of them written in his Bookham days: *Dymer,* a narrative poem, was published in 1926, the fruit of much pain and effort during a peculiarly difficult period. During all these early years, he thought of himself (though with no great confidence) as essentially a poet. A certain feeling of alienation from the poetic currents of his time led him to publish pseudonymously: those first two books were by 'Clive Hamilton' (his own first name, and his mother's maiden surname), and the many poems that he published in later years were signed 'Nat Whilk' (Anglo-Saxon for 'I know not who') or, more simply, 'N.W.'

In 1933 he published *The Pilgrim's Regress* and in 1936 *The Allegory of Love.* This latter book, on which he had been working since 1928, was immediately and permanently a success by every standard: and from that time on, my brother's life was one of continual writing and continual publication for an ever-increasing and ever more appreciative audience. It may be observed at this point that to become a best-selling author does not necessarily involve full success in the task of 'communication'. The two books into which Jack put most of himself—*The Pilgrim's Regress* and *Till We Have Faces*—were in his own estimation failures, misunderstood or ignored by the public.

It was with the publication of *The Screwtape Letters* in the autumn of 1942, that Jack first achieved wide public success of the kind that brings money rolling in. He was not used to this—his early penury had not trained him for relative affluence—and he celebrated by a lavish and improvident scattering of cheques to various societies and individual lame dogs. Before the situation got completely out of hand, his solicitor intervened: a charitable trust was set up into which two-thirds of his royalties was thereafter paid automatically, and from which payments both large and numerous were made for all manner of charitable purposes. The financial side of his charity was by no means limited to this particular arrangement, and the total of his benefactions will never be known; but over and above this, he had in an extraordinary degree the deeper charity that can perhaps best be described as a universal and sympathetic neighbourliness to all and sundry, strangers as well as acquaintances.

Two examples of this quality come to my mind. One summer day he heard it mentioned casually that there was a sick man in a field some distance away. Jack said 'poor devil' and continued to write; then he suddenly jumped up in distress and said, 'I have sinned; I have shown myself lacking in all charity'. Out he went, found the man, brought him to the house, gave him a drink, heard his story, and then—being satisfied that the man was able to look after himself—saw him off, not (I am sure) forgetting the Samaritan's twopence. Then, on another occasion, he met a tramp while walking on Shotover—a tramp who turned the conversation to the subject of poetry, quoting Fitzgerald with gusto. Jack went home, armed himself with bottles of beer and a verse anthology, trudged up to the top of the hill again, gave book and beer to the tramp, and bade him a cordial farewell.

During all these Magdalen years until Mrs Moore's death in 1951, the domestic circumstances of Jack's life continued to impose a heavy strain upon this habit of charity. Relations with his father were peaceful but distant. Jack wrote home in regular and informative style, but visits to 'Little Lea' had always a sad penitential character: in his later years my father became more and more of an inquisitor and tyrant, prying into every detail of his sons' lives, interfering blindly in even the most personal matters. We were always glad to get away. The three of us were at home together for the last time in 1927: it is pleasant to record that my father noted this in his journal as 'a very pleasant holiday—roses all the way'. In 1929 he died: I was in China at the time, and it fell to Jack to make the immediate arrangements for winding up the household at 'Little Lea'.

And at Oxford, for more than three decades, Jack continued to live under the autocracy of Mrs Moore—an autocracy that developed into stifling tyranny, as I experienced myself during the years of my inclusion within this incomprehensible ménage. Mrs Moore was one of those who thrive on crisis and chaos; every day had to have some kind of domestic scene or upheaval, commonly involving the maids: the emotional burden so created had then to be placed squarely on the uncomplaining shoulders of Jack. In this atmosphere the physical inconveniences of the household seemed relatively unimportant: notable among them was the total unpredictability of any meal-time.

Jack's servitude was made more burdensome, as the years passed, by Mrs Moore's senility and invalidism: it was only broken by her admission to a nursing home in April 1950 and her death there nine months later.

Four years after this Jack's whole life changed, and for six years he was to experience first peace and then a delight and fulfilment which had never previously come to him.

In 1954 Jack accepted the offer of a new chair at Cambridge. He finished his last Oxford tutorial—with a certain sense of relief—on 3 December, and the New Year found him installed at Cambridge as Professor of Mediaeval and Renaissance English. His inaugural lecture, later printed under the title of *De Descriptione Temporum*, was a crowded and memorable occasion: it added a new phrase to the colloquial jargon of the time, and many people could be heard for a while thereafter proclaiming stoutly that they were, or were not, specimens of 'Old Western Man'. Dr G. M. Trevelyan, who was then Master of Trinity, presided on this occasion: he introduced Jack by revealing that this was the only university appointment in the whole of his experience for which the electing committee had voted unanimously.

Jack found the life at Cambridge and the company at Magdalene congenial, mentally stimulating yet relaxed. His years there were happy years. The break with his old life was not complete: he continued to live at The Kilns, passing there not only his vacations but also many week-ends in term. He necessarily resigned his Fellowship at Magdalen, but was immediately reelected to an Honorary Fellowship: and with his Cambridge chair went a Fellowship there under the same patronage, at Magdalene.

Meanwhile he had met the woman who was to bring him so much happiness in love and marriage. Joy Davidman was American by birth and Jewish by race. She and her husband, William Lindsay Gresham, were avid admirers of Jack's work and became Christians partly under his influence. She met Jack for the first time in 1953, having already corresponded with him at some length. Later, and free now to marry again, she returned to England with her two sons, intending to live there permanently. By 1955 she was on close terms with Jack. For Jack the attraction was at first undoubtedly intellectual. Joy was the only woman whom he had met (although as his letters show, he had known with great affection many able women) who had a brain which matched his own in suppleness, in width of interest, in analytical grasp, and above all in humour and sense of fun. Further, she shared his delight in argument for argument's sake, whether frivolous or serious, always good-humoured yet always meeting him trick for trick as he changed ground. A woman of great charity, she had an unbounded contempt for the sentimental. Setting herself high standards, she could laugh at the seeming absurdities to which they sometimes carried her. With all this, she was intensely feminine.

Joy had cancer, and on 21 March 1957 they were married, not in church but at the bride's bedside in the Wingfield Hospital, a civil ceremony having taken place in April of 1956. Both knew she was a dying woman. Yet she did not then die: she made a temporary recovery and Jack brought her home to The Kilns. There were now for him three years of complete fulfilment. To his friends who saw them together it was clear that they not only loved but were in love with each other. It was a delight to watch them, and all the waste of Jack's years which had gone before was more than recompensed. Nevill Coghill has told how Jack at this time said to him, looking at his wife across a grassy quadrangle, 'I never expected to have, in my sixties, the happiness that passed me by in my twenties'.

Then on 13 July, 1960, after a return to hospital, she died.

A short episode, of glory and tragedy: for Jack, the total (though heartbreaking) fulfilment of a whole dimension to his nature that had previously been starved and thwarted. Joy's death was entirely expected. Even though her temporary recovery had made possible certain travels, including holidays to Ireland and Greece, none the less, the parting when it came was a shattering blow to him. His notes on the experience of those black days were later published, pseudonymously, as *A Grief Observed:* to this harrowing book, anyone can be referred who feels curiosity about the character and flavour of this love, this marriage.

It may not be amiss if I place on record here my own reaction to this side of Jack's life. For almost twenty years I had shared (to some degree) in his submission to matriarchal rule: the attitude that I have already expressed towards this rule, and towards Mrs Moore in person, may predispose some readers towards a suspicion that I may have been a possessive brother, jealous and resentful if any other person had importance in Jack's eyes. If this had been the case, I would have resented this marriage of his intensely: and in fact, my earlier experience did lead me to the preparation of plans for withdrawal and for the establishment of a home of my own in Eire.

But Jack and Joy would not hear of this; and so I decided to give the new régime a trial. All my fears were dispelled. For me, Jack's marriage meant that our home was enriched and enlivened by the presence of a witty, broad-minded, well-read and tolerant Christian, whom I had rarely heard equalled as a conversationalist and whose company was a never-ending source of enjoyment: indeed, at the peak of her apparent recovery she was at work on a life of Mme de Maintenon, which unfortunately never got further than several books of notes and an explanatory preface.

It would be an impertinence for me to compare my own sorrow at her death with his: nevertheless, I still continue to miss her sadly.

To speak temperately of the greater loss that overtook me three years later is difficult indeed. Jack was already in poor health by the time of his marriage: afterwards it became apparent that he needed an operation but was too weak to undergo it. In this situation, his health was bound to deteriorate steadily: no success attended the attempts to 'fatten him up' as he put it, 'for the sacrifice', and in July 1963 he very nearly died. He made some beginning of a recovery; but by early October it became apparent to both of us that he was facing death.

In their way, these last weeks were not unhappy. Joy had left us, and once again—as in the earliest days—we could turn for comfort only to each other. The wheel had come full circle: once again we were together in the little end room at home, shutting out from our talk the ever-present knowledge that the holidays were ending, that a new term fraught with unknown possibilities awaited us both.

Jack faced the prospect bravely and calmly. 'I have done all I wanted to do, and I'm ready to go', he said to me one evening. Only once did he show any regret or reluctance: this was when I told him that the morning's mail included

an invitation to deliver the Romanes lecture. An expression
of sadness passed over his face, and there was a moment's
silence: then 'Send them a very polite refusal'.

Our talk tended to be cheerfully reminiscent during these
last days: long-forgotten incidents in our shared past would
be remembered, and the old Jack would return for a moment,
whimsical and witty. We were recapturing the old schoolboy
technique of extracting the last drop of juice from our holidays.

Friday, 22 November 1963, began much as other days:
there was breakfast, then letters and the crossword puzzle.
After lunch he fell asleep in his chair: I suggested that he
would be more comfortable in bed, and he went there. At
four I took his tea and found him drowsy but comfortable.
Our few words then were the last: at five-thirty I heard a
crash and ran in, to find him lying unconscious at the foot
of his bed. He ceased to breathe some three or four minutes
later.

The following Friday would have been his sixty-fifth
birthday. Even in that terrible moment, the thought flashed
across my mind that whatever fate had in store for me, nothing worse than this could ever happen to me in the future.

'MEN MUST ENDURE THEIR GOING HENCE.'

*

In making this selection from my brother's correspondence,
I have kept in mind not only those interested in the literary and religious aspects of his mind, but also—and perhaps
more urgently—those who want to know what manner of

man he was, and who may derive from these letters some idea of the liveliness, the colour and wit displayed throughout his life by this best of brothers and friends.

I should perhaps stress that this book is a selection. Not all the letters that Jack wrote were of permanent and public interest; he sometimes repeated himself; and a few letters, or parts of letters, must be held back on grounds of charity or discretion. In certain cases, the name of his correspondents have been altered or suppressed, for sufficient reason. In general, omissions have only been indicated where the reader might otherwise be misled or bewildered: I have considered the general reader's convenience, not aiming at any scholarly punctiliousness.

I am deeply grateful to those who passed Jack's letters to me, with permission to reprint; and also to Walter Hooper and Christopher Derrick for help in preparing the typescript for publication.

Warren H. Lewis

THE LETTERS

It seems appropriate to begin this selection from my brother's correspondence with his own first account of a major turning-point in his life, a major influence upon his thought and work. —W.H.L.

TO ARTHUR GREEVES: from Great Bookham, Surrey*

[7 March 1916]

I have had a great literary experience this week . . . The book, to get to the point, is George Macdonald's 'Faerie Romance', *Phantastes*, which I picked up by hazard . . . Have you read it? . . . At any rate, whatever the book you are reading now, you simply MUST get this at once . . . Of course it is hopeless for me to try and describe it, but when you have followed the hero Anodos along the little stream of the faery wood, have heard about the terrible ash tree . . . and heard the episode of Cosmo, I know you will quite agree with me. You must not be disappointed at the first chapter, which is rather conventional faery tale style, and after it you won't be able to stop until you finish. There are one or two poems in the tale . . . which, with one or two exceptions are shockingly bad, so don't TRY to appreciate them . . .

I quite agree with what you say about buying books, and love the planning and scheming beforehand, and if they come by post, finding the neat little parcel waiting for you on the hall table and rushing upstairs to open it in the privacy of your own room . . . I have at last come to the end of

---

* Lewis's occasional eccentricities and inconsistencies of spelling have been retained.

the Faerie Queene: and though I say 'at last', I almost wish
he had lived to write six books more as he hoped to do—so
much have I enjoyed it. The two cantos of 'Mutabilitie' with
which it ends are perhaps the finest thing in it . . . I well remember the glorious walk of which you speak, how we lay
drenched with sunshine on the 'moss' and were for a short
time perfectly happy—which is a rare enough condition,
God knows . . .

TO ARTHUR GREEVES: from Great Bookham
(The 'Mrs K.' referred to here is Mrs Kirkpatrick.)

[14 March 1916]
I am afraid our Galahad [Arthur] will be growing a very
stodgy mind if he reads nothing but Trollope and Goldsmith
and Austen. Of course they are all very good, but I don't
think myself I could stand such a dose of solidity. I suppose you will reply that I am too much the other way, and
will grow an unbalanced mind if I read nothing but lyrics and faery tales. I believe you are right, but I find it so
hard to start a fresh novel: I have a lazy desire to dally with
the old favourites again . . . I have found my musical soul
again—you will be pleased to hear—this time in the pre-
ludes of Chopin. I suppose you must have played them to
me, but I never noticed them before. Aren't they wonderful? Although Mrs K. doesn't play them well, they are so
passionate, so hopeless, I could almost cry over them: they
are unbearable . . .

TO ARTHUR GREEVES: **from Great Bookham**
[30 May 1916]

I cannot urge you too strongly to go on and write some-thing, anything, but at any rate WRITE. Of course everyone knows his own strength best, but if I may give any advice, I would say as I did before, that humour is a dangerous thing to try: as well, there are so many funny books in the world that it seems a shame to make any more, while the army of weird and beautiful or homely and passionate works could well do with recruits ... And by the way, while I'm on this subject, there's one thing I want to say: I do hope that in things like this you'll always tell me the absolute truth about my work, just as if it were by someone we didn't know: I will promise to do the same for you. Because otherwise there is no point in sending them, and I have sometimes thought that you are inclined not to. (Not to be candid I mean) ...

TO ARTHUR GREEVES: **from Great Bookham**
[6 June 1916]

I was rather surprised to see the note paper of your last letter and certainly wish I could have been with you: I have some vague memories of the cliffs round there and of Dunluce Castle, and some memories which are not vague at all of the same coast a little further on at Castlerock, where we used to go in the old days. Don't you love a windy day at a place like that? Waves make one kind of music on rocks and another on sand, and I don't know which of the two I would rather have ... I don't like the way you say 'don't tell anyone' that you thought 'Frankenstein' badly written, and at once draw in your critical horns with the 'of course I'm no judge' theory. Rot! You are a very good judge for me because our tastes run in the same direction. And you ought to rely more on yourself than on anyone else in matters of books—that is if you are out for enjoyment and not for improvement or any nonsense of that sort . . .

TO ARTHUR GREEVES: from Great Bookham

[14 June 1916]

I have now read all the tales of Chaucer which I ever expected to read, and feel that I may consider the book as finished: some of them are quite impossible. On the whole with one or two splendid exceptions such as the Knight's and the Franklin's tales, he is disappointing when you get to know him. He has most of the faults of the Middle Ages—garrulity and coarseness—without their romantic charm . . .

I hope that you are either going on with 'Alice' or starting something else: you have plenty of imagination, and what you want is practice, practice, practice. It doesn't matter what we write (at least in my view) at our age so long as we write continually as well as we can. I feel that every time I write a page either of prose or of verse, with real effort, even if it's thrown into the fire next minute, I am so much further on . . .

TO ARTHUR GREEVES: from Great Bookham

[20 June 1916]

What is nicer than to get a book—doubtful both about reading matter and edition, and then to find both are topping? By the way of balancing my disappointment in 'Tristan' I have just had this pleasure in Sidney's 'Arcadia'. Oh Arthur, you simply must get it . . . I don't know how to explain its peculiar charm, because it is not at all like anything I ever read before: and yet in places like all of them. Sometimes it is like Malory, often like Spenser, and yet different from either . . . The story is much more connected than Malory: there is a great deal of love making, and just enough 'brasting and fighting' to give a sort of impression of all the old doings of chivalry in the background without becoming tedious . . .

TO ARTHUR GREEVES: **from Great Bookham** (after a holiday spent together at Portsalon in County Donegal)
27 September 1916

As you say, it seems years and years since I left: I have quite dropped back into the not unpleasant, though monotonous routine of Bookham, and could believe I never left it. Portsalon is like a dream . . . One part of my journey I enjoyed very much was the first few miles out of Liverpool: because it was one of the most wonderful mornings I have ever seen—one of those lovely white misty ones when you can't see ten yards. You could just see the nearest trees and houses, a little ghostly in appearance, and beyond that everything was a clean white blank. It felt as if the train was alone in space, if you know what I mean . . .

Have you reached home yet? . . . The country at home was beginning to look nice and autumn-y, with dead leaves in the lanes and a nice nutty smell . . . Here it is horrible bright summer, which I hate. Love to all our friends such as the hedgepig etc.

TO ARTHUR GREEVES: from Great Bookham

4 October 1916

The beastly summer is at last over here, and good old Autumn colours & smells and temperatures have come back. Thanks to this we had a most glorious walk on Saturday: it was a fine cool, windy day & we set out after lunch to go to a place called 'Friday Street' which is a very long walk from here through beautiful woods and vallies that I don't know well. After several hours wandering over fields & woods etc. with the aid of a map we began to get lost and suddenly at about 4 o'clock—we had expected to reach the place by that time—we found ourselves in a place where we had been an hour before! . . . We had a lot of difficulty in at last reaching the place, but it was glorious when we got there. You are walking in the middle of a wood when all of a sudden you go downwards and come to a little open hollow just big enough for a little lake and some old, old red-tiled houses: all round it the trees tower up on rising ground and every road from it is at once swallowed up in them. You might walk within a few feet of it & suspect nothing unless you saw the smoke rising up from some cottage chimney. Can you imagine what it was like? Best of all, we came down to the little inn of the village and had tea there with—glory of glories—an old tame jackdaw hopping about our feet and asking for crumbs. He is called Jack and will answer to his name. The inn has three tiny but spotlessly clean bedrooms, so some day, if the gods will, you & I are going to stay there . . .

TO ARTHUR GREEVES: from Great Bookham

12 October [1916]

You ask me my religious views: you know, I think, that I believe in no religion. There is absolutely no proof for any of them, and from a philosophical standpoint Christianity is not even the best. All religions, that is, all mythologies to give them their proper name, are merely man's own invention—Christ as much as Loki. Primitive man found himself surrounded by all sorts of terrible things he didn't understand—thunder, pestilence, snakes etc: what more natural than to suppose that these were animated by evil spirits trying to torture him. These he kept off by cringing to them, singing songs and making sacrifices etc. Gradually from being mere nature-spirits these supposed being[s] were elevated into more elaborate ideas, such as the old gods: and when man became more refined he pretended that these spirits were good as well as powerful.

Thus religion, that is to say mythology, grew up. Often, too, great men were regarded as gods after their death—such as Heracles or Odin: thus after the death of a Hebrew philosopher Yeshua (whose name we have corrupted into Jesus) he became regarded as a god, a cult sprang up, which was afterwards connected with the ancient Hebrew Jahweh-worship, and so Christianity came into being—one mythology among many, but the one that we happened to have been brought up in . . .

TO ARTHUR GREEVES: from Great Bookham
25 October 1916

I don't know when I shall buy some new books, as I am at present suffering from a flash of poverty—poverty comes in flashes like dullness or pleasure. When I do it will be either *Our Village*, or *Cranford* or Chaucer's *Troilus and Cressida*, if I can get a decent edition of it. By all accounts it is much more in my line than the *Canterbury Tales*, and anyway I can take no more interest in them since I have discovered that my Everyman is abridged & otherwise mutilated. I wish they wouldn't do that (*Lockhart*, you say, is another case) without telling you. I can't bear to have anything but what a man really wrote.

I have been reading the quaintest book this week, *The Letters of Dorothy Osbourne to Sir William Temple* in Everyman. I suppose, as a historian you will know all about those two, but in case you don't they lived in Cromwell's time. It is very interesting to read the ordinary everyday life of a girl in those days, and, tho' of course they are often dull there is a lot in them you would like: especially a description of how she spends the day and another of a summer evening in the garden . . . I have read today—there's absolutely no head or tale in this letter but you ought to be used to that by now—some ten pages of *Tristram Shandy* and am wondering whether I like it. It is certainly the maddest book ever written or 'ever wrote' as dear Dorothy Osbourne would say. It gives you the impression of an escaped lunatic's conversation while chasing his hat on a windy May morning. Yet there are beautiful serious parts in it though of a sentimental kind, as I know from my father . . .

Tang-Tang there goes eleven o'clock 'Tis almost faery time'. Don't you simply love going to bed. To curl up warmly in a nice warm bed, in the lovely darkness, that is so restful & then gradually drift away into sleep . . . I'm turning out the gas. Bon soir!

TO ARTHUR GREEVES: from Great Bookham

[1 November 1916]

I can't let it pass unchallenged that you should put 'Beowulf' and 'Malory' together as if they belonged to the same class. One is a mediaeval, English prose romance and the other an Anglo-Saxon epic poem: one is Christian, the other heathen: one we read just as it was actually written, the other in a translation. So you can like one without the other, and anyway you must like or dislike them both for different reasons. It is always very difficult of course to explain to another person the good points of a book he doesn't like.

TO HIS FATHER: from 1 Mansfield Road, Oxford
(a scholarship candidate's first impressions of Oxford)

[7 December 1916]

This is Thursday and our last papers are on Saturday morning: so I will cross on Monday night if you will kindly make the arrangements. We have so far had General Paper, Latin Prose, Greek and Latin unseen, and English essay. The subject for the latter was Johnson's 'People confound liberty of thinking with liberty of talking'[1]—rather suggestive, tho' to

---

[1] James Boswell, *The Life of Samuel Johnson*, 7 May 1773 (1791).

judge by faces, some did not find it so. I don't know exactly how I am doing, because my most dangerous things—the two proses—are things you can't judge for yourself . . . The place has surpassed my wildest dreams: I never saw anything so beautiful, especially on these frosty moonlight nights: tho' in the Hall of Oriel where we do our papers it is fearfully cold at about four o'clock on these afternoons. We have most of us tried with varying success to write in our gloves. I will see you then on Tuesday morning.

TO HIS BROTHER: from Belfast

Postmark: 8 January 1917

Many thanks indeed for the letter, and the most acceptable enclosure, which arrived, thank goodness, while P[apy] was out, and so was saved from going the same road as my poor legacy. For you know I got £21 (is that the amount?) the same as you, but of course I have never seen a penny of it: my humble suggestion that I might have a pound or two was greeted with the traditional 'Ah, such nonsense.'

Congers on being made a real Lieut., which of course I suppose is far more important than the temporary Captaincy. Is there any chance of your being made a real Captain when this war is over—which I hope to God will be before my valuable person gets anywhere near it . . .

Oxford is absolutely topping, I am awfully bucked with it and longing to go up, tho' apparently I am not to do this until next October . . .

TO HIS FATHER: from Great Bookham

[28 January 1917]

At about half past 11 on the Saturday morning I went to Univ. and was led across two quads, one behind the other, to a house in a beautiful old walled garden. This was the ogre's castle. He was a clean shaven, white haired, jolly old man, and was very nice indeed.[2] He treated me to about half an hour's 'Oxford Manner', and then came gradually round to my own business. Since writing last, he had made enquiries, and it seems that if I pass Responsions in March I could 'come up' in the following term and join the O.T.C. [Officers' Training Corps]. This plan he thinks the best, because I should have far more chance of a commission from the Oxford O.T.C. than from anything else of the sort . . . After that he made me stay to lunch with his wife and niece and 'so to the station'. I am very pleased with my ogre after all . . .

TO HIS FATHER: from University College (on first taking up residence in wartime Oxford)

Postmark: 28 April 1917

The effect of the war here is much more startling than I could have expected, and everything is very homely and out of order. The College at present numbers six men, of whom four are freshmen! Others are coming all the time, but I do not think we shall be more than eleven all told. Last night we had dinner not in Hall but in a small lecture room, and

---

[2] Reginald Walter Macan (1848–1941), the Master of University College.

none of the dons appeared. Hall is in possession of the blue-coated wounded, who occupy the whole of one quad . . . The first thing that strikes you is the enormous size of the rooms. I imagined a 'sitter' something smaller than the little end room. The first one they showed me was rather larger than our drawing room and full of most beautiful oak. I wasn't left there however, and am now in a much humbler, and very nice set, on the other side of the quad. It is a pity in a way that all the furniture and pictures really belong to a man who may be coming back after the war—it saves me expenses, but it prevents me from having what I want.[3]

I have been to see the Dean, who turns out to be a beard-less boy of about twenty-five, and also my tutor, who is also the bursar.[4] They don't appear to suggest any real read-ing while I am in the Corps, but the Bursar has promised to find me a coach for elementary mathematics, if possible.[5] Corps does not begin till Monday evening for which respite I am very thankful. I think it will be quite cheap living in this 'vast solitude': the only serious expenses so far have been £2.10.0 for uniform (which seems very reasonable), and £1.9.0 for cap and gown (which does not) . . .

---

[3] He was in set number 5 on staircase 12 of the Radcliffe Quad. Most of the rooms in this quad were occupied by the wounded.

[4] John Clifford Valentine Behan (1881–1957) was the Dean 1914–17. He was the first Rhodes Scholar to come from the State of Victoria, Australia, and he was made a Fellow of Law at University College in 1909. Jack's tutor was Arthur Blackburne Poynton (1876–1944). He was the Master of University College 1935–37.

[5] Jack had failed algebra in his Responsions in March. Shortly after this letter was written he began tutorials in this subject with Mr John Edward Campbell (1862–1924) of Hertford College.

TO HIS FATHER: from University College

Postmark: 17 May 1917

Our 'military duties' are as light as they well could be. We have a morning parade from 7 till 7.45, and another from 2 till 4, with occasional evening lectures on map reading and such like subjects . . . The early morning parade of course makes it impossible for us to go to chapel, except to the Celebration on Sundays. I am afraid that I usually find the place in possession of us freshers and the dons. As to St Mary's, I have not been yet. The last two Sundays were so fine that having been to the early service, I felt justified in going off to bathe after 'brekker'. I have however found out enough about it to realize that it is rather different from what we imagine. There are only a few prayers, and a very long sermon, usually more of a philosophical and political than of a religious nature: in fact it is more a Sunday lecture room than a church in the true sense. The best place to go for a fine service is the Cathedral at 'The House' as Christ Church is called: it is typical of the House that it should have the Cathedral of the diocese for its chapel!

TO HIS FATHER: from University College

[3? June 1917]

I am glad to find that my money 'pans out' quite sufficiently, and is indeed just about the average. I mean the amount of pocket money is about the same as that of other people, though of course many have an allowance out of which they pay all their own bills—in which case the actual pocket money will vary with the ups and downs of their Battels. To give you some idea of the latter, I enclose mine as supplied so far . . . The first week was necessarily expensive chiefly through ignorance, 'in which accomplishment', as De Quincey says, 'I excel'.

My scout is a very fatherly old man who has been here for forty-six years, and is really exceedingly good about keeping my expenses down: he once even told me to change my socks when they were wet!!![6] His only failing is an impentrible (or -able) deafness which causes many conversations of the 'It's a fine day'—'No, not much to pay' type.

I am afraid you must not build anything on the idea of my rowing, as I have almost given it up in favour of canoeing. You see a row boat can be used only on the big river, where you run into all the real rowing men, as the Cherwell (much prettier and more interesting) soon gets too narrow for rowers to pass each other. Besides, there is to me something very attractive about one of these little canoes—so very light and so all-to-yourself. Perhaps when we all come back again from the war, and there is no O.T.C., I will take up rowing again.

The O.T.C. gets more interesting as we go on. We spend a good deal of our time in 'the trenches'—a complete model system with dug outs, shell holes and—graves. This last touch of realistic scenery seems rather superfluous . . .

I have nearly finished Renan, whom I find delightful.[7] He seems to have written a good many other books on different subjects. I am going to borrow Wells's new book[8] from a man in College called Edwards, who is thinking of becoming a Catholic. He is an ardent Newmanite, and we have some talk

---

[6] 'Jo', as everyone called this college scout, was Cyril Haggis.
[7] Joseph Ernest Renan, *La Vie de Jésus* (1863).
[8] H. G. Wells, *God the Invisible King* (1917).

on literary subjects.[9] Someone pointed me out our present poet-laureate, Bridges (1), on the river last Wednesday.
(1) Its just occurred to me that you might have known the name anyway. Apologies! — J.

[Keble College, Oxford, had been used since 1 January 1915 for the training of officers. Jack was one of the many from Oxford and other places who arrived there on 7 June 1917. He shared a room with Edward Francis Courtenay ('Paddy') Moore, who came into the Oxford O.T.C. from Clifton College, Bristol. In their Introduction to the *Oxford University Roll of Service* (Oxford, 1920), the editors, E. S. Craig and W. M. Gibson, said this about the colleges which made up Oxford University: 'By the end of the year 1917 there were only three hundred and fifteen students in residence. Of these some fifty were Oriental students, twenty-five were refugees, chiefly Serbians, some thirty were medical students, and about a hundred and twenty were members of the Officers' Training Corps, waiting till their age should qualify them for admission to a Cadet Battalion. The military history of Oxford, during the latter years of the War, is to be read among the records of the battle fronts, from Flanders to Mesopotamia' (pp. x–xi). In order to help these young men from other universities and schools who were also quartered in Keble, Leonard

---

[9] John Robert Edwards (1897–) became a teacher after leaving Oxford. He was the Headmaster of the Liverpool Institute High School from 1935 until his retirement in 1961.

Rice-Oxley published a booklet entitled *Oxford in Arms: With an Account of Keble College* (1917).]

TO HIS FATHER: from **Keble College, Oxford**

Postmark: 8 June 1917

Just a line in a hurry, to let you know how things go. I have not been able to write to you before. Well of course this is not an agreeable change, but it was the natural next step in any pilgrimage towards a commission. The cadet batallion, which I joined yesterday (of course it has nothing to do with the varsity) is quartered in Keble. There are several gentlemen among it, and I am fortunate in sharing a room with one. It is a great comfort to be in Oxford, as I shall still be able to see something of my Univ. friends and Cherry.[10] As to Responsions, I may or may not be able to persuade them to give me three days' leave to do it in: if they do, I should not think that under the circumstances my chances of passing would be very bright. At any rate, six months' service with the colours will exempt me from it. As to the artillery, I am afraid that only those who have 'some special knowledge of mathematics' will be recommended. About leave we don't know anything yet. I am sorry I can't write any more to cheer you up, but we must both of us thole for a while. My tips etc. on leaving College have cleared me out, so could you let me have something to go on with? . . .

---

[10] Charlotte Rose Rachael ('Cherry') Robbins (1888–1978), Lewis's cousin, was with the Voluntary Aid Detachment at a military hospital in Oxford.

TO HIS FATHER: from Keble College

[10? June 1917]

And now for some account of the new life. Well at first when I left my own snug quarters and my own friends at Univ. for a carpetless little cell with two beds (minus sheets or pillows) at Keble, and got into a Tommy's uniform, I will not deny that I thought myself very ill used. However, as What's-his-name said, 'I have had many misfortunes in life, but most of them never happened to me'. I have quite recovered, and am now leading a very happy life, tho' not of course the life I would have chosen. In many ways it is a better life: I have never worked until now, and it is high time that I began.

As to my companions, they are really divided into three lots. The first and largest lot consists of rankers who have been out for some time and have come here to get commissions. These are mostly jolly good chaps: clean, honest, infinitely good natured. As they have come here to be made into 'officers and gentlemen' their own naïve conceptions of how gentlemen behave among themselves lead them into an impossible politeness that is really very pathetic. Most of our set get on very well with them. The next lot (about one third of the whole) consists of cads and fools pure and simple. They don't need much description: some of them are vicious, some merely doltish, all vulgar and uninteresting. They drop their h's, spit on the stairs, and talk about what they're going to do when they get to the front—where of course none of them has been. Then comes the third lot, our own set, the public school men and varsity men with all their faults and merits 'already ascertained'.

My chief friend is Somerville, scholar of Eton and scholar of King's, Cambridge, a very quiet sort of person, but very booky and interesting. Moore of Clifton, my room companion, and Sutton of Repton (the company humourist) are also good fellows. The former is a little too childish for real companionship, but I will forgive him much for his appreciation of Newbolt. I must not pass over the knut, De Pass, also of Repton, our regnant authority on all matter of dress, who is reported to wear stays: nor Davy, the Carthusian, who remembers my Sinn Fein friend as a prefect at Charterhouse.[11]

The daily round is of course pretty strenuous, and leaves little time for dreaming or reading. However, I eat and sleep as I have never done before, and am getting rid of some adipose tissue . . .

TO HIS FATHER: from Keble College

Postmark: 18 July 1917

Life here goes on pretty much in the usual way, except that the work gets rather more interesting and involves less actual 'sweat of the brow' than at first. We do a good deal of night work, which I rather like, and which leads to getting up later in the morning . . . You are allowed week end leave here every week, provided that you do not go out of

---

[11] This group of friends, all born in 1898, were: Martin Ashworth Somerville, 'Paddy' Moore, Alexander Gordon Sutton and Denis Howard de Pass of Repton School, and Thomas Kerrison Davey of Charterhouse School. The 'Sinn Fein' friend was Theobald Richard Fitzwalter Butler (1894–1976) who had just taken his final examinations. He was to achieve great distinction as a lawyer.

Oxford. The last four weeks I have spent it over at Univ., enjoying all my old luxuries over again. Now however the Dean—Who as I remarked is a superior person—has vetoed the plan; on the ground that College is kept open in vacation for men who want to read 'and not for use as an hotel'. I suppose he is quite right in a way, but it is rather a pity.

You can't imagine how I have grown to love Univ., especially since I left. Last Saturday evening when I was sleeping there alone, I spent a long time wandering over it, into all sorts of parts where I had never been before, where the mullioned windows are dark with ivy that no one has bothered to cut since the war emptied the rooms they belong to. Some of these rooms were all dust sheeted, others were much as the owners had left them—the pictures still on the wall and the books dust covered in their shelves. It was melancholy in a way, and yet very interesting. I have found one room that I have mapped out to be my own when I come back.

At present I am reading a countrymen of ours, Bishop Berkely, 'that silly old man' as Andrew Lang calls him: in fact, one of our few philosophers and a very interesting fellow, whom I always admired for the courage with which you find him standing up to the ogre in Boswell[12] ... Could you

---

[12] Jack was deeply impressed at this time by the 'Subjective Idealism' of Bishop George Berkeley (1685–1753) as propounded in his *Principles of Human Knowledge* (1710). The Bishop held that when we affirm material things to be real, we mean no more than that they are perceived. What annoyed Jack about 'the ogre in Boswell' was the famous remark of Dr Johnson's recorded in Boswell's *Life of Samuel Johnson*. On 6 August 1763 Boswell wrote: 'After we came out of the church, we stood talking for some time together of Bishop Berkeley's ingenious sophistry to prove the non-existence of matter, and that every thing in

let me have some money to get boots for my officer-pattern uniform. I find the cadet school so far much more expensive than the Varsity. When does W. get his leave?

TO HIS FATHER: from Keble College
Postmark: 22 July 1917

Pay there was none at first, except for the old soldiers: but the War Office has at last discovered our existence, and on Friday I drew 7/-, the first money I have earned. It ought to be hung on a watch chain. You say that you should talk to me 'not of the Muse'. Indeed the reverse is quite the truth, for I make every effort to cling to the old life of books, hoping that I may save my soul alive and not become a great, empty headed, conceited military prig. I am finding out that the military ideal in our army differs from the German one only in degree and not in kind. The Sergeant Major told us the other day that 'soldiering is more than 'arf swank. You've got to learn to walk out as if the bloody street belonged to you. See?' We are also encouraged in every way to be pharisees

---

the universe is merely ideal. I observed, that though we are satisfied his doctrine is not true, it is impossible to refute it. I never shall forget the alacrity with which Johnson answered, striking his foot with mighty force against a large stone, till he rebounded from it, "I refute it *thus.*"'

As Bishop Berkeley never met Dr Johnson, he had no chance of 'standing up' to him. Jack has confused the Bishop with his son, who was also named George. This George (1733–95) met Dr Johnson shortly after he came up to Oxford in 1752, and when Dr Johnson made fun of the Bishop's abortive scheme for a missionary college in Bermuda the young George walked out of the room. He subsequently refused Dr Johnson's repeated requests for permission to write a 'Life of Bishop Berkeley.'

and pat ourselves on the back for being in khaki, and stare rudely at apparently eligible young men whom we meet in mufti. Well I hope that neither I nor any of my friends—and I have done well here in the way of friends—will ever attain to that degree of soldierhood. The promised four days' leave will come in about a fortnight's time: I am sorry that I cannot let you know more definitely. I shall of course come home the quickest way, there being no question of 'lucre' when a paternal government provides you with a pass . . .

On Saturday I drank tea with a dear old gentleman named Goddard, formerly an undergrad of Balliol and now a don at Trinity.[13] What interested me most was his opinion of Jowett[14] (here usually pronounced to rhyme with 'poet') who, he said, had spoiled the scholarly tone of Balliol by a vulgar running after lions . . .

Of Swinburne's prose, I have read the book on Charlotte Bronte, and the smaller one on William Blake.[15] It is undoubtedly very bad prose (I did not find the coarseness) but it is so vigorous that you can forgive it. Don't forget to keep Wells's *God the Invisible King* in the house, as I am longing to read it.

---

[13] He must have misunderstood the name. There was no don named 'Goddard' at Trinity College in 1917.

[14] Benjamin Jowett (1817–93) was the Master of Balliol College 1870–93). He was ordained a priest in 1845 but his theological liberalism, particularly evident in his essay 'The Interpretation of Scripture', was hotly debated. Jowett's classical learning was, however, almost unrivalled during his years in Oxford. He was an Oxford figure and the subject of innumerable stories.

[15] Algernon Charles Swinburne, *Note on Charlotte Bronte* (1877); *William Blake* (1868).

TO HIS FATHER: from **Keble College** (having visited his
father in Belfast 9–11 August)

Postmark: 27 August 1917

You must have been wondering what had come over me,
but the crowded time I have been having since I left home
will serve as some excuse. First of all came the week at
Warwick, which was a nightmare. I was billeted with five
others in the house of an undertaker and memorial sculptor. We had three beds between six of us, there was of
course no bath, and the feeding was execrable. The little
back yard full of tomb stones, which we christened 'the
quadrangle', was infinitely preferable to the tiny dining
room with its horse hair sofa and family photos. When
all six of us sat down to meals there together, there was
scarcely room to eat, let alone swing the traditional cat
round. Altogether it was a memorable experience. We
came back on Saturday, and the following week I spent
with Moore at the digs of his mother who, as I mentioned,
is staying at Oxford.[16] I like her immensely and thoroughly

---

[16] Mrs Jane ('Janie') King Moore was born in Dunany, Co. Armagh, in
1872, the eldest of the three daughters and two sons of the Revd William
James Askins (1842–95) and his wife Jane King Askins (1846–90). Mrs
Moore's father was the Vicar of Dunany 1872–95, and in 1894 he was
made Prebendary of Ballymore. In 1898 Janie married Courtenay
Edward Moore (1870) from whom she had two children, 'Paddy'
(b. 1898) and Maureen (b. 1906) who is now the baronetess, Lady
Dunbar of Hempriggs. When Jack met the Moores in June of 1917, Mrs
Moore had been separated from her husband for some time, and she
had come to Oxford from her home in Bristol to see as much as she
could of 'Paddy' before he left for the Front.

enjoyed myself. On Wednesday as you know, Warnie was up here and we had a most enjoyable afternoon and evening together, chiefly at my rooms in Univ. How I wish you could have been there too. But please God I shall be able to see you at Oxford and show you my 'sacred city' in happier times . . .

TO HIS FATHER: from Keble College

Postmark: 10 September 1917

I was very glad to get your letter, for, though my own sins in that line are as scarlet, I must admit that I was beginning to get a little bit anxious. It was such a pity that Warnie and I could not be home together—and yet too, in a way, it spread out the 'invasion' of your young hopefuls longer for you. Warnie seems to have thoroughly enjoyed his leave, and I am sure the 'drag' exists only in your imagination . . .

The next amusement on our programme is a three days bivouac up in the Wytham hills. As it has rained all the time for two or three days, our model trenches up there will provide a very unnesseccarily good imitation of Flanders mud. You know how I always disapproved of realism in art! . . .

As time gets on towards the end of our course, we are more and more crowded and live only in hope for the fabulous amounts of leave we are going to get before we're gazetted. Tell Arthur I simply CAN'T write.

TO HIS FATHER: from **Keble College**

Postmark: 24 September 1917

I hope I was not grousing in my last letter, for though this may not be the life I had chosen, yet a little hard work never did any one any harm, and I might be much worse off. The sleeping out on Cumnor hills (there were only two nights of it) illustrated some old theories of anticipation etc.—but I needn't go through it. In point of fact, sleeping out of doors proved delightful. You have a waterproof groundsheet, two blankets, and your haversack for a pillow. There was plenty of bracken to make a soft bed, and I slept excellently. You wake up in a flash without any drowsiness, feeling wonderfully fresh. Both nights were fine, but of course it would be horrible in the wet.

Our final exam comes off next Tuesday: and remembering my wonderful faculty for failing in easy exams (vide Smalls[17]) I don't feel too confident. There seems some doubt as to when we get away after it, but probably before the end of this week. In any case I shall stay on here with the Moores over the Sunday, and wire exact date of my crossing to you later. We get a free warrant home, but I should be glad if you would send me the Samaritans 'two pence' for oil and wine en route . . . [18]

---

[17] A colloquial term for Responsions.

[18] On 25 September Jack was gazetted into the 3rd Somerset Light Infantry and given a month's leave. It would appear from the next letter that he went with the Moores to their home in Bristol on Saturday 29 September.

TO HIS FATHER: from 56 Ravenswood Road, Redlands, Bristol

3 October [1917]

I suppose you must have been wondering what had become of your prodigal son all this time. Rather a chapter of adventures has occurred, and I will hasten to recount them—in the best journalese style.

We got away from Keble on the Saturday, and instead of staying in Oxford with the Moores I came down here to their home at Bristol—within a mile or so of Clifton school. On the Sunday we went and saw the latter, including the Chapel where I failed to find *Qui procul hinc ante diem* etc,[19] which in fact does not exist. The place is fine, but inferior to Malvern.

On Monday a cold (complete with sore throat) which I had developed at Oxford, went on so merrily that Mrs Moore took my temperature and put me to bed, where I am writing this letter (Wednesday). I am quite looking forward to seeing you soon again . . .

[Albert Lewis wrote in his diary: 'Friday 12 October. Jacks arrived from Oxford. News arrived that Jacks gazetted Somerset Light Infantry. He had stayed with Moore at Bristol for three weeks, leaving one week for home.' 'Thursday 18 October. Jacks left by Holyhead to join regiment at Crownhill, S. Devon.' As Mr Lewis was to learn later, Jack was separated from 'Paddy' Moore who was sent to France with the Rifle Brigade.]

---

[19] 'Who far from here before day . . .'

TO HIS FATHER: from 3rd Somerset Light Infantry, Crownhill, South Devon

Monday, 5.5 P.M.
[22 October 1917]

I have waited till now so that I could tell you what an ordinary working day here is like. Incidentally the phrase 'working day' is merely *façon de parler*: but more of that anon, as you will first be anxious to hear what sort of thieves I have fallen among. I should say the gentlemen are about sixty-five per cent of the whole crowd of officers, which is quite as large a majority as one has a right to expect now-a-days. One or two of them I think I shall like, though of course it is hard to say at present. It must be admitted that most of them are hardly after my style: the subjects of conversation are shop (Oh! for the ancient taboo that ruled in officers messes in the piping times of peace), sport and theatrical news recurring with a rather dull regularity—that is in the few moments of conversation which interrupt the serious business of bridge and snooker. However, they are for the most part well bred and quite nice to me. So that if this new life rouses no violent enthusiasm in me, it is on the other hand quite bearable or even pleasant.

The 'work' is a very simple matter. All the men nearly are recruits, and the training is carried on by N.C.O.s. All you do is to lead your party onto parade, hand them over to their instructor, and then walk about doing nothing at all. This you do for several hours a day. It is a little tiring to the legs and I think will finally result in atrophy of the brain. However, it is very much better than hard work, and I am quite satisfied.

I was a bit too previous in wiring from Plymouth station that Crownhill was a barracks. It turns out to be a village of wooden huts, set up in the hills amid really very beautiful scenery. Besides the officers' mess—which is a sort of glorified golf club-house—we each have our own room, with a stove in it. When this is lit, it is really very snug . . . So my verdict you see is quite favourable. The life, so long as I am in England, will be rather dull, but easy and not unpleasant. There is no need to transfer into any other infantry regiment. So at least I think now: of course I may change . . .

[For weeks it was rumoured that Jack's battalion would almost certainly be sent to Ireland to fight either the Sinn Fein or the Germans, said to be landing there. However, on 15 November they were ordered to the front following a 48-hour leave. As it was impossible for him to go to Belfast, Jack went to Mrs Moore's home in Bristol from where he sent a telegram to his father saying: 'Have arrived in Bristol on 48 hours leave. Report Southampton Saturday. Can you come Bristol. If so meet at station. Reply Mrs Moore's address 56 Ravenswood Road Redlands Bristol. Jack.' Mr Lewis wired back: 'Don't understand telegram. Please write.']

TO HIS FATHER: **telegraphed from Bristol**
15 November 1917
I have just got your wire. I am sending off another to explain things more clearly: I'm awfully sorry, but I can't

think how I failed to make it plain in the first. It is perfectly wretched giving me such short leave—forty-eight hours is no earthly use to a person who lives in Ireland and would have to spend about two days and nights travelling. Please don't worry, I shall probably be a long time at the base as I have had so little training in England. Can't write more now: must go and do some shopping. I return the proofs. I should like one of each I think. I'll let you know my address in France as soon as I can.[20]

TO HIS FATHER: from France

21 November 1917

This is really a very sudden and unpleasant surprise. I had no notion of it until I was sent off on my forty-eight hours final leave, in fact I thought they were ragging me when they told me. I am now at a certain very safe base town where we live comfortably in huts as we did at Crownhill. I am being innoculated this afternoon and have forty-eight hours off duty afterwards . . . I suppose we have no reason to grumble: this was bound to come sooner or later. There is no need to worry for a good time yet, and I'll try and let

---

[20] The proofs were of photographs of Mr Lewis taken with his sons. On Friday 16 November Jack sent the following telegraph to his father: 'Orders France. Reporting Southampton 4 P.M. Saty. If coming, wire immediately. No need alarm. Shall be at base. Jack.' Jack Lewis, having been commissioned a 2nd Lieutenant, was suddenly transferred from the 3rd to the 1st Battalion of the Somerset Light Infantry and he crossed to France on 17 November.

you hear every day when there is. Have got to go on parade in a few minutes, so must stop. Shall be able to write you a proper letter off duty tomorrow.

[Mr Lewis was desperately worried about Jack's safety. Upon receiving the above letter he wrote to Colonel James Craig, later Viscount Craigavon (1871–1940), who was M.P. for the East Division of Co. Down, asking for his help in getting Jack transferred from the Infantry to the Artillery. He believed Jack would be safest with the gunners. Colonel Craig replied that it would be necessary for him to have a letter from Jack expressing his wish to be transferred, as well as a recommendation from his Commanding Officer. Mr Lewis then sent a copy of this correspondence to Jack.]

TO HIS FATHER: **from France**

13 December 1917

The letter of which you forwarded me a copy is rather a surprise, and I hope you will not be disappointed at my answer to it. Some arguments in favour of staying in the infantry have arisen since we were last together. In the first place, I must confess that I have become very much attached to this regiment. I have several friends whom I should be sorry to leave and I am just beginning to know my men and understand the work. In the second place, if the main reason for going into the gunners is their supposed safety, I hardly think it is enough. On this part of the front the guns are exposed to almost as heavy shelling (and it is shells that count far more than rifle fire) as the infantry: if their casualties are fewer that must be because their total strength is so much smaller. Then, again, nobody holds out any hopes of my getting recommended by the C.O. He would be sure to reply (and not without reason) that it would be expensive and wasteful to take a half-trained infantry officer home again and turn him into a gunner. Our C.O.—a Lt Colonel Majendie—is a splendid fellow for whom I have a great admiration, and I should be sorry to cut so poor a figure in his eyes as I must do in trying to back out as I get nearer the real part of my job.[21] Of course I fully understand that it is rather late for me to talk thus; and beyond the right which you have to guide me in any case, you have ample grounds for claiming that I should stick to our arrangement. Yet I think you will sympathize with what I have said above.

I am at present in billets in a certain rather battered town somewhere behind the line. It is quite comfy, but of course the work is hard and (which is worse) irregular. I have just finished *Adam Bede*[22] which I liked immensely—but don't send me any more of hers as I know a shop (or rather canteen here) that has them—in the Tauchnitz edition . . .

---

[21] Vivian Henry Bruce Majendie (1886–1960) had been educated at Winchester College and Sandhurst. As Commander of the 1st Battalion of the Somerset Light Infantry he was eminently suited for writing *A History of the 1st Battalion, the Somerset Light Infantry (Prince Albert's) July 1st 1916 to the end of the War* (1921). He ended his long and useful career in the Army as a Major-General, and he retired in 1946.

[22] By George Eliot (1859).

TO HIS FATHER: from France

4 January 1918

I have thought a good deal about the question that is uppermost in both our minds, and talked it over with some of my friends. The arguments in favour of staying where I am seem overwhelming, and I have finally made up my mind to do so. I am very sorry that you should have taken trouble unnecessarily, and I hope that my decision will not be a disappointment to you. From what you say in your last letter, I think you agree with me that the gunners are not really preferable for safety or society. I have been up in the trenches for a few days (which I will speak about later on) attached to a company for instruction, and the number of shells that went singing over our heads to fall on the batteries far away behind, did not—as you may imagine—weaken my affection for the infantry!

I am now back again on a course of bombing, where I live with the bombing officer, a very nice fellow, of literary tastes, in a quite comfortable billet. The work, involving a good deal of chemical and mechanical questions, is not of the sort my brain takes to readily, but as long as one is safe and has an unbroken night's sleep, there is nothing to grouse about I suppose.

You will be anxious to hear my first impressions of trench life. This is a very quiet part of the line and the dug outs are very much more comfortable than one imagines at home. They are very deep, you go down to them by a shaft of about twenty steps: they have wire bunks where a man can sleep quite snugly, and brasiers for warmth and cooking. Indeed, the chief discomfort is that they tend to get TOO hot, while of course the bad air makes one rather headachy. I had quite a pleasant time, and was only once in a situation of unusual danger, owing to a shell falling near the latrines while I was using them.

I think I told you that I had read *Adam Bede* and am now at *The Mill on the Floss*,[23] which I like even better. Do you know of any life of George Eliot published in a cheap edition? If you find one, I should like to read it.

Thank you muchly for the smokeables. The pipes have been soaked in whisky, according to the dictum of experts, and are going very well. I also thank you from my heart for your last letter that defies definition. I am very proud of my father . . .

[On 2 February 1918 the War Office in London sent the following message to Albert Lewis: 'The Military Secretary presents his compliments to Mr Lewis and begs to inform him that the following report has just been received. 2nd Lieutenant C. S. Lewis, Somerset Light Infantry, was admitted to 10th Red Cross Hospital, Le Tréport on February 1st., suffering from slight Pyrexia. Further news will be sent when received.']

---

[23] By George Eliot (1860).

TO HIS FATHER: from No. 10 British Red Cross Hospital, Le Tréport

16 February 1918

Your letter has remained unanswered for some time, and if I had literally fulfilled my promise of 'writing when I got up', I fear the time would have been longer still. 'Trench fever' sounds a formidable name enough—like 'prison fever' in the days of the Bloody Assize I always think, but it is not usually a troublesome business. In this country it is called P.U.O. which, I am told, stands for 'Pyrexia unknown origin': which in plain English means merely a high temperature arising from the general irregularity of life at the front. In my case however, after they had got me down to normal, I had a relapse, and was pretty ill for a day or two. I am now however on the highroad to recovery, though still in bed. I consider this little turn as an unmixed blessing: even if I get no leave by it—and I'm afraid that is not very likely—I shall have had a comfortable rest from the line. The place where I have been dropped down is a little fishing village so far as I can make out. There are cliffs and a grey sea beyond—which one is very glad to see again—and from my own window pleasant wooded country. They tell me Dieppe is about eighteen miles away: and that makes one remember ... *eheu fugaces!*[24]

By the way (I can't remember whether I told you before or not) the Captain of the Company I am in is the Harris

---

[24] 'Alas! How the years fly by!' He and Warren had gone on holiday with their mother at Berneval, near Dieppe, in September 1907.

who used to be a master at Cherbourg: I think you met him once. He impressed me in those days, but I find him very disappointing. I wonder is it my own fault that so many of my old acquaintances I have run up against since leaving my shell at Bookham 'Please me not'? I suppose these things are to be expected.[25]

---

[25] This meeting of the extremely colourful Harris again after five years is worthy of a footnote in red ink. While I can understand Jack's disenchantment with this man at this time, I have discovered enough about Percy Gerald Kelsal Harris to cause me to like him very much. He is the master at Cherbourg House whom Jack refers to as 'Pogo' in *Surprised by Joy* (ch. IV). Of his arrival at the school in May 1912, Jack wrote: '"Sirrah", as we called him . . . was succeeded by a young gentleman just down from the University whom we may call Pogo. Pogo was a very minor edition of a Saki, perhaps even a Wodehouse hero. Pogo was a wit, Pogo was a dressy man, Pogo was a man about town. Pogo was even a lad. After a week or so of hesitation (for his temper was uncertain) we fell at his feet and adored. Here was sophistication, glossy all over, and (dared one believe it?) ready to impart sophistication to us . . . After a term of Pogo's society one had the feeling of being not twelve weeks but twelve years older.'

P. G. K. Harris was born in Kinver, Staffordshire, on 31 August 1888. From King's School in Taunton he went up to Exeter College in 1907. That he left Oxford without taking a degree may be explained by those very qualities which delighted his pupils at Cherbourg House. He was commissioned a Lieutenant in the Somerset Light Infantry in February 1915, and had been promoted to Captain by the time Jack was assigned to his command. If Harris wasted his time in Oxford and made a flashy but poor showing at Cherbourg, he cuts an heroic and dashing figure in Everard Wyrall's official *History of the Somerset Light Infantry (Prince Albert's) 1914–1919* (1927). Wyrall describes the bravery at Verchain which caused Harris to receive the Military Cross with this Citation: 'For conspicuous gallantry near Verchain on 24 October 1918. At the river bank, in the darkness, considerable confusion and difficulty were experienced in throwing the bridges, owing to the heavy machine-gun fire. It was entirely due to his example and efforts that the bridges were thrown and that the men were able to cross. He subsequently led his company to a further objective, and carried out a personal reconnais-

You kindly ask if there is anything you could send. The next time you are in Mullan's, I should be 'beholden' if you would ask them to look out some cheap edition of Burton's *Anatomy of Melancholy* and send it to me, or the 1st volume of it. You remember it used to be a fancy of mine, and somebody has recommended it to me lately. If the only edition is in a fairly large book, let them send it all the same — I can find room for it. What are you reading? You see I make some desperate attempt to keep in touch with a life beyond the one which we lead here. I hope you keep well in body: so long as I am in hospital you may keep easy in mind. How I wish your hopes about leave could be realized. Of course it is possible, but I don't think there is much chance. By the

---

sance across the open under heavy machine-gun fire, obtaining very valuable information.' A bar was added to that Cross as a result of Harris's gallantry at Preseau on 1 November 1918. Wyrall wrote of it: '"Preseau"—it was here that the 1st Somerset Light Infantry ended its glorious record of fighting in the Great War . . . Assisted by Company Sergeant-Major R. Johnson, Captain P. G. K. Harris rallied his men and ordered them to charge. The whole line sprang forward with a cheer and, with the bayonet, flung the Germans back' (p. 356).

It is, however, in Lt Col. Majendie's *History of the 1st Battalion, the Somerset Light Infantry* that the Cherbourg 'Pogo' of uncertain temper is seen as a man, not less glossy perhaps, but far more admirable than the one Jack remembered. 'During the clearing of Preseau,' wrote Lt Col. Majendie, 'Captain P. G. K. Harris, M.C., was the chief performer in an incident which gave rise to some merriment. He was standing at the top of some cellar steps collecting prisoners, when a German came up from below "kamerading" with such enthusiasm that he collided with Captain Harris and knocked him down. Captain Harris sat down violently on top of a dead German, and in his efforts to rise put his hand on the dead man's face. This was too much for Light Company's Commander; he leapt at the offender and, mindful of his Oxford days, caught him such a left under the jaw that the unhappy German did not recover consciousness for a long time' (p. 120).

way, offer Warnie all my congratulations upon his recent glories when next you write. That at least is a blessing: he won't be doing badly in the soldiering line if he is to be a Captain after the war at his age . . .

TO HIS FATHER: from No. 10 British Red Cross Hospital, Le Tréport

22 February 1918

Your letter of the 17th has just arrived, with the enclosure, for which many thanks: a widening experience of other people's parents has taught me to value these things more than I once did, both for themselves and what they mean. That suggests literary possibilities: there is already a book called *Other people's children*,[26] but why not a companion volume *Other people's parents*?—in our schooldays we have most of us suffered from time to time at the hands of these irrelevant beings.

It is one of the punishments—to be sure, richly deserved—of a bad correspondant, that when at last he does write, his letter usually crosses the next one from his victim. I hope that you have before this got the longer letter which apparently had not come when you wrote yours.

I don't think there is need to worry if at any future time you hear of my being in hospital merely with illness. Even supposing it to be fairly serious, it is a more natural and easy kind of danger than that of the front: as well, there is always the rest, the unaccustomed comforts, and at the end of the possibility of leave. In this case I am afraid I have not been bad enough.

---

[26] By John Habberton (1877).

I am sending you in this two photographs of my room at Univ. They were taken by my friend Moore shortly before I left Oxford, but remained undeveloped for a long time and have lately been sent to me by his mother. The room is not of much personal interest, as everything in it belonged to another man—I think I mentioned that at the time. But I daresay you may care to see them. Do you remember it used to be one of my dreams that I might some day entertain you and the Knock [W. T. Kirkpatrick] there together. As you said, 'That would be a symposium of the gods'. What crack there would have been! With what an added zest we would have drunk in the man's 'statements of fact' in the hope of chuckling over them between ourselves later on. Who knows? At any rate we can hope that you and I will some time see Oxford together.

The picture of our Warnie attending an A-murican professor's lecture from the chair of Poker is good. But I'm afraid the psychology of the card player will always baffle me as it has baffled you. I had as soon spend the evening building card houses—much sooner watch the picture in the red of the fire.

I have discovered that optimism about the war increases in an inverse ratio to the optimist's proximity to the line. Was our Colonel so hopeful a month ago?[27] But indeed I'm afraid I must

---

[27] The 'Colonel' referred to here is Warren. He had been trying to prevent Mr Lewis from worrying so much about Jack, and in writing to his father on 9 February 1918 he said: 'I wish Papy that I could convince you that your depression is almost entirely due to your solitary life: Jacks is very seldom from my thoughts now, but still I am for some reason convinced that all will be well with him. Surely you are giving way to mere pessimism when you say that you can see no early end to the war . . . It is a pity you never played poker or you would appreciate the situation bet-

live up to our family reputation, for certainly I can't see any bright prospects at present. The conditions at home are almost as bad as anything we once fabled of starvation in Germany: spirits will be more pacific every day on short commons: there seems to be 'spiritual wickedness in high places'. . . .

I am ordering a couple of books of Vergil from my bookseller in London, and if I find that I get on with these I shall order something equally pleasant and simple in Greek. German and Italian I fear must go to the wall: of course I read a French book from time to time and seek opportunities of speaking it—but one sees very little of the natives. I am also still at Boswell, and have also begun *Middlemarch*. You see I am quite 'caught' by George Eliot's books.

I have now almost written my pen out of ink, and—perhaps my reader out of patience: but 'out of the abundance of the heart' and as well there will be days when I cannot write much. I have been out once or twice, and can't say how much longer I shall be here. Write as often and as long (grammar!) as you can.

[Jack was discharged from the hospital on 28 February. He rejoined his battalion at Fampoux. Then after being on the front line of the Battle of Arras 21–24 March he returned to Fampoux, from where he wrote the following letter.]

---

ter: the Bosche holds a fairish hand, but not so good as ours: unfortunately for him however, he is so badly dipped that he CANNOT afford to pay up and drop it: therefore he is naturally bluffing all he can in the hope of frightening us out.'

TO HIS FATHER: from France

[25 March 1918]

I have been living at such a rush since I left hospital that it needed this battle and your probable anxiety to make me write. I am out of the fighting area, but of course we are not enjoying the old peaceful trench warfare I knew before Le Tréport. We have just come back from a four days' tour in the front line during which I had about as many hours' sleep: then when we got back to this *soi-disant* rest, we spent the whole night digging. Under these conditions I know you will excuse me from much letter writing: but I will try and let you know that I am safe from time to time.

[Jack Lewis was among those who were wounded on Mount Bernenchon during the Battle of Arras on 15 April by an English shell which burst behind him. Wyrall records in his *History of the Somerset Light Infantry* (p. 295): 'The casualties of the 1st Battalion between the 14th and 16th April were: 2/Lieut. L. B. Johnson died of wounds (15/4/18) and 2/Lieuts. C. S. Lewis, A. G. Rawlence, J. R. Hill and C. S. Dowding wounded: in other ranks the estimated losses were 210 killed, wounded and missing.' It is not known whether Lewis learned of the death of his friend Laurence Johnson before he was taken to the Liverpool Merchants Mobile Hospital at Etaples. On 24 April Warren learned from Mr Lewis that Jack was 'severely wounded'. Such was his anxiety that he borrowed a bicycle and rode the fifty miles from near Doullens to Etaples to see him. He then had to cycle back to his camp.]

TO HIS FATHER: from the Liverpool Merchants Mobile Hospital at Etaples

4 May [1918]

Many thanks for the smokes and also for the letter which I was particularly glad to get, as I had not heard from you for so long. I am very sorry—and angry—that you have been through a lot of unnecessary worry and anxiety owing to the carelessness of some fool at the War Office, who—as Arthur informs me—told you some rubbish about my being hit in both arms and in the face. As a matter of fact I was really hit in the back of the left hand, on the left leg from behind and just above the knee, and in the left side just under the arm pit. All three were only flesh wounds. The myth about being hit in the face arose, I imagine, from the fact that I got a lot of dirt in the left eye which was closed up for a few days, but is now alright. I still can't lie on my side (neither the bad one nor the other one) but otherwise I lead the life of an ordinary mortal and my temperature is alright. So there is no need for any anxiety at all.

TO HIS FATHER: from Etaples

[14 May 1918]

I expect to be sent across in a few days time, of course as a stretcher case: indeed whatever my condition they would have to send me in that way, because I have no clothes. This is a standing joke out here—the mania which people at the dressing stations have for cutting off a wounded man's clothes whether there is any need for it or not. In my case the tunic was probably beyond hope, but I admit that I mourn the undeserved fate of my breeches. Unfortunately I was unconscious when the sacrilege took place and could not very well argue the point.

I am doing exceedingly well and can lie on my right side (not of course on my left), which is a great treat after you have been on your back for a few weeks. In one respect I was wrong in my last account of my wounds: the one under my arm is worse than a flesh wound, as the bit of metal which went in there is now in my chest, high up under my 'pidgeon chest' as shown: this however is nothing to worry about as it is doing no harm. They will leave it there and I am told that I can carry it about for the rest of my life without any evil results.

Aunt Lily keeps up a sharp fire of literature — Browning, Emerson, Mill (on 'the subjection of women')[28] and *The Scotsman*. How on earth can I be supposed to be interested in *The Scotsman*? However there are one or two Scotch patients here to whom I hand it over: so I can truthfully tell her that they 'are read and enjoyed'.[29]

My friend Mrs Moore is in great trouble — Paddy has been missing for over a month and is almost certainly dead. Of all my own particular set at Keble he has been the first to

---

[28] John Stuart Mill, *The Subjection of Women* (1869).
[29] Mrs Lily Hamilton Suffern (1860–1934) was the sister of Jack's and Warren's mother. Warren described her as 'an ardent suffragette' who had quarrelled with everyone in her family, including his parents. Although the lady was constantly on the move, she was especially fond of Jack whom she bombarded with books and a pseudo-metaphysical correspondence.

go, and it is pathetic to remember that he at least was always certain that he would come through.[30]

TO HIS FATHER: from Endsleigh Palace Hospital, Endsleigh Gardens, London (after arriving there on 25 May)

30 May 1918

I hope that you got my telegram and that I will soon hear from you, and not only hear but receive a visit in the aristocratic neighbourhood of Euston. You will be able to come over, will you not, if only for a few days? We must get Kirk up to meet you and have a famous crack. In the meantime, will you please send me my new brown suit, and also, if possible, a pair of black brogue shoes: I ought to have several. It is allowed to wear ordinary clothes here until I can get a uniform made. This is merely a note, as you are already heavily in my debt in the matter of letters . . .

---

[30] The story of 'Paddy's' part in the war was summarized, from information supplied by Mrs Moore, in his school magazine *The Cliftonian*, No. CCXCV (May 1918), p. 225: '2nd-Lieutenant E. F. C. Moore. He joined the Rifle Brigade after the usual training, and was in action in France in the great German attack which began on March 21. He was reported missing on March 24, and it is now feared that he cannot have escaped with his life. The Adjutant of his battalion writes: "I have to tell you that your very gallant son was reported missing on the 24th of last month. He was last seen on the morning of that day with a few men defending a position on a river bank against infinitely superior numbers of the enemy. All the other officers and most of the men of his company have become casualties, and I fear it is impossible to obtain more definite information. He did really fine work on the previous night in beating off a party of Germans who had succeeded in rushing a bridgehead in our lines. We all feel his loss very deeply, and I cannot express too strongly our sympathy with you."'

TO HIS FATHER: from Endsleigh Palace Hospital

12 June 1918

Thank you for both the letters, as the 'essay with enclosures' has followed me here, and indeed arrived shortly after the one I wrote, venturing to suggest that my score of letters was still one up. *Peccavi:* I most humbly apologise. 'And you wid a bronchitis in you.' (By the way it is not a whole shell in me, only a bit of one.) Seriously, I hope that before this you have got over any suggestion of the old trouble: you cannot be too careful in warding it off . . .

I am now up and dressed and have been out a few times: you can well imagine how delightful it is for me to wear decent clothes again—to have pockets without buttons, and to be able to change one's tie from day to day. I have written to the transport officer of the battalion about my valise, but so far there is no answer: poor man, I expect he has other things to think about than my kit. And—who knows— perhaps even now a Teutonic *unter offizier* is sleeping in my blankets and improving his English on my bits of books.[31] Which reminds me, though the reproach is usually the other way, on the only occasion when we took any prisoners, I was able to talk a little German to their officer, though he could speak no English to me[32] . . .

---

[31] Warren wrote to his father on 7 June saying: 'It is splendid to know that our 'IT' [Jack] is safely home at last. I confess it made me very uneasy when I heard that those damned hounds had been bombing base hospitals. And talking about that, did you see that the fellow who was caught red handed was admitted into the hospital he had bombed, and had his wound treated. I'd have given him treatment forsooth.'

[32] This occurred the day before Jack was wounded. Wyrall records in his *History of the Somerset Light Infantry* (p. 293) the taking of 135 prison-

I have since added to my new knowledge of Trollope *The Warden* and *Dr Thorne*. Although it may seem strange that Warnie and I both neglect books that are at home and then afterwards read them elsewhere, there is a reason. A book must find you in the right mood, and its mere presence on a shelf will not create that mood, tho' it lie there for years: as well, when you meet 'in a strange land' a book that is associated with home, it has for that very reason an attraction which it would not have at ordinary times. I am now at work, and very much at work on Hume's *Treatise of Human Nature*, a new Maeterlinck and a new volume of Swinburne. I keep up a very brisk fire of correspondence on Literary and pseudo-scientific subjects with my Aunt Suffern: at this distance she is entertaining, but in a *tête à tête* 'no, a thousand times no' . . .

It is a great pity that you are laid up: there would be points about London for us two — I should like to go with you to the Abbey and the Temple and a few other places. (Just as I am making Arthur green with envy by my accounts of Charing Cross Road, 'a mile of bookshops'.) On Sunday I am going down to Bookham to see the sage: if only you could make the same pilgrimage! . . .

---

ers: 'As the leading Somerset men approached the eastern exits of Riez, the enemy launched a counter-attack from east of the village and the northern end of the Bois de Pacaut. This counter-attack was at once engaged with Lewis-gun and rifle fire and about 50 per cent of the attacking German were shot down: of the remainder about half ran away and the other half ran towards the Somerset men with their hands in the air crying out "Kamerad!" and were made prisoners.'

TO HIS FATHER: **from Endsleigh Palace Hospital** (after visiting Mr W. T. Kirkpatrick)

[20? June 1918]

On Sunday [16 June] I made my pilgrimage. Even to go to Waterloo was an adventure full of memories, and every station that I passed on the way down seemed to clear away another layer of the time that passed and bring me back to the old life. Bookham was as its best: a mass of green, very pleasing to one 'that has been long in city pent'. As I walked up to Gastons the familiar road was crowded with good people coming back from church, and I passed many a stuffy old couple whom I remembered well, though none of them recognised me. It was like being a ghost: I opened the gate of Kirk's garden almost with stealth and went on past the house, to the vegetable garden and the little wild orchard with the pond, where I had sat so often on hot Sunday afternoons, and practised skating with Terry when the long frost began two years ago. And there among the cabbages, in his shirt and 'Sunday' trousers, there sure enough was the old man, still digging and smoking his villainous pipe. His back was towards me and I had come within a few paces of him before he turned and saw me. And so I was led into the house with much triumph and displayed to Mrs K., whom we found fussing with the maid just as of old. I have seldom spent a more delightful afternoon: what 'crack' we had, what reminiscences, how often my opinions were shown to be based ('bazed' as the sage pronounces it) on an insufficient knowledge of the subject! When I told him that it was by an English shell I was hit, it called forth a magnificent Tirade on the 'simple mathematical problem' of calculating how a gun's range would shorten as it got heated by firing—on the 'every school boy knows' lines.

I have bought an edition of Yeats which I ordered the bookseller to send home and which should have arrived by this time.[33] Of course I need not add that you are welcome to open the parcel, if you would care to. Arthur at any rate would like to see it, and if you replace the books in their boxes they will be safe from dust and damp until I come home. I hope you do not think it extravagant in me to have bought such a thing, for I knew it was a limited edition which would be very much dearer in a few years' time. In the same shop where I made this purchase, I'm afraid I gave myself away badly. What first tempted me to go in was a battered copy of Burton's *Anatomy:* as you know, I had been looking for this and thought here was an opportunity of picking up a cheap second hand copy. I went in and requested a courtly old gentleman to let me see it. 'H'm', said I, glancing over the dirty little volume, 'it seems rather worn: haven't you a newer copy?' The gentleman looked at me in rather a pained way and said that he had not. 'Well, how much is it?' I asked, expecting a considerable reduction. 'Twenty-five guineas', said my friend with a bland smile. Ye Gods! Just think of it: there was I for the first time in my life fingering a really valuable old edition and asking for a 'NEWER' copy. I turned hot all over: and even you as you read, will blush for the credit of the clan. However,

---

[33] This was probably *The Collected Works of William Butler Yeats in Verse and Prose* in 8 volumes, published in 1908 by the Shakespeare Head Press.

the old gentleman was very forgiving: he turned his treasury inside out for me. He showed me priceless old copies of Vergil and Rabelais, books from the Kelmscott Press, including the Chaucer at £82 and strange forgotten waifs of French literature with stiff engravings 'from the age of snuff boxes and fans'. And so what could I do but bring away the Yeats? Apropos of Beardsley,[34] he told me that the 'fleshly' artist had often been in that shop and had finally gone the way of all mortal things without paying his account. Well, *et ego in Arcadia vixi*,[35] it is something to have been in the shop of James Bain even for an hour.

It seems that now-a-days one is sent from hospital to be kept for some time in a 'convalescent home' before going on leave. Of course I have asked to be sent to an Irish one, but there are only a few of these and they are already crowded: we must not therefore expect too much. But wherever I am I know that you will come and see me. You know I have some difficulty in talking of the greatest things: it is the fault of our generation and of the English schools. But at least you will believe that I was never before so eager to cling to every bit of our old home life and to see you. I know I have often been far from what I should in my relations to you, and have undervalued an affection and a generosity which (as I said somewhere else) an experience of 'other people's parents' has shown me in a new light. But, please God, I shall do better in the future. Come and see me. I am homesick, that is the long and the short of it.

---

[34] Aubrey Vincent Beardsley (1872–98).
[35] 'I too have lived in Arcadia.'

I have been once or twice to the English Opera at Drury Lane and seen among other things my long desired *Valkyrie* and *Faust* again—full of reminiscences of course. This week Mrs Moore has been up on a visit to her sister who works at the War Office, and we have seen a good deal of each other. I think it some comfort to her to be with someone who was a friend of Paddy's and is a link with the Oxford days: she has certainly been a very, very good friend to me . . .

TO HIS FATHER: **from Ashton Court, Long Ashton, Clifton, Bristol** (after his arrival there on 25 June)

[29 June 1918]

Surely this is the most unfortunate thing that ever happened to us! I was prepared to be disappointed in my efforts to be sent to an Irish convalescent home, but this is the very acme of ill luck. When they finally told me in London that I could not go to Ireland, they asked me to choose some part of England: at first I said London, thinking that this would be more convenient for you than any provincial town, but this could not be done. I then elected Bristol, where I could have the society of Mrs Moore, and also of Perrett of the Somersets, whose being wounded some days before myself I mentioned to you.[36] Little could I foresee what was going to happen: we are still close prisoners . . .

---

[36] Frank Winter Perrett (1898–) had known Jack at Malvern College where he had been a pupil 1912–15. He, too, had served with the 1st Battalion of the Somerset Light Infantry and he was wounded on 29 March 1918.

All the 'gilded youth' among the patients, who have no interests in themselves, of course grow more troublesome being confined. The place echoes to the crack of their billiard balls and their loud, tuneless whistling: I was very miserable for the first few days until I discovered a little, almost disused writing room at one end of the house. Here I can sit in comparative safety and read Burton's anatomy which I have had sent from town.[37]

If I should happen to get the disease I suppose all my bits of things will be burned. I could sit down and cry over the whole business: and yet of course we have both much to be thankful for. When a man can sleep between sheets as long as he will, sit in arm chairs, and have no fears, it is peevish to complain. If I had not been wounded when I was, I should have gone through a terrible time. Nearly all my friends in the Battalion are gone.

Did I ever mention Johnson who was a scholar of Queens? I had hoped to meet him at Oxford some day, and renew the endless talks that we had out there. *Dis aliter visum*, he is dead.[38] I had had him so often in my thoughts, had so often

---

[37] Richard Burton's *The Anatomy of Melancholy* was published in 1621. Jack's copy is one brought out by Chatto & Windus in 1907 and some of its many annotations were probably made at Ashton Court.

[38] 'It seemed otherwise to the gods.' Laurence Bertrand Johnson was elected a Scholar of Queens' College, Oxford, in 1917 but he was sent to the Front with the Somerset Light Infantry before he could matriculate. Jack says of Johnson in *Surprised by Joy* (ch. XII): 'In him I found dialectical sharpness such as I had hitherto known only in Kirk, but coupled with youth and whim and poetry. He was moving toward Theism and we had endless arguments on this and every other topic whenever we were out of the line.' Johnson was killed by the shell which wounded Jack.

hit on some new point in one of our arguments, and made a note of things in my reading to tell him when we met again, that I can hardly believe he is dead. Don't you find it particularly hard to realise the death of people whose strong personality makes them particularly alive: with the ordinary sons of Belial who eat and drink and are merry, it is not so hard.

But I must not enlarge on a melancholy subject: I have no doubt that we are all three of us pretty low. However, 'better luck next time': this cannot last for ever and I hope yet to have a visit from you. As for my own health it is pretty good, although the wound in the leg—the smallest of the three—is still giving some trouble.

The house here is the survival, tho' altered by continual rebuilding, of a thirteenth-century castle: the greater part is now stucco work of the worst Victorian period (à la Norwood Towers) but we have one or two fine old paintings and a ghost. I haven't met it yet and have not much hope to—indeed if poor Johnson's ghost would come walking into the lonely writing room this minute, I should be glad enough. Greatly to my chagrin the library is locked up. The park is several miles in extent, very pleasant and stocked with deer: once or twice while wandering in the bracken I have suddenly come upon the solemn face and branching antlers of a stag, within a few feet of me. He examines me for a moment, then snorts, kicks up his heels, and is gone: a second later, head after head comes up—his panic has reached the rest of the herd, and they too scamper off after him like the wind.

A most generous and welcome consignment of smoke-ables came this morning. Communication with the town is scanty now of course, and this is a most welcome addition to our diminishing stocks: what is more, such little attentions are infinitely cheering when one is dull, lonely and disappointed . . .

TO HIS FATHER: from Ashton Court

[29? July 1918]

You can imagine how mystified I was by an envelope from the U.V.F.—the contents too were unexpected.[39] In some ways this scheme has given me to think: you see the Board which sate upon me in London gave me two months convalescence which will be finished on the 24th of August. It appears however in this hospital, if you are quiet and inoffensive and keep yourself well out of the notice of the authorities, you may be often left for several weeks after your time. The great danger about this change would be that of getting the reply 'If you are so anxious to move, we will have you boarded at once and discharged from hospital.' Such a procedure would of course hasten my return to France. The amount of leave I get after hospital (whatever it may be) will not be influenced by the time which I have spent in the former, and it is therefore to our interest to prolong the hospital period to the utmost. The smaller Irish hospitals are notoriously strict and up to time with their Boards. I must admit too, I should be sorry to give up the idea of your coming to visit me here: it would give me great pleasure for you

---

[39] Mr Lewis was trying to get Jack into the Ulster Volunteer Force, hoping this way to get him transferred to Ireland.

to meet Mrs Moore, and I feel that this visit to me is the only excuse on which you will ever get away for a while from Belfast and the office. If you were at the office all day and I had to be back at the hospital at 6 or 7 every night, it would be hardly worth while coming to a hospital at home. Here we could have a delightful little holiday together . . .

TO HIS FATHER: from Ashton Court

3 September 1918

Ever since my last letter to you I have been almost daily expecting to hear from you, and I am rather surprised that neither my answer to your proposal nor my suggestion that you should come over here has met with any reply. Have you not yet decided on a date for coming over? It is four months now since I returned from France, and my friends laughingly suggest that 'my father in Ireland' of whom they hear is a mythical creation like Mrs Harris.[40]

As to my decision, I think you will agree that it has already justified itself. I am now nearly a month over my time, and even if I were boarded tomorrow this would be so much to the good. Of course in the present need for men, being passed fit by a board would mean a pretty quick return to France. I am afraid there is not much possibility of the 'job at home' which you once thought might be the result of my wounds: although not quite well I am almost 'fit' now in the military sense of the word, and depend only on the forget-

---

[40] The mythical friend of Mrs Gamp in Charles Dickens's *Martin Chuzzlewit* (1843–44).

fulness of the authorities for my continued stay in hospital. Of course this has nothing to do with my leave.

I hope there is nothing wrong and that I shall soon hear from you again and see you here. I know there are difficulties in the way, but I suppose they are no more serious now than when Warnie was at home . . .

TO HIS FATHER: from Ashton Court

9 September 1918

I write in haste to give you a piece of news which I hope will please you not much less than it did me. You are aware that for some years now I have amused myself by writing verses, and a pocket book collection of these followed me through France. Since my return I have occupied myself in revising these, getting them typed with a few additions, and trying to publish them. After a refusal from Macmillans they have, somewhat to my surprise, been accepted by Heinemann. Wm. Heinemann thinks it would 'be well to reconsider the inclusion of one or two pieces which are not perhaps on a level with my best work'. I have sent him some new ones as substitutes for these and things are going on well, although his absence from town on a fortnight's holiday will cause a delay in coming to a definite arrangement about money. I don't know when I may hope actually to see the book, but of course I will send you a copy at once. It is called *Spirits in Prison: a cycle of lyrical poems by Clive Staples*. The paper and printing will probably be detestable, as they always are now-a-days. This little success gives me a pleasure which is perhaps childish and yet akin to greater things . . .

TO HIS FATHER: from Ashton Court

14 September 1918

I am sorry that you should have been so troubled as you were when you last wrote to me, and sorrier still that I should have been to any extent the cause of it. At the same time it is only fair to add that I do not entirely acquiesce in the blame which you lay upon me. Above all, the joking reference to 'Mrs Harris' which you take *au pied de la lettre* was quite harmlessly meant. I do not choose my friends among people who jeer, nor has a tendency to promiscuous confidence ever been one of my characteristic faults. However, perhaps it was tactless, and there is no need to go into it further.

Many thanks for the 'monies numbered' and the parcel. Those Virginian cigarettes which you have sent me several times are a good brand. Are matches obtainable at home? We are very badly off for them here: hardly any tobacconist will give you a box, and grocers only give a small weekly allowance to their regular customers.

I was very much cheered by your telegram. Such things are the most valuable part of the successes which they accompany. I hope I have not led you to expect too much: the publisher is only the first fence in our steeplechase—the book may still be badly reviewed or not reviewed at all, may fail to sell, or your own taste and judgement may be disappointed in it. The news I need hardly say should be communicated with discretion to the 'hoi polloi' . . .

TO HIS FATHER: from Ashton Court

18 September 1918

It had quite escaped my notice that Hichens had written a novel called *Spirits in Prison,* but now that you mention it, I think that you are right—or perhaps it is *A Spirit in Prison*—the resemblance at any rate is close enough to hit that title on the head.[41] I don't know whether I shall be able to find another that expresses so aptly the general scheme of the book, but we must do our best. The subtitle 'A cycle of lyrical poems' was not given without a reason: the reason is that the book is not a collection of really independant pieces, but the working out, loosely of course and with digressions, of a general idea. If you can imagine *In Memoriam*[42] with its various parts in different metres it will give you some idea of the form I have tried to adopt. Such merit as it has depends less on the individual than on the combined effect of the pieces. To call it a cycle is to prepare the reader for this plan and to induce him to follow the order of the poems as I have put them. Probably he will not, but we must do our best. At the same time I admit that the word 'cycle' is a very objectionable one. The only others which I know to express the same thing are 'series' and 'sequence' and of these the former is hardly definite enough and the latter in my opinion more affected and *precieux* than 'cycle' itself. Of course one could dispense with a sub-title altogether, but I rather approve of

---

[41] Robert Hichens, *A Spirit in Prison* (1908).
[42] Alfred, Lord Tennyson, *In Memoriam A. H. H.* (1850).

the old practice by which a book gives some account of itself—as *Paradise Lost—a heroic poem in twelve books—The Pilgrim's Progress—being an account of his journey from this world to the next.* Perhaps you can suggest some simpler and more dignified way of saying that the book is a whole and not a collection.

My only reason for choosing a pseudonym at all was a natural feeling that I should not care to have this bit of my life known in the regiment. One doesn't want either officers or men to talk about 'our b****y lyrical poet again' whenever I make a mistake . . .

Mrs Moore had received news at last of her son's death: I suppose it is best to know, and fortunately she never cherished any hopes[43] . . .

[For some time Warren had been asking his father if he had been to see Jack. In his letter to Warren of 19 September Mr Lewis praised Jack's success in having his poems accepted by Heinemann. He went on to say: 'I am sorry—I won't say ashamed—to say that I have not been over to see him yet. Nor do I see a prospect of going soon. I have never been so awkwardly—or at least more awkwardly—placed in the office and Court than I am at the present time. I cannot be certain any morning that my managing man will turn up. If I left home and went on the spree, the result to my little

---

[43] For a detailed account of the Second Battalion of the Rifle Brigade with which Paddy Moore served see William W. Seymour, *The History of The Rifle Brigade in The War of 1914–1918*, Vol. II (1936).

livelihood would be disastrous. Indeed the worry and overwork is beginning to tell on me. The last holiday I had was my visit to Malvern and some water has flowed under the bridge since then. I have never felt as limp and depressed in my life I think, as I have for the last few weeks. I have no doubt that Jacks thinks me unkind and that I have neglected him. Of course that fear makes me miserable. One night about ten days ago I went to bed worrying about it, and I heard every hour strike from eleven to seven.']

TO HIS FATHER: from Ashton Court

Postmark: 3 October 1918

I think 'Spirits in Bondage' would be a good substitute for the old title and would sound well: 'Spirits in Bonds' would not do so well, and suggests tiresome jokes about whiskey. I think it is only natural to describe it as a Cycle of poems, just to say 'a cycle' is rather unintelligible. After all I'm not claiming that they are good poems—you know the schoolboy's definitions, 'Prose is when the lines go on to the end of the page: poetry is when they don't.'

The more I think of it the less I like anonymity. If it wasn't for the army I'd let my own name take its chance. Don't you think Clive is too famous a surname to take as a nom de plume (just as we thought Staples too notorious)? Of course we must always remember that the people who are most likely to talk to 'our *b****y* poet' are also the least likely to hear anything about it; they don't haunt bookshops, nor do they read literary papers.

I read and posted the letter which you enclosed for Mrs Moore. It seemed to me up to the high standard of your usual letters on such occasions. I have heard lately that Somerville, whom I have mentioned to you, is gone too. With him the old set completely vanishes . . . "

TO HIS FATHER: from Officers Mess, No. 3 Camp, Perham Down, Andover, Hampshire

18 October 1918

I have had a board at last, and been moved to this 'Command Depot' for an unspecified period. This is the usual step after leaving hospital, unless one is well enough to be passed for general service. Of course I am still far from this, but one doesn't usually remain here very long. It is a sort of a glorified hospital here, although we live in a mess and wear uniform: the best feature is that we have rooms to ourselves, which is a pleasant change after hospital wards.

" Those who made up 'the old set' are mentioned in Jack's letter of 10 (?) June 1917. Paddy Moore died at Pargny in March 1918. Martin Ashworth Somerville, also of the Rifle Brigade, served in Egypt and Palestine and he was killed in Palestine on 21 September 1918. Alexander Gordon Sutton, who was with Paddy in the 2nd Battalion of the Rifle Brigade, was killed in action on 2 January 1918. Thomas Kerrison Davey, of the 1st Battalion of the Rifle Brigade, died of wounds received near Arras on 29 March 1918. Jack assumed that Denis Howard de Pass—'our regnant authority on all matters of dress, who is reported to wear stays'—had died as well. He was reported 'wounded and missing' on 1 April 1918. As it turned out, de Pass of the 12th Battalion of the Rifle Brigade, had been taken prisoner by the Germans. Following his repatriation in December 1918 he not only continued to serve in the First World War but he fought in the Second as well. From 1950 until his death in 1973 this once fashionable dresser was a dairy farmer at Polegate in Sussex.

I have just had a letter from Heinemann's which has taken some time to come round through Ashton Court. He accepts some new pieces I had sent him and mentions a few he wants rejected. He also objects to a 'too frequent use of certain words' and points to one or two places that seem weak and which I might alter. 'After that' he suggests we might come to terms, a point on which I am quite ready to agree with him. I am hoping to get a day off some time next week and run up to town and see him . . .

Of course I remembered the text about 'the spirits which are in prison'[45] and it is that which seemed to give the old title its significance which 'Spirits in bondage' could never have. I think perhaps we should stick to 'Prison'. I shall ask Heinemann whether that novel by Hichens really exists; he ought to know.

By the way, what about Clive Hamilton for a pseudonym? It will be a complete disguise to outsiders, transparent to 'our ain folk', and will be a name which we have the best of reasons to love and honour.

TO HIS FATHER: from Perham Down Camp

27 October 1918

I succeeded in getting my day off to see Heinemann yesterday, after being stopped last week through a very ridiculous incident of a kind that is common in the army. In order to get leave for a day you have to write down your name, the time of leaving, and your destination in the book which

---

[45] 1 Peter 3:19.

is then signed by the medical officer. Last week the book was lost: no objection was made to my going on either military or medical grounds, but—how could I go without the book? A suggestion that I might write the particulars on a slip of paper which could then afterwards be put in the book was treated as a sort of sacrilege. After a week however it occurred to the Adjutant (who must be a man of bold originality and signal generosity) that we might spend half a crown on a new book, and so I was able to go after all.

Heinemann was out when I reached the office and I was shown in to the Manager, a man called Evans, quite a young fellow and very agreeable.[46] Afterwards Heinemann himself came in and I was with him for about three-quarters of an hour. He produced a typed agreement of which, with many 'hereinafter's and 'aforesaid's, the gist is that they are to publish the book 'at their own expense, in such style and to be sold at such price as they deem best' and that I am 'to receive the following royalty: 10% of the profits on the published price of 12 out of every thirteen copies sold'. It concludes with a stipulation that they should have the refusal of my next work, if any. Whether I am being well or ill treated I am of course too ignorant to say: but I suppose, poetry being such an unprofitable branch of publishing, I have no reason to be dissatisfied. He also told me that John Galsworthy (who publishes with them) had seen my MS

---

[46] William Heinemann (1863–1920) had founded the publishing house which still bears his name in 1890. His manager at this time was Charles Sheldon Evans (1883–1944). The meeting took place in 20–21 Bedford Street, London.

and wanted to publish a certain poem in a new monthly called *Revielle* which he is bringing out in aid of disabled soldiers and sailors. I naturally consented, both because it is pleasant *laudari a laudato viro* and because it is an excellent advertisement. Before I left he said he would go on with the printing at once and might be able to have the proofs ready for me in three weeks. He is a fat little man with a bald head, apparently well read, and a trifle fussy—inclined to get his papers mixed up and repeat himself . . .

TO HIS FATHER: **from Perham Down Camp**
3 Sept. [November] 1918
You may make your mind easy on the question of the War Office's 'tricks', as my removal to a command depot is quite in order. At the same time I am afraid I shall have to disappoint you on the two months leave as I am not likely to get nearly so long. The idea doubtless arose in your mind from the fact that officers discharged from hospital and still convalescent, were formerly sent home and told to report for a board again in two, three or even six months' time. This however was

> *'In the olden*
> *Time long ago'*

It was found that the average uniformed bounder had only two interests—alcohol and women—and that two months' undisturbed indulgence in his natural tastes left him very much less fit than when he began. As well, men were continually being forgotten, and there were even cases of officer's desertion: consequently tho' Majors *et hoc genus omne* still get their sick leave, we unfortunates convalesce in hospitals and depots and get some leave as a sop after we are cured. As usual, the innocent suffer for the guilty, but this is too common an event to surprise either you or me. Any attempt to 'work' things is dangerous: we had a hopelessly unfit man at Ashton, who, on trying to be sent to a different hospital was boarded and sent to France. It's a way they have in the army . . .

Yes—a year and six days is a long stretch enough: indeed my life is rapidly becoming divided into two periods, one including all the time before we got into the battle of Arras, the other ever since. Already last year seems a long, long way off. However, there appears to be some prospect of the whole beastly business coming to an end fairly soon . . .

TO HIS FATHER: **from Perham Down Camp**
10 November 1918
Although one does not wish to live in a fool's paradise or be foolishly confident, yet I do think the present course of events is such as to render the question of trying to get a home job rather less important than it was a month ago. In twenty-four hours' time it may have ceased to have any meaning at all. Of course even it we do get peace, I suppose I shall take some time in escaping from the army. But in no position should I stand a better chance of a speedy discharge, than in my present one of convalescent officer at a Command Depot. Our attitude therefore must simply be to 'stand by' . . .

Of course the question whether Heinemann is treating me well or no has often been in my mind, and I have come to the conclusion that such an agreement is all that we have a right to expect. We must remember that even when poetry has a *succès fou* it is still less profitable to the publisher than even fairly good fiction. As Evans said to me, 'We don't expect to make a commercial success out of poetry: we only publish it—well simply because its good.' . . . Since you ask, such compliments as I was payed by Heinemann were of a somewhat peculiar nature—their object being to impress upon me the great honour that was being done me, and the majesty of the firm. 'Of course Mr Lewis we never accept poetry unless it is really good' and more in that strain—with mental reservations on my part as I remembered some specimens. He merely said that Galsworthy 'admired' the one he wanted for *Reveille* . . .

[The following day, Monday 11 November 1918, Albert Lewis wrote in his diary: 'Armistice signed. War ended. Thanks be to God.']

TO HIS FATHER: **from Officers' Command Depot, Eastbourne**

[17? November 1918]

As you see, I have been moved again. That is to say I have in the literal sense covered several hundreds of miles of country, but in the military sense I have not moved at all. In other words, 'Command Depot' itself has moved: as a step towards demobilisation the officers who were scattered at various depots over the country have been collected into a special depot for officers here. As to the great news which is uppermost in our minds, I can only echo what you have already said. The man who can give way to mafficking at such a time is more than indecent—he is mad. I remember five of us at Keble, and I am the only survivor: I think of Mr Sutton, a widower with five sons, all of whom have gone. One cannot help wondering why. Let us be silent and thankful.

The question of how to get most quickly out of the army has of course occupied me too. I wrote to Macan explaining my position and asking whether Colleges propose to make any representations to the powers on behalf of the Sam-Browne'd freshmen who wanted to get back—for I had heard that something of that kind was being done. He replied in a kind and even cordial letter that I was not likely, so far as he knew, to be discharged for several months, and that the head of the U.T.C. [University Training Courses] was writing to me. The latter wrote to me saying that if I could get passed by a board as 'unfit for at least three months' I could go back to Oxford in khaki and on army pay, for what they call 'an intensive course of University training' on the chance of not being disturbed again. This seems to me however rather a cat and mouse business . . .

We're a nice pair! In the same letter you say—quite truly—that I have never told you to what extent I am likely to be disabled by the wound, and also that you are in Squeaky's hands for trouble—unspecified.[47] Well let's make a bargain. Here is

---

[47] 'Squeaky Dick', as Richard Whytock Leslie, M.D. (1862–1931) was known to many, was the Lewis family doctor.

my health report, and in return I shall look for a full account of your own bother. The effects of the wound in general movement are practically nil. I can do everything except hold my left arm straight above my head, which I don't want to do anyway. The effects on general health are very small: I have had one or two stoppages of breath which I am told are not unusual after a chest wound and which will soon disappear, and of course I still get tired easily and have a few headaches in the evenings. On the nerves there are two effects which will probably go with quiet and rest . . . The other is nightmares—or rather the same nightmare over and over again. Nearly everyone has it, and though very unpleasant, it is passing and will do no harm. So you see I am almost *in status quo . . .*

TO HIS FATHER: **from Eastbourne**

8 December 1918

As you have probably seen in the papers, we are all going to get 12 days' 'Christmas leave'. I use the inverted commas advisedly as mine seems likely to be in January. I suppose it would be unreasonable to expect them to let us all go at the same time, and you and I won't quarrel with dates. It has been a long time coming and a time unpleasantly and wastefully spent, but thank God it is over at last. By the way although, as I understand, I am entitled to a vote, I have not yet received any of the 'Election Communications' which have fallen to the lot of most men I know. Perhaps you can advise the constituency that it is in danger of losing the support of an influential voter! I suppose we are all voting for the Coalition, though I must confess I distrust them most heartily and look for no liberty as long as they are in power. Most of us here would be ready to vote for Lucifer himself if he rose up in red velvet and sulpher whispering the word 'Discharged'. But I see we are not to be 'discharged' but 'demobilized' and kept on a leash for the rest of our lives ...

At my suggestion Mrs Moore has come down here and is staying in rooms near the camp, where I hope she will remain until I go on leave. It is a great relief to get away from the army atmosphere, although for that matter I have been lucky in finding several decent fellows, including even another aspirant for poetical laurels—a most amusing card. It is fine country down here and I am glad that chance has given me its hills and cliffs to walk on. Certainly, if nothing else, the army has shown me some bits of England that I would not otherwise have seen ...

TO HIS FATHER: from Eastbourne

[16?] December 1918

I have already wired to you the dates of my leave: a list of the periods alloted to each of us has been posted up here, and, as was to be expected, the coveted dates which would include Christmas fall to the Majors and Captains *et hoc genus omne*. If however you can let Warnie know in time, I should think he would have no difficulty in getting his leave postponed. Everyone of course will be trying to get home for Christmas day, and it ought to be easy to change with someone who had got a later date against his will. I quite agree with you that it would be most disappointing if even now our little gathering were broken up.

Of course I shall be only too pleased if any influence of yours could succeed in getting me a discharge, though at the same time I am afraid it will be a very difficult business. As you have probably seen in the papers, we are to be drafted on our demobilization in 'Class Z Reserve' where I suppose we shall remain ready for the next scrape that some Labour government in the future may get the country into. I don't want to be pessimistic, but there does not seem much hope of ever being quite free of the army again. To get a discharge might be possible on the score of unfitness, but I do not think that my degree of military unfitness will be sufficient to serve our turn . . .

So far my readings both in Latin and Greek have been a pleasant surprise: I have forgotten less than I feared, and once I get the sound and savour of the language into my head by a spell of reading, composition should not come too hard either. In English I have started friend Trollope again—*The Small House at Allington* . . .

[In his wire Jack told his father that his leave was 10–22 January. Warren was, however, unable to alter the dates of his and he arrived home on 23 December. Suddenly Jack found himself demobilized from the Army. There was no time to tell his father. Mr Lewis and Warren were in the study of 'Little Lea' on 27 December when a cab drove up the drive and Jack got out. As Warren says in his Memoir, they drank champagne to celebrate the occasion. Following this reunion with his family, Jack returned to Oxford on 13 January 1919 to begin the 'Honour Mods' course in

Greek and Latin literature. Mrs Moore and Maureen found rooms nearby in 28 Warneford Road, Oxford.]

TO HIS FATHER: from University College, Oxford
27 January 1919

After a quite comfortable journey (which showed me that 1st Class travelling is very little different from 3rd) I arrived here somewhat late in the evening. The moon was just rising: the porter knew me at once and ushered me into the same old rooms (which by the way I am going to change). It was a great return and something to be very thankful for. I was also pleased to find an old friend, Edwards, who was up with me in 1916, and being unfit, has been there all the time.

There is of course already a great difference between this Oxford and the ghost I knew before: true, we are only twenty-eight in College, but we DO dine in Hall again, the Junior Common Room is no longer swathed in dust sheets, and the old round of lectures, debates, games, and whatnot is getting under weigh. The reawakening is a little pathetic: at our first [meeting of the J.C.R.] we read the minutes of the last—1914. I don't know any little thing that has made me realise the absolute suspension and waste of these years more thoroughly.

The Mugger[48] preached a quite memorable sermon on the first Sunday evening. It was very plain, even homely in style, not what one expected, but it grew on one, and I admire the restraint where 'gush' would have been so fatally easy. By

---

[48] The Master of University College, R. W. Macan.

the way, I have not been asked to see the Mugger yet, but I gather he has a waiting list and is working slowly through it. We have quite a number of old members who were up before the war and are a kind of dictionary of traditions.

Now as to work: I am 'deemed to have passed' Responsions and Divinity and it was open to me either to take Honour Mods or go straight on to 'Greats'—as you know, the final fence. In consideration of my wish to get a fellowship, Poynton, who is my tutor, strongly advised me not to avail myself of this opportunity of slurring over Mods. I presume I was acting as I should when I followed his advice. Except for the disadvantage of starting eighteen books of Homer to the bad I find myself fairly alright: of course the great difference after Kirk's is that you are left to work very much on your own. It is a little bit strange at first, but I suppose hard work in any lines will not be wasted. The best thing I go to is the series of lectures by Gilbert Murray, which are very good indeed: I always feel much the better for them.[49]

The coal difficulty is not very serious. We have all our meals in Hall, which, if it abolishes the cosy breakfast in one's rooms and the interchange of 'decencies and proprieties' is a little cheaper: we shall go back to the old arrangement as soon as we can. The library, one lecture room, and the Junior Common Room are always warm, and the two former are quite quiet: then for the evening we can afford a modest

---

[49] Gilbert Murray (1866–1957) was Regius Professor of Greek at Oxford 1908–36. His translations of Greek plays are as notable as his interpretation of Greek ideas.

blaze at one's 'ain fireside'. Our little body gets on very well together and most of us work. The place is looking more beautiful than ever in the wintry frost: one gets splendid cold colouring at the expense of tingling fingers and red noses.

TO HIS FATHER: from University College

4 February 1919

I find the work pretty stiff, but I think I am keeping my head above water. Poynton is, so far as I can judge, quite an exceptionally good tutor, and my visits to him are enjoyable as well as useful—although he objects to my style of Greek prose—'I don't care very much for treacle OR barley sugar myself'. So you have bequeathed to me some remnant of the old Macaulese taint after all. I drank tea with him last Sunday. Another man from Univ. went with me and the party consisted of Mrs and Miss Poynton, two girl undergraduates, and ourselves. As a matter of fact our host did nearly all the talking and kept us very well amused: he is an excellent if somewhat unjust raconteur. He came up to Balliol under Jowett and had a lot to say of the great man. It's funny you know, they all laugh at him, they all imitate his little mannerisms, but nobody who ever met him forgets to tell you so.

Much to my surprise I have had 'greatness thrust upon me'. There is a literary club in College called the Martlets, limited to twelve undergraduate members: it is over three hundred years old, and alone of all College Clubs has its minutes preserved in the Bodleian. I have been elected Secretary— the reason being of course that my proposer, Edwards, was afraid of getting the job himself. And so if I am forgotten as

all else, at least a specimen of my handwriting will be preserved to posterity. Someone will read a paper on Yeats at
our next meeting: we are also going to have one on Masefield
and we hope to get Masefield himself (who lives just outside
[Oxford]) to come up and listen to it and give a reply.[50]

I have a very bad piece of news for you: Smugy is dead.
Sometime in the middle of last term he fell a victim to flu. I
suppose I am very inexperienced but I had come to depend
on his always being there[51] ...

TO HIS FATHER: from University College

5 March 1919

I don't think that anyone who takes the trouble to read
my book through will seriously call it blasphemous, whatever criticism he may make on artistic grounds.[52] If he

---

[50] The Martlets somehow acquired the reputation of dating 'from dim
antiquity' but their first meeting was in 1892. The Minute Books are in
the Bodleian under the shelfmark MS. Top Oxon. d. 95/1–5. There is an
article on 'The Martlets' by P. C. Bayley in the *University College Record*
(1949–50). My essay called 'To the Martlets' in *C. S. Lewis: Speaker and
Teacher*, ed. Carolyn Keefe (1971), contains the minutes of the papers
Jack read to the Martlets between 1919 and 1940.

[51] 'Smugy' or 'Smewgy' was Harry Wakelyn Smith (1861–1918) who
taught Classics and English to the Upper Fifth at Malvern College. In the
tribute paid him in *Surprised by Joy* Jack speaks of this teacher as good
'beyond expectation, beyond hope'.

[52] The book is *Spirits in Bondage: A Cycle of Lyrics* which was published on 20 March 1919 under the pseudonym 'Clive Hamilton'. Mr
Lewis and Warren had read the manuscript of it, and on 28 January
Warren wrote to his father saying: 'While I am in complete agreement
with you as to the excellence of parts of 'IT'S' book, I am of opinion
that it would have been better if it had never been published. Even at 23

does not, we need not bother about his views. Of course I know there will be a number of people who will open it by chance at some of the gloomiest parts of Part I and decide 'Swinburnian Ballads' and never look at it again. But what would you do? If one writes at all—perhaps like Talleyrand many 'don't see the necessity'—one must be honest. You know who the God I blaspheme is and that it is not the God you or I worship, or any other Christian. But we have talked over this before. Arthur tells me that you have a copy of *Reveille* with my thing in it.[53] They have omitted to send me one—'who am I?' as Knowles said.

I look like having a busy time next week: I am reading in Chapel, saying grace in Hall, writing a paper on Morris for the Martlets, finishing the *Iliad,* and dining with the Mugger. I hope to be able to eat and sleep a little as well! As the time goes on I appreciate my hours with Poynton more and more. After Smugy and Kirk I must be rather spoiled in the way of tutors, but this man comes up to either of them, both as a teacher and as a humorous 'card'. Gilbert Murray is, I'm afraid, not very much good for exams., tho' his literary merits are unsurpassed . . .

---

one realizes that the opinions and convictions of 20 are transient things. Jack's Atheism is I am sure purely academic, but even so, no useful purpose is served by endeavouring to advertise oneself as an atheist. Setting aside the higher problems involved, it is obvious that a profession of a Christian belief is as necessary a part of a man's mental make up as a belief in the King, the Regular Army, and the Public Schools.' *Spirits in Bondage* was reprinted under Lewis's name in the United States by Harcourt Brace Jovanovich in 1984.

[53] 'Death in Battle' from *Spirits in Bondage* appeared in *Reveille*, No. 3 (February 1919).

TO HIS FATHER: **from University College**

15 [March 1919]

I am writing to tell you that the 'Varsity term ends today and the College term on Monday. I shall be staying up for a week more, following Poynton's instructions. After that I shall go down to help Mrs Moore with her move at Bristol: she has had to come back to clear out the house. There seems to be considerable difficulty about getting anywhere else. London and Bristol are both hopeless: I have suggested here, but that seems equally impossible. I can't understand where the influx of people is coming from. Of course the expences of the journey I shall pay myself . . .

TO HIS BROTHER: **from University College**

[2? April 1919]

The reason for my silence in general is that I have got to work like Hell here—I seem to have forgotten everything I know. If you are on the look out for a cheap modern edition of Chesterfield's letters, I will see what I can do, but I feel inclined to reply in Tommy's irreverent style, 'Wot 'opes'. About St Simon you will find it much easier to write to Paris for a French edition: when you had finished with it you could send it on to me to be bound and pressed—after which you would find it as good as new. I don't know of a crib to it.[54] To

---

[54] Warren, still stationed in France, was probably looking for the whole of the Duc de Saint-Simon's *Mémoires*. In later years he was to write six books on Louis XIV and the *Grand Siècle*. So memorable was his discovery of Saint-Simon that forty-five years later he told me he could still recall buying an abridgement of the *Mémoires* at St Omer on 3 March 1919.

take up P's style, have you ever noticed a book at home 'very much on the same lines', the Memoirs of Count Gramont, written in French by a Hamilton who was a hanger on of the grand monarque, and translated?[55]

In the name of all the gods why do you want to go into the 'Russian Expeditionary Force'? You will drag on a post-less, drink-less, book-less, tobacco-less existence for some months until the Bolshevists finally crush us and then prob-ably end your days at a stake or on a cross.

The typewriting of private letters is the vile invention of business men, but I will forgive you on the ground that you were practising . . . Did you see the 'very insolent' review of me on the back page of the *Times Literary Supplement* last week?[56] . . .

TO HIS FATHER: **from University College**

25 May 1919

I have not written to Evans, as I found a circular from a Press cutting Association to which I have replied, enclosing 10/-. The results so far have been a very interesting review on 'The Principles of Symbolic Logic' by C. S. Lewis of the University of California. I am writing back to tell them that they have got rather muddled. Symbolic Logic forsooth!

---

[55] *Memoirs of Count Grammont*, ed. Gordon Goodwin (1903).

[56] *The Times Literary Supplement* (27 March 1919), p. 167: 'These lyrics are always graceful and polished, and their themes are chosen from those which naturally attract poets—The Autumn Morning, Oxford, Lullaby, The Witch, Milton Read Again, and so on. The Thought, when closed with, is found often not to rise above the commonplace . . .'

I started reading it without noticing the title and was surprised to find myself—as I thought—being commended for
a 'scholarly elucidation of a difficult subject'.

As nearly everyone here is a poet himself, they have naturally no time left for lionizing others. Indeed the current
literary set is one I could not afford to live in anyway, and
tho' many of them have kindly bought copies of the book,
their tastes run rather to modernism, *vers libre* and that sort
of thing. I have a holy terror of coteries: I have already been
asked to join a Theosophist, a Socialist, and a Celtic society.

By the way, the distinction which one finds in such books
as *Tom Brown* by which the poor, the industrious, and the
intellectual, are all in one class, and the rich, brainless and
vicious, all in another, does not obtain. Some 'poor scholars'
are bad lots, and some of the 'gilded youth' are fond of literature . . .

[Increasingly, Mr Lewis and Warren worried about the
prominent position of Mrs Moore in Jack's life. Writing
to Warren on 20 May, Mr Lewis said: 'I confess I do not
know what to do or say about Jacks' affair. It worries
and depresses me greatly. All I know about the lady
is that she is old enough to be his mother—that she
is separated from her husband and that she is in poor
circumstances. I also know that Jacks has frequently
drawn cheques in her favour running up to £10—for
what I don't know. If Jacks were not an impetuous,
kind hearted creature who could be cajoled by any
woman who has been through the mill, I should not
be so uneasy. Then there is the husband whom I have

always been told is a scoundrel—but the absent are always to blame—somewhere in the background, who some of these days might try a little aimable blackmailing. But outside all these considerations that may be the outcome of a suspicious, police court mind, there is the distraction from work and the folly of the daily letters.' On 3 June Warren wrote to his father, saying: 'I am greatly relieved . . . to hear that Mrs Moore HAS a husband: I understood that she was a widow; but as there is a Mr Moore, the whole complexion of the business is altered. We now get the following very unsatisfactory findings. (1) Mrs Moore can't marry Jacks. (2) Mr Moore can't blackmail him because "IT" hasn't enough money to make it a paying risk. (3) YOU can't be blackmailed because you wouldn't listen to the proposition for one moment. But the daily letter business DOES annoy me: especially as I have heard from Jacks ONCE since January of this year.']

TO HIS BROTHER: from University College

9 [June 1919]

'Sir,' said Dr Johnson, 'you are an unsocial person.' In answer to the charge I can only plead the general atmosphere of the summer term which is the same here as it was at school: whatever energy I have has to be thrown into work and, for the rest, the seductive influence of the river and hot weather must bear the blame. Term ends some time in July, but I shall be staying up for part of the vac. Would the early part of September do for your leave: one doesn't get any chance of fine weather or of endurably warm sea water any earlier in Donegal. I quite agree with you that we could have quite an excellent time together at Portsalon—if we were 'both' there, if, as you suggest, we were 'all' there, I suppose we could endure as we always have endured.

You ask me what is wrong with P . . . which he describes as exceedingly painful and horribly depressing. I don't meet the doctors myself and therefore, in the case of a man who would hold precisely the same language about a boil or a wasp's sting, it is impossible to say how bad he is: I am afraid however it is rather a serious bother. There is also a second thing wrong with him—namely that he is fast becoming unbearable. What the difficulties of life with him always were, you know: but I never found it as bad as when I was last at home. I needn't describe the continual fussing, the sulks, the demand to know all one's affairs—you might think I was exaggerating as you have been out of it for so long . . .

TO HIS BROTHER: from University College

22 [July 1919]

I have just got your letter to which I am replying immediately. Of course I quite see your point, and am greatly relieved to hear from you as I had—of course—lost your address and wanted to get into touch with you. Now will you please wire to me at Univ. and let me know the day and approximate time of your arrival at Oxford: I will then report at the station at a suitable hour. If by any chance I am absent from parade you must drive to Univ. and wait for me, even if I do not turn up at once. The porter will have means of getting on to me if I am out. The programme you sketch is very attractive and it would be grand to have ignorance exposed by the Knock again. You understand why I behave so queerly—the effort to avoid being left alone at Leeborough. With you to back me up however, I have no doubt that we shall depart up to scheduled time. I doubt if this letter will reach you before you leave . . .

[Warren arrived in Oxford on 23 July to begin his holiday with Jack. They were in London for the next two days, and on the 25th they visited Mr Kirkpatrick in Great Bookham. On 26 July they crossed to Ireland to stay with their father until 22 August. The already uneasy relations between Jack and his father were considerably worsened by an event described by Mr Lewis in his diary on 6 August: 'Sitting in the study after dinner I began to talk to Jacks about money matters and the cost of maintaining himself at the University. I asked him if he had any money to his credit, and he said about £15. I happened to go up to the little end room and lying on his table was a piece of paper. I took it up and it proved to be a letter from Cox and Co stating that his a/c was overdrawn £12 odd. I came down and told him what I had seen. He then admitted that he had told me a deliberate lie. As a reason, he said that he had tried to give me his confidence, but I had never given him mine etc., etc. He referred to incidents of his childhood where I had treated them badly. In further conversation he said he had no respect for me—nor confidence in me.' This rupture was to last for quite a long time. On

5 September Mr Lewis wrote in his diary: 'I have during the past four weeks passed through one of the most miserable periods of my life—in many respects the most miserable. It began with the estrangement from Jacks. On 6 August he deceived me and said terrible, insulting, and despising things to me. God help me! That all my love and devotion and self-sacrifice should have come to this—that 'he doesn't respect me. That he doesn't trust me, and cares for me in a way.' He has one cause of complaint against me I admit—that I did not visit him while he was in hospital. I should have sacrificed everything to do so and had he not been comfortable and making good progress I should have done so . . . The other troubles and anxieties which have come upon me can be faced by courage, endurance, and self-denial. The loss of Jacks' affection, if it be permanent, is irreparable and leaves me very miserable and heart sore.']

TO HIS FATHER: **from University College**

9 October [1919]

Once again, in the words of the immortals, we have resumed our round of steady work, relieved and sweetened by hearty play. I would have written earlier but I have been rather incapacitated by a bite from a playful cat—merely a scratch at the end of my forefinger, but enough for a while to prevent one laying it to a pen with any comfort. It is now alright.

I was sorry to see the other day news of our friend Heineman's sudden death. The papers have been so covering him with eulogy since he went that I begin to feel glad I met him, if only for once—*Vergilium vidi tantum!*[57] In this case however I think the virtues are not wholly of the tombstone nature: a great publisher is really something more than a mere machine for making money: he has opportunities for doing things for the best of motives, and if one looks round most of our English houses, I think he avails himself of them as well as anyone can expect. I always put up a fight for the tribe of publishers here where so many young men with manuscripts have nothing too bad to say of them ...

TO HIS FATHER: from University College

Postmark: 20 October 1919

I had already seen about the death of Cousin Quartus in the *Times* before I got your telegram.[58] For this I suppose one should have been prepared, and indeed for himself, poor man, it was no tragedy. Yet I had come to think of his always being there: it will be a sad thing to go to Glenmachan now. As far back as I can remember he has always had a big place in our life—always the same kindly, courteous old gentleman. I am of course writing to Cousin Mary, although I think such letters are of little use. There is a great deal that we could all say, and say honestly, but it usually sounds conventional on paper ...

---

[57] 'I have seen the so great Vergil!'

[58] This was Sir William Quartus Ewart (b. 1844) who died on 17 October. His wife, Lady Ewart, was first cousin to Jack's mother. Their home, 'Glenmachan', was very near "Little Lea" and there is a pleasing picture of the Ewarts and their children in the chapter of *Surprised by Joy* entitled 'Mountbracken and Campbell'—'Mountbracken' being a ficticious name for Glenmachan.

As regards the other matter of which you spoke in your letters, I must ask you to believe that it would have been much easier for me to have left those things unsaid. They were as painful to me as they were for you. Yet, though I have many things to blame myself for, I should blame myself still more if I had tried to establish the relations you refer to by any other means than that of saying frankly what I thought. I did not speak in anger; still less for the purpose of giving pain. But I am sure you will agree with me that the confidence and affection which we both desire are more likely to be restored by honest effort on both sides and toleration—such as is always necessary between imperfect human creatures—than by any answer of mine which was not perfectly sincere . . .

TO HIS FATHER: from University College

Postmark: 4 February 1920

I am preparing to wait upon my great aunt Warren this afternoon, with transports as moderate as those of the Colonel. I think this particular form of introducing strangers by letter, on the theory that blood is thicker than water ('and a good deal nastier' as someone added) is one of the most irritating of social amenities. It always reminds me of two hostile children being shoved into a room and told to 'have a nice game' together . . .

I am inclined to agree with you—and Mrs Ward—about the lack of charm in Wells: but there are other qualities as important, if less delightful. I am now reading *Lavengro*[59] at

---

[59] By George Borrow (1851).

breakfast every morning and should like it very much if one could cut out the anti-Catholic propaganda . . .

TO HIS FATHER: from 22 Old Cleve, Washford, Somerset

4 April 1920

I am glad to be able to begin with a bit of good news. I did get a First [in Honour Mods] after all. Unfortunately that is almost all I can tell you, as the names in each class are given only in alphabetical order and I can see no possibility of finding out places or marks.

Now as to our movements: as this is the shortest vac., and also as I felt in need of some 'refresher' I thought it a good opportunity of paying off an engagement with a man who has been asking me for some time to go and 'walk' with him. We are at present at this tiny little village in a perfectly ideal cottage (which is, so to speak, his people's Teigh-na-mara) from which base we shall set out when the weather clears.[60]

We are quite alone and live an idyllic life on eggs, bully beef and—divine treasure—an excellent ham which Aunt

---

[60] Jack was hiding a good deal from his father. He was in Somerset, not with a male friend, but with Mrs Moore and Maureen. Since Mrs Moore and Maureen had moved to Oxford in January 1919 they had lived in four different places. They had gone for a month's holiday with Jack in Somerset because of a disagreement with the landlady, Mrs John Jeffrey, from whom they had been renting a flat over what was then, and still is, a butcher's shop in 58 Windmill Road. Having spent a year in college, Jack was allowed to live in rooms approved by the University. Upon their return to Oxford at the beginning of May, Jack went to live with the Moores in 'Court Field Cottage' in 131 Osler Road, Headington.

Lily very opportunely sent. The country is delightful, consisting of high moors with charming valleys full of orchards between them, and everything is a mass of white blossom. It is on the borders of Somerset and Devon. Our address will of course be moveable but letters sent here will reach me after some delay. I am sorry to desert you for the present, but it had to be polished off sooner or later.

I am just getting over a rather tiresome cough and cold and am beginning to feel much better than I have done for a long time. I have brought *Waverley*[61] to clean out my mind— there is great comfort in these solid old books . . .

TO HIS FATHER: from Washford

11 April 1920

I had quite forgotten about Aunt Warren. She must be pretty old, and dresses (with cap and white collar) in a style which makes her look rather more so. At the same time there is nothing senile in her conversation or manner. We talked chiefly about Glenmachan and Irish politics. The only one of 'the girls' present was Daisy, who is, I suppose, over forty. She struck me as being ecclesiastical in a high degree: for instance from her point of view the chief argument in favour of expelling the Turks from Europe was 'that it would re-establish the Patriarch at Constantinople and thus create a balance to the Papacy'. After the Armenian massacres, not to mention the war, THAT would hardly have appeared to me—nor to you I presume—the most important reason.

---

[61] By Sir Walter Scott (1814).

There was a very attractive child whose parents are in India: but I like the old lady the best of the three.

As you see, we have not yet moved: indeed the weather has not encouraged us to set out, though it has not prevented us from a great deal of walking. It is more beautiful here almost than any place I have ever seen — whether in the valleys full of orchards or up on the big heathery hills from which one looks down on the sea and the Welsh coast away on the horizon.

You need not have any fears about our cuisine here. Remember we are almost in Devon and the clotted cream of the country is a host in itself: also — shades of Oldie — the real 'Deevonshire' cider in every thatched and sanded pub.[62]

A few miles away is a little fishing town called Watchet, which saw at least one interesting scene in its obscure history: it was here that Coleridge and the Wordsworths slept (or 'lay' as they would have said) on the first night of their walking tour. During that afternoon the germ of the Ancient Mariner occurred in conversation and in the inn at Watchet the first lines were jotted down . . .

TO HIS FATHER: from University College

1 May 1920

I have two tutors now that I am doing 'Greats', one for history and one for philosophy. Of course I am sorry to have parted brass rags with old Poynton: the other two are much

---

[62] 'Oldie' was the nickname of Robert Capron (1851–1911), a native of Devon and the Headmaster of Wynyard School. Wynyard is the dreadful school referred to in *Surprised by Joy* as 'Belsen'.

younger men, but seem quite nice.[63] We go to the philosophy one in pairs: then one of us reads an essay and all three
discuss it. I wish you could hear the 'crack', it is very amusing. Luckily I find that my previous dabbling in the subject
stands me in good stead and for some time I shall have only
to go over more carefully ground through which I have
already meandered on my own.

I expect that what you feel about travel would be endorsed
by a great many other people of your own age, who, as you
say, have never really wanted a shilling in their lives. As far
as I can see it is only the few who can do it without the least
sacrifice who bother to see the world at all: the majority will
not give up anything for it and would sooner afford a car
to go round Stangford on, than see Greece or Cathay—if
there really is a Cathay. One is amazed at the resolution of
a real traveller like Herodotus, whom I am reading at present: knowing apparently no language but his own and relying on merchant caravans and dragomans with a smattering
of Greek, he had yet penetrated to Babylon and seen the
hanging gardens and the temple of Bel-Baal I suppose—and
up the Nile as far as Elephantine where there were rumours
of the land of dwarfs beyond—the Pygmies of course. Or
Marco Polo—whom you should read: books of travel are a
great resource.

---

[63] His tutor in History was George Hope Stevenson (1880–1952) who,
after taking a B.A. in 1904 as a member of Balliol, was Fellow and
Praelector in Ancient History at University College 1906–49. Jack's
tutor in Philosophy was Edgar Frederick Carritt (1876–1964). Following
his undergraduate years at Hertford College he was elected Fellow and
Praelector in Philosophy at Univ. in 1898.

I can't understand the Irish news at all. One of the most curious things is the *rapprochement* which seems probable between English Trades Unionism and Sinn Fein. I was always confident that the religious differences, the *odium theologicum* would prevent a junction between the two. If they really do work together I think it is all up for England and Ireland . . .

TO HIS FATHER: from University College

6 June 1920

I thought I had said something about the Anthology. It is being got up as a kind of counterblast to the ruling literary fashion here, which consists in the tendencies called 'Vorticist'. Vorticist poems are usually in *vers libre* (which means they are printed like verse, but neither rhyme nor scan, a line ending wherever you like). Some of them are clever, the majority merely affected, and a good few—especially among the French ones—indecent: not a sensuous indecency, but one meant to nauseate, the whole genus arising from the 'sick of everything' mood. So some of us others who are not yet sick of everything have decided to bring out a yearly collection of our own things in the hope of persuading the gilded youth that the possibilities of metrical poetry on sane subjects are not yet quite exhausted because the Vorticists are suffering from satiety. Of course we may end by proving just the opposite, but we must risk that: there will be a polemical preface and the first number is to appear in the autumn. We call it *The way's the way* which is a quotation from Bunyan (a writer of books you know)![64] ...

We have had a bus strike here. The President of the Liberal Club and the President of the Labour Club, with followers, very foolishly addressed the world at large from chairs the other evening: and a warm scene between mixed workers and undergraduates on each side was only interrupted by the appearance of the Proctors: whereupon the undergraduates fled from the Proctors and the Proctors, with less success, fled from the mob. This, you see, is true democracy ...

TO HIS FATHER: from University College

25 July 1920

I should have answered you before but I have been engaged in entertaining the colonel [Warren]. He, despite the efforts of a tyrannical and slave driving general staff, is still managing to keep body and soul together and to sustain his labours with that equanimity for which he is justly famed. Contrary to your fears he, as yet, [has] only one car: which he proposes to sell and buy another. As soon as his leave begins he is going to motor me to Liverpool, via Malvern, and so home. I am still debating whether I can sufficiently brace my nerves to such an ordeal ...

---

[64] This volume of poems was to be published by Basil Blackwell. It turned out, however, that the poets themselves would have to raise the money for having it printed. As this was impossible the project had to be abandoned.

I had nearly forgotten to tell you that Uncle and Aunt Hamilton were here for a night on their tour.[65] If any man has ever been successful in screwing the honey out of life it is he. One cannot help admiring the skill with which he knows exactly how far selfishness can go without rebounding on himself: he has learned to a nicety how much every plank will bear. At the same time this worldly wisdom which has an appetite for everything and yet can be content with little, which knows what can be got out of life and does not expect more, would be almost a virtue, so pleasant is it and so sensible, if it were not centred completely on self. He made one good *mot* here—that 'England would be an excellent country to tour in were it not for the Cathedrals.'[66] . . .

TO HIS FATHER: from University College

Postmark: 8 December 1920

My journey to Cambridge was on this wise. You will remember that a society of Martlets at Pembroke, Cambridge sent representatives to our society of that name: on this occasion four of us were sent to play a return match. The trip was rendered both cheaper and pleasanter by the fact that one of the four lives there, and very kindly put us all up. I read them a paper on narrative poetry. Of course I

---

[65] The relatives were Jack's maternal uncle, Augustus Warren Hamilton (1866–1945), and his much-loved Canadian wife, Anne Sargent Harley Hamilton (1866–1930).

[66] Warren, unable to afford a car, bought a motorcycle with a sidecar instead. He and Jack went to Belfast on it, arriving there on 26 August. They were with their father until 23 September.

don't know what they thought of it, but at any rate nothing was thrown at me.[67] We dined with them first. It was a wretched night, which having attempted to freeze, had finally decided instead on a sleety rain. The old library of their college, where we had dinner, was very badly heated, and what between that and going about their quadrangle in the chilliness of evening dress and the rain, I got rather a nasty chill — whereof I am just now recovered.

It was very interesting next day to see Cambridge. In many ways it is a contrast: there is something, I can hardly say whether of colour or of atmosphere, which at once strikes a more northern, a bleaker and a harder note. Perhaps the flatness of the country, suggesting places seen from the railway beyond Crewe, has something to do with it. The streets are very narrow and crowded: the non-university parts depressing enough. Some things — such as King's College Chapel, in which I was prepared to be disappointed — are indeed beautiful beyond hope or belief: several little quadrangles I remember, with tiled gables, sun dials and tall chimnies like Tudor houses, were charming. One felt everywhere the touch of Puritanism, of something Whiggish, a little defiant perhaps. It has not so much Church and State in its veins as we. The stained windows in the Halls show figures like Erasmus and Cranmer. Oxford

---

[67] Jack had been elected President of the Martlets on 15 October 1919 and he was prevailed upon to retain the position until 13 June 1921. The paper which he read in Cambridge on 'Narrative Poetry' was read to the Oxford Martlets on 3 November 1920. The paper has not survived, but the minutes written about it are reproduced in my essay 'To the Martlets', *op. cit.*, pp. 44–45.

is more magnificent, Cambridge perhaps more intriguing. Our characteristic colour is the pale grey, almost the yellow of old stone: their's the warm brown of old brick. A great many Cambridge buildings remind one of the Tower of London. Most of the undergraduates whom I met I liked very much. Their dons, as judged by those who were at the 'do', are certainly inferior to ours in charm of manners and geniality. One I thought hardly a gentleman.

I am afraid you took my remark about 'a small book' rather too literally—I meant only an essay for my tutor: I am hardly up to writing historical monographs (for publication) just yet. I have however been recommended to try for the Vice Chancellor's Essay Prize next April. The subject is 'Optimism' under which heading one could include almost anything one wanted to write about. My point of view will be mainly metaphysical and rather dry. It would be a splendid advertisement if I could pull it off, but of course competition is very keen . . . [68]

TO HIS FATHER: from the Oxford Union Society

21 January [1921]

My history tutor has handed me over to a gentleman at Magdalen whom he recommended by telling me that he was

---

[68] On 15 December Warren was granted a leave of absence until his departure from Sierra Leone. He and Jack arrived in Belfast together on 24 December. Jack returned to Oxford on 13 January. Warren, however, remained with his father until 8 March. He sailed for Sierra Leone the next day.

a grandson of Mendelsohn's: a trifle irrelevant I thought.[69]
The exchange was presented to me in the form of a compliment and I am quite satisfied with it. The reason I mention it
is because the new man deserves to be known to fame. I had
not been many minutes in his room until I had an uneasy
sense of strange yet familiar neighbours. When he went out
for a moment I discovered what it was—pigs! Do not mistake me: not live pigs: but pigs of china, of bronze, of clay,
of wood, of stuff and of stone: pigs jovial and pigs quizzical,
kindly pigs and severe pigs, Falstaffian pigs and pigs philosophical. I counted twenty-eight in a few seconds and had
still not got beyond the mantelpiece. The porcine seraglio of
a lonely old batchelor is one of the little comedies I would
not have missed for a good deal. And yet how wise! Here
are companions for every mood, who need practically no
upkeep and are never untrue or unkind. I think I must give
him a new one: perhaps one of those balloon pigs filled with
gas, so that it could hover against the ceiling—and be drawn
down by a windlass at nights to rest, like a Zeppelin in some
little 'hangar'.

I am very sorry to hear that you were laid up so long,
and hope that you now have quite shaken it off. I have had
a bit of a cold, but it is now gone, and beyond the perennial

---

[69] Paul Victor Mendelssohn Beneke (1868–1944) was the great-grandson
of the composer Felix Mendelssohn. He became a Fellow of Magdalen
College in 1893 and taught Classics until his retirement in 1925. He lived
in Magdalen (with his vast collection of pigs) for the rest of his life.
Lewis's reminiscences of Beneke can be found in Margaret Denecke's
Paul Victor Mendelssohn Beneke (1868–1944) (Oxford [1954]), pp. 31–34.

need of having my hair cut, I think you would pass me as 'all present and correct'. I am still smoothing and varnishing the work on Optimism.

Here is a story that will please the Colonel. The other night at the 'Martlets' old Carlyle read a paper.[70] He is a foxy old gentleman with a cleanshaven face as red as a berry and straight hair the colour of snuff—a very comical face and a high croaking voice. He began by saying that he ought to apologize for his paper 'because—h'm—to tell you the truth—I had meant to publish it—but h'm—h'm—it was so unsatisfactory that—I—I just sent it to an American magazine.' That's the proper spirit! . . .

TO HIS BROTHER: from University College (a serial letter, written on various dates)

I am waiting to hear your address from M. L'Oiseau Pomme de Terre,[71] and in the meantime have begun—tho' with what

---

[70] The Rev. Alexander James Carlyle (1861–1943) was the Chaplain of University College. He was an undergraduate at Exeter College, and following his appointment as Chaplain of Univ. in 1893 he became an active member of the Martlets.

[71] The Lewis brothers were enthusiastic nicknamers. Since boyhood they had been amused by their father's 'low' Irish pronunciation of 'potatoes' as 'p'daytas'. As a result, he became 'The P'dayta' or 'The P'daytabird'— and now, with Warren in Sierre Leone, 'Monsieur L'Oiseau Pomme de Terre'. The brothers had nicknames for one another as well. When I observed Jack addressing his brother in letters as 'APB' and being addressed by Warren as 'SPB' I asked what the initials meant. He told me that when they were very young their nurse, Lizzie Endicott, when drying them after a bath, threatened to smack their 'piggiebottoms'. In time the brothers decided that Warren was the 'Archpiggiebotham' and Jack the 'Smallpiggiebotham'.

promise of continuance I don't know — my journal letter. As nothing ever happens to me it will be filled, if at all, with trivialities and things that have interested me from day to day. As we talk a good deal of odd fragments out of books when we are together, there's no reason why we should not reproduce the same sort of tittle-tattle. Perhaps one of the reasons why letters are so hard to write and so much harder to read is that people confine themselves to news — or in other words think nothing worth writing except that which would not be worth saying. All that should be said by way of preamble has already been better said by Lamb in his letter to a friend at the Antipodes. I feel the same difficulty: I cannot imagine in what kind of melodramatic setting you will be reading this. I hear that your 'preposterous box' on the 'East Indiaman' was not to your liking. Well, you would be a soldier: you must keep a stiff upper lip about it and button up your coat. Here we have sleet and that sort of wind that freezes you when you go out drest for summer: if you do otherwise, 'the wild winds whist' and the sun comes out a good 80. But I will be on with my journal: the dates are only approximate.

1 March 1921

Going into College today I met Hamilton-Jenkin in the porch, who carried me to his rooms in Merton Street.[72] Jenkin is a little, pale person with a smooth green face, not unlike a lizard's. He was too young for the war and I always look on him as rather a child, though some people think I

---

[72] Alfred Kenneth Hamilton Jenkin (1900–80) matriculated at Univ. in 1919 and after completing his B.A. he took a B.Litt. degree. *The Cornish Mines* (1927) was the first of his many interesting books on Cornwall.

am wrong in this. I mention him for the amusing passages he showed me from two books. One was *A Tour of the County of Cornwall* written in the 17th Century: an admirable codology. Under the heading of Beastes we find (after those of Venerie and Draught) Rats. These are described as 'not only mischievious by day for their devouring of clothes, writings and meats, but cumbersome by night for their rattling and jaunting as they gallup their galliards in the roof'. This sentence I at once learnt by heart. 'The slow six legged crawler' which in Cornwall infest all but the 'cleanly home bred' are also worth recording.[73]

Jenkin himself is an enthusiastic Cornishman and some are bored with his persistency in talking of his native scenery, habits, language and superstitions. I rather like it. He put on a little linen cap which he wears when 'he goes down mines'. Cornwall of course is all mines: they are full of beings called Nackers whom one hears knocking at the ends of the lonelier galleries. The workmen leave little bits of their food for them, for they are terrible bringers of good and bad luck—rather like Leprechauns as I understand. Jenkins has only one vice: that of writing very sad poetry which he sometimes shows me. It is usually about Cornwall.

12 March 1921

Everyone was going down today. Such days have all the atmosphere of a school end of term with its joy taken out of it—body without soul. I hate it: and lest empty rooms and stacks of suit cases should not be sufficiently offensive, we have the

---

[73] Although the passages are slightly misquoted they come from Richard Carew's *The Survey of Cornwall* (1602), p. 22.

intolerable institution of Collections. This is the worst relic of barbarism which yet hangs about the University. From 9 until noon the Master with all his 'auxiliar fiends' sits at the high table in Hall and one by one sheepish or truculent undergraduates, as their names are called, walk up the long emptiness, mount the dais and stand foolishly gaping while he delivers a little homily. In my case he always used to say the same thing. 'Well Mr Lewis, I—ah—I—have nothing but—ah—satisfaction to express as regards—ah—ah. We expect great things of you.' Apparently he has now given up expecting great things of me.

Now you, lolling in your punkah while the lotuses fly over a pagoda coloured sky etc, may think me very weak: but it is extraordinary that any ceremony which is destined to make you feel like an inky schoolboy will succeed in making you feel like an inky schoolboy. I doubt if even the P'daytabird could have invented anything more subtly undermining of one's self-respect than that early morning procession up a big hall to be complimented by an old gentleman at a table. Try to imagine it and then add the idea of nine o'clock in the morning: and that your collar has broken loose from its stud at the back: and that there's a smell of last night's dinner about: a fly on your nose: a shaving cut beginning to bleed—but no, it is too painful . . .

13 March 1921

It being Lord's Day I waited after breakfast on Pasley in his rooms at Unity House: that is a cottage in a lane by Headington Church where the buildings are so ruinous that it looks like a bit of France as the cant goes—well FAIRLY like it. Pasley is my oldest ally: he used to write poetry but is now too engrossed in history and he has also become engaged—that fatal tomb of all lively and interesting men[74] ... Unity House is ruled by a strangely ugly woman ... I had an excellent walk with Pasley: he described to me the humours of the new constitution of TzechoSlovakia, which I wish I cd. remember. We sat in a wood full of primroses. Damnit, how generations of P'dayta's have teased the language till the very name of a primrose sounds sentimental: when you come to look at them, they are really rather attractive. I walked Pasley off his legs and we lunched *chez moi* on rabbit pie—our common fare at present—Pasley and Mrs Moore having a lively conversation on money in view of his intent shortly to try 'this marrying business'.

14 March 1921

I received this morning a letter from my obliging friend Stead.[75] Stead is rather a punt: I think you saw me stop to speak to him one day in the Corn. He is an undergraduate but also curate of a parish in Oxford. He writes poetry. The

---

[74] Sir Rodney Marshall Sabine Pasley (1899–1982), who succeeded to a Baronetcy in 1947, took his B.A. from University College in 1921. His first position was as a Master at Alleyn's School, 1921–25; then Vice-Principal of Rajkumar College at Rajkot, India, 1926–28. He was the Headmaster of Barnstaple Grammar School 1936–43 and the Headmaster of Central Grammar School, Birmingham from 1943 until his retirement in 1959. When Jack wrote this letter Pasley was engaged to Miss Aldyth Werge Hamber.

[75] William Force Stead (1884–1967) was born in Washington, D.C., and attended the University of Virginia before coming to England. He was ordained a priest in the Church of England in 1917 and he became a member of Queen's College, Oxford, in 1921. After taking his degree in 1925 he served as the Chaplain of Worcester College from 1917 to 1933. Besides publishing a great many poems, he knew many famous poets. He baptized his friend T. S. Eliot in 1927.

annoying thing is that it's exactly like mine, only like the bad parts of mine: this was my own original opinion and it has been confirmed by others. Perhaps you can imagine the sensation I experienced in reading it. Stead's letter was to say that he had mentioned to Yeats—whom he knows—'my double claim to distinction as an Irishman and a poet' and would I come along this evening and see him?

I accordingly repaired after dinner to Stead's lodging in Canterbury Street. He is a married man: his wife is an American: she is the sister of a woman who is married to a brother of Mrs Moore's.[76] She was a woman of implacable sullenness who refused even to say good evening to me: beside her at the fire sat an American gentleman who was apparently left to console her for the absence of her husband. This was a very amiable person: he was 'studyin'' when I entered, but politely laid his book down. You know the sort of face in which a long promontory of nose (eagle build) projects from between two rounded hills of cheek (cherub build)? Picture this surmounted by a pair of horn spectacles and made of a texture rather like cod's roe: then add that this face beams but can contribute to the crack only by saying 'That's right' at the end of everyone's remark. In these rather nasty surroundings Stead was finishing a very nasty meal of cold fish and cocoa: but he soon put on his coat and after asking his lady why there were no stamps in the house and receiving no answer, swung out with me into

---

[76] Mrs Stead's sister, the former Mary Goldsworthy, was married to Dr John Hawkins Askins (1877–1923). The Askins were living just outside Oxford in the village of Iffley.

the usual Oxford theatrical night. Trusting soul to leave his wife unguarded in such society!

Yeats lives at the end of Broad St, the first house on your right as you leave the town. I can assure you I felt a veritable Bozzy as I reflected that I was now to meet at last WILLIAM BUTLER YEATS! But enough of that. We were shown up a long stairway lined with rather wicked pictures by Blake—all devils and monsters—and finally into the presence chamber, lit by tall candles, with orange coloured curtains and full of things which I can't describe because I don't know their names.

The poet was very big, about sixty years of age: 'awful' as Bozzy says: grey haired, clean shaven. When he first began to speak I would have thought him French, but the Irish sounds through after a time. Before the fire was a circle of hard antique chairs. Present were the poet's wife, a little man who never spoke all evening, and Father Martindale.[77] Father M. is a Catholic Priest, a little twinkling man like a bird, or like Puck, whom I take to be an atheistical dog. I used to go to his lectures in the old days: he is a mocker. Everyone got up as we came in: after the formalities I was humbly preparing to sink into the outlying chair leaving the more honourable to Stead, but the poet sternly and silently motioned us into other ones. The meaning of this I have not fathomed: 'twas very Pumblechookian.

---

[77] Father Cyril Charles Martindale SJ (1879–1963) was a member of Campion Hall and he lectured in the faculty of *Literae Humaniores*. He wrote as both a scholar and a popular apologist.

Then the talk began. It was all of magic and cabbalism and 'the Hermetic knowledge'. The great man talked while the priest and Mrs Yeats fed him with judicious questions. The matter I admit was either mediaeval or modern, but the manner was so XVIII Century that I lost my morale. I understood how it is possible for a man to terrify a room into silence: and I had a ghastly presentment that something would presently impel me to up like that 'unknown curate' and say 'Were not Vale Owen's revelations, Sir, addressed to the passions?' And then as Max Beerbohm says 'Bang' the suddenness of it! However I remembered that Johnson WAS really dead and controlled myself. Indeed some good angel guided me: for presently I really had something to say—a case mentioned by Coleridge which was most apposite and indeed crying for quotation on something just said. But thank God I didn't: for a minute later the priest did.

YEATS (thumping his chair): 'Yes—yes—the old woman in Coleridge. That story was published by Coleridge without the slightest evidence. Andrew Lang exposed it. I've never had a conversation on the subject that SOMEONE didn't bring in Coleridge's old woman. It is anonymous in the first place and every one has taken it over without question. It just shows that there's no limit to the unscrupulousness that a sceptical man will go to—'

MARTINDALE: 'Oh surely Mr Yeats—'

YEATS: 'Yes! There is a Professor living in Oxford at this moment who is the greatest sceptic in print. The same man has told me that he entered a laboratory where X (some woman whose name I didn't catch) was doing experiments: saw the table floating near the ceiling with X sitting on it: vomited: gave orders that no further experiments were to be done in the laboratories — and refused to let the story be known.'

But it would be only ridiculous to record it all: I should give you the insanity of the man without his eloquence and presence, which are very great. I could never have believed that he was so exactly like his own poetry.

One more joke must be recorded. Stead presently told us a dream he had had: it was so good that I thought it a lie. YEATS (looking to his wife): 'Have you anything to say about that, Georges?' Apparently Stead's transcendental self, not important enough for the poet, has been committed to Mrs Yeats as a kind of ersatz or secondary magician.

Finally we are given sherry or vermouth in long and curiously shaped glasses, except Martindale who has whiskey out of an even longer and more curiously shaped glass, and the orgy is at an end. Try to mix Pumblechook, the lunatic we met at the Mitre, Dr Johnson, the most eloquent drunk Irishman you know, and Yeat's own poetry, all up into one composite figure, and you will have the best impression I can give you.

21 March 1921

Having met Stead yesterday in the Broad with his wife and of course with our friend of the nose, I was told that the great man had expressed himself sorry not to have been able to see more of me owing to his argument with the priest, and would I come again with Stead next night?

This night we were shown to a study up in the ceiling and entertained by him alone: and, would you believe it, he was almost quite sane, and talked about books and things, still eloquently and quite intelligently? Of course we got on to magic in the end—that was only to be expected. It was really my fault, for I mentioned Bergson. 'Ah yes,' said he, 'Bergson. It was his sister who taught me magic.' The effect of this statement on Aunt Suffern (already in paroxysms of contempt over what I had already told her about Yeats) ought to be amusing.

We spoke of Andrew Lang. YEATS: 'I met him once—at a dinner somewhere. He never said a word. When we began to talk afterwards, he just got up and took his chair into a corner of the room and sat down facing the wall. He stayed there all the evening.' Perhaps Lang didn't like wizards!

Of the 'great Victorians' he said: 'The most interesting thing about the Victorian period was their penchant for selecting one typical great man in each department—Tennyson, THE poet, Roberts, THE soldier: and then these types were made into myths. You never heard of anyone else: if you spoke of medicine it meant . . . (some "THE Doctor" whose name I've forgotten): if you spoke of politics it was Gladstone.'

This is especially interesting to us as explaining the mental growth of a certain bird we wot of. ('Well all said and done boys, he was a GREAT man.') So home to bed more pleased with our poet than I had been on the last occasion: and rather thankful that L'Oiseau Pomme de Terre hadn't been there to explain that 'you can see he's a disappointed man' after every adverse criticism on any living writer. Oh, before I leave it, Stead told me he had shown Yeats a poem: Yeats said he thought 'IT WOULD DO VERY WELL' to set to music! Stead thinks this is a compliment. H'mh!

TO HIS FATHER: from University College

28 March 1921

I am glad that you sent me the wire. I am a poor reader of papers and should have been very sorry, through ignorance, to let such a thing pass in silence. Poor old Kirk![78] What shall one say of him? It would be a poor compliment to that memory to be sentimental: indeed, if it were possible, he would himself return to chide the absurdity. It is however no sentiment, but plainest fact to say that I at least owe to him in the intellectual sphere as much as one human being can owe another. That he enabled me to win a scholarship is the least that he did for me. It was an atmosphere of unrelenting clearness and rigid honesty of thought that one breathed from living with him—and this I shall be the better for as long as I live. And if this is the greatest thing, there are others which none of us will forget: his dry humour,

---

[78] Mr William T. Kirkpatrick, who was born in 1848, died on 22 March 1921. He became the Headmaster of Lurgan College in Lurgan, Co. Armagh, shortly after its founding by Samuel Watts in 1874. It was during his twenty-five years as Headmaster that Albert Lewis became one of his pupils. In 1900 he moved with his wife, Louise, and their son, Louie, to Northenden, Cheshire, so that Louie could train as an electrical engineer in Manchester. A few years later he and Mrs Kirkpatrick moved to Great Bookham where he gave Warren and Jack, along with a few others, private tuition.

his imperturbable good temper and his amazing energy—
these it is good to have seen. He was a unique personality
with nothing inconsistent about him—except the one foi-
ble about the Sunday suit: the more one sees of weakness,
affectation and general vagueness in the majority of men,
the more one admires that rigid, lonely old figure—more
like some ancient Stoic standing fast in the Roman deca-
dence than a modern scholar living in the home countries.
Indeed we may almost call him a great man, tho', as it happened, his greatness was doomed to reach so small a circle.
I should have liked to have seen him once again before this
happened. I have of course written to Mrs K.

You ask whether I am satisfied with my Optimism, and
I am afraid I hardly know. For one thing I almost know it
by heart, and consequently can least of all judge it impar-
tially . . . At any rate, it has given me, in parts, as much trouble as anything I have ever done and I shall be glad to have
it launched into the registrar's box for good and all and to
leave the rest on the knees of the gods. Only don't expect any
results. You see I am afraid I have rather fallen between two
stools: it has to aim at being both literary and philosophical, and, in the effort to accomplish the double object, I have
made it too literary for the philosophers and too metaphysical for the dons of English Literature. These are the pitfalls
with which the walks of Academe are digged. Such things are
written for a tiny public of appointed judges, and you never
know what their particular point of view is going to be: they
are only human beings and must have tastes and tempers of
their own, but one can't find these out. It must be difficult

to be quite fair to an essay which expresses some view that you have been denouncing to a submissive Senior Common Room for the last half century, however good it may be . . .

TO HIS BROTHER: from University College
(a continuation of the serial letter)

20? April [1921]

About the coal strike itself you have, I suppose, heard AD NAUSEAM from the papers: what it means to me personally is that I have done a good deal of wood sawing. Have you ever sawed wood? If not, you probably have an idea that one sets the saw lightly on the log, gets to work, and continues steadily deepening until the two halves fall apart. Not a bit of it: you set the saw lightly on the log and then try to move it. It darts aside with a sound like a swallow, and you wrap a handkerchief round your hand: when the blood has soaked through this you go into the house and get some court plaster. Next time you go more cautiously and after the saw has chirped a whole song, a bit of bark comes off: by this time you are fairly warm. Then you really get to it: back and forward you go, changing uneasily from your left to your right feeling the blisters arise on your hand, while the shadows lengthen and the sweat pours down. When you go to bed that night, the 'big push' has got about as far as you see in the cut, and you get visions of getting through that log on your thirtieth birthday. I have now become quite good at it and sometimes even get a degree of enjoyment out of it when the day is fine and it goes well. Pasley has turned up the other day: everyone has drifted in since.

Many thanks for your most interesting letter. What a queer end of the world backwater—just like the places we used to imagine out of God knows what sea stories but, still more 'all made out of the carver's brain'. I certainly never thought to hear anything like *H.M.S. Dwarf* in real life: and how very homely to have a telescope and a Lloyd's register!

You will have plenty more to tell me in your next letter: I haven't quite got my picture yet. What type of mountains are they? I assume they don't rise to snow: I know they can't be heathery: and I have a suspicion they are not smooth green like the hills at Malvern. So you see I am at a loss for them ...

I am very glad you have become a convert to Milton: what put you on to him and what parts have you been reading? I wonder will you ever get to the end of the Bible: the undesirable 'primitives' around you will enable you to appreciate the Hebrews who were Class A primitives after all ...

TO HIS FATHER: from University College

23 April [1921]

I can of course appreciate your feelings about poor Kirk's funeral.[79] Stripped of all wherewith belief and tradition have clothed it, death appears a little grimmer—a shade more chilly and loathsome—in the eyes of the most matter of fact.

---

[79] The Lewises had long known that Mr Kirkpatrick was an atheist. However, writing to Warren on 21 April, Mr Lewis told him how painful he found the arrangements for Mr Kirkpatrick's body: 'There was not to be a funeral—no service, no ceremony, no flowers, and he was to be cremated. My whole soul rose in revolt at the thought. The dear old man to be spirited away furtively—like an unclean thing—and burned!'

At the same time, while this is sad, it would have been not only sad but shocking to have pronounced over Kirk words that he did not believe and performed ceremonies that he himself would have denounced as meaningless. Yet, as you say, he is so indelibly stamped on one's mind once known, so often present in thought, that he makes his own acceptance of annihilation the more unthinkable. I have seen death fairly often and never yet been able to find it anything but extraordinary and rather incredible. The real person is so very real, so obviously living and different from what is left that one cannot believe something has turned into nothing. It is not faith, it is not reason—just a 'feeling'. 'Feelings' are in the long run a pretty good match for what we call our beliefs.

TO HIS FATHER: from University College

9 May [1921]

I am beginning my period of Roman history and this has sent me back to Tacitus whom I read with Kirk. It is the strangest and in a way the pleasantest sensation. The old phrases come up inevitably in his own voice and manner, not only by the usual force of association, but also because Tacitus is a grim, sardonic author whose hardest sayings Kirk relished and made his own. One seems to remember those days in the little upper room with the photograph of Gladstone and the gas stove all the more often now that they are absolutely finished and shut up.

The weather continues pretty cold here and there are still a good many soldiers passing to and fro. I don't know that the Colonel's letter to me was very discursive: the Lloyd's

Register in his office and his dislike of the natives and cock-chafers were the chief points. But for the climate it would not be a bad job for troglodytes and readers like ourselves: fortunately he has a streak of that in him. For the average officers with no mind and no resources it must be a terrible business and a nurse of all the solitary vices: it is a curious necessity that always casts these sort of jobs—Lighthouses, wireless stations etc.—on the men least fitted for them by nature.

There is still no news of Optimism, and by now little optimism among those who await the news. I should have thought they could have decided on the productions before this: an unsettled possibility like that becomes in the end a nuisance at the back of one's mind.

TO HIS BROTHER: from University College

10 May [1921]

Here term is still new enough to be interesting. It is still pleasant to see fewer foreign visitors pacing the High with guide books and taking photos of spires—where I know they'll get them crooked—and to see one's friends again instead. Pasley was the first to wait upon us, in a blinding snow shower, a few days before term began . . .

A great friend of mine, Baker of Wadham, has come up again after being down for a couple of terms.[80] I often amuse

---

[80] Leo Kingsley Baker (1898–1986) matriculated at Wadham College in 1917. He served as a Flight Lieutenant in the RAF and was awarded the distinguished Flying Cross in 1918. He returned to Oxford in 1919 and took his B.A. in 1922.

myself by thinking how you and he would worry each other: not so much by direct antagonism as by being absolutely unable to understand one another. Have you ever met a person who talks habitually in metaphors and doesn't know that they are metaphors? He has certainly the perverseness and troublesomeness of speech which betoken greatness: his poems are like rooms full of exotic and insolent ornaments, but with nowhere to sit down . . .

The only strictly social function I have attended so far this term was tea with the Carlyles in their most charming house in Holywell.[81] It is a place I greatly envy: long uneven rooms with beams in the ceiling and wide stone grates where a little kind of brazier sits in a deep cave of Dutch tiles. I need hardly say that in Oxford houses all such things were unearthed only fairly recently: the XVIII Cent. wd doubtless have said 'elegance and civility for Gothic rudeness'.

The principles on which tea fights are conducted at the Carlyles is this: you are given a seat by someone and when you have had a reasonable time to get to the interesting part of the conversation, Mrs C., a rather fatuous woman, gets up and says, 'Mr Lewis, go and talk to Professor Smith' or 'Mr Wyllie, I think you know my daughter' or whatever it may be: then every single pair is shuffled. When you've got fairly settled, the same thing happens again: as some one said, it is like nothing so much as a game of cricket with nothing in it but an umpire calling 'over'. I had my longest 'spell' between Pasley and a lady whom the elder Miss C. describes as 'my little sister' . . . By the rule of the house

---

[81] Dr and Mrs A. J. Carlyle lived with their family in 29 Holywell Street.

of course Pasley and I had scarcely started trying to instil a little pessimism when she said, 'Oh, I must get Father to talk to you'. OVER!

When that had subsided I recovered consciousness beside Dr Carlyle. He has every reason to be an optimist: a man who can hold a parish AND a College Chaplaincy (you remember Poynton's remark 'Dr Carlyle repeats as much of the service as he can remember') without being a Christian, and who has lived on the bounty of a Royal Foundation for the last century while being a Socialist, ought to be. All the same he's a dear old man with a thin brick red face and very straight white hair and never takes anything seriously.

People talk about the Oxford manner and the Oxford life and the Oxford God-knows what else: as if the undergraduates had anything to do with it. Sitting beside this worthy priest I felt that it is really a thing we are quite outside: the real Oxford is a close corporation of jolly, untidy, lazy, good for nothing humorous old men, who have been electing their own successors ever since the world began and who intend to go on with it: they'll squeeze under the Revolution or leap over it somehow when it comes, don't you worry.

When I think how little chance I have of ever fighting my way into that unassuming yet impregnable fortress, that modest unremovability, that provokingly intangible stone wall, I think of Keats's poison.

Brewed in monkish cell
To thin the scarlet conclave of old men.[82]

---

[82] John Keats, *The Fall of Hyperion*, I, pp. 49–50. Slightly misquoted.

. . . Today the 11th, little Jenkin appeared after lunch and bade me go for a bike ride. As I had decided to work, I thought this would be an excellent opportunity of breaking my resolution. Jenkin has his own principles of push biking, the maxim being that 'where I go my machine can go'. He rides over moors and once carried it down a cliff in Cornwall.

After stopping for a drop of the negus at Garsington in the same little pub whither I went (v. last letter) on Easter Monday, we rode along the top of a long hill where you look down into a good, woody English valley with the Chilterns, rather sleek and chalky—like greyhounds—on the horizon. It was a grey day with clouds in muddled perspective all round. Just as the first drops of rain began to fall, we found a young man looking as if he were going to be hanged, crossing a field.

He turned out to be one Groves of Univ., who is now gone down and incarcerated at a High Church Theological Seminary in the neighbouring village of Cuddesdon.[83] 'He would have liked to ask us in to tea, but couldn't—indeed oughtn't to be talking to us—because they were having a QUIET DAY.' Ye gods: a lot of young men shut up together, all thinking about their souls! Isn't it awful?

After this it was quite fresh and lively to investigate an old wind mill near Wheatley: it has the sort of atmosphere we felt at Doagh and a little copper place over the door with a figure of a bird on it. Under it was a word variously read

---

[83] Sidney John Selby Groves (1897–1970) was ordained in 1922. He was Vicar of Sonning 1942–65 and a Canon of Christ Church.

by Jenkin and myself as *County* and *Cointy*. I do not know what this all was about. Jenkin keeps on picking up stones and telling you that it is iron here.

We rode over Shotover Hill: through sandy lanes with gorse on each side and passing occasional warm comfortable English barns and haystacks. Most attractive sign posts, 'Bridle path to Horsley'—a bridle path always sounds mysterious. And dozens of rabbits and whole bunches of bluebells: and a view far off between the two slopes of Forest Hill and the little house where the first Mrs Milton used to live. About the time he wrote *L'Allegro* and *Il Penseroso* he would often be riding over here from his home to court her—God help her! . . .

TO HIS FATHER: **from University College**
(after 'Optimism' had been awarded the Chancellor's Prize for an English Essay)

29 [May 1921]

Thank you very much for your wire and the letter: I am very glad to have been able to send you good news. I had almost lost heart about the thing, it dragged on so long. Everyone has been very nice about it, particularly the Mugger who is delighted, and this ought to be of use to me later on.

Some of my congratulations indeed have made me feel rather ashamed, coming from people whom I have been used to class generically as 'louts'. By louts I denote great beefy people unknown to me by name, men with too much money and athletic honour, who stand blocking up passages. If looks could kill I'm afraid they would often have been in danger as I shouldered my way through them. Now they have weighed in with polite remarks and gratified my vanity with the grand-paternal 'No. Does HE know ME?' I suppose the explanation is that in their view we have done so badly on the river that any success—even in so unimportant a field as letters—should be encouraged.

I have also had a letter from Blackwell offering to see me about publishing it, and have, as a formality, written to Heinemann's. In any case I am not sure what to do about that: I shall certainly not spend any money (nor allow you to, tho' I know you gladly would) on forcing it into print if publishers won't take the risk. I have always thought that a bad thing to do. Perhaps publication in some periodical might provide a compromise: it would remind people that I exist and yet it would not give too permanent a form to any opinion or argument that I may outgrow later on. At worst, if any one would like it, it would mean a five pound note and enable you and everyone else to read it decently printed instead of in type. If all these plans fall through, or if they are likely to take a long time, I will get another copy done and send it to you. You must not expect too much: the trains of argument are rather dull and I am afraid this effect is not neutralized by anything more than adequacy in the form. No purple patches—hardly a faint blue. But I must drop the annoying habit of anticipating your judgement . . .

I have been reading the oddest book lately—Newman's *Loss and Gain*.[84] I never knew that he had written a novel.

---

[84] John Henry Newman, *Loss and Gain* (1848).

As fiction or drama it is of course beneath contempt, but it has some real satirical humour. Do you know it? The picture of the then Oxford, with its ecclesiastical controversies etc., is something more remote from my experience whether real or imagined, than ancient Britain or modern Cathay.

I haven't heard anything about the prize—I think it is in money—not very much—and there are some books from College. I too thought about Kirk. We are all old, disillusioned creatures now, and look back on the days of 'buns and coffee' through a long perspective and only seldom come out of our holes: the young men up from school in their immaculate clothes think we have come to clean the windows when they see us. It happens to everyone here. In your first year you drink your sherry and see people: after that your set narrows, you haunt the country lanes more than the High, and cease to play at being the undergraduate of fiction. 1919 seems further off than France at times . . .

TO HIS FATHER: from University College

27 [June 1921]

The event of last week was one of the unforseen consequences of my winning 'Optimism'. I had almost forgotten, if I had ever known, that 'prizemen' have to read portions of their compositions at our ceremony of the Encaenia.[85] Being

---

[85] The Encaenia is Oxford University's annual Commemoration of founders and benefactors. This one took place on 22 June.

of the troglodytic nature I have never before exerted myself so far as to assist at this show: but having been now compelled, I am glad.

It is a most curious business. We unhappy performers attend (tho' it is at noon) in caps, gowns, and FULL EVENING DRESS. It was held in the Sheldonian Theatre: I think Macaulay has a purple passage about 'the painted roof of the Sheldonian' under which Charles held his last parliament. During the long wait, while people trickled in, an organ (much too large for the building) gave a recital. The undergraduates and their guests sit round in the galleries: the 'floor' is occupied by the graduates *en masse*, standing at barriers in all their war paint. At noon the Vice Chancellor enters with his procession of 'Heads of Colleges, Doctors, Proctors, and Noblemen'—a very strange show they make, half splendid and half grotesque, for few don's faces are fit to bear up against the scarlet and blue and silver of their robes.

Then some 'back chat' in Latin from the Vice Chancellor's throne and the Public Orator led in the persons who were to receive honorary degrees: with the exception of Clemenceau and Keyes (the Zeebruge man), they were not well known to the world at large. Keyes was a very honest looking fellow and Clemenceau the tough, burly 'people's man' whom one expected: but what was beyond everything was the Canon of Notre Dame, a great theologian apparently, with some name like Raffitol.[86] Such a picture of a

---

[86] Georges Clemenceau (1841–1929) was the Prime Minister and Minister for War of France, 1917–20. Vice-Admiral Sir Roger Keyes (1881–1929)

great priest with all the pale dignity that one had imagined, I never saw. If the words 'love at first sight' were not tied down to one kind of feeling only, I would almost use them to express the way this man attracted me. He would have appealed to you immensely.

After the honorary degrees, the Professor of Poetry made an 'oration' in Latin, chiefly about colleagues who had died during the last year: this was my first experience of spoken Latin and I was pleased to find that I could follow and enjoy it.

The performance of us prizemen was of course very small beer after all this. We had been instructed to read for about two minutes each: I had some difficulty in finding a short passage which would be intelligible by itself. I was, of course, nervous: I am also told that I was the first of our little band whom Clemenceau looked at: but as I do not know WITH WHAT EXPRESSION he looked, nor whether he speaks English, we must remain in doubt whether this was a compliment or not.

I have had a good lesson in modesty from thus seeing my fellow prize men. I was hardly prepared for such a collection of scrubby, beetle-like, bespectacled oddities: only one of them appeared to be a gentleman. Any I spoke to sounded very like fools, perhaps like Goldsmith, they 'writ like an angel and talked like poor Poll'.[87] It brings home to

---

was Admiral of the Fleet 1920–29 and the hero of Zeebruger. The Canon of Notre-Dame de Paris was the Rt Rev. Monseigneur Pierre Batiffol (1861–1929), a distinguished Church historian.

[87] David Garrick's imaginary epitaph on Oliver Goldsmith.

one how very little I know of Oxford: I am apt to regard my own set, which consists mainly of literary gents, with a smattering of political, musical and philosophical—as being central, normal, and representative. But step out of it, into the athletes on one side or the pale pot hunters on the other, and it is a strange planet . . .

TO HIS BROTHER: from 28 Warneford Road, Oxford

1 July [1921]

I was delighted to get your letter this morning; for some reason it had been sent first to a non-existent address in Liverpool. I had deliberately written nothing to you since those two you mention: not that I was tired of the job, but because I did not feel disposed to go on posting into the void until I had some assurance that my effusions would reach you. That seemed a process too like prayer for my taste: as I once said to Baker—my mystical friend with the crowded poetry—the trouble about God is that he is like a person who never acknowledges one's letters and so, in time, one comes to the conclusion either that he does not exist or that you have got the address wrong. I admitted that it was of great moment: but what was the use of going on despatching fervent messages—say to Edinburgh—if they all came back through the dead letter office: nay more, if you couldn't even find Edinburgh on the map. His cryptic reply was that it would be almost worth going to Edinburgh to find out . . .

Here another term has blossomed and faded: that time moves has I believe been observed before. I have lived my usual life: a few lectures, until—as happens about half way through the term—I got tired of them all: work, meetings with friends, walks and rides, solitary or otherwise, and meetings of the Martlets. These birds by the by were all invited to dinner by the don Martlets a few weeks ago, and I again had the opportunity of peeping into the real Oxford: this time through the medium of a very excellent meal ('with wine' as Milton says with the air of a footnote) in cool, brown oaky rooms. I have been thinking of a formula for it all and decided on 'Glenmachan turned male and intellectualized' as fairly good.

The great event of MY term was of course 'Optimism'. I must thank you for your congratulations before going on: THEY were provoked by the event, but the consequences of it will move your ribaldry. 'Prizemen', the Statues say, 'will read at the Encaenia portions of their exercises (I like that word)—their exercises chosen by the Professor of Poetry and the Public Orator.' Sounds dam' fine, doesn't it? But the Statues omit to mention the very cream of the whole situation—namely that the prizemen will appear in full evening dress. Fancy me entering the Sheldonian at 11.30 A.M. on a fine June morning in a cap, gown, boiled shirt, pumps, white tie and tails. Of course it was a 'broiling' day as the P'daytabird would say, and of course, for mere decency I had to wear an overcoat.

However, I managed to make myself audible, I am told, and beyond nearly falling as I entered the rostrum, I escaped with success. (They DO actually call it a rostrum, so that I was delighted: for the whole gallery of the Damerfesk seemed to gaze at me, and the jarring ghosts of Big, Polonius and Arabudda to lend me countenance.)[88] This was really the fault of one not unlike our Arabudda—old Ker the professor of poetry,[89] who, having earlier in the proceeding delivered his Latin oration, decided to remain sitting in the rostrum instead of going back to his own stall. This (in the language of Marie Stopes) 'made entry difficult if not impossible' for us prizemen: in my anxiety to avoid the burly professor, I stumbled over a raised step and nearly fell backwards. This must have appeared curiously enough to those who were on a level with, or higher than the rostrum: but the best effect of all was from the floor, from which, owing to the height of the front barrier and the big velvet cushion on it, I appeared simply to sink through a trap and rise again like a jack-in-the-box. However, I rallied my sang froid and bawled defiant remarks on the universe for two minutes. It is a good thing that the P'daytabird was not present or he would have been sorely put to it—especially if you had been beside him, giddy with laughter (You can imagine his asking me afterwards 'Did you do it to annoy me?').

I will send you a copy of my essay, since you ask for it, though I do not think it will be much in your line. Some of the insolent passages may amuse you: I hope you will like

---

[88] Lord Big (a frog), Polonius Green (a parrot) and Sir Charles Arabudda (a fish) are characters from the world of 'Boxen' which Jack and Warren created as boys. They are still to be found in the stories Jack wrote about them and now published as *Boxen: The Imaginary World of the Young C.S. Lewis,* ed. Walter Hooper (London, New York, 1985).

[89] William Patton Ker (1855–1923), Fellow of All Souls' College, Oxford, Professor of Poetry, and Quain Professor of English Literature in London, was the author of many books on English, Scottish and Scandinavian literature.

the way I dealt with the difficulty of 'God or no God'. To admit that person's existence would have upset my whole applecart: to deny it seemed inadvisable, on the off chance of there being a Christian among the examiners. I therefore adopted the more Kirkian alternative of proving—at any rate to my own satisfaction—that it 'really made no difference whatsoever' whether there was such a person or no. The second part of my essay you may use as a mild test whether you are ever likely to come to metaphysics or not. I look forward with some trepidation to discussing it at home: for his 'reading of the thing' will doubtless differ vastly from my writing of it[90] . . .

I had not meant, in my other letters, to bring any serious charge against the Oxfordshire country. Tried by European standards it takes a lowish rank: but I am not such a fool as to deprecate any decent country now, and rather wrote in deprecation for fear you'd fancy I was 'writing up' a place [in] which you would remember no particular beauties. Of landscapes, as of people, one becomes more tolerant after one's twentieth year (which reminds me to congratulate you on your birthday and ask what age it makes you. The rate at which we both advance towards a responsible age is indecent). We learn to look at them not *in the flat* as pictures to be seen, but *in depth* as things to be burrowed into. It is not merely a question of lines and colours but of smells, sounds and tastes as well: I often wonder if professional artists don't lose something of the real love of earth by seeing it in eye sensations exclusively?

---

[90] 'Optimism' was never published, and no copies seem to have survived.

From the house where we are now living there are few good walks, but several decent rides. Last Saturday we rode to Strandlake. In the heat of the day—we are having drought here too—it was an heroic undertaking. Don't come down on me with any traveller's tale about 'what real heat is': I know *with my intellect* that it is much hotter in Africa, but put any honest man on a treeless road, uphill, in an English summer, and he can't really *imagine* anything is hotter.

We had to begin by climbing the 'warm green muffled Cumnor hills': a long pull, all on foot. You have a fine, but conventional view of Oxford as you look back: but we really enjoyed nothing until beyond Cumnor we sunk into the long grass by the side of the road under one of the deplorably rare trees and tackled our luncheon basket. A local pub supplied beer for me and lemonade for the children, and we had a basket of cherries.[91] After this it became better and when after a long and pleasant decline through corkscrew lanes full of meadowsweet (that's the white, dusty stuff with a nice smell, you know) we reached Bablocke Hythe, it was quite delightful. Beyond this the country is very flat, but tree-y: full of villages rather too 'warm and muffled': they make you feel like a bumble bee that has got into damp cotton wool.

Our objective was a cottage in Strandlake about the letting of which during the summer Mrs Moore was going to see. Here (tho' our purpose failed) we were rewarded by meeting a wonderful old woman, the owner, Mrs Penfold,

---

[91] Although Maureen was fifteen, and a pupil at Headington School, Jack continued to refer to her when writing to Warren as 'the child'. 'The children' meant Maureen and one or more of her friends.

who talked of her husband as 'Penfold' without the Mr, just like a character in Jane Austen. This I am afraid you will hardly credit, but it is true all the same. Although flat and almost too blankety for a man to strike a match in, this country is much favoured of the Muse.

A few miles beyond us was Kelmscott, where Wm Morris lived and built that 'red house' whose brick nudity first defied the stucco traditions: from it, all the pretty villas of our day are directly descended. A little to our right at Stanton Harcourt (where Jenkins is always going to take me) is an old Manor with a tower room where Pope wrote his famous parody—which he called a translation—of the *Iliad*. And of course, as you know, every mile smells of Arnold. We were not far from 'the Fyfield elm': we had 'crossed the stripling Thames' and saw in the distance near Cumnor what I took for the 'plot of forest ground called Thessaly'.

Oh by the way I have found the ideally bad edition of [Matthew Arnold's] *Thyrsis* and the *Scholar Gipsy*. It was lying in Blackwells between grey boards with very black type: illustrated with photographs—one to almost every two stanzas. For 'what sedged brooks are Thames's tributaries' you had a bed of rushes taken close, as you would for a plate in a natural history handbook, with a water rat in the middle: but best of all—there's a line somewhere I can't remember, about a 'battered merchant-man coming into port': for this we had two cutter racing yachts!! How are such things possible: and yet people will buy this and like it and be very proud of it. I am writing in our little strip of garden at five past ten and it is getting too dark to see: I will in and drink some of the eveningmilch . . .

The steps by which you became a Miltonian are very interesting. Can one quite have done by labelling him a republican and a puritan? Puritanism was after all (in some of its exponents) a very different thing from modern 'dissent'. One cannot imagine Milton going about and asking people if they were saved: that intolerable pride is the direct opposite to sentimentalism. He really had the vices and virtues of the aristocracy—writing for 'fit audience tho' few'. He always seems to look down on the vulgar from an almost archducal height. 'How charming is divine philosophy. Not harsh and crabbed as dull fools suppose.' The *dull fools* are the ordinary mass of humanity, and though it has its ridiculous side, that deliberate decision of his, taken at my age 'to leave something so written that posterity wd not willingly let it die' takes a little doing. *Paradise Regained* I only read once: it is a bit too much for me. In it the Hebrew element finally gets the better of the classical and romantic ingredients. How can people be attracted to things Hebrew? However, old Kirk really summed up Milton when he said 'I would venture to assert that no human being ever called him Johnnie'.

By the way, on a ride the other day I passed an inn which the landlord had seen fit to call 'The Olde Air Balloon'. What a splendid name for the P'daytabird—who, by the way, is threatening to come here in a few days, thanks to the persistent endeavours of Uncle and Aunt Hamilton, backed, according to his account, by your advice. I wish you'd mind your own business, Master P. B. I have told him I've been moved out of College, so the business resolves itself into my presenting my abode here as ordinary digs—

and keeping him out of them as much as may be. Luckily Pasley will be up for his *viva* and 'a friend sharing with me and working very hard' ought to be a sufficient deterrent. I think too, that if I walk the Old Air Balloon out here in the present insupportable heat, once will be enough for him.

The temperature is over 90 in the shade: even the water at Parson's Pleasure has reached 71. Though still the only comfortable place (where I spend many a happy hour) this takes the real bite and shock out of a bathe. One great beauty at present is that they are mowing the meadows on the far side, and as you splash along with your nose just above the dark brown water, you swim into the smell of hay. But to expiate over the delights of an English river would be really unkind to you.

You will probably await my next with interest, in which you will hear of the success or failure of the paternal visit. What an anachronism he will be here . . .

[On 20 July 1921 Mr Lewis set off from Belfast with Augustus and Annie Hamilton on one of his very rare holidays. Travelling in the Hamiltons' car, they traversed Wales and arrived in Oxford on 24 July.]

TO HIS BROTHER: from 28 Warneford Road

7 August [1921]

You heard in my last letter of the consternation into which our little household was thrown by the threatened and hardly precedented migration of the P'daytabird. I have so much history to record that I must bustle on from that point. By rights I should tell you of all the preparations that were made: how Pasley came up at a whistle, like the faithful comrade in arms he is, to be the man who was digging with me and to 'lend artistic verisimilitude': how the little back room was dressed up in the semblance of an undergraduate's digs, where women never set foot. But the story would be too long. The gods spared me the need of this Palais Royal farce with its uneasy tendency to degenerate into something more like Grand Guignol.

It so worked out that the Irish party only stopt at Oxford for their midday eating and then took me with them for a week. My compulsory holiday took me through so much good country and supplied me with such a rare crop of P'daytisms that it gives me really too much epic matter to write about. I shall try to give you any information that may interest you as prospective pilot of the Dawdle through the same parts: but of course you must not take it for as accurate as Michelin.

The first and by far the funniest piece of scenery I saw was my first glimpse of the Old Air Balloon himself, outside the Clarendon in Cornmarket. You've no idea how odd he looked, almost a bit shrunk: pacing alone with that expression peculiar to him on a holiday—the eyebrows half way up his forehead. I was very warmly greeted by all; and with the exception of Aunt Annie, we took a short stroll before lunch. I was in a great flutter for fear of meeting some fool who might out with any irrelevance, but everything passed off well.

I learned that he found the heat intolerable, that he had not slept a wink since he left home, that he had a feather

bed last night at Worcester—which Uncle Hamilton
thought a great joke. He seemed dazed by his surroundings
and showed no disposition to go and see my rooms, tho'
he observed that College had 'treated me very shabbily as
they distinctly mentioned free rooms as one of the privileges of scholars'—a statute by the by completely unknown
at Oxford, however familiar at Leeborough. We lunched
heavily at the Clarendon: I succeeded in getting some cold
meats (suitable to a shade temperature of near 90) in spite of
the frequently advanced proposition that it would be 'better' (how or why?) for us 'all to have the table d'hôte'.

We addressed ourselves to the road as soon as the meal
was over. Uncle Hamilton's car is a 4-seater Wolsley: I have
forgotten the horse power. It is pale grey and wears a light
hood. Our direction was South and West, so we ran out
over Folly Bridge and towards Berkshire, thro' pleasant but
tame wooded country. The weather was oppressively hot,
even in an open car which our uncle keeps almost permanently over thirty-five miles an hour: when you dropped to
twenty at a turn or a village a stifling heat leaps up round
you at once. This first run was almost the only one where
Excellency [Mr Lewis] sat behind me, and it was about half
an hour south of Oxford that he made his first mot, and one
of the best of his life, by asking 'Are we IN CORNWALL
YET?' Honest Injun, he did!

I don't know if you have a map with you: we drove by
Nailsworth, Cirencester, Tetbury (I think) to Malmesbury
('MAWMSbury, Gussie' from the O.A.B.) where we hoped
to lie. The people here have a very barbarous, uncivil custom
of closing hotels, even to resident visitors, on a Sunday—

this being Sunday. In this quandary various proposals were raised: the P'daytabird was in favour of going on to Bath and going to the largest hotel there—being reduced to a painful uneasiness when we told him that he could get supper, not dinner, of a Sunday evening in these small towns. Here and elsewhere through the tour Uncle H. displayed great skill in his family tactics of amusing all parties with a frivolous appearance of a discussion while he was preparing his own plans.

It ended by our pushing on to a place called Chippenham, which we made about five o'clock, and, liking the house where we had tea, we took rooms for the night. Aunt A. and I were sent to look at them, and the O.A.B., despite of all his pother of the feather bed overnight refused (of course) to look at them. 'If they satisfy you, Annie, they'll satisfy me.' Chippenham is one of (I suppose) a thousand English towns that one has never heard of, but once having seen, remembers kindly. It is perhaps about the size of Wrexham, but as different as the south from the north. Here are quiet streets with nice old ivied houses, at a strange variety of levels, so that you can look into their gardens, with a little river running through them, and very fine trees. These streets widen occasionally into what are called squares, being, after the manner of English country towns, any other shape in Euclid rather than a square.

Our hotel was very comfortable and nearly empty. After dinner of course we 'strolled'. I had some Leeburian talk with the O.A.B. and afterwards some, of another sort, with our uncle—about God: a monstrous unlikely subject under such conditions. He finds the proof of intelligible work, of a mind something like his own in the universe, because the universe does after all work: it is not all higgledy piggledy. The conversation was perhaps not worth saving, but he has great merits as a talker: he has many gaps in his thinking, but it is all absolutely his own—he never takes anything over. If he covers familiar ground he still uses maps of his own making.

I found him a wonderful antidote to the P'daytabird: the latter was made happily miserable by a Salvation Army band which played the Dead March from Saul up and down the streets—why I don't know. When we got back to our hostel we sat for a time in the dark hall on a very comfortable sort of benching, and the O.A.B. offered us drinks.

Uncle H. wd have some beer and so would I. *O.A.B.* (in his 'desperate' voice): 'I'll have a bottle of soda water. Here! Waitress: two half pints of bitter beer and a bottle of soda water—(pause)—and if you'd just put a little Scotch whiskey in it.' (The waitress goes and returns.) 'Here you are Gussie. Is that my soda water?' *Waitress:* 'Yes sir—with the whiskey in it.' *O.A.B.:* 'Hm'h.' (Roars of laughter from Uncle H.) This was truly in our best manner, wasn't it?

The next morning I was early astir, after an excellent night and a bath, to buy some aspirin surreptitiously at the nearest chemist's, having had a headache the night before: but I never used it again. What is pleasanter than a hotel breakfast in a strange town—porridge, crisp fried fish, and an ample plinth? I have never outgrown the child's belief that food grows better with every mile further from our usual table (except tea, which I can never get good outside my Oxford residentiary).

On this second day I had a typed itinerary to keep me right: the Oxford journey, being unrehearsed, was not on it. In our seats at about ten. We drove through a hilly country, the weather being a little cooler, by Bath, Farrington Gurney and Chewton Mendip to Wells. The landscape has everything, tho' on a small scale: rocks, hills, woods and water. Chiefly you run along the sides of winding valleys. The villages and their churches are very pleasant.

At Wells I distinguished myself in a way to make you laugh: (should I remind you that it is the Cathedral city of the diocese of Bath and Wells?) We were not quite certain of our whereabouts, and seeing a military looking old gentleman standing on the pavement, I lean out and shout 'What's this place, sir?' M.O.G. (in a tone of thunder) 'The City of Wells!' A minute later an irreverent little boy jerked a finger at the M.O.G. and informed us 'E's the Mayor'.

The whole street seemed to be in laughter. As Uncle H. said, it must have been the word 'place' which stuck in his gorge: we should have asked 'What great city are we now approaching?' I profited however by this lesson, and after Uncle H. had given me an itinerary and a look at the maps he had I steered our course very satisfactorily. The P'daytabird only advanced so far as to get hold of the Michelin every day and look up hotels: usually he looked up some place *he* thought suitable to lie at: very often it was wrong—once or twice it was a place we had stopped at the night before.

We lunched at Wells after seeing the Cathedral. I do not know whether such things come into your horizon: I at any rate am no architect and not much more of an antiquarian. Strangely enough it was Uncle H. with his engineering more than the O.A.B. with his churchmanship that helped me to appreciate them: he taught me to look at the single end-less line of the aisle, with every pillar showing at once the strain and the meeting of the strain (like a ships frame work inverted): it certainly is wonderfully *satisfying* to look at. The pleasure one gets is like that from rhyme—a need, and the answer of it following so quickly, that they make a single sensation. So now I understand the old law in architecture 'No weight without a support, and no support without an adequate weight'. For the rest, Wells is particularly rich in a wilderness of cloisters all round the Cathedral where one can cut the cold and quiet with a knife. There is a fine castle with the only *real* drawbridge I ever saw, just across the Close.

We lunched pretty well in this city (I daren't call it a town) and were on the road by two. Henceforward the P'daytabird nearly always took the front seat since this seemed to please him. We ran through Westbury, Cheddar ('Are we in Cheshire, Gussie?' asked the Balloon), Axbridge, Highbridge, Bridgewater etc., into Somerset. All this was country I knew (towards the end), having stayed twice in the village of Old Cleeve: for this reason I had been able to name Dunster to Uncle H. as a likely stopping place. I had at first been rather troubled lest my apparent knowledge of the place should lead to long and tedious questioning from the P'daytabird: but I found him advancing from his own resources that I had got to know it while stationed at Plymouth ('They're both in Devonshire aren't they?')—and did not pursue the subject.

Here it begins to be very beautiful. Through the village of Nether Stowey we climbed up through the Quantocks: they are a tremendous barrier of moor, with the most wonderful valleys, called 'combes', running up them. From the high ground we looked down into the last valley in Somerset—a little piece of ground that I love as well as any I have ever walked in. On your right is the Bristol Channel with the faint line of the Welsh coast beyond it. Ahead are the enormous hills of [the] Devonshire border, the beginnings of Exmoor, with Minehead just this side of them where they go down to the water. On the left are the lower moors, known as the Black Hills, and all between the pleasantest green country with no end of red iron streams, orchards, thatched villages and buried lanes that wind up the hills in leafy cuttings.

I pointed the Welsh coast out to the O.A.B. He replied, 'Ah, the thing's got twisted. It ought to be round to our left.' How I should like to draw a P'daytamap of England! It was a curious sensation for me to scoot down the Quantocks into Williton and on through Washford, passing at forty miles an hour through country that I had often walked.

We made Dunster at about 4 o'clock, and had our first engine trouble just as we drew up at the Luttrell Arms: my ignorance reduces me to saying that it 'was the gear jammed somehow'. Later on you may be able to gather what was really the matter. Uncle H. treated the business with admirable *sang froid:* his faculty of never being ruffled is a great virtue in a companion, and if life was confined to this kind of intercourse I really think it would cover all his other sins. The O.A.B. insisted on standing by with an expression like a pirate flag, making irritating suggestions: I made one or two attempts to remove him, in sympathy with our uncle, but of course they were unsuccessful. Later on he discussed the situation with me in private. I remarked that Uncle Gussie took it very well. O.A.B.: 'Ah Jacks, you don't know the fellow as I do. Making a mess of things like this just hits him on his sore point: he's as vain as a peacock. He's just fuming under the surface. That's why I waited: just to smooth things over.' Why by the way is any misfortune that happens to anyone but himself always described in P'daytesque as the sufferer's 'having made a mess of something'? It was finally arranged to have the car towed into Minehead, about two miles further on, where there is a well appointed garage: Uncle Hamilton was afraid that he would have to get a new part from Birmingham: the P'daytabird was strongly in favour of taking a 'day of rest tomorrow'.

For the present, however, we could do nothing but wait: and it was fortunately in the most delightful place. One of the many mountain valleys that I mentioned before ends in a small wooded hill attached to the main mountain by a sort of isthmus. The little hill is crowned by Dunster Castle: the village of Dunster winds up the isthmus, consisting chiefly of a very broad lazy street with old houses. The Luttrell Arms itself is a sixteenth-century building with embrasures for musketry fire on either side of the porch. Just opposite its door is a curious octagonal erection with a tiled roof, used I suppose for market purposes in wet weather. It was 'pierced by a ball' from the Castle during the Civil Wars. I remarked that this gave one a visible specimen of the trajectory of the old cannon: to which Uncle Hamilton very shrewdly replied that unless one knew whether it was *aimed* at the thing or not, it told one nothing.

I am afraid that from my description this may sound a

typical guide book village: as a matter of fact there is nothing really curious enough in it to attract the tourist, and it is more completely tucked away than anywhere. Wherever you look, through every V left by two meeting gables, you see the hills, so close that they seem to go straight up and the rare paths in the heather look perpendicular: it gives one a great sense of snugness. Only from the little garden at the back of the hotel do you get an unexpected view across to the cliffs by Watchet and the Bristol Channel. Nobody talks loud, nobody walks fast, rooms are deep and shady, chairs have their backs well broken so that you can't sit down without an 'Ah!', hotels are never crowded at Dunster. It has a personality as definite as, though antithetical to, Doagh. It has changed hands only once; from the De Mohuns to the Luttrells in almost mediaeval times. It's off the main road: nobody goes there: when I saw the car towed off to Minehead I had a notion that nobody ever leaves it either. Oh what a place for a soak—but not for a 'day of rest' with the P'daytabird.

After an excellent dinner we strolled: Aunt Annie and I both climbed the nearest ridge—a very stiff scramble—and left the uncles behind, being rewarded with a fine view over Exmoor and the Channel: then, after the evening beer in the little garden, to bed.

Next morning was very warm again: the male section of the party—one of them most unwillingly, to wit myself— walked to Minehead to see if the car was done: the mechanic thought it would be quite alright. We drove it back and decided to take the road after lunch. The P'daytabird was now quite in love with Dunster (which he called 'Dernster', 'Deemster' and other weird names) and was still talking of a

day of rest. I noticed that he was usually in love with somewhere we had left: after anything good he could hardly be
brought to admit merits anywhere else, and when he was,
the whole process began over again. Thus for the first days,
if you ventured to praise anything, you were told it was
not to be compared with the Welsh mountains: after that it
was Dunster that blotted every other halt: then Land's End:
when I left him he had settled down to the view that 'none
of these places come up to' Salisbury.

But to proceed, we ran very comfortably through Minehead and immediately began to climb, tho' still on tolerable surfaces. We passed one barrier and saw the first real
Exmoor ahead—tremendous mountains and awful gradi-
ents: but we weren't there yet and dropped into Porlock, a
very pleasant town at the bottom of the moors. All though
Devon and Cornwall a valley and a town are synonymous:
'they all live in holes' as Uncle Gussie said. At Porlock we
had [a] choice of two roads: one the 'old' road and the other
a private venture which the local lord of the soil supports
by a shilling toll.

We paid our toll and Uncle G. was just changing gear in
preparation for the next appalling hill when it stuck again.
Telephoned back to Minehead for the same mechanic. More
buttoning up of coats and stiffening of upper lips as per
previous night. Aunt Annie and I went and looked at the
Church—we found it cooler both psychologically and
physically—for the sun was terrific (none of your traveller's advice here!). Apparently there is a bar that fits into
a hollow cylinder where the gear works: and the Wolseley
people 'have a catch of' making everything a perfect fit:

which means that everything is just a little too tight when the metal gets hot. The bar was reduced by sand paper when the relief car came, and we had no more trouble with it. We were held up there for some three-quarters of an hour, greatly to the annoyance of the other traffic: and the heat as we stood still made us very glad to be in motion again.

Our objective was now Lynmouth, a very short run which would be occupied entirely in climbing up and down over the next shoulder of Exmoor into the next hole. Let me here solemnly warn you against ever attempting this ride on the Dawdle. The toll road is generally detestable in surface and hardly anywhere — after the first hundred yards — broad enough for two cars to pass: it ascends at a gradient which is habitually worse than Broadway hill and which seems all but impossible, especially at the inner corners of the twenty odd hairpin bends by which it reaches the top. The humourist who owns it has also left it without any kind of barrier at the outside, and everywhere the banking is all wrong.

I must confess that mountain scenery is often seen most impressively when I for one wd be least ready to enjoy it. To look back as you attack an almost perpendicular corner, down an enormous cliff: to see other hills piled up on the far side of the gorge and, in their unusual perspective from such a position, giving the whole scene a gauchmaresque appearance: to look forward at the same moment and see the road getting even worse ahead to the next bend: to remember that the cheery man from the garage told us that a car backed over into the sea further along this road a few days ago: to wonder what exactly you'd do if one of those char-a-banc came down — on my life I had the wind up.

We did reach the top somehow, where nature played another practical joke by plunging us into a cold winter's day with a misting rain. It was fine here all the same: an enormous stretch of moor all round you, and a car going all out over a single road, which was not straight if it was rough. It reminded me of the opening chapter of Meriman's *Sowers*. The descent from this into the next hole was even worse than the ascent. You just wind down the cliff edge on a road about seven ft wide, which touches, at times, the pleasant gradient of $1/41/2$. That's not my own conjecture, it's from some guide book of Uncle H. The view over the sea below you wd be very fine — on foot.

We were exceedingly glad to drop into Lynmouth, a little town wedged into this next wooded gorge round the edge of a broad, brown, stony river: the heights all round are perhaps too beetling, and to live there permanently would be like living at the bottom of a well. Our hotel had a veranda above the river, where we sat very pleasantly after the four o'clock and watched a water rat manoeuvering from stone to stone.

I had to share a room with Excellency here, and I am not likely to forget the fact that it was the scene of a typical episode. We all walked out after dinner and up the road which we were to follow next day. Uncle Hamilton and I outstripped the others. It was a fine evening, delightfully cool and dewy. The road was good: it wound up the sides of big gorges that kept opening out of one and other into mysterious and chaotic landscape — 'forest on forest piled'. Looking back you saw the sea in the V shaped opening between the hills. Whenever you were still the sound of that stream under the trees many feet below and the EEE-eee of

bats worked a kind of counterpoint on the general theme
of silence. We walked faster: we talked most entertainingly.
Finally we reached the top where these valleys, getting shallower and shallower, at last come out on the surface of the
moor. We sat under a haystack enjoying the smell and the air
of a good starless, moonless English country night.

We arrived back at the Hotel about eleven, and, incredible to relate, our Uncle gave me a drink. But when I reached
my room, 'twas to be greeted by the O.A.B. in shirt and
'drawers' with the apostrophe 'Jacks, why did you do it?'
How much real nervousness, how much pique and desire
for drama went, and in what proportions, to making up a
scene at once ridiculous and unpleasant, I cannot say. But
the sound of the stream under our window drowned the
puffings and blowings of the O.A.B. In fairness I should
record how earlier that day, P'daytism had blossomed into
something like grandeur: which it reaches at times, because
of rather than in spite of its absurdity. After arriving there
had been some discussion as to which hotel we should lie
in. Aunt Annie suggested that the one we finally chose was
rather too big. O.A.B.: 'IT'S NO BIGGER THAN WE
ARE.' If only he had the right, no one could quarrel with
his power to assume the grand manner.

I find that I have very few distinct images left of the next
day's run, but I know that it was wild and beautiful. From
this [point] onwards all the roads are bad. We ate *Mittagessen*
[lunch] at Clovelly. It carried the West Country tradition of
living in holes to its logical conclusion, consisting simply of
a stairway some 250 yards long with whitewashed houses on
each side, ending in a cove and a jetty. The local tramway con-

sists of a dozen well cared for donkeys on which lazy people travel up and down: goods are carried or trailed in a kind of wooden sledge. The bump bump from step to step is one of the most characteristic sounds of the place. Commercial enterprise has made the place convenient as a halt, for there are several eating places varying from the trimly modest and artificially rural where you can get galantines, salad and wines, to the frankly 'vulgar, easy, and therefore disgusting' where you can get—I suppose—mutton pies and brandy balls.

The O.A.B. strongly disapproved of going down to the cove before lunch, or indeed afterward over that infinite staircase: and it certainly was a very slippery and tedious journey of which you could say in Miltonic phrase

> '*Each stair* mysteriously was meant, *nor stood*
> *There always'—where one's foot expected it.*

Arrived at the beach, he sternly refused the unanimous advice of his companions to facilitate his ascent by mounting one of the donkeys. Doubtless because he thought it unbecoming to his dignity: we continued to press him, for precisely the same reason: but he would not. After a hearty lunch, we proceeded.

This day we passed into Cornwall. I have always imagined Cornwall a place of rocky heights and gulfs. At first I was very disappointed: for, to be candid, it is so like county Down or parts of Antrim that it felt uncanny. The same absence of bright colours, the same cottages, the same sloping, somewhat bare hills, grey rather than green. The only thing that disturbs the illusion is the continual engine houses of the tin and copper mines . . . some in use and more half decayed. I can hardly remember a landscape which had not a dozen of these silhouetted on the horizon: they rather increase the general celtic dreariness and 'oddness' (you know what I mean) which bring it so close at times to our own country — a thing by the by far more insidious than the sensuous idleness of richer scenery. Are any 'flower coloured fingers' of the tropics half so numbing as the tepid morsels of putty that such places 'put down into your brain'?

The hills never rise into mountains, but are heaped together like eggs as far as the eye can reach, and the road winds on and on between them. The gates are coming off their hinges: the loose stones that divide the fields are all getting scattered. 'They'll do rightly — ach, never bother your head.' Then every little while you drop on one of the mining settlements: a valley probably, not unlike the back areas in France, splashed with great dirty pools and ringed round with enormous conical piles of shingle: and narrow gauge railways threading in and out like fussing insects among the debris. Why does a metal mine have such a glamour and a coal mine not?

The show parts of Cornwall — the parts one has read about — are all on the coast. We lay this night at Tintagel, storied name. There is a generally diffused belief that this place is connected with King Arthur: so far as I know from Malory, Layamon and Geoffrey of Monmouth, it is not: it is really the seat of King Mark and the Tristram story. This has not however deterred some wretch, hated by the muse, from erecting an enormous hotel on the very edge of the cliff, built in toy Gothic, and calling it the King Arthur's Hotel. The interior walls are made of cement with lines stamped on them to represent stone. They are profusely illustrated with toy armour from Birmingham: a Highland target, suitable for Macbeth, jostles a reproduction of late Tudor steel plate and is lucky to escape a Cromwellian helmet for its next door neighbour. In the centre of the lounge, with the Sketch and Tatler lying on it, is—of course—THE Round Table. Ye Gods!! Even the names of the Knights are written on it. Then there are antique chairs—on which very naturally we find the monogram K. A. stamped.

I have not yet exhausted the horrors of the place: I was glad to see a book case in the lounge. All the books were uniformly bound, and I was surprised to see such unlikely titbits as the *Ethics of Aristotle* and the works of the Persian epic poet Firdausi. I solved the mystery by finding out that they were a uniform series of Lubbock's *Hundred Best Books*!!! How I abominate such culture for the many, such tastes ready made, such standardization of the brain. To substitute for the infinite wandering of the true reader thro' the byways of the country he discovers, a char-a-banc tour. This whole place infuriated me.

But the coast was wonderful: very like the Antrim coast only better: foreland after foreland stretching away on each side, and just in front of us, joined by a narrow ridge of rock and grass the huge Tintagel rock. There is a little sandy bay between it and the mainland. There are some remains of fortification on it, but not very old: nature has however so marked it for a stronghold that I could imagine its having been a fort almost immemorially.

In the evening I extracted honey even from the hundred best books by reading an excellent play of Molière's. I cannot remember the title but it is the one from which the famous phrase *'Tu l'as voulu, Georges Dandin'* comes. Do you know him at all? We left Tintagel after breakfast. By the way it is of course pronounced Tingtagj-le: which was a sufficient reason for the P'daytabird's insisting on calling it TIntagEL, with a hard G. I find (like Bozzy) that 'I have preserved no record of the O.A.B.'s conversation during this period'.

We passed through a perfectly abominable town, Redruth. It was about here that a stinging rain, that might equally be described as a fast moving fog, attacked us. At Penzance we put up our side screens and excluded the view but nothing would deter Uncle Hamilton from going on to Land's End: I indeed thoroughly agreed, but I was his only supporter. Of the last bit of England I saw nothing. Hot clothes began to steam under the screen and hood: outside there was only a genuinely celtic greyness: the road winds abominably and has no surface. My chief recollection is of Aunt Annie shouting 'Gus, don't run into that post!' We began to pass several hotels, nearly every one of which announced that it was the 'last hotel in England'. Some of them looked as if this was perfectly true. Our Uncle scorned them all and drove ahead till we reached the real end of the world where the road stops on a cliff outside the really last hotel.

It was pouring with rain and blowing a terrific gale. It is a place well worth seeing. The cliffs go down sheer, and one is so to speak in a salient. The same driving mist continued all the time we were there, clearing up for ten minute intervals with extraordinary suddenness every now and then. When this happens the blue suddenly leaps out of the grey and you see the clouds packing all along the cliff for miles, while a light house or some rocks about three and a half miles out turns up from nowhere. Indeed the appearance and disappearance of this place is what I most remembered. It has almost the regular phases of a revolving light: first the blank mist—then the outlines rather ghostly in it—then golden—then quite clear with hard outlines and waves breaking on it—then blurred again and so back into the fog. Watching it from behind the thick plate windows of the very snug hotel, I found there was something curiously soporific about it—this most 'debatable land' that comes and goes, as if it winked at you with confiding solemnity. Whenever the rain thinned we went out and climbed as near the cliffs as was safe and watched the enormous breakers.

We had—A big lacuna occurs here: some pages of journeying have been lost and you will perhaps be relieved to hear that I do not propose to rewrite them. Dartmoor and New Forest must remain unsung. Three more vignettes I give and then I will leave the tour.

The first is simply to record our monster run in one day from Lyndhurst in the New Forest, thro' Camberley, Maidenhead and Oxford to Warwick, including our only headlight voyage.

The second is a good P'daytism—or shall I report as Minister of Experimental Philology a new word for an old thing—shall a P'daytism be a Balloon play or *Ballonenspeil*?—which occurred at Warwick. Uncle Hamilton could get no cover for the car which had to spend the night—a threatening night, in an open yard. When I lamented this fact, the O.A.B. replied 'Ah well, the holiday's nearly over now'. This remark contains so many distinct trains of thought and pure P'dayta ethics that you may spend a wet afternoon in disentagling them.

My third—as the Acrostics say—is connected with a certain Cathedral city in the North Midlands where I found the masterpiece of comic or satiric statuary. It represents a little eighteenth-century gentleman with a toy sword. I cannot explain how cunningly a kind of simpering modesty is combined with a certain profound vanity in this figure. Perhaps the eyes looking down the nose and the smug smile have something to do with it—perhaps it is the stomach thrust forward or the conventionally statuesque pose of the feet, as if to support a figure of heroic proportions, and then at once belied by the stiff little doll to which they really belong. Or, on second thoughts, perhaps it owes something to the colossal figure on the other pedestal, older and less ingenious work, obviously meant to be the centre and obviously made into the fool of the piece by its compulsory second. At any rate the effect is too funny for laughter: real genius went to make it. Need I add that the town was Lichfield and that the statue bore the mystic name—BOSWELL.

From Lichfield I returned to Oxford by train: I am going home in a few days, but you had better send your next as usual to Univ. I was delighted with your letter and have much to say in answer which must at present wait. I liked particularly your description of the rains—I can see that. Just one word about *Paradise Regained*—surely the real reason for the shrinkage of Satan is the very proper one that since the great days of *P. Lost*, he has spent sixty centuries in the Miltonic Hell? It comes out in his great speech beginning ''Tis true—I am that spirit unfortunate.' . . .

TO HIS FATHER: **from University College**

31 August 1921

As you say, the change from society for which 'lively' would at times have been too mild an epithet, and from the constant variety of our moving seats to the routine of ordinary work, is one that we are rather acutely conscious of at first.

I still feel that the value of such a holiday is still to come—in the images and ideas which we have put down to mature in the cellarage of our brains, thence to come up with a continually improving bouquet. Already the hills are getting higher, the grass greener, and the sea bluer than they really were: and, thanks to the deceptive working of happy memory, our poorest stopping places will become haunts of impossible pleasure and Epicurean repast.

As to myself, I do not propose, as you may be sure, to spend the whole vac. here. I will do what I can: but I must 'sit to my book' for a little while yet. The fault of our course here is that we get so little guidance and can never be sure that our efforts are directed exactly to the right points and in the right proportions. I suppose that is part of the education—part at any rate of the game.

I expect you have heard from Warnie before this. I had a letter since my return, the first for a considerable time. I am sorry to hear that he has had a bad attack of boils, followed by prickly heat: but he seems better now and is in excellent spirits and reading Dante. The revolutions which Africa has produced in his literary policy are really amazing.

I am still working whenever I have half an hour to spare, at my account for him of our journey. It would be amusing and *will* no doubt be amusing for him to compare the two versions. We shall differ in selection and (so confused does one get) even on matters of fact, where a map will often show both authorities equally wrong. Uncle Hamilton on the other hand would be able to give exact information about every stage and distance—but totally incapable of describing anything at all . . . [92]

TO HIS FATHER: from the Oxford Union Society

Postmark: 30 November 1921

I am afraid that my weakness in yielding to the Colonel's request for a copy of 'Optimism' had reduced the poor man to permanent silence. I must try to get some sort of letter off to him before Christmas.[93] . . .

---

[92] Warren was able to compare Jack's version of this famous motor tour with that supplied by his father. Mr Lewis's account is found in two long letters to Warren, one written in August, and the other during the weeks Jack spent at 'Little Lea' over the last part of September and the early weeks of October. In the second of these undated letters Mr Lewis said of their visit to Lichfield: 'Such a city! The ugliest and dowdiest place by far we came across . . . And the statues of Johnson and Boswell are in a mean street. But Bozzy's statue is a magnificent piece of work. In every feature, in the cock of the hat and the pose of the body, in every line and curve it is the man as he must have been in life.' (*Lewis Papers,* vol. VII, p. 87.)

[93] Writing to Jack on 22 November, Warren said: 'I have by the way read your essay twice, but as on neither occasion could I make the slightest glimmer of meaning out of it, I have put it away in despair for perusal in the cold tang of a saner climate . . .' Warren was to remember years later lending 'Optimism' to a fellow officer in Sierra Leone who, after reading it, said 'Tell me, Lewis, strictly between ourselves, does your brother *drink*?'

A dread portent has arisen above our horizon here—an immortalist, nihilist, determinist, fatalist. What are you to do with a man who denies absolutely everything? The joke is that he's an army officer on a course. He talks you blind and deaf. The more I see of him the clearer does my mental picture become of his brother officers *en masse* imploring him to take advantage of a two years course at Oxford—or Cathay or the Moon . . .

FROM HIS DIARY: **while still living at 28 Warneford Road**

1 April 1922

I walked to Iffley in the morning and called in at the Askins [Dr and Mrs John Hawkins Askins]. The doc. has foolishly knocked himself up by walking too far and cd not come to Headington in the afternoon. He talked about Atlantis, on which there is apparently a plentiful philosophical literature: nobody seems to realize that a Platonic myth is fiction, not legend, and therefore no base for speculation . . .

2 April 1922

A beautiful spring day. D.[94] busy cutting oranges for marmalade. I sat in my own bedroom by an open window in bright sunshine and started a poem on Dymer in rhyme royal . . .

5 April 1922

I . . . got the two poems (typed v. accurately for 1/-) and saw Stead in order to get the address of the *London Mercury*. He told me with a solemn face and admirable naïvety how he

---

[94] Mrs Moore is nearly always referred to as 'D' in Jack's Diary.

had got his accepted. Two or three were sent back by return post, whereupon he went up to London and called on the Editor, saying, 'Look here Mr Squire, you haven't taken these poems of mine and I want to know what's wrong with them!!' If the story ended there, it would be merely a side light on Stead, but the joke is that Squire said, 'I'm glad you've come to talk it over: that's just what I want people to do' and actually accepted what he'd formerly refused. Truly the ways of editors are past finding out! ...

7 April 1922

I wish life and death were not the only alternatives, for I don't like either: one could imagine a *via media* ...

15 April 1922

Tried to work at Dymer and covered some paper: but I am very dispirited about my work at present—especially as I find it impossible to invent a new opening for the Wild Hunt. The old one is full of clichés and will never do. I have learned much too much on the idea of being able to write poetry and if this is a frost I shall be rather stranded ... A dissatisfying day, but, praise God, no more headaches ...

18 April 1922

In the afternoon I walked into Oxford and looked up Civil Service examination papers in the Union. 'Greats' is child's play compared with them ... Before supper I called and saw Arthur Stevenson and his mother, hoping to hear something of the Civil Service. He tells me there is no vacancy this year in the Home Civil, and that probably there will be none next ... Thus ends the dream of a Civil Service career as suddenly as it began: I feel at once that I have been in alien territory—not mine, and deep down, impossible ...

21 April 1922

Got up shortly before seven, cleaned the grate, lit the fire, made tea, 'did' the drawing room, made toast, bathed, shaved, breakfasted, washed up, put the new piece of ham on to boil, and was out by half past ten . . . Washed up after lunch. Worked at Gk History notes until tea when Miss Baker came. Had got settled to work when D called me down 'for five minutes' to talk about Maureen's programme for next term. This would not have mattered, but before I could make my escape, Miss Baker began to be 'just going' and continued so. When she finally got away it was time to get supper and to clear the tea things which Maureen had kindly left *in statu quo*. A good hour thus wasted altogether . . .

3 May 1922

Went into town after lunch, and after looking in vain for Jenkin in Merton St., met him in the High. It had now cleared and we walked down St Aldate's and over the waterworks to Hincksey. I talked of staying up for another year and lamented that all my friends would be down: he said he had not got to know any new people who had any interest in literature and who were not, at the same time, dam'd affected dilettanti talking *l'art pour l'art* etc., etc., was almost impossible—in fact he put Baker, Barfield[95] and me as the only exceptions in his own circle: and even the 'hearty' men were preferable to the usual literary sort . . .

---

[95] Arthur Owen Barfield (1898–1997) came up to Oxford in 1919 after being elected to a Classical Scholarship at Wadham College. He met Jack in 1919 through their mutual friend Leo Baker and they became life-long friends There is an engaging description of him in ch. XIII of *Surprised by Joy*.

TO HIS FATHER: from University College

18 May 1922

And now I want to talk about my plans. You will remember a talk we had when I was last at home. On that occasion I repeated to you a conversation which had taken place some time before between one of my tutors and myself. I had asked him for a testimonial, preparatory to giving my name to the employment agency. Instead of giving me one he advised me very earnestly not to take any job in a hurry: he said that if there was nothing for me in Oxford immediately after Greats, he was sure that there would be something later: that College would almost certainly continue my scholarship for another year if I chose to stay up and take another school, and that 'if I could possibly afford it' this was the course which he would like me to take. He ended with some complimentary remarks.

I was not particularly keen at the time about doing so: partly on your account, partly because I did not care to survive most of my contemporaries. At this time there seemed to be one or two things in view—a vacant fellowship at Lincoln, another at Magdalen. Soon however it 'transpired' (I know you love the word) that one of these was to lapse and the other be filled from its own college without open election. I thought of the Civil Service: but as my tutor says, 'There is no Civil Service now'. Thanks to the Geddes axe there are no vacancies in the Home Civil this year, and there probably will be none next.

The advice of my first tutor was repeated by my other one: and with new points. The actual subjects of my own Greats school are a doubtful quantity at the moment: for no one quite knows what place classics and philosophy will hold in the educational world in a years time. On the other hand the prestige of the Greats School is still enormous: so that what is wanted everywhere is a man who combines the general qualification which Greats is supposed to give, with the special qualifications of any other subjects. And English Literature is a 'rising' subject. Thus if I cd take a First or even a Second in Greats, *and* a First next year in English Literature, I should be in a very strong position indeed: and during the extra year I might reasonably hope to strengthen it further by adding some other University prize to my 'Optimism'.

'While I yet pondered' came the news of a substantial alteration in the English Schools. That course had formerly included a great deal of philology and linguistic history and theory: these are now being thrown over and formed into a separate school, while what remains is simply literature in the ordinary sense—with the exception of learning to read a very few selected passages of Anglo-Saxon, which anyone can do in a month. In such a course, I should start knowing more of the subject than some do at the end: it ought to be a very easy proposition compared with Greats. All these considerations have tended to confirm what my tutor advised in the first place.

You may probably feel that a subject of this sort ought to be left for discussion by word of mouth: but, while I do not want to hurry you, my decision must be taken in the near future, as, if I stay up, I must apply to College for permission to do so and for the continuation of my scholarship; if not, I must beat up the agency at once. And after all, I do not know what discussion can do beyond repeating the same points over again. The facts—I hope my account is intelligible—naturally suggest all the pros and cons. I ought, in fairness, to say that I am pretty certain I can get a job of some sort as I am: but if it comes to schoolmastering, my inability to play games will count against me. Above all, I hope it is clear that in no case will Greats be wasted.

The point on which I naturally like to lean is that the pundits at Univ. apparently don't want me to leave Oxford. That is rather a loathsome remark for any man to make about himself—but no one overhears us, and it really is relevant. Now if, on all this, you feel that the scheme is rather a tall order and that my education has already taken long enough, you must frankly tell me so, and I shall quite appreciate your position. If you think that the chance thus offered can and ought to be taken, I shall be grateful if you will let me know as soon as may be . . .

FROM HIS DIARY: at 28 Warneford Road

19 May 1922

After tea I bussed back to College and called on the Mugger. He had just had a letter from 'Mr Wyllie' asking him to recommend some one for a studentship tenable for one year in Cornell University [New York State]. He said I was the only person he would care to offer: but as the money, tho' adequate for the year out there, did not include the travelling expenses, it was hardly to be considered. We then talked of my plans. He said the days were past when one could walk out of the schools into a Fellowship: even in minor universities there was a demand for men who had done something . . . He advised me however to take the extra year. He said that College was very hard up, but that he thought that they could manage to continue my scholarship. I asked him whether if I 'came a cropper in Greats' he would still advise the extra year, and he said he would . . . A dear old man, but the inexhaustible loquacity of educated age drove me to the City and University to recoup on a Guinness . . .

[On 22 May Jack received a wire from Mr Lewis saying: 'Letter of 18 just received. Stay on. Father.']

FROM HIS DIARY: at 28 Warneford Road

24 May 1922

Bussed into Oxford, meeting Barfield outside the Old Oak. After finding a table we decided to go to the Good Luck instead. An excellent lunch . . . From there we walked to Wadham gardens and sat under the trees. We began with Christina dreams: I condemned them—the love dream made a man incapable of real love, the hero dream made him a coward. He took the opposite view and a stubborn argument followed. We then turned to Dymer which he had brought back: to my surprise, his verdict was even more favourable than Baker's. He said it was 'by streets' the best thing I had done, and 'Could I keep it up?' He did not feel the weakness of the lighter stanzas. He said Harwood had 'danced with joy' over it and had advised me to drop everything else and go on with it.[96] From such a severe critic as

---

[96] Alfred Cecil Harwood (1898–1975) had known Owen Barfield since 1909. He came up to Oxford in 1919 on a Classical scholarship to Christ Church and, like his friend Barfield, had met Jack through Leo Baker. At

Barfield the result was very encouraging. We then drifted
into a long talk about ultimates. Like me, he has no belief
in immortality etc., and always feels the materialistic pessimism at his elbow . . .

27 May 1922

I called on [G. H.] Stevenson and asked him to let me know
of any tutorial work for the vac., which he might hear of. I
then called on [A. B.] Poynton and made the same request of
him. He also promised to give my name to the *Manchester
Guardian* for some reviewing. In the course of the morning
I met Blunt who said he was sure he could get me a school
boy to coach from Lynhams's[97] . . . I also visited Williams,
who is the local agent for Trueman & Knightley: he gave
me a form and said that by narrowing the field to Oxford
I reduced my chances, but that if there was anything my
qualifications would get it. He advised me also to put an
advertisement in the *Oxford Times* . . .

[Jack took his examination for Greats 8–14 June.]

TO HIS FATHER: from University College

[21 June 1922]

I have waited for some days to try and get a birds eye view
from a distance before telling you anything—only to find

---

this time he and Owen Barfield were living in 'Bee Cottage' in the village
of Beckley. There is a portrait of him in ch. XIII of *Surprised by Joy*.
[97] Herbert William Blunt (1864–1940) was Tutor in Philosophy and
Librarian at Christ Church from 1888 to 1928.

how difficult it is to form or keep any opinion of what I've done. With the history papers where I can look up facts and see how near or far I was, it is easier: and on these I think I have done pretty fairly—in one case, very much better than I expected. But my long suit is the philosophy and here it is like trying to criticise an essay you wrote a week ago and have never seen again, nor ever read over. Sometimes I feel I have done badly, sometimes that I have done brilliantly. Last night however, I got a little light from my tutor who repeated the following conversation he had had with one of the examiners. 'One of your young men seems to think that Plato is always wrong'—'Oh! Is it Simpson?' 'No.' 'Blunt? Hastings?' 'No, a man called Lewis: seems an able fellow anyway.'

On the whole I may sum up: I don't at all know whether I have got a first or not, but at least I know that there was nothing in the nature of a débacle. Of course the *viva* is still ahead, and there the family ability to bluff on paper will be no use . . . Luckily we had a spell of cool weather for the exam, which for six hours writing a day for six days is a great blessing . . .

FROM HIS DIARY: **at 28 Warneford Road** (after being interviewed for a Classical Lectureship at University College in Reading)

24 June 1922

Breakfasted before 8 and cycled to the station to catch the 9.10 to Reading: I read the Antigone during the journey. Arriving at Reading I found my way to University College

and left my bike at the Lodge. I saw a great many undergraduates of both sexes walking about: a nice looking lot.
I then strolled until 11 o'clock when I was taken to the
Principal's rooms. Childs, de Burgh and Dodds were present.[98] All were very nice to me, but Childs very firmly ruled
out my idea of living anywhere else than at Reading . . .
[Dodds] then showed me round the college which is pleasant and unpretentious, and left me in the Senior Common
room, to wait for lunch . . .

I left the College at 2 and cycled to Bradfield [*to see
Sophocles' 'Antigone' performed in Greek at Bradfield
College*] . . . [The theatre] is perfectly Greek—simple stone
steps to sit on and incense burning on the altar of Dionysus
in the orchestra. Unfortunately the weather was perfectly
English . . . most of the actors were inaudible and as the
rain increased (beating on the trees) it completely drowned
them . . . The audience were spectacle enough: rows of unhappy people listening to inaudible words in an unknown
language and sitting bunched up on stone steps under a
steady downpour . . . I then noticed that Jenkin was stand-

---

[98] University College in Reading was later to become The University
of Reading. William Macbride Childs (1869–1939) was the Principal of
University College, Reading, 1903–26, and the first Vice-Chancellor of
the University of Reading, 1926–29. William George de Burgh (1866–
1943) was Professor of Philosophy at the University of Reading, 1907–
34. Eric Robertson Dodds (1893–1979) was a fellow Ulsterman and he
took his B.A. from University College, Oxford, shortly after Jack
arrived there in 1917. Dodds was Lecturer in Classics at University
College, Reading, 1919–24, Professor of Greek in the University of
Birmingham, 1924–36, and the Regius Professor of Greek in the
University of Oxford, 1936–60.

ing on the last tier where the amphitheatre merged into the hillside—a steep bank of ivy overhanging the stone work. Crept up to join him—'Oh, think of a cup of steaming hot tea' said he. We exchanged a pregnant glance: then I led the way and in a trice we had plunged into the bushes, plugged our way on all fours up the ivy bank, and dropped into a lane beyond. Never shall I forget J. shaking streams off his hat and repeating over and over again, 'Oh, it *was* a tragedy'. We then repaired to a marquee and had tea ...

30 June 1922

After lunch I packed up my things for the night and biked into Oxford: failing to see Poynton in College I went on to Beckley through wind and rain. I was warmly welcomed by Barfield and Harwood ... We got into conversation on fancy and imagination: Barfield cd not be made to allow any essential difference between Christina dreams and the material of art. In the end we had to come to the conclusion that there is nothing in common between different people's ways of working, and, as Kipling says, 'every single one of them is right'.

At supper I drank Cowslip Wine for the first time in my life. It is a real wine, green in colour, bittersweet, as warming as good sherry, but heavy in its results and a trifle rough on the throat—not a bad drink however.

After supper we went out for a walk, into the woods on the edge of Otmoor. Their black and white cat, Pierrot, accompanied us like a dog all the way. Barfield danced round it in a field—with sublime lack of self-consciousness and wonderful vigour—for our amusement and that of three horses. There was a chilling wind but it was quite warm in the wood. To wander here as it got dark, to watch the cat poising after imaginary rabbits and to hear the wind in the trees—in such company—had a strange de la Mare-ish effect. On the way back we started a burlesque poem in *terza rima* composing a line each in turn: we continued it later, with paper, by candle light. It was very good nonsense. We entitled it the 'Button Moulder's story' and went to bed.

2 July 1922

In the evening D and I discussed our plans. It was hard to decide yes or no about the Reading job and D was so anxious not to influence me that I cd not be quite sure what her wishes were—I am equally in the dark as to what my own real wishes are ...

TO HIS FATHER: from University College

20 July [1922]

I am now close to my viva and of course on that subject I have nothing new to tell you. The details of the examination for the Magdalen Fellowship have however been published at last. The subjects are, as was expected, identical with those of Greats: but it is also notified that candidates may send in a dissertation on any relevant subject in addition to competing on the papers. I felt at once that this gave me a great pull. To choose your topic at your ease, to stake out your own line and display a modicum of originality—these, for men of our ilk, are more promising roads to victory than mere answering of questions. Indeed this condition is a rare bit of luck and of course I am all agog to begin. Naturally I shall not sit seriously to the work until my viva is over.

Under these circumstances you will understand that I cannot promise an early return home. I must see how I get on. No doubt this is disappointing for us all: but apart from that—on the score of health—you need have no misgiving. I am in excellent form at the moment and I shall not play the fool: midnight oil and ten hours a day were never my passion, and I am careful about the daily walk. Being confident on that score I feel it would be folly to throw away any chances for the sake of an immediate holiday. Also—odious factor—in my present position it is advisable to be on the spot, to be seen, to let people remember that there's a young genius on the look out for a job.

In the meantime I find the financial waters a trifle low. I have had examination fees and a few old wardrobe repairs to pay and I look forward to more expenses, including tipping, when I take my degree. The dates of terms naturally make a long interval between my spring and autumn allowances, but it has not been worth bothering you about before, and last year the Chancellors Prize helped to fill up. I had hoped to combine a little light tutoring with my own work—which would have been useful experience apart from the scheckels—but I was too late and the possible jobs in Oxford were filled up. Could you then let me have £25? I am sorry to 'out and come again' but you will understand the reasons.

I thought I had got hold of a temporary job for next year the other day. It was before I knew full details of the Magdalen fellowship, and consisted of a classical lectureship at University College, Reading. For geographical reasons I had hoped that this would combine—by means of a season ticket—the diplomatic or 'advertizement' advantages of keeping in touch with Oxford with the advantages of a salaried post. This however turned out impossible. As well, pure classics is not my line. I told them quite frankly and they gave the job to some one else. Perhaps I was too young. My pupils would nearly all have been girls. The funny thing was that the head of their classical department and one of the committee who interviewed me was Eric Dodds. I had lunch with him in Reading and some talk. He is a clever fellow, but I didn't greatly take to him somehow.

Arthur [Greeves] has been staying in Oxford. He was painting and I was working, but we saw a good deal of one another. He is enormously improved and I didn't feel the qualms which I once should have about introducing him to people. He is not a brilliant talker and he seldom sees a joke, but his years in London are brightening him up amazingly. His painting is getting on and he did one landscape here which I thought really good . . .

FROM HIS DIARY: at 28 Warneford Road

24 July 1922

At about 2.30 Baker came. He had been at Tetsworth yesterday with the Kennedys, to see Vaughan Williams. As if by arrangement, he was at work on his new symphony when they arrived, and was quite ready to talk of music. He is the largest man Baker has ever seen—Chestertonian both in figure and habits. He eats biscuits all the time while composing. He said that after he had written the first bar on the page of a full score, the rest was all mechanical drudgery and that in every art there was 10% of real 'making' to 90% of spade-

work. He has a beautiful wife who keeps a pet badger—
Baker saw it playing both with the dog and the kittens and it
licked his hand . . .

TO HIS FATHER: from University College

26 July [1922]

Very many thanks for the enclosure. 'There's a power of
washboards in that' as Mehawl Macmurrachu said when he
found the crock of gold. It is very kind of you to tell me to
possess my soul in patience, when the patience has rather to
be practised on your side. But let us hope that my unique
merits will soon be appreciated and that I shall be able to
rely on the inexhaustible patience of the tax payer and the
sainted generosity of dead benefactors. In the meantime
thank you and again thank you.

I have wondered, as you suggest in your letter, whether
I unduly decried my own wares before the Readingites. I
think, on the whole, that I behaved wisely: I am, after all,
nothing remarkable as a pure scholar, and there is no good
hiding what is so easily in their power to find out. As well
one produces only misery for oneself, don't you think, by
taking on jobs one is not up to. Biting off more than you can
chew is about the most poisonous sensation I know . . .

It is a strange irony that Dodds who is a born pure
scholar, spends his time lecturing on philosophy. As you
say however, the loss is hardly to be regretted: but there is
a mean spirit somewhere in most of us that strives under
all circumstances to explain away the success of the other
fellow . . .

FROM HIS DIARY: at 28 Warneford Road

28 July 1922

Up betimes in white tie and 'subfusc' and into my viva. We all presented ourselves (I knew none of the others) at 9.30. Myers, looking his most piratical, called over our names and read out the times at which we were to come, but not in alphabetical order. Two others and myself were told to stay and I was immediately called out, thus being the first victim of the day. My operator was Joseph. He was very civil and made every effort to be agreeable . . . The whole show took about five minutes . . .

[On 1 August Jack, Mrs Moore and Maureen moved into a large, furnished house in Headington, where they were to remain until 5 September. The house is named 'Hillsboro' and it is located on what was called Western Road but has since been altered to 14 Holyoake Road.]

FROM HIS DIARY: at 'Hillsboro', 14 Holyoake Road, Headington (where he, Mrs Moore and Maureen had lived since 30 April 1923)

2 August 1922

I bussed into College and called on Farquharson.[99] Apparently I am not too late to take my B.A. on Saturday . . . He also discussed exams and kept saying that everyone knew

---

[99] Arthur Spenser Loat Farquharson (1871–1942), who had been elected a Fellow of Univ. in 1898, held the positions of Senior Tutor, Praelector in Logic, and Dean of Degrees.

my abilities and would not change their opinions if I happened to get a second. From a don, such talk has its uncomfortable side—I hope there is nothing behind it more than his general desire of flattery . . .

I then returned and took my share of getting things straight . . . This house is full of unnecessary ornaments in the sitting rooms: beyond them, in the kitchen etc., we found a state of indescribable filth: bottles of cheap champagne in the cellar. Trash for the drawing room, dirt for the kitchen, second rate luxury for the table—an epitome of a 'decent English household' . . .

[Warren was on leave from West Africa. He arrived in Oxford on the morning of 3 August and took a room at the Roebuck Hotel in Cornmarket Street.]

3 August 1922

After tea I hastened into town and met Warnie at the Roebuck; dined with him at Buols with a bottle of Heidsick. He has certainly grown enormously fat. He was in excellent form. I mooted the proposal of his coming out here: he did not seem inclined to take it up. I left him my diary to read to put him *en rapport* with the life.

4 August 1922

I . . . met W[arnie] and we strolled to the Schools to see if my lists would be out in the evening. It gave me rather a shock to find them already up. I had a first, Wyllie a second: everyone else from College a third. The whole thing was rather too sudden to be as pleasant as it sounds on paper. I wired at once to P[apy] and went to lunch with W. at Buols.

During the meal I thought I had arranged for him to come and meet the family at tea: but quite suddenly while sitting in the garden of the Union he changed his mind and refused pertinaciously either to come to tea or to consider staying with us. I therefore came back to tea . . . after which I returned to W., and dined. He was now totally changed. He introduced the idea of coming to stay off his own bat and promised to come out tomorrow . . .

5 August 1922

Went to College after breakfast and saw Poynton about money matters . . . I then bussed out to Headington, changed rapidly into white tie and subfusc suit, and returned to lunch with W. at Buols. At 2 o'clock I assembled with the others at Univ. porch to be taken under Farquharson's wing for degrees. A long and very ridiculous ceremony making us B.A.s. . . .

I met W. again at the Roebuck and came up here. Everyone present for tea and [Warnie] got on well . . .

6 August 1922

W. came out with his luggage. Bridge in the afternoon. A wet night.

25 August 1922

W. and I did most of our packing before breakfast. We were delayed for a few minutes to have a photo taken by Maureen, and then departed, carrying his tin trunk between us. His visit here has been a great pleasure to me—a great advance too towards connecting up my real life with all that is pleasantest in my Irish life. Fortunately everyone liked him and I think he liked them . . .

[Warren visited his father in Belfast after leaving Oxford. He was joined at 'Little Lea' by Jack who was there from 11 to 21 September. On 6 October Warren reported at his new station in Colchester.]

FROM HIS DIARY: at 28 Warneford Road

30 September 1922

After breakfast I washed up and did the dining room. I then went to my own room and started to work again on the VIth Canto of Dymer. I got on splendidly—the first good work I have done since a long time . . . An absurd episode after lunch. Maureen had started saying she didn't mind which of two alternative sweets she had: and D, who is always worried by these indecisions, had begun to beg her to make up her mind in rather a weary voice. Thus developed one of those little mild wrangles about nothing which a wise man accepts as in the nature of things. I however, being in a sublime mood, and unprepared for jams, allowed a silent irritation to rise and sought relief in jabbing violently at a piece of pastry. As a result I covered myself in a fine shower of custard and juice: my melodramatic gesture was thus deservedly exposed and everyone roared with laughter.

13 October 1922

Shortly before one I saw Farquharson. He told me to go to Wilson of Exeter for tuition in English.[100] He then gave me

---

[100] Frank Percy Wilson (1889–1963) was at this time a Fellow of Exeter College and a university lecturer in English Literature. He was the Merton Professor of English Literature at Oxford from 1947 to 1957.

a paternal lecture on an academic career which was not (he said) one of leisure as popularly supposed. His own figure however lessened the force of the argument. He advised me, as he has done before, to go to Germany for a time and learn the language. He prophesied that there would soon be a school of modern European literature and that linguistically qualified Greatsmen would be the first to get the new billets thus created. This was attractive, but of course circumstances make migration impossible for me . . .

15 October 1922

Worked all morning in the dining room on my piece in *Sweet's Reader* and made some progress. It is very curious that to read the words of King Alfred gives more sense of antiquity than to read those of Sophocles. Also, to be thus realizing a dream of learning Anglo-Saxon which dates from Bookham days . . . After [supper] and washing up and more Troïlus up till nearly the end of Book III. It is amazingly fine stuff. How absolutely anti-Chaucerian Wm Morris was in all save the externals . . .

16 October 1922

Bicycled to the Schools after breakfast to a 10 o'clock lecture: stopping first to buy a batchelor's gown at the extortionate price of 32/6. According to a usual practice of the schools we were allowed to congregate in the room where the lecture was announced, and then suddenly told that it would be in the North School: our exodus of course fulfilled the scriptural condition of making the last first and the first last. I had thus plenty of time to feel the atmosphere of the English School which is very different from that of Greats. Women, Indians, and Americans predominate and—I can't say how—one feels a certain amateurishness in the talk and look of the people. The lecture was by Wyld on the History of the language.[101] He spoke for an hour and told us nothing that I haven't known these five years . . . After lunch I bicycled again to Schools to seek out the library of the English school. I found it at the top of many stories, inhabited by a strange old gentleman who seems to regard it as his private property . . .

18 October 1922

Bicycled to Schools for a 12 o'clock lecture on Chaucer by Simpson, who turns out to be the old man I found in the English school library.[102] Quite a good lecture . . . Jenkin arrived and I went to him in the drawing room. We talked of Troilus and this led us to the question of chivalry. I thought the mere ideal, however unrealized, had been a great advance. He thought the whole thing had been pretty worthless. The various points which I advanced as good results of the Knightly standard he attributed to Christianity. After this Christianity became the main subject. I tried to point out that the mediaeval knight ran his class code and his church code side by side in watertight compartments. Jenkin said that the typical example of the Christian ideal at work was Paul, while admitting that one would probably have disliked him in real life. I said that one got very little definite teach-

---

[101] Henry Cecil Kennedy Wyld (1870–1945) was a Fellow of Merton College and the Merton Professor of English Literature 1920–47. One of the books used at this time for the study of English was Wyld's *A Short History of English* (1921) which Jack found a very muddled piece of writing and of which he complained often.

[102] Percy Simpson (1865–1962) had been a Lecturer in English Literature at Oxford since 1913. He was Librarian of the English School 1914–34 and a Fellow of Oriel College 1921–36.

ing in the gospels: the writers had apparently seen something overwhelming, but been unable to reproduce it. He agreed, but added that this was so with everything worth having . . .

TO HIS FATHER: **from University College** (after failing to be elected to the Fellowship in Philosophy at Magdalen College)

28 [October 1922]

I judged that you would see my fate in the *Times*. This needs little comment. I am sorry for both our sakes that the 'hastings days fly on with full career and my late spring no bud nor blossom showeth'. But there's no good crying over spilt milk and one must not repine at being fairly beaten by a better man. I do not think I have done myself any harm, for I have had some compliments on my work. One examiner, at any rate, said I was 'probably the ablest man in for it', but added that my fault was a certain excess of caution or 'timidity in letting myself go' . . . For the rest, except for the extra drain on you, I should be glad enough of the opportunity or rather the necessity of taking another School. The English may turn out to be my real line, and, in any case, will be a second string to my bow.

I very much appreciate your enquiries about the adequacy of my allowance, and hasten to assure you that it leads to no such privations as you imagine. I will be quite frank with you. It is below the average, but that is balanced by the longer period of time over which it has been spread. It leaves no margin for superfluities, but I am lucky in having found cheap digs and, as my tastes are simple and my friends neither rich nor very numerous, I can manage alright—specially as you have been always very ready to meet any extraordinary charges. I am very grateful of the slow period of incubation which you have made possible—and have no mental reservations on the subject.

On the contrary, I very often regret having chosen a career which makes me so slow in paying my way: and, on your account, would be glad of a more lucrative line. But I think I know my own limitations and am quite sure that an academic or literary career is the only one in which I can hope ever to go beyond the meanest mediocrity. The Bar is a gamble which would probably cost more in the long run, and in business, of course I should be bankrupt or in jail very soon. In short you may make your mind easy on this subject. As to looking run down—I suppose I am turning from a very chubby boy into a somewhat thinner man: it is, at all events, not the result of a bun diet . . .

I am drumming ahead like anything with my Anglo-Saxon, and it is great fun. One begins it in a Reader constructed on the admirable system of having nearly all the text in one dialect and nearly all the glossary in another. You can imagine what happy hours this gives the young student—for example, you will read a word like 'Wado' in the text: in the glossary this may appear as Wedo, Waedo, Weodo, Waedu, or Wiedu. Clever bloke, ain't he? The language in general, gives the impression of parodied English badly spelled. Thus the word 'Cwic' may baffle you till you remember the 'quick and the dead' and suddenly realize that it means 'Alive'. Or again 'Tingul' for a star, until you think of 'Twinkle, twinkle little star'.

By the way I was quite wrong about Miss Waddell: it turns out to be Miss Wardale—an amazing old lady who is very keen on phonetics and pronounciation.[103] I spend most of my hours with her trying to reproduce the various clucking, growling and grunted noises which are apparently an essential to the pure accent of Alfred—or Aelfred as we must now call him . . .

FROM HIS DIARY: at 28 Warneford Road

29 October 1922

[Aunt Lily] has been here for about three days and has snubbed a bookseller in Oxford, written to the local paper, crossed swords with the Vicar's wife, and started a quarrel with her landlord . . . Her conversation is like an old drawer, full both of rubbish and valuable things, but all thrown together in great disorder. She is still engaged on her essay, which starting three years ago as a tract on the then state of woman suffrage, is still unfinished and now embraces a complete philosophy on the significance of heroism and maternal instinct, the nature of matter, the primal one, the value of Christianity, and the purpose of existence. That purpose by the way is the return of differences to the One through heroism and pain. She thus combines a good deal of Schopenhaur with a good deal of theosophy: besides being indebted to Bergson and Plotinus. She told me that ectoplasm was done

---

[103] Edith Elizabeth Wardale (1863–1943) had been educated at both Lady Margaret Hall and St Hugh's College, Oxford, and she had been appointed a Fellow of St Hugh's College in 1920. Jack went to her for tuition in Anglo-Saxon because there was no one in his college who taught that subject.

with soap bubbles, that women had no balance and were cruel as doctors, that what I needed for my poetry was a steeping in scientific ideas and terminology, that many prostitutes were extraordinarily purified and Christ-like, that Plato was a Bolshevist . . . that the importance of Christ could not have lain in what He said, that Pekinese were not dogs at all but dwarfed lions bred from smaller and ever smaller specimens by the Chinese through ages innumerable, that matter was just the stop of motion and that the cardinal error of all religions made by men was the assumption that God existed for, or cared about us. I left Dymer with her and got away, with some difficulty, at one o'clock . . .

2 November 1922

Went to the Schools library. Here I puzzled for the best of two hours over phonetics, back voice stops, glides, glottal catches and open Lord-knows-whats. Very good stuff in its way, but why physiology should form part of the English school I really don't know . . .

FROM HIS DIARY: on his way to Belfast

23 December 1922

Shortly before 4 I returned to the Central hall at Euston and there was met by W[arnie], when we immediately went and had tea in the refreshment room. He gave me a most favourable account of Colchester which, he said, was a very old world town in an Arthur Rackham country. We caught the 5.30 for Liverpool: what between dinner, drinks, and conversation the journey passed very quickly: we succeeded in sitting in the dining car the whole way. We had two single berth rooms in the boat, with a communicating door. I was greatly worried all day by the pain in my armpit. A rough night, but we both slept well.

FROM HIS DIARY: at 'Little Lea' in Belfast
24 December 1922

We got out to Leeborough in the grey of the morning, not in the best of spirits. My father was not up yet. When he finally appeared, he was in poor form and rather shaky—for whatever reason. He approved of my new suit. Then followed breakfast and the usual artificial conversation. We vetoed churchgoing and went out for a walk at twelve o'clock . . . The path was so narrow that the other two walked ahead and I was left, not to my own thoughts, for in Ireland I have none, but to the undisturbed possession of my lethargy. We came back and had some sherry: W. and I have often remarked on the extraordinary effect of this sherry. Last night I drank four whiskies without any undue result: today, in the study, my own glass of sherry led to a dull and cheerless shadow of intoxication. We had a heavy midday dinner at 2.45. The rest of the day was spent entirely in the study: our three chairs in a row, all the windows shut . . .

25 December 1922

We were awakened early by my father to go to the communion service. It was a dark morning with a gale blowing and some very cold rain . . . As we walked down to church we started discussing the time of sunrise: my father saying rather absurdly that it must have risen already, or else it wouldn't be light.

In Church it was intensely cold. W. offered to keep his coat on. My father expostulated and said 'Well at least you won't keep it on when you go up to the Table'. W. asked why not and was told it was 'most disrespectful'. I couldn't help wondering why. But W. took it off to save trouble . . .

Another day set in exactly similar to yesterday. My father amused us by saying in a tone, almost of alarm, 'Hello, it's stopped raining. We ought to go out' and then adding with undisguised relief 'Ah no. It's still raining: we needn't.' Christmas dinner, a rather deplorable ceremony, at quarter to four.

Afterwards it had definitely cleared up: my father said he was too tired to go out, not having slept the night before, but encouraged W. and me to do so—which we did with great eagerness and set out to reach Holywood by the high road and there have a drink. It was delightful to be in the open air after so many hours' confinement in one room. Fate however, denied our drink: for we were met just outside Holywood by the Hamilton's car and of course had to travel back with them. Uncle Gussie drove back along the narrow winding road in a reckless and bullying way that alarmed W. and me . . .

Early to bed, dead tired with talk and lack of ventilation. I found my mind was crumbling into the state which this place always produces: I have gone back six years to be flabby, sensual and unambitious. Headache again.

11 January 1923

After this I read Macdonald's *Phantastes* over my tea, which I have read many times and which I really believe fills for me the place of a devotional book . . .

FROM HIS DIARY: **at 28 Warneford Road** (having left
Belfast on 12 January)

25 January 1923

I went to Schools at 10 o'clock to hear Onions on Middle
English.[104] ... Onions gave a delightful lecture: the best part
being the quotations, which he does inimitably. Once he
repeated nearly a whole poem with much relish and then
observed 'That wasn't what I meant to say'. A man after my
own heart.

26 January 1923

Got home in time for tea and read Donne and Raleigh till just
before supper when I began my essay. I was just sitting down
to it again after supper when I heard a knock and going out,
found Barfield. The unexpected delight gave me one of the
best moments I have had since the even better ones of leaving Ireland and arriving home ... We went at our talk like a
dogfight: of Baker, of Harwood, of our mutual news ...

[Barfield] is working with Pearsall Smith who is genuinely *trivious* and an utter materialist.[105] He (Smith) and De
la Mare are fast friends ... Barfield hopes soon to meet De
la Mare. He sees Squire fairly often. He says Squire is a man
who promises more than he can perform, not through flattery but because he really believes his own influence to be

---

[104] Charles Talbut Onions (1873–1965), lexicographer and grammarian,
joined the staff of the Oxford English Dictionary in 1895. He was a lecturer in English at Oxford 1920–27 and Reader in English Philology
1927–49.
[105] Logan Pearsall Smith (1865–1946) was born in Philadelphia but spent
most of his life in England, devoting himself to a study of the English
language. He taught on the English Faculty at Oxford and his many
books include three volumes of *Trivia* (1918, 1921, 1933).

greater than it is . . . He said it had always surprised him that my things were as good as they were, for I seemed to work simply on inspiration and did no chipping. I thus wrote plenty of good poetry but never one perfect poem. He said that the 'inspired' percentage was increasing all the time and that might save me in the end . . . I thought his insight was almost uncanny and agreed with every word . . . I walked back to Wadham with him in the moonlight . . .

4 February 1923

Went off on my bike to have tea with Miss Wardale . . . I found Miss W. alone. After we had talked for a few minutes I was pleasantly surprised by the arrival of Coghill[106] . . . Miss W., apart from a few sensible remarks on Wagner, was content to sit back in a kind of maternal attitude with her hands on her knees. Coghill did most of the talking, except when contradicted by me. He said that Mozart had remained like a boy of six all his life. I said nothing could be more delightful: he replied (and quite right) that he could imagine many things more delightful. He entirely disagreed with my love of Langland and of Morris . . . He said that Blake was really inspired. I was beginning to say 'In a sense—' when he said 'In the same sense as Joan of Arc'. I said 'I agree. In exactly the same sense. But we may mean different things.' He: 'If you are a materialist.' I apologized for the appearance of quibbling but said that 'materialist' was too ambiguous . . .

---

[106] Neville Henry Kendall Aylmer Coghill (1899–1980) matriculated at Exeter College in 1919. He was a Fellow of Exeter College 1925–57 and the Merton Professor of English Literature 1957–66. See his essay 'The Approach to English' in *Light on C. S. Lewis*, ed. Jocelyn Gibb (1965).

When I rose to go he came with me and we walked together as far as Carfax. It was very misty. I found out that he had served in Salonika: that he was Irish and came from near Cork . . . He said (just like Barfield) that he felt it his duty to be a 'conchy' if there was another war, but admitted that he had not the courage. I said yes—unless there was something really worth fighting for. He said the only thing he would fight for was the Monarchy . . . I said I didn't care twopence about monarchy—the only real issue was civilization against barbarism. He agreed, but thought with Hobbes that civilization and monarchy went together . . . Before parting I asked him to tea: he said he had just been going to ask me, and we finally arranged that I should go to him on Friday. I then biked home. I thought Coghill a good man, quite free from our usual Oxford flippancy and fear of being crude . . .

9 February 1923

On getting into bed I was attacked by a series of gloomy thoughts about professional and literary failure—what Barfield calls 'one of those moments when one is afraid that one may not be a great man after all'.

15 February 1923

Again today—it is happening much too often now—I am haunted by fears for the future, as to whether I will ever get a job and whether I shall ever be able to write good poetry . . .

21 March 1923

Got home very tired and depressed: D made me have some tea. I told her (what had been on my mind all afternoon) that I didn't feel very happy about the plan of staying here as a more or less unattached tutor. I do not want to join the rank of advertisements in the Union—it sounds so like the prelude of being a mere grinder all my days. If it wasn't for Maureen I think I should plump for a minor university if possible. We had rather a dismal conversation about our various doubts and difficulties ...

22 March 1923

I went to Carritt's room and returned his Aristotle. I then went and saw Stevenson, whom I found sitting in his rooms by a hot fire, very miserable with a bad throat and not able to talk much. I asked him what prospects there were of my being able to exist as a free lance tutor until something turned up. He said there was practically no such work to be had in my subject ... He said he thought I was pretty sure to get a fellowship soon ... In the mean time he advised me to get a job at a minor university ...

I then came home ... and discussed the situation with D. We are both greatly depressed. If one cd be sure of my coming back to a fellowship after a term or two at some minor University we could take the Woodstock Rd house—but if not? ... It was certainly a damnably difficult situation. Thence we drifted into the perennial difficulty of money, which would be far more acute if we had to separate for a time ...

TO HIS FATHER: from University College

27 May [1923]

I do not care to think how long it is since I last wrote to you. I have made some attempts to do so before this, but they have all collapsed under the pressure of work, or of the mere trifling and lassitude which is the reaction to work. You wrote to me that a disinclination to write letters was 'one of the marks of approaching old age' which you felt or thought you felt. If that were true, what a premature senility is mine! It is a very ridiculous and a very wretched confession that I can hardly remember any period since I was a child at which I have not had a crowd of unanswered letters nagging at the back of my mind: things which would have been no trouble if answered by return but which hang on for weeks or months, getting always harder to write in the end, and contributing their share to the minor worries that lay hold of us when we have the blues or lie awake. That anyone should let himself maintain such a standing army of pinpricks would be incredible if it were not fairly common . . . Our Colonel, on the principle of 'diamond cut diamond' knows how to defeat this laziness in another because he is so familiar with it himself. At Whitsun he wrote to me saying he would arrive for the weekend unless he heard to the contrary: that at any rate means that no one can keep him waiting for a reply!

He came from Friday evening to Monday. He is at present deep in Gibbon and is very enthusiastic about it. I envy him his routine work—in itself apparently not uninteresting and finished definitely at four o'clock with the rest of the day free for general reading, with no uncertainties or anxieties. Despite the frittering away of time over drinks and gossip in the mess and the low mental level of the society I cannot help feeling that for him the military life has solved the problem of existence very well . . .

Our summer here consists of sleet, frost and east winds: tho' the summer invasion of Americans has come punctually enough. I mention this because they introduce a good

American story which you may not have heard. In the old days of primitive sheriff rule in the western states a man was hanged and shortly afterwards his innocence was proved. The local authorities assembled and deliberated on the best method of conveying the news to the inconsolable widow. It was felt that a too sudden statement would be a little 'brutal' and the Sheriff himself, as the man of greatest refinement, was finally deputed to wait upon the lady. After a few suitable remarks on the figs and the maize, he began with the following, 'Say, Ma'am, I guess you've got the laugh of us this time!' . . .

FROM HIS DIARY: at 'Hillsboro'

1 June 1923

A cold day. I spent the morning working on my essay . . . Coming back to College I heard with interest what is I suppose my nickname. Several Univ. people whom I don't know passed me. One of them, noticing my blazer, must have asked another who I was, for I heard him answer 'Heavy Lewis' . . .

20 June 1923

I . . . rode home. Found D and Dorothy polishing in D's room. Had hardly left them when I heard an awful crash and rushed back thoroughly frightened and half believing that the wardrobe had fallen on D. I found however that it was only she herself who had fallen and hurt her elbow: she was badly shaken. All attempts to get her to stop polishing and rest on her laurels were treated in the usual way . . . This put me into such a rage against poverty and fear and all the infernal net I seemed to be in that I went out and mowed the lawn and cursed all the gods for half an hour . . .

22 June 1923

In the morning I read *Venice Preserved*[107] which contains more loathsome sentimentality, flat language, and bad verse than I should have imagined possible. Later I scraped and began to stain the exposed passages of floor in the hall, which was work both hot and hard. After lunch I finished the hall and did the same for the drawing room and helped D with some changes of furniture in the dining room . . . At six I walked out to find a new field path that I had heard of . . . This brought me up [a] hill beside a very fine hedge with wild roses in it. This, in the cool of the evening, together with some curious illusion of being on the slope of a much bigger hill than I really was, and the wind in the hedge, gave me intense pleasure with a lot of vague reminiscences . . . I got back about 8 and watered the garden . . .

TO HIS FATHER: from **University College** (after taking Schools in English Literature)

1 July [1923]

Before everything else let me thank you very heartily . . . I hope some day to repay these long years of education in the only way in which they can be repaid—by success and distinction in the kind of life which they aim at. But that is partly in the power of fortune and in the meantime I can only record that I am not foolish enough to take these things for

---

[107] Thomas Otway, *Venice Preserv'd* (1682).

granted and that the thought of how much you are doing for me is often, even insistently, before my mind . . .

I should not be a son of yours if the prospect of being adrift and unemployed at thirty had not been very often present to my mind: for of course the worrying temperament of the family did not end in your generation, and to quote Jeremy Taylor 'we were born with this sadness upon us' . . .

But, shaking off all that is temperamental and due to momentary fits of optimism and pessimism, I can only put the situation thus. I have, and of course, shall always have, qualifications that should, by all ordinary probability, make a tolerable schoolmastering job practically certain whenever we decide to give up Oxford as hopeless. The same qualifications also put me fairly high in the rank of candidates for academic jobs here. The Magdalen people told my tutor quite recently that they thought my work for their fellowship quite on a level with that of the man who won it, except that it was 'more mature'. But of course the number of hungry suitors with qualifications equal to mine, tho' not very large, is large enough to put up a well filled 'field' for every event: and the number of vacancies depends, as in other spheres, on all sorts of accidents.

What it comes to is that there is a pretty healthy chance here which would, on the whole, be increased by a few years' more residence in which I should have time to make myself more known and to take some research degree such as B. Litt. or Doc. Phil. and which would be, perhaps indefinitely or permanently lost if I now left. On the other hand, even apart from the financial point of view, I very keenly realize the dangers of hanging on too long for what might not come in the end. Speaking, for the moment, purely for myself, I should be inclined to put three years as a suitable term for waiting before beating a retreat . . .

The English School is come and gone, tho' I still have my viva to face. I was of course rather hampered by the shortened time in which I took the school and it is in many ways so different from the other exams that I have done that I should be sorry to prophesy . . .

FROM HIS DIARY: at 'Hillsboro'

7 July 1923

I went to the Station where I met Harwood. He is working on a temporary job connected with the British Empire Exhibition and says that he is becoming the complete business man. He was in excellent form . . . We walked to Parson's Pleasure to bathe. It was the first time I have been there this year. They had finished mowing the meadows beyond the water: all was cool and green and lovely beyond anything. We had a glorious bathe and then lay on the grass talking of a hundred things till we got hot and had to bathe again. After a long time we came away and back to the Union where he had left his suitcase and thence bussed up to Headington. D and Maureen had of course got home before us and we all had tea on the lawn. Afterwards Harwood and I lay under the trees and talked. He told me of his new philosopher, Rudolf Steiner who has 'made the burden roll from his back'.

Steiner seems to be a sort of panpsychist, with a vein of posing superstition, and I was very much disappointed to hear that both Harwood and Barfield were impressed by him.

The comfort they got from him (apart from the sugar plum of promised immortality, which is really the bait with which he has caught Harwood) seemed something I could get much better without him. I argued that the 'spiritual forces' which Steiner found everywhere were either shamelessly mythological *people* or else no-one-knows-what. Harwood said this was nonsense and that he understood perfectly what he meant by a spiritual force. I also protested that Pagan animism was an anthropomorphic failure of imagination and that we should prefer a knowledge of the real unhuman life which is in the trees etc. He accused me of a materialistic way of thinking when I said that the similarity of all languages probably depended on the similarity of all throats. The best thing about Steiner seems to be the Goetheanum which he has built up in the Alps . . . Unfortunately the building (which must have been very wonderful) has been burned by the Catholics . . .

10 July 1923

Up betimes and dressed in subfusc and white tie . . . At 9.30 we entered the viva room and after the names had been called, six of us were told to stay, of whom I was one. I then sat in the fearful heat, in my gown and rabbit skin, on a hard chair, unable to smoke, talk, read, or write, until 11.50 . . . Most of the vivas were long and discouraging. My own—by Brett Smith—lasted about two minutes. I was asked my authority, if any, for the word 'little-est'.[108] I gave it—the Coleridge-

---

[108] Herbert Francis Brett-Smith (1884–1951) took his B.A. from Corpus Christi College in 1907. In 1922 he became a lecturer in English Literature at Pembroke College and, in time, a lecturer at a number of the other colleges of Oxford.

Poole correspondence in *Thomas Poole and his friends*. I was then asked if I had not been rather severe on Dryden and after we had discussed this for a little Simpson said that they need not bother me any more. I came away much encouraged, and delighted to escape the language people—one of whom, not a don, was a foul creature yawning insolently at his victims and rubbing his small puffy eyes. He had the face of a pork butcher and the manners of a village boy on a Sunday afternoon, when he has grown bored but not yet quite arrived at the quarrelsome stage . . .

[On 16 July the examination results of the English School were posted and the next day Jack sent a wire to his father saying 'A First in English'. The next few weeks he made a little money correcting English essays for School Certificates. This was followed by a visit to his father in Belfast during 22 September—10 October.]

FROM HIS DIARY: at 'Hillsboro'

11 October 1923

I crossed last night from Ireland after nearly three weeks at 'Little Lea'. In two respects my compulsory holiday was a great improvement on most that I have had, for I got on very well with my father and held the usual mental inertia at arm's length by working steadily at my Italian . . . In revenge, I was never really well, suffering from headaches and indigestion. In the loneliness of that house I became hypochondriacal and for a time imagined that I was getting appendicitis or something worse. This worried me terribly, not only chiefly for its own sake but because I didn't see how I could manage to get back here in time. I had one or two dreadful nights of panic.

I did many long walks hoping to make myself sleep. I was twice up the Cave Hill where I intend to go often in future. The view down the chasm between Napoleon's Head and the main body of the cliffs is almost the best I have seen. I had one other delightful walk over the Castlereagh hills where I got the real joy—the only time for many years that I have had it in Ireland.

This morning I was called at 7 . . . On getting out at Oxford I found myself in a crisp wintry air and as I bussed up to Headington I felt the horrors of the last week or so going off like a dream . . . So home, full of happiness, and early to bed, both being very tired and sleepy.

TO HIS FATHER: **from University College**
22 November [1923]
I have a certain amount of news to give you, all of an inconclusive character. To get the least agreeable item over first, I am afraid old Poynton has proved a broken reed in the matter of pupils: I believe, because he put off the job too long. He is an oldish man and habitually overworked so I do not judge him hardly, tho' I was rather disappointed . . .

I have got quite recently *one* pupil, tho' not through Poynton. He is a youth of eighteen who is trying to get a Classical scholarship. I am to coach him in essay writing and English for the essay paper and general papers which these exams always include. I fear we shall win no laurels by him. I questioned him about his classical reading: our dialogue was something like this:

SELF: 'Well Sandeman, what Greek authors have you been reading?'

SAND (cheerfully): 'I never can remember. Try a few names and I'll see if I get on to any.'

SELF (a little damped): 'Have you read any Euripides?'

SAND: 'No.'

SELF: 'Any Sophocles?'

SAND: 'Oh yes.'

SELF: 'What plays of his have you read?'

SAND (after a pause): 'Well—the Alcestis.'

SELF (apologetically): 'But isn't that by Euripides?'

SAND (with the genial surprise of a man who finds £1 where he thought there was a 10/-note): 'Really. Is it now? By Jove, then I *have* read some Euripides!'

My next is even better. I asked him if he were familiar with the distinction that critics draw between a *natural* and a *literary* epic. He was not: you may not be either, but it makes no difference. I then explained to him that when a lot of old war songs about some mythological hero were handed down by aural tradition and gradually welded into one whole by successive minstrels (as in the case of 'Homer') the result was called a natural epic: but when an individual poet sat down with pen in hand to write *Paradise Lost,* that was a literary epic. He listened with great attention and then observed 'I suppose Grey's Elegy is the natural kind.'

What idiots can have sent him in for a Scholarship? However, he is one of the cheeriest, healthiest, and most perfectly contented creatures I have ever met with . . .

FROM HIS DIARY: at 'Hillsboro' (part of a summary of events from 22 October to the end of December 1923)

[December 1923]
It was shortly after this that I read Flecker's *Hassan*. It made a great impression on me and I believe it is really a great work. Carritt (whom I met at the Martlets shortly after) thinks that its dwelling on physical pain puts it as much outside literature as is pornography in another: that it works on the nervous system rather than the imagination. I find this hard to answer: but I am almost sure he is wrong. . . .

TO HIS FATHER: from University College

4 February [1924]
You will explain your long silence as an answer to mine — at least I hope there is no more serious reason for it than that and the desultoriness in correspondence which you claim as one of the penalties, if it is not rather one of the privileges, of the years beyond fifty. I, like the judge, have other reasons.

As soon as I had met people here I heard of a new will-o-the-wisp, a poor Fellowship at St John's now vacant and calling out for candidates. The warning that preference would be given to 'founder's kin and persons born in the

County of Stafford' did not seem sufficient to deter me from trying my luck. At first I thought of sending them my old dissertation which I had written for Magdalen: but no man cares greatly for his own things when once the bloom is off them, and I decided in the end to write a new one. I was in pretty good form, but I was pressed for time: and of course there is a waste of time when one flings oneself back into work which one has abandoned for a few months—the old harness will not at once sit easily.

It was only after I had sent this in that I discovered how small my chances must necessarily be. I had supposed—and who would not—that the preference for natives of Staffordshire etc., meant only a preference, other things being equal. I find however that if any candidate appears who claims such preference and who has in addition either a *Second* in Greats or a *First* in any other final school, he must be elected. I do not of course know in fact whether there is such a candidate in the field, for Stafford is a large county, and we may be sure that the founder was some philoprogenitive old fellow who, like Charles II in Dryden, 'scattered his Maker's image through the land'. In short we may expect a defeat with almost complete certainty . . .

This then occupied my first weeks. And I had hardly looked about me when a most irritating thing happened. I got chicken pox and am only now out of quarantine. I have of course been quite well enough to write for some time but I don't know whether you have had this complaint and thought it better not to chance infecting you: I am told that the older you are the less likely it will be to 'take', but the worse if it does. I had a pretty high temperature at the beginning and some very uncomfortable nights of intense perspiration, but it soon passed off. The danger of cutting any of the spots on my face of course made shaving impossible till this very day and I had a fine beard. I have left the moustache which would excite 'poor Warren's' envy, but I shall probably get tired of it in a few weeks. It is very stiff, and all the hairs grow in different directions and it is thicker on one side than on the other . . .

You know of course that my Scholarship is at an end. It was nominally a scholarship of £80 a year. What I actually got out of it was about £11 a term. Sometimes it would be a little more or a little less, but it generally averaged out to £33 a year . . . I had hopes of being able to make up that in other ways—pupils and the like—but they have not been realized and I am afraid I must ask for help. I do not like increasing your charges—but as Kirk said, 'All this has been said before'.

I have lost Sandeman. He got good marks in his English in the Scholarship he tried for near Christmas and his mother and his other coach said the nicest things of me, when dash it if the fool doesn't go and break his leg . . .

FROM HIS DIARY: at 'Hillsboro'

29 February 1924

Shortly after tea, which was very late, I went up to dress, preparatory to dining with Carritt . . . At dinner Carritt put into my hand the notice of the vacancy at Trinity—an official Fellowship in Philosophy, worth £500 a year . . . I walked home, looking at the details of the Trinity Fellowship as I passed the lamps. For some reason the possibility of getting it and all that would follow if I did came before my mind with unusual vividness. I saw it would involve living in [Trinity College] and what a break up of our present life that would mean, and also how the extra money would lift terrible loads off us all. I saw that it would mean pretty full work and that I might become submerged and poetry crushed out. With deep conviction I suddenly had an image of myself, God knows when or where, in the future looking back on these years since the war as the happiest or the only really valuable part of my life, in spite of all their disappointments and fears. Yet the longing for an income that wd free us from anxiety was stronger than all these feelings. I was in a strange state of excitement—and all on the mere hundredth chance of getting it . . .

17–25 March 1924

During this time it was unfortunate that my first spring flood of Dymer should coincide with a burst of marmalade making and spring cleaning on D's part which led without intermission into packing. I managed to get in a good deal of writing in the intervals of jobbing in the kitchen and doing messages in Headington. I wrote the whole of a last canto with considerable success, tho' the ending will not do. I also kept my temper nearly all the time.

Domestic drudgery is excellent as an alternative to idleness or to hateful thoughts—which is perhaps poor D's reason for piling it on at this time: as an alternative to the work one is longing to do and able to do (*at that time* and heaven knows when again) it is maddening. No one's fault: the curse of Adam.

TO HIS FATHER: from University College

27 April [1924]

I have been exercised in the slightly unpleasant duty of getting all things in readiness for my application for the Trinity Fellowship—getting testimonials and talking to one or two people who will write unofficially for me. I also went to a dinner where I met the present philosophy man from Trinity whose successor I should become if I were elected. This was done no doubt to give me an opportunity of impressing him with my unique social and intellectual qualifications.

Unhappily the whole conversation was dominated by a bore who wanted to talk (and *did* talk) about the state of India, and I suppose I hardly exchanged ten words with the Trinity man. However, it may have been just as well. A man who knows he is on show can hardly be at his best: and I am told that this Trinity man is a very shy, retiring, moody old man and difficult to talk to. In the meantime I send in my application and wait—reminding myself that the best cure for disappointment is the moderation of hopes . . .

I can't remember if I told you about my last visit to Aunt Lily. I went out by bus. The conductor did not at once understand where I wanted to stop, and a white bearded old farmer chipped in, 'You know, Jarge—where that old gal lives along of all them cats'. I explained that this was exactly where I did want to go. My informant remarked, 'You'll 'ave a job to get in when you *do* get there'. He was as good as his word, for when I reached the cottage I found the fence supporting a wire structure about nine feet high which was continued even over the gate. She does it to prevent her cats escaping into the main road. On this occasion she presented me with a print of an old picture: 'St Francis preaching before Pope Honorius' because, she said, the Pope was a portrait of me. It is not one of her fads, for I do really see the likeness myself. I suppose nature has only a limited number of faces to use after all . . .

TO HIS FATHER: from University College

[11 May 1924]

I have a bit of good—or fairly good—news. Some nights ago I was summoned to call on the new Master after dinner, there to meet Farquharson and my old philosophy tutor Carritt, and when I arrived the following 'transpired'. Carritt it appears is going for a year to teach philosophy in the University of Ann Arbor, Michigan, and it was suggested that I should undertake his tutorial duties here during his absence and also give lectures. As soon as I heard the proposal I said that I was already a candidate for the vacancy at Trinity. To this they replied that they had no intention of asking me to sacrifice the possibility of a permanent job: it would be understood that if I were elected to Trinity I should be released from my engagement to Univ.—unless indeed Trinity were willing to let me do both tasks and I felt able to do so. This being settled, I of course accepted their offer.

I was a little disappointed that they only offered me £200—specially as I anticipate that when living in and dining at high table I shall hardly be able to economise as much as I do now. I am afraid that I shall still need some assistance from you. Of course Carritt's job must be worth more than that: I imagine he is keeping his *fellowship* and I am getting his *tutorial* emoluments and of these, Farquharson, who is 'taking a few of the senior men' is getting a share.

Being under Farquharson's superintendance will be in some ways troublesome: and indeed I have already had a specimen of his fussy futility. I sent in to the Master as the title of my proposed lectures for the next term 'The Moral Good—its place among the values'. Within an hour I had a notice brought out to my digs by special messenger 'Farquharson suggests "position" instead of "place". Please let me know your views at once.' There's glory for you, as Humpty Dumpty said! Well, it is poorly paid and temporary and under the shadow of Farquharson, but it is better to be inside than out, and is always a beginning. The experience will be valuable.

You may imagine that I am now pretty busy. I must try to get through most of the Greats reading before next term and do it more thoroughly than ever I did when I was a candidate myself. I must be ready for all comers and hunt out the bye ways which I considered it safe to neglect in my own case. There can be no throwing dust in the examiner's eyes this time. Preparing my lectures will however be the biggest job of all. I am to lecture twice a week next term, which comes to fourteen hours' talking in all. You who have been so much on your legs, can tell better than I what a lot of talking a man can do in one hour. I rather fancy I could really tell the world everything I think about everything in five hours—and, Lord, you hear curates grumbling because they have to preach for twenty minutes a week. However, as Keats remarks somewhere, 'Demme, who's afraid?': we must learn that slow deliberate method dear to the true lecturer. As Farquharson remarked (without the ghost of a smile) 'Of course your first lecture would be *introductory*'. I felt like replying, 'Of course: that's why I always skipped *your* first lectures!'

As a perspective candidate I dined at Trinity the other night . . . I was very favourably impressed with the Trinity people. In the smoking room after dinner we were just of a number for conversation to be general and I had one of the best evenings imaginable, the 'crack' ranging over all things . . . So if Trinity don't give me a Fellowship, at least they gave me a very good time . . .

FROM HIS DIARY: at 'Hillsboro'

15 June 1924

After supper I bussed in to Exeter and went to Coghill's rooms where, after a short wait, I was joined by Coghill and Morrah.[109] The latter is a Fellow of All Souls . . . He told us a good story of how H. G. Wells had dined at All Souls and said that Oxford wasted too much time over Latin and Greek. Why should these two literatures have it all to themselves? Now Russian and Persian literature were far superior to the classics. Someone (I forget the name) asked a few questions. It soon became apparent that Wells knew neither Greek, Latin, Persian, nor Russian. 'I think', said someone, 'I am the only person present here tonight who knows these

---

[109] Dermot Macgreggor Morrah (1896–1974) took his B.A. from New College in 1921 and he was a Fellow of All Souls College 1921–28. He was a leader writer for a number of newspapers, including *The Times*, and he published several books on the Royal Family.

four languages: and I can assure you, Mr Wells, that you are mistaken: neither Russian nor Persian literature are as great as the literatures of Greece or Rome' . . .

3 July 1924

Today I went to Colchester in order to travel back in W[arnie]'s sidecar . . . A brisk shower of rain came down as I reached Colchester where I was met at the station by W. and driven to the Red Lion where I had tea. This is one of the oldest hotels in England, curiously and beautifully beamed. W. tells me that the American who insulted Kipling at the Rhodes dinner in Oxford has made a great name for himself (of a sort) in the army. W. had just been reading *Puck of Pook's Hill* for the first time: he praised it highly and I agreed with him.

While we were sitting under the roof of a kind of courtyard after tea waiting for the rain to stop, a Major came up, to whom W. introduced me, telling me afterwards that he was a very well preserved specimen of the real old type of army bore. When it cleared a little we walked out to see the town which is a very pleasant sprawling old world place, not unlike Guildford. The Roman castle is very fine in a kind quite new to me, as also the remains of the old gate of Camolodunum. There is also a pleasant old house (now an office but it ought to be a pub) bullet marked from the civil wars. After all this we motored up out of the town to a higher, windy land, full of camps. W.'s camp consists of a small old country house ('a Jorrocks house' he called it) and its park, now filled with huts. The C.O. lives in the Jorrocks house.

I was taken to the Mess (Lord, how strange to be in such a place again!) and of course given a drink. The 'Orficers' were really very nice to me. It was odd to me to see a mess full of people in mufti. We then motored back to town to a civilian club of which W. is a member, where he had provided a royal feast of the sort we both liked: no nonsense about soup and pudding, but a sole each, cutlets with green peas, a *large* portion of strawberries and cream, and a tankard of the local beer which is very good. So we gorged like Roman Emperors in a room to ourselves and had good talk . . .

We drove back to camp. W. had turned out into another hut and I had his bedroom. He has two rooms for his quarters. The sitting room with stove, easy chair, pictures, and all his French books, is very snug. I notice that a study in a hut, or a cave, or a cabin of a ship can be snug in a way that is impossible for a mere room in a house, the snugness there being a *victory,* a sort of defiant comfortableness—whereas in a house of course, one demands comfort and is simply annoyed at its absence. He 'put into my hands' Anatole France's *Revolt of the Angels* in a translation, which seems an amusing squib.

4 July 1924

We started on our Oxford journey after breakfast in the mess. The day looked threatening at first, but we had fair weather. I do not remember the names of the villages we passed, except Braintree and Dunmow (where the flich lives). At St Albans we stopped to see the Cathedral: I had been there once before in my Wynyard days about 1909 or 1910 to sit and kneel for three hours watching Wyn Capron (whom God reject!) ordained a deacon or priest, I forget which. Yet, in those days, that day without work, the journey to St Alban's, the three hour's service and a lunch of cold beef and rice in an hotel was a treat for which we counted the days beforehand and felt *nessum maggior dolore* when the following day brought us back to routine.

I was rather glad to find the Cathedral quite definitely the poorest English cathedral I have yet seen. In the town we bought two pork pies to supplement what W. considered the Spartan allowance of sandwiches given us by the mess, and drank some beer. I think it was here that W. formed the project of going far out of our way to eat our lunch at Hunton Bridge on the L.N.W.R. where we used to sit and watch the trains when out on our walk from Wynyard. I assented eagerly. I love to exult in my happiness at being forever safe from at least one of the major ills of life—that of being a boy at school.

We bowled along very merrily in brilliant sunshine, while the country grew uglier and meaner at every turn, and therefore all the better for our purpose. We arrived at the bridge and devoured the scene—the two tunnels, wh. I hardly recognized at first, but memory came back. Of course things were changed. The spinney of little saplings had grown quite high. The countryside was no longer the howling waste it once looked to us. We ate our egg sandwiches and pork pies and drank our bottled beer. In spite of W.'s fears it was as much as we could do to get through them all. But then, as he pointed out, this was appropriate to the scene. We were behaving just as we would have done fifteen years earlier. 'Having eaten everything in sight, we are now finished.' We had a lot of glorious reminiscent talk. We developed our own version of *si jeunesse savait:* if we could only have seen as far as this out of the hell of Wynyard. I felt a half comic, half savage pleasure

(Hobbes's sudden glory) to think how by the mere laws of life we had completely won and Oldy had completely lost. For here were we with our stomachs full of sandwiches, sitting in the sun and wind, while he had been in hell these ten years.

We drove on and had tea at Aylesbury—dizzy by now and stupid with fresh air—and got to Oxford before seven. On Saturday . . . W. and I (after I had done the lunch wash up) biked to Wantage Road where he wanted to take a photo of the fastest train in England. We did this successfully and looked out for a suitable place for tea on the return journey. A countryman told us that there was no pub near, but that we could get tea at the—it sounded like Dog House. We both felt sure there could be no place called the dog house, yet presently found it. Here we had strange adventures. I rang at the closed door—it is a little red house under a woodside— and waited for ten minutes: then rang again. At last a very ancient beldame appeared. I asked if we could have some tea. She looked hard at me and asked 'Are you golfers?': on my answering 'no' she shut the door softly and I could hear her hobbling away into the bowels of the house. I felt like Arthur at Orgoglio's Castle. Anon the ancient dame appeared again and looking even harder at me asked me a second time what I wanted. I repeated that we wanted some tea. She brought her face closer to mine and then with the air of one who comes at last to the real point asked '*How long* did you want it for?' I was quite unable to answer this question but by God's grace the witch left me *multa parantem dicere* and hobbled away once more. This time she left the door open and we walked in and found our way to a comfortable dining room where a plentiful and quite unmagical tea was presently brought us.

We sat here for a very long time. A storm of wind got up (raised, I make no doubt, by our hostess, who by the by, may have been the matriarchal dreadfulness) and the ivy lashed the windows. On the next day, Sunday, we went to bathe at Parson's Pleasure ... W. left us on Monday ...

9–16 July 1924

I spent most of this time looking up the books I was to examine in ... This was the first time I had looked into Macaulay for many years: I hope it will be many years before I read him again. It's not the style (in the narrower sense) that's the trouble—it's a very good style within its own limits. But the man is a humbug—a vulgar, shallow, self-satisfied mind: absolutely inaccessible to the complexities and delicacies of the real world. He has the journalist's air of being a specialist in everything, of taking in all points of view and being always on the side of the angels: he merely annoys a reader who has had the least experience of *knowing* things, of what knowing is like. There is not two pence worth of real thought or real nobility in him. But he isn't dull ...

TO HIS FATHER: **from University College** (after reading and correcting many School Certificate essays)

[27 July 1924]

I should have answered your last generous letter earlier but for the last three weeks I have been busy from morning to night examining. To examine is like censoring letters in the army or (I fancy) like hearing confessions if you are a priest. Beforehand it seems interesting—a curious vantage point from which to look into the minds of a whole crowd of people 'as if we were God's spies': but it turns out to be cruelly dull. As the censoring subaltern finds that every man in his platoon says the same things in his letters home, and as the priest, no doubt, finds that all his penitents confess the same sins, so the examiner finds that out of hundreds of girls and boys of all social classes from all parts of England, scarcely a dozen make themselves memorable either for original ideas or amusing mistakes.

The paper which I corrected most of was on *David Copperfield* and Kinglake's *Eothen:* and the first question was 'Contrast the characters of Uriah Heep and Mr Micawber'. So one takes up one's first sheet of answers and reads 'Uriah Heep is the finished type of a rogue: Mr Micawber on the other hand is the portrait of a happy go lucky debtor.' Then one plods on to the same question answered by the next candidate and reads 'Mr Micawber is the finished portrait of a happy go lucky debtor, while Uriah Heep is a typical (or perhaps "typicle") rogue.' And so it goes on through all the weary hours of the day till one's brain reels with Uriah Heep and Mr Micawber and one would willingly thrash the editor or whoever it is who has supplied them with that maddening jargon about the 'finished portrait of a rogue'.

I must set down on the credit side the fact of having been thus forced to read *Eothen*. I know of course that it has stood in red cloth, skied near the ceiling in the bookcase nearest the study door, since I can remember—unmoved by twenty spring cleanings, the Russian Revolution and the fall of the German Monarchy. I don't know whether this is one of the books you have advised me to read or not. It is even possible (such things have been known) that *Eothen* has lived there all these years in the study bookcase undisturbed not only by the Russian revolution, but equally by the hand of its owner . . . At any rate I most strongly advise you to give yourself a very pleasant evening by taking down Kinglake. If you don't feel a stomach for the whole thing at least read the interview between the Pasha and the 'possible policeman of Bedfordshire' in the first chapter and the Surprise of Sataleih in the last, for humour: and for ornate prose I should recommend the opening of the chapter on Constantinople, the part beginning 'the stormy bride of the Doge is the bowing slave of the Sultan'. The Colonel was over here shortly before my durance began and I have converted him to my new idol: so you must by all means 'come in' and share the spoil—unless of course you really had read it already . . .

I had almost forgotten to say that on the occasion of W.'s last visit I went over to Colchester for the night in order to come back with him in the sidecar. The new bike is a noble machine and we stopped to eat our lunch at a railway bridge near Watford which used to be the regular goal of our walks when we were at Wynyard. Here we sat on the slope of the cutting looking down on the L.N.W.R. main line on which we used to gaze in the old days when it was the only object of interest in the landscape. It was strange to find that the said landscape was quite an ordinary, even pleasant English countryside: and it was almost impossible to realize the appalling blankness and hostility which it once wore. In those days we had not grown used to the English colouring (so different from Ulster): our interests and appreciation of nature were limited to the familiar: rivers might wind and trees bloom in vain—one saw it all only as an abominable mass of earth dividing one by hundreds of miles from home and the hills and the sea and ships and everything a reasonable man could care for. We were puzzled for some time as to why the line was invisible from a fence on which we used to sit to watch it: until W. hit on the simple truth that some trees which had been little trees in 1909 had become big trees in 1924. That's the sort of moment that makes the youngest of us feel old . . .

TO HIS FATHER: from University College
Postmark: 28 August 1924

When I came to the part in your letter where you speak of how God does temper the wind to the shorn lamb I fairly laid it down and laughed. A joke by letter seldom has this effect: it usually arrives but the ghost of the spoken joke—it reaches the intellect without disturbing the face. But the image of Warnie as a shorn lamb, and of the expression with which he would say 'What d'you mean?' if you tried to explain to him *why* he was funny as a shorn lamb, was too much for me. But though you didn't mention it, I know very well *who* tempered the wind in the present case.

I am plodding on with my fourteen lectures—I am at number five, or rather have just finished it. I think I said before that I am not writing them *in extenso,* only notes. The extemporary element thus reproduced is dangerous for a beginner, but *read* lectures send people to sleep and I think I must make the plunge from the very beginning and learn to *talk,* not to recite. I practise continually, expanding my notes to imaginary audiences, but of course it is difficult to be quite sure what will fill an hour. Perhaps I will experiment on you when I come home! The laborious part is the continual verifying of references and *quoting*. As Johnson says 'a man can write pretty quickly when he writes from his own mind: but he will turn over one half a library to make one book.'[110] And of course when one is trying to *teach* one can take nothing for granted. Hitherto I have always talked or read to people to whom I could say 'You remember Bradley's stunt about judgement' or 'The sort of business you get at the beginning of Kant'. But of course that won't do now—and the deuce of it is that when you actually look the passage up you always find that they either say more or less than you want. Consequently I spend my days running from library to library, or hunting things from the index of one book to another. By the way, in *oral* instruction, how many times do you have to say the same thing before people tumble to it? You should be able to answer that.

While it comes into my head—a propos of the photo of Warnie bathing—I take it it is the one of him *floating* which he showed me: telling me at the same time that one of his colleagues had remarked 'It is one of the sights of the summer to see Lewis *anchored* off the coast' . . .

TO HIS FATHER: from University College

[15 October 1924]
My maiden lecture yesterday went off alright in a sense— the only difficulty was the audience. They put me down for

---

[110] James Boswell, *The Life of Samuel Johnson*, 6 April 1775 (slightly misquoted).

the same time at which a much more important lecture by an established man was being held elsewhere. They also, by a misprint, put me down as lecturing at Pembroke, not at Univ. In these conditions it is not to be wondered at if no one came at all. As a matter of fact *four* people turned up! This of course is not very encouraging. But I shall not let it come between me and my rest. Better men than I have begun in the same way and one must be patient. As long as Mr Pritchard's highly essential lectures are held at the same time as mine, I can hardly expect anyone to come to me.[111] Don't be worried about it.

Otherwise everything goes well. All my new colleagues are kindness itself and everyone does his best to make me feel at home—especially dear old Poynton. I find the actual tutoring easy at the time (tho' I am curiously tired at the end of the day) and have already struck some quite good men among my pupils. I have seen only one real dud so far—a man who celebrated his first hour with me by telling me as many obvious lies as I have ever heard in a short space . . . I have the College football captain among my pupils and am busy making up *that* subject also in order to be able to talk to him.

[Jack and Warren travelled to Belfast by motorcycle and sidecar and were with their father from 23 December to 10 January 1925. They took a few days' excursion in

---

[111] Harold Arthur Pritchard (1871–1937) who was lecturing on Philosophy was a Fellow of Hertford College 1895–98, a Fellow and Tutor of Trinity College 1898–1924, and White's Professor of Moral Philosophy 1928–37.

the South of England before returning to Oxford on 13 January.]

TO HIS FATHER: from University College

Postmark: 11 February 1925

You should have heard from me before, but I have hardly been in a position to write. I spent the first fortnight of the term in bed with flu. I am very much afraid my organism is acquiring the *habit* of getting this troublesome complaint every time it becomes prevalent. As you have had it yourself and as you doubtless remember the curious psychological results it produces in the convalescent stage—the depression and dead alive feeling—I need not describe them . . .

W. and I had a magnificent ride back and I was sorry he had not his camera with him. From Shrewsbury to Oxford was all perfect: an orgy of woods, hills, broad rivers, grey castles, Norman abbeys and towns that have always been asleep. I wish I could describe Ledbury to you. It consists of about four broad streets in which every second house is of the Elizabethan type, timbered and white, with gables to the front. It is set in the middle of delightful rolling country and the end of the Malvern hills comes down to the town end. Best of all, no one has yet 'discovered' it: it has not become a show place and the inhabitants are quite unaware that there is anything remarkable about it. Ludlow too I would like you to see: with its castle, former seat of the Earl of the Marches, where *Comus* was first performed. But after all where can you go in the South and West of England without meeting beauty?

I don't think I have much news. All goes on as usual here—that is to say very pleasantly on the whole though with some sense of strain and little leisure. My lectures have gone off rather better this term though it's still very much a case of 'fit audience though few'. My most persevering auditor is an aged parson (I can't imagine where he comes from) who takes very copious notes and darts dagger glances at me every now and then. Some one suggests that he is a spy sent out by the board of faculties to detect young lecturers in heresy—and that he keeps on coming with the idea that if he gives me enough rope I shall hang myself in the end. There is also a girl who draws pictures half the time—alas, I have done so myself! ...

TO HIS FATHER: from University College

[April 1925]

I am sorry to hear of your 'rotten Easter': mine was redeemed by the glorious two days trip with Warnie. Otherwise I was pretty well hustled during the vacation, working against time to prepare for this term, which, to tell the truth I begin in rather a tired state. As you once said to me, 'Talking is the most exhausting of all occupations'.

The trip was delightful. I was pleased to revisit Salisbury and see it more thoroughly. I well remember my former visit. 'It was a Sunday' and *not* very early in the morning, as you doubtless recollect, when we stopped for a few minutes in Uncle Hamilton's headlong career and heard morning prayer going on in the Cathedral. At that time I did not agree with you and cared for it less than Wells or Winchester.

This time as we came into sight of Salisbury, where, on those big rolling downs that spire can be seen from fifteen miles away, I began to have my doubts. Later, when we had had tea and strolled into the Close I decided that it was very good in its own way but not in my favourite way. But when we came out again and saw it by moonlight after supper, I was completely conquered. It was a perfect spring night with the moon nearly full, and not a breath of wind stirring nor a sound from the streets. The half light enhanced its size, and the sharp masses of shadow falling in three great patches from the three main faces of one side emphasized the extraordinary simplicity in which it differs so from say, Wells.

That is the real difference I think, and what repelled me at first: the others, mixed of a dozen styles, have grown from century to century like organic things and the slow history of secular change has been built into them. One feels the *people* behind them more: the nameless craftsmen in this or that gargoyle which is different from every other.

Salisbury, on the other hand, is the idea of a master mind, struck out at once for ever. Barring mechanical difficulties it might have been built in a day. Doesn't Kipling talk of the Taj-Mahal as 'a sigh made marble'? On the same metaphor one might say that Wells is an age made into stone and Salisbury a petrified moment. But what a moment! The more one looks the more it satisfies. What impressed me most—the same thought has come into everyone's head in such places—was the force of Mind: the thousands of tons of masonry held in place by an idea, a religion: buttress, window, acres of carving, the very lifeblood of men's work, all piled up there and gloriously *useless* from the side of the base utility for which alone we build now. It really is typical of a change—the mediaeval town where the shops and houses huddle at the foot of the cathedral, and the modern city where the churches huddle between the sky scraping offices and the appalling 'stores'. We had another good look at it in the morning light after breakfast—when the plump and confident members of the feathered chapter cooing in the very porch added a new charm. W. says that Salisbury is Barset: if so, we must have been standing near where the Warden said 'I'm afraid I shall never like Mrs Proudie' and the Archdeacon took off his hat to 'let a cloud of steam escape'.

On our run that day we stopped at Stonehenge—a very fine morning and intensely quiet except for a battery practising over the next ride. It was the first time I had heard a gun fired since I left France, and I cannot tell you how odd the sensation was. For one thing it seemed much louder and more sinister and generally unpleasant than I had expected: as was perhaps natural for the general tendency of memory to minimize, and also from the solitude and quiet of the place.

I thought (as I had thought when we revisited Watford) how merciful it would be if we could sometimes forsee the future: how it would have carried me through many a long working night in the trenches if I could have seen myself 'seven years on' smoking my pipe in the oldest place in the old, safe, comfortable English fields where guns fire only at targets. But on the whole, however, it would not be a comfortable priveledge: though I have no doubt at all that it is accorded to some—but like all these mysterious leaks through of Something Else into our experience it seems to come without rhyme or reason, indifferently chosen for the trivial or the tragic occasion. I don't know why I have blundered into this subject, which may not interest you: you must put it down as a momentary eruption of that sense of irremediable ignorance and bewilderment which is becoming every year more certainly my permanent reaction to things. Whatever else the human race was made for, it at least was not made to know.

This is my last term 'in the bond' at Univ. and there is still no word of the Fellowship. I begin to be afraid that it is not coming at all. A Fellowship in English is announced at Magdalen and of course I am applying for it, but without any serious hopes as I believe much senior people including my own old English tutor are in for it. If he gets it I may get some of the 'good will of the business': I mean some of the pupils at Univ., Exeter and elsewhere whom he will have to abandon. These continued hopes deferred are trying, and I'm afraid trying for you too. About money, if you will put in £40—if you think this is reasonable—I shall be on the pig's back.

My best pupil is in great trouble. He went down in the middle of last term to attend his father's deathbed. He came up late at the beginning of this term, having been detained at home while his mother was operated on for cancer. To make matters worse the poor fellow has been left very badly off by his father's death, and it was even doubted last term whether he would be able to go on with his course. It is really extraordinary how long troubles are in letting go when they have once fastened on an individual or a house. If only he had a decent chance he would almost certainly get a first: he is in addition a very modest decent chap. One feels very helpless in coming continually into contact with such a case. If I were an older man, or again if I were his contemporary I might be able to convey some sense of sympathy: but the slight difference in age, or some defect in myself makes an insurmountable barrier and I can only feel how trivial or external and even impertinent my 'philosophy' must seem to him at such a moment.

I am sorry if this is rather a scrappy letter—and likewise rather smudged and meanly written. I have been writing in pauses between pupils, and odd moments. You must not think that I am forgetful in my long silences. I have often things to say to you day by day, but in the absence of *viva voce* conversation they die away and the time and mood for a set letter do not come so easily.

I have been into Hall and common room afterwards and heard an interesting thing. Do you remember Mrs Asquith's saying in that detestable autobiography that she once asked Jowett if he had ever been in love? He replied 'Yes' and being asked what the lady was like, replied 'Violent—very violent.'[112] Apparently the lady was really Florence Nightingale. Poynton and Farquharson both knew of it. For her 'violence' see Strachey in *Eminent Victorians*. The story—a strange tragicomedy—seems to have been common property. Both the parties were irascable and opinionated and quarrelled nearly as often as they met: and yet the affair hung on for a long time . . .

[On 20 May 1925 Mr Lewis recorded the following incident in his diary:

---

[112] *The Autobiography of Margot Asquith* (1920), vol. I, p. 118.

While I was waiting for dinner Mary came into the study and said 'The Post Office is on the phone'. I went to it.

'A telegram for you.'

'Read it.'

'Elected Fellow Magdalen. Jack.'

'Thank you.'

I went up to his room and burst into tears of joy. I knelt down and thanked God with a full heart. My prayers have been heard and answered.]

TO HIS FATHER: from University College

26 May 1925

First, let me thank you from the bottom of my heart for the generous support, extended over six years, which alone has enabled me to hang on till this. In the long course I have seen men at least my equals in ability and qualifications fall out for the lack of it. 'How long can I afford to wait' was everybody's question: and few had those at their back who were both able and willing to keep them in the field so long. You have waited, not only without complaint but full of encouragement, while chance after chance slipped away and when the goal receded furthest from sight. Thank you again and again. It has been a nerve racking business, and I have hardly yet had time to taste my good fortune with a deliberate home felt relish.

First of all, as I told you, I thought that I had my own tutor Wilson as a rival, which would have made the thing hopeless. But that I found to be a false rumour. Then I wrote to Wilson and Gordon (the Professor of English Literature)[113] for testimonials, relying on them as my strongest supports. Within twenty-four hours I had the same answer from both. They were very sorry. If only they had known I was going in for it ... they thought I had definitely abandoned English for philosophy. As it was, they had already given their support to my friend Coghill of Exeter. Once more, they were exceedingly sorry, and remained mine sincerely etc.

This was enough to make anyone despair: but mark how the stars sometimes fight for us. Two days later came news that Coghill had been offered a fellowship by his own College and had withdrawn from the field. Wilson's testimonial—a very good one—came by the next post. Gordon said he wouldn't write anything as he was going to be consulted personally by the Magdalen people, but he would *back* me. This of course was much better than the testimonial. Still, I hardly allowed myself to hope. Then came a letter from Gordon—'CONFIDENTIAL'. 'I was asked my opinion about the candidates yesterday and I put my money on you. I think your chances good, but of course one never knows what the spin of the coin may do in such things.' This, I said to myself, is at least nearer than I've ever got before: but don't hope, don't build on it.

Then came an invitation to dine at Magdalen on Sunday a fortnight ago. This showed only that I was one of the

---

[113] George Stuart Gordon (1881–1942) had been Fellow in English at Magdalen College from 1907 until he became a professor of English in Leeds. He returned to Oxford to become Merton Professor of English 1922–28 after which he was President of Magdalen College from 1928 until he died.

possibles. Then came the little problems that seem so big at the time. Was Magdalen one of the Colleges where they wore white ties and tails, or did they wear dinner jackets and black ties? I asked the Farq. and he advised white tie and tails: and of course when I got there I found every one in black ties and dinner jackets. These dinners for inspection are not exactly the pleasantest way of spending one's evening—as you may imagine. You can hardly say 'He'll enjoy it when he gets there'. But I must say they carried off as well as could be asked a situation which must be irksome to the hosts as well as to the guest. So far so good.

Then came a spell of thundery weather of the sort that makes a man nervous and irritable even if he has nothing on his mind: and the news that Bryson and I were the two real candidates.[114] Bryson comes from home and knows Arthur: but of course I mention his name in the strictest possible secrecy. One afternoon, in that week, I saw the said Bryson emerging from Magdalen and ('so full of shapes is fancy')[115] felt an unanswerable inner conviction that he had won and made up my mind on it.

On the Saturday Warren (I) met me in the street and had a vague tho' kindly conversation with me.[116] On Monday I had a very abrupt note from him asking me to see him

---

[114] John Norman Bryson (1896–1976) was educated at the Queen's University in Belfast and at Merton College, Oxford. He was a lecturer at Balliol, Merton and Oriel Colleges from 1923 to 1940, and then Fellow and Tutor in English Literature at Balliol College 1940–63.

[115] Shakespeare, *Twelfth Night*, I, i, 14.

[116] Sir Thomas Herbert Warren (1853–1930) had taken Firsts in Mods and Greats at Balliol College. He became a Fellow of Magdalen in 1877 and was President 1885–1928.

on Tuesday morning, with the curious addition 'It is most important'. I didn't like it at all: it suggested some horrible hitch. Was I going to be viva-d on Anglo–Saxon verbs or asked my views on the Thirty Nine Articles? We had thunder that night, but a poor storm and not enough to clear the air: and Tuesday rose up a grey clammy morning when one sweats every time one moves and the big blue bottles settle on your hands. This sounds like writing it up to an exciting conclusion: but it *was* a nasty morning and it *was* quite exciting enough for me at the time.

I got to Magdalen, and, would you believe it, he kept me waiting for *half an hour* before he saw me. The choir boys were practising in the tower close by. When he did see me it turned out to be all formalities. They were electing tomorrow and thought me the 'strongest and most acceptable candidate'. Now *if* I were elected would I agree to this, and would I be prepared to do that, and did I understand that the terms of the fellowship implied so and so. The only thing of the slightest importance was 'would I be prepared in addition to the English pupils, to help with the philosophy'. (This, I imagine, stood me in good stead: probably no other candidate had done English as well as philosophy.) I need hardly say that I would have agreed to coach a troupe of performing bagbirds in the quadrangle: but I looked very wise and thought over all his points and I hope let no subservience appear. He then gave me a long talk about the special needs of Magdalen undergraduates—as if they were different from any others!—all as if I had been elected, but without saying I had been. During the whole interview he was cold and dry and not nearly so agreeable as he had been on the Saturday. He finally dismissed me with a request that I would hang about Univ. the following afternoon in case I were called for.

And then next day—about 2.30—they telephoned for me and I went down. Warren saw me, told me I had been elected and shook hands: since, he has written me a very nice letter of congratulations saying that he believes they may congratulate themselves. It is a fine job as our standards go: starting at £500 a year with 'provision made for rooms, a *pension,* and dining allowance'. The election for five years only in the first case of course means only that in five years they have the chance of getting rid of you if you turn out 'hardly one of our successes'. One hopes, in the ordinary course of events, to be re-elected.

A cat 'met me in the day of my success' and bit me deeply in the right thumb while I was trying to prevent it from attacking a small dog. In fact, to go on with the Shakespearian allusion, I came 'between the fell incensed points of mighty opposites'.[117] By dint of poultices I have now reduced the inflammation, and this is the first day I have been able to write with ease. It would have been better sooner if I had not been forced daily to answer as best I could the kind congratulations which have reached me. I must cut it short now. It has been an egotistical letter, but you asked for it. Once more, with very hearty thanks and best love . . .
(1) I mean the President of Magdalen of course, not Big Brother.

---

[117] *Hamlet,* V, ii, 60–61.

TO HIS FATHER: from University College

14 August [1925]

The only other event of importance since I last wrote has been my formal 'admission' at Magdalen. It is a formidable ceremony and not entirely to my taste. Without any warning of what was in store for me, the Vice-President (a young fellow called Wrong whom I have since got to know on the Cambridge jaunt)[118] ushered me into a room where I found the whole household—it is large at Magdalen. Warren was standing and when Wrong laid a red cushion at his feet I realized with some displeasure that this was going to be a kneeling affair. Warren then addressed me for some five minutes in Latin. I was able to follow some three-quarters of what he said: but no one had told me what response I ought to make and it was with some hesitation that I hasarded *do fidem* as a reply—copying the formula for taking your M.A. This appeared to fill the bill. I was then told (in English) to kneel. When I had done so Warren took me by the hand and raised me with the words 'I wish you joy'. It sounds well enough on paper but it was hardly impressive in fact: and I tripped over my gown in rising. I now thought my ordeal at an end: but I was never more mistaken in my life. I was sent all round the table and every single member in turn shook my hand and repeated the words 'I wish you joy'. You can hardly imagine how odd it sounded by the

---

[118] Edward Murray Wrong (1889–1928), a scholar of Balliol, took a First Class in Modern History in 1913 and was elected a Fellow of Magdalen in 1914. He was Vice-Principal of Manchester College of Technology 1916–19 after which he returned to Magdalen.

twenty-fifth repetition. English people have not the talent for graceful ceremonial. They go through it lumpishly and with a certain mixture of defiance and embarrassment as if everyone felt he was being rather silly and was at the same time ready to shoot the first man who said so. In a French or Italian university now, this might have gone off nobly . . .

In a way I share your regret that when the opening came it did not come at Univ. I shall never find a common room that I did not like better: and every break in the continuity of ones associations is in some degree unpleasant. No one likes, even at my age, to see any slice of life being finally turned over to the past.

As to the other change—from Philosophy to English—I share your feeling less. I think you are mistaken in supposing that the field is less crowded in Philosophy: it seems so to you only because you have more chance of seeing the literary crowd. If you read *Mind* and one or two other periodicals of the sort as regularly as you read the *Literary Supplement,* you would probably change your view. I think things are about equal in that way. On other grounds I am rather glad of the change. I have come to think that if I had the mind, I have not the brain and nerves for a life of pure philosophy. A continued search among the abstract roots of things, a perpetual questioning of all that plain men take for granted, a chewing the cud for fifty years over inevitable ignorance and a constant frontier watch on the little tidy lighted conventional world of science and daily life—is this the best life for temperaments such as ours? Is it the way of health or even of sanity? There is a type of man, bull necked and self satisfied in his 'pot bellied equanimity' who urgently needs that bleak and questioning atmosphere. And what is a tonic to the Saxon may be a debauch to us Celts. As it certainly is to the Hindoos.

I am not condemning philosophy. Indeed in turning from it to literary history and criticism, I am conscious of a descent: and if the air on the heights did not suit me, still I have brought back something of value. It will be a comfort to me all my life to know that the scientist and the materialist have not the last word: that Darwin and [Herbert] Spencer undermining ancestral beliefs stand themselves on a foundation of sand; of gigantic assumptions and irreconcilable contradictions an inch below the surface. It leaves the whole thing rich in possibilities: and if it dashes the shallow optimisms it does the same for the shallow pessimisms. But having once seen all this 'darkness', a darkness full of promise, it is perhaps best to shut the trapdoor and come back to ordinary life: unless you are one of the really great who can see into it a little way—and I was not.

At any rate I escape with joy from one definite drawback of philosophy—its solitude. I was beginning to feel that your first year carries you out of the reach of all save other professionals. No one sympathizes with your adventures in that subject because no one understands them: and if you struck treasure trove no one would be able to use it. But perhaps this is enough on this subject. I hope you are well and free from corns, sore gums and all other 'crosses' . . .

[On Jack's next visit with his father they got on better than they had in a long time. In his diary for 13 September Mr Lewis wrote: 'Jacks arrived for

holiday. Looking very well and in great spirits.' On 1
October he wrote: 'Jacks returned. A fortnight and a
few days with me. Very pleasant, not a cloud. Went to
the boat with him. The first time I did not pay his passage money. I offered, but he did not want it.'

Following his return to Oxford Jack divided his
time between Magdalen and 'Hillsboro'. During term
he slept in his college rooms—Staircase 3, Number
3, of New Buildings—and visited the 'family' at
'Hillsboro' in the afternoons. When term ended this
was reversed and he spent his nights at 'Hillsboro'
and came into Magdalen whenever there was a need
to do so.]

TO HIS FATHER: from Magdalen College

21 October 1925

When we discussed the question of furnishing my rooms
before I left, I thought it a very remote contingency.
It was rather a crushing blow to find that I had to get
everything—and for three spacious rooms: the extent of
College's bounty being some linoleum in the smaller sitting
room and a washstand in the bedroom. It is hard to say on
what principle fellows are provided with washstands but
left to provide their own beds: unless it is a symbol of the
combined *vigilance* and purity which is so characteristic of
their corporate life. Carpets, tables, curtains, chairs, fend-
ers, fire irons, coal boxes, table covers—everything—had
to be bought in haste. It has cost me over £90, although I
was able to pick up some things second hand. It sounds an

alarming total, but I do not think I have been extravagant; the rooms certainly do not look as if they had been furnished by a plutocrat.

My external surroundings are beautiful beyond expectation and beyond hope. To live in the Bishop's Palace at Wells would be good but could hardly be better than this. My big sitting room looks north and from it I see nothing, not even a gable or spire, to remind me that I am in a town. I look down on a stretch of level grass which passes into a grove of immemorial forest trees, at present coloured with autumn red. Over this stray the deer. They are erratic in their habits. Some mornings when I look out there will be half a dozen chewing the cud just underneath me, and on others there will be none in sight—or one little stag (not much bigger than a calf and looking too slender for the weight of its own antlers) standing still and sending through the fog that queer little bark or hoot which is these beasts 'moo'. It is a sound that will soon be as familiar to me as the cough of the cows in the field at home, for I hear it day and night. On my right hand as I look from these windows is 'his favourite walk'.[119] My smaller sitting room and bedroom looks out southward across a broad lawn to the main buildings of Magdalen with the tower across it. It beats Bannaher!

As to the 'College' in the other sense—as a human society—I can say little yet. One's first impressions of a new set are changed many times in the first month. They are all very nice to me. The general tone of the place strikes

---

[119] The favourite walk of Joseph Addison (1672–1719) who had been both a pupil and a fellow at Magdalen College.

me as rather slack and flippant—I mean among the Dons—
but I may very well be mistaken. Sambo [the President]
hardly ever appears. The most surprising thing is that they
are much less formal than Univ. They don't dress for dinner
except when the President dines on which occasion a warning notice is sent round to our rooms. Again, there are an
enormous number of us compared with Univ., and we meet
much more often. Thus we breakfast and lunch in Common
Room; meals in your own rooms (which I had thought universal at Oxford) being unknown here either for Dons or
undergraduates. The latter are a little aloof from the rest
of Oxford: not entirely thro' affectation but because as a
matter of geography we are 'at the town's end': or, as someone said, we are the beginning of suburbia. I have very few
pupils at present, wh. of course is helping me to improve
my reading. They are quite nice fellows . . .

TO HIS FATHER: from Magdalen College

4 December [1925]
I have had a nasty blow—don't be alarmed, it concerns neither life, limb or reputation. I was already rather worried
about the difficulty of preparing an English lecture in the
time at my disposal, but by dint of choosing a short subject which I know well (XVIII century precursors of the
Romantic movement) I hoped to be able to acquit myself
well enough. What was my displeasure on finding, when
the rough draft of next term's lecture list was sent me, that
my old tutor Wilson was lecturing on 'English Poetry from
Thomson to Cowper'. Now of course my 'precursors', with

the exception of some critics and other prose writers, are just the poets from Thomson and Cowper. It is in fact the same subject under a different name. This means that, being neither able nor willing to rival Wilson, I am driven to concentrate on the prose people of whom at present I know very little. I have as hard a spell cut out for me between now and next term as I have ever had. Of course all the more easy and obvious subjects which will leap to your mind are long since occupied by the bigwigs.

The immediate consequence is that I am afraid I shall scarcely be able to take more than a week at home this Christmas. To compensate for this I shall try to get across at Easter. I am sorry to disappoint you (and myself): but it is only one of the many evils which I see following from this bad luck about the lecture. At the very best it means working much harder for a much poorer result. Of course no one, least of all Wilson himself, is to blame . . .

TO HIS FATHER: **from Magdalen College** (Following a visit with their father in Belfast 20–28 December Warren was posted to Woolwich.)

[5 January 1926]

Warnie and I had a rather interesting journey back. First there was the episode of the friendly and intoxicated stranger in the smoking room of the Liverpool boat: but I feel that the Colonel's pen will do that story more justice than mine. Secondly there was the amazingly erudite fellow traveller in the train. I suppose he had gathered from our conversation—W. was reading Evelyn's diaries—that we were bookish people, but he let several hours pass before he quite suddenly chipped in, in a rather apologetic manner. I surmise that he lives among people who do not share his tastes and it is a relief to him to talk about them. He did not speak with the voice of an educated man, but his reading was curious: Pepys, Evelyn, Burnet, Boswell, Macaulay, Trollope, Thackeray, Ruskin, Morris and *The Golden Bough*. He seemed to be some kind of architect or decorator.

Now this is the sort of thing I like. To have a literary conversation in the study at Leeborough or the common room at Magdalen is (by comparison) nothing, because one remains in the charmed circle of ones own set and caste: there is nothing to refute the accusation of being out of the world, of playing with things that perhaps derive a fictitious value from the chatter of specially formed groups. But to talk over the same things with a man whose aitches are uncertain in a third class carriage—this restores ones faith in the value of the written word and makes one feel suddenly at home in ones country. It is the difference between grapes in a greenhouse and a hillside of vines.

The other interesting thing in our journey was the new scenery produced by the floods. Round about Warwick (you remember Warwick) for miles at a time there was nothing but water between one hedgerow and the next—and then the little hills made into islands. A village on a rise with 'the decent church that fronts (or is it *crowns*) the neighbouring hill' has a very fine effect.

You probably spotted the enclosed picture [of Magdalen College] in today's *Times,* but I send it in case you have not. The long building to the right of the tower is 'New

Building' which Gibbon, who lived in it, called 'a stately pile' . . . You can imagine from the picture what a magnificent view I now have when the park has been converted into a lake. On a fine day when the sky makes the water blue and the wind fills it with ripples, one might almost take it for an arm of the sea. Of course I am not forgetting the serious side of the floods: but after all, what would you? I can't save the life of Dutch peasants or the pockets of Warwickshire peasants by refusing to enjoy the beauty of the thing as it appears from my window . . .

TO HIS FATHER: from Magdalen College

Postmark: 25 January 1926

As to the German measles—will you think me affected if I number a small illness among the minor pleasures of life? The early stages are unpleasant but at least they bring you to a point at which the mere giving up and going to bed is a relief. Then after twenty-four hours the really high temperature and the headache are gone: one is not well enough to get up, but then one is ill enough not to want to get up. Best of all, work is impossible and one can read all day for mere pleasure with a clear conscience.

I re-read some of my favourite Jane Austens and read for the first time that jolly, unexpected tale, *Quentin Durward.* I even took the chance of going on with my neglected Italian and got through several cantos of Boiardo: an interminable fairy-tale kind of a poet, full of dragons and distressed damsels, without the slightest moral or intellectual significance. It is suited to the atmosphere of a day in bed with the snow falling outside: the drift, the holiday from all sublunary cares. Then one returns to a primitive and natural life as regards sleeping and waking. One dozes when the doze comes unsought and if one lies castle building at night one does not mind because there is no getting up in the morning.

But of course all these delights have to be paid for: the first few days back to work when legs still ache and hours are long, are an unwelcome shock of earth—and that, I think, is the really bad part of it. I hope you are now past that stage . . .

I have given my first lecture. I suppose my various friends in the English Schools have been telling their pupils to come to it: at any rate it was a pleasant change from talking to empty rooms in Greats. I modestly selected the smallest lecture room in College. As I approached, half wondering if anyone would turn up, I noticed a crowd of undergraduates coming into Magdalen, but it was no mock modesty to assume that they were coming to hear someone else. When however I actually reached my own room it was crowded out and I had to sally forth with the audience at my heels to find another. The porter directed me to one which we have in another building across the street. So we all surged over the High in a disorderly mass, suspending the traffic. It was a most exhilirating scene. Of course their coming to the first lecture, the men to see what *it* is like, the girls to see what *I* am like, really means nothing: curiosity is now satisfied—I have been weighed, with results as yet unknown—and next week I may have an audience of five or none. Still it is something to be given a chance . . .

FROM HIS DIARY: at Magdalen College

27 May 1926

Betjemann and Valentin came with O. E. [Old English].[120]
Betjemann appeared in a pair of eccentric bedroom slippers
and said he hoped I didn't mind them as he had a blister. He
seemed so pleased with himself that I couldn't help saying
that I should mind them very much myself but that I had
no objection to *his* wearing them—a view which I believe
surprised him . . .

TO HIS FATHER: from Magdalen College

5 June 1926

I hear with delight from Warnie that you propose to visit
England this summer. Let us determine that no light reason shall be allowed to upset this plan, and no difficulty be
made into an impossibility. My idea is that I should cross to
Ireland for part of my usual time and that we shd then return
to Oxford and you spend some days with me in College.
There is a set of guest rooms on this very staircase, so we
should be very snug and able to hob nob a' nights without
going out of doors. We could dine in Common Room (not
dressed) or go to an ordinary in the town as we preferred,

---

[120] This entry gives an early glimpse of the pupil of Jack's who became the
most famous. John Betjeman (1906–85) came up to Oxford from
Marlborough. He matriculated at Magdalen in 1925 and he left in
December 1928 without a degree. His well-deserved fame as a poet led to
a Knighthood in 1969 and he was made Poet Laureate in 1972. Deric
William Valentin (1907–) was at Magdalen 1925–27. He was with Naval
Intelligence 1942–44 and is living in Italy.

and you would have an opportunity of sauntering about the city and its fields with more leisure than Uncle Hamilton's peremptory programme allowed us. Then, if possible, W. could come up for a week and we might proceed to London or elsewhere. Do make every effort to realize this plan. Now that I am in College we have a *pied à terre* in England which seems to have all the advantages and none of the drawbacks of a hotel, and which certainly ought to make visits more possible than they have ever been before. It is rather important to try and fix a date, and I should be glad to know when you think you could get away.

But I know what I do in raising the point of 'date'. At least I presume it is from you that I inherit a peculiar tendency by which a chill comes over the happiest designs as soon as a definite detail of time or place is raised. At first all is attractive and like a floating island, detached from the actual world: at the mention of a date, obstructions crowd upon the mind: arrangements to be made, difficulties to be overcome, and all the repellent lumber of packings, boats, time tables and interrupted habits rush in and 'quench the smoking flax'. The odds are that the whole scheme, if injudiciously pressed at that moment becomes a sort of bugbear. Is this a true bill? It is of me, I know only too well. The only remedy seems to be to remember that every happiness we have attained in the past depended on the lucky moments when we were not cowed by the 'lumber'. (Lord! Was there ever such a young fellow for preaching at his elders? He cannot take up his pen but a steady flow of doctrine begins. Perhaps it comes from taking pupils.)

A heavy responsibility rests on those who forage through

a dead man's correspondence and publish it indiscriminately. In those books of Raleigh's we find, as you say, letters like 'a glass of good champagne' side by side with mere squibs thrown off in high spirits or mere grumbles written when he was liverish.[121] Notice how Liverpool, India and Oxford all come up for castigation in turn. Much of this should never have seen print. The antireligious passages are odd. Something must be allowed for the mere turn of his language which was always violent and dogmatic—like Johnson . . . When all allowance has been made for the haphazard nature of casual letter writing, it remains true that there must be a flaw in a man who is always blessing or damning something or other. There are *too many exstasies* and the opposite . . .

I have been bothered into the last job I ever expected to do this term: taking a class of girls once a week at one of the women's Colleges. However, I am not engaged to be married yet, and there are always seven of them there together, and the pretty ones are stupid and the interesting ones are ugly, so it is alright. I say this because as a general rule women marry their tutors. I suppose if a girl is determined to marry and has a man alone once a week to whom she can play the rapt disciple (most fatal of all poses to male vanity) her task is done . . .

The best strike story I have heard was about engines. A train (with amateur driver) set out from Paddington for Bristol, first stop Bath. When it reached Bath *half an hour* earlier than normal express time, every single passenger got

---

[121] *The Letters of Sir Walter Raleigh (1879–1922)*, ed. Lady Raleigh, with a Preface by D. N. Smith, 2 vols (1926).

out of that train and refused to enter it again. Apparently the genius in the engine had just opened the throttle full, said to the stoker 'Carry on', and left the rest to fate . . .

FROM HIS DIARY: at Magdalen College

6 June 1926

As Hardie[122] and I were coming across to New Building we were overtaken by J. A.[123] who proposed a stroll in the walks. We went in [and] sat in the garden till it was quite dark. He was very great, telling us about his travels in the Balkans. The best things were (a) the masterful ladies (English of course) on a small Greek steamer who made such a nuisance of themselves that the Captain said 'Have you no brothers? Why have they not got someone to marry you?' and went on muttering at intervals for the rest of the evening 'It ought to have been possible to get *someone*'. (b) The Austrian minister at some unhealthy town who took J. A. and his party out for a walk on the railway line, which was the only place level enough to walk on, and beginning to balance himself on the rails, remarked sadly '*C'est mon seul sport*'. (c) The Greek clergyman who asked J. A. and his sister to tea and when they departed, accompanied them

---

[122] William Francis Ross Hardie (1902–1990) read Classics at Balliol College and was a Fellow of Magdalen 1925–26, a Fellow and Tutor in Philosophy at Corpus Christi College 1926–50 and President of Corpus Christi 1950–69.

[123] John Alexander Smith (1863–1939), who was also a Classicist, was a Fellow of Balliol from 1891 until he became Waynflete Professor of Moral and Metaphysical Philosophy 1910–36 and a Fellow of Magdalen.

back to their hotel repeating 'You will remember me?' 'Yes, certainly' said J. A. The clergyman repeated his touching request about fifteen times and each time J. A. (tho' somewhat surprised) assured him with increasing warmth that he would never forget him. It was only afterwards that they realized that the reverend gentleman was asking for a tip . . .

13 June 1926

D tired but I hope none the worse. The chief excitement today was over Henry, Dotty's tortoise, who was discovered about two hundred yards from the gate, working his passage towards the London road. He was brought back and tethered by a cord across his body, and supplied with lettuce leaves and snails, in which he took no interest. He escaped repeatedly during the day. When I buy a tortoise I shall say I want a quiet one for the ladies. Began G. K. Chesterton's *Eugenics and Other Evils.*

4 July 1926

Beginning to re-read *The Well at the World's End.* I was anxious to see whether the old spell still worked. It does — rather too well. This going back to books read at that age is humiliating: one keeps on tracing what are now quite big things in one's mental outfit to curiously small sources. I wondered how much even of my feeling for external nature comes out of the brief convincing little descriptions of mountains and woods in this book.

6 July 1926

Home for tea, with a sharp headache, at 4.30 and changed socks and shoes. Poor D felt too ill to take even a cup of tea. Afterwards I went over the revised proofs of Dymer wh. arrived today from Canto I, 30, to the end of the whole. I never liked it less. I felt that no mortal could get any notion of what the devil it was all about. I am afraid this sort of stuff is very much hit or miss, yet I think it is my only real line . . .

[Jack was unable to persuade his father to travel to Oxford for a visit. He was, however, on a holiday at 'Little Lea' 11–20 September and, so, with Mr Lewis when his long narrative poem, *Dymer,* was published by J. M. Dent on 18 September under the pseudonym 'Clive Hamilton'.

On 19 September Warren learned that he had been selected to attend a six months' course in Economics at London University beginning 4 October. He was able to travel with Jack to Belfast on 21 December to be with their father for Christmas. On 8 January 1927 Mr Lewis wrote in his diary: 'Warnie and Jacks returned tonight by Fleetwood. As the boat did not sail until 11. o.c. they stayed with me to 9.30. So ended a very pleasant holiday. Roses all the way.']

FROM HIS DIARY: at 'Hillsboro'

10 January 1927

It was a most extraordinary afternoon. Most of the sky was very pale creamy blue, and there were clouds about, of the coldest shade of dark blue I have ever seen. The further hills were exactly the same as the clouds in colour and texture. Then near the sun the sky simply turned white and the sun itself (its outline was invisible) was a patch of absolutely pure white light that looked as if it had no more power of heating than moonlight—tho' it was quite a mild day in fact. I got into a tremendously happy mood . . .

3 February 1927

Dined in and sat in common room beside J. A. who told me of a lady who had long worried him by coming up at the end of lectures to ask questions, and finally wrote offering him her hand. 'She pretended it was a joke afterwards' he said, shaking his white head. 'But it wasn't. And she wasn't the only one either. A man who lectures to women takes his life in his hand' . . .

8 February 1927

Spent the morning partly on the Edda, partly on the Realtetus. Hammered my way through a couple of pages in about an hour, but I am making some headway. It is an exciting experience when I remember my first passion for things Norse under the initiation of Longfellow (Tegner's Drapa and the Saga of K. Olaf) at about the age of nine: and its return, much stronger, when I was about thirteen, when the high priests were M. Arnold, Wagner's music, and the Arthur Rackham *Ring*. It seemed an impossible [thing] then that I shd ever come to read these things in the original. The old authentic thrill came back to me once or twice this morning: the mere names of god and giant catching my eye as I turned the pages of Zoega's dictionary was enough . . .

9 February 1927

[A. J. Carlyle] told me a lot more about the murderer of Rasputin, who had been incapable of passing any exam and had suggested to the Fark. that 'of course, he presumed, there wd be no difficulty in arranging these things in the case of a person of quality'. Being told that the organization of our exams was inflexibly democratic he exclaimed 'But what am I to do? My parents will not let me marry unless I get some sort of certificate or diploma. They will only send me to some other university.' Finally Farquharson and Carlyle made him out a parchment v. solemnly, a sort of certificate of their own ...

10 February 1927

I went on to Corpus—Hardie having sent me a note to say that the *Theaetetus* was off, but would I come round and talk. We had an evening of pleasant and desultory tomfoolery, enriched later on by the arrival of Weldon.[124] Someone started the question 'whether God can understand his own necessity': whereupon Hardie got down St Thomas's *Summa* and after ferreting in the index suddenly pronounced, without any intention of being funny, 'He doesn't understand anything'. This lead to great amusement, the best being an imaginary scene of God trying to explain the theory of vicarious punishment to Socrates. We left Hardie at about 10 to 12, and found Corpus in total darkness. Escaped in the end with difficulty ...

15 February 1927

Spent the morning on Trevelyan's *England in the Age of Wycliff* and partly in reading Gower, a poet I always turn to for pure, tho' not for intense pleasure. It's a rum thing that Morris shd have wanted so desperately to be like Chaucer and succeeded in being so exactly like Gower ...

---

[124] Thomas Dewar Weldon (1896–1958) had served in the RAF during 1915–18. He took a B.A. from Magdalen in 1921 and he was a Fellow and Tutor in Philosophy at Magdalen from 1923–58.

Back to College and read Gower till dinner time: after dinner to meet D and Maureen at the theatre where the OUDS were doing *Lear*. We decided that we wd give up going to them hereafter. It was all that sort of acting wh. fills one at first with embarrassment and pity, finally with an unreasoning personal hatred of the actors. 'Why should that damned man keep bellowing at me?' They nearly all shouted hoarsely and inarticulately. Bussed with the others to Magdalen gate, all v. cheery in spite of our wasted evening . . .

1 April 1927

I am entertaining the Mermaids tonight, drat 'em.[125] They are nothing but a drinking, guffawing cry of barbarians with hardly any taste among them, and I wish I hadn't joined them: but I don't see my way out now . . . Back to College, and had to spend most of the time getting things ready for the sons of Belial. The evening passed off alright I think: Tourneur's *Revenger's Tragedy* was read, a rotten piece of work whose merits, pretty small to begin with, were entirely lost in the continual cacking wh. greeted every bawdy reference (however tragic) and every mistake made by a reader. If one spent much time with these swine one wd blaspheme against humour itself, as being nothing but a kind of shield with which rabble protect themselves from anything wh might disturb the muddy puddle inside them.

---

[125] The Mermaid Club was founded on 19 June 1902 'to promote the reading and study of the Elizabethan and post-Elizabethan drama'.

TO HIS FATHER: from Magdalen College

30 March 1927

I was very sorry both to hear of the eclipse of the visit scheme and of your disappointing state of health. As to the former, if it stood by itself, I would reply (adapting Falstaff) 'Are there not trains? Are there not motor busses? Are there not men of war in side cars?' Why should your movements depend on the erratic and extremely hazardous aurigations of a boiler maker [Gussie Hamilton]? On the score of economy, trains have it every time. On the score of safety I can think of no method of travelling which is not superior to a seat in Uncle Gussie's car. Your account of the swelling on the right knee elicited the word 'gout' from the only knowledgeable person I mentioned it to . . .

The scene of Squeaky in the office is a masterpiece and made me roar with laughter . . . It reminds me of the President's latest exploit, when we met to elect a Proctor (it falls to each College in turn to choose one of its own Fellows as Proctor). When the election had been made the President said that a formal notice had to be sent to the Vice-Chancellor at once 'so perhaps Mr Benecke' (Benecke is about sixty years of age) 'you wouldn't mind going round: and then you must ring at the door and hand it to the maid'. As some one said, it only needed the additional injunctions, 'and remember to wipe your feet and take a clean handkerchief' to make it really complete. While I'm on this, I must tell you another. We are putting up a new building. In the committee that met to discuss it, someone suggested an architect's name, adding by way of explanation, 'that's the man who built Liverpool Cathedral'. To which the

President at once retorted with an air of closing the matter, 'Oh, I don't think we want anything quite so large as that'.

He has at last announced his intention of retiring, so I suppose we shall live in the excitement of an election for the next year. He has certainly had a wonderful run for his money, and tho' a very laughable, is also a very loveable old fellow. He had the ludicrous, without the odious side of snobbery. He may have reverenced a Prince or a Duke too much, but never in his life did he despise or snub a poor scholar from a grammar school. When snobbery consists *only* of the admiring look upward and *not* of the contemptuous look downward, one need not be hard on it. A laugh—no unfriendly laugh—is the worst it deserves. After all, this kind of snobbery is half of it mere romance . . .

We live in the most absurd age. I met a girl the other day who had been teaching in an infant school (boys and girls up to the age of six) where the infants are taught the theory of Evolution. Or rather the Headmistress's version of it. Simple people like ourselves had an idea that Darwin said that life developed from simple organisms up to the higher plants and animals, finally to the monkey group, and from the monkey group to man. The infants however seem to be taught that 'in the beginning was the Ape' from whom all other life developed—including such dainties as the Brontosaurus and the Iguanadon. Whether the plants were supposed to be descendants of the ape I didn't gather. And then people talk about the credulity of the middle ages!

A propos of this can you tell me who said 'Before you begin these studies, I should warn you that you need much more *faith* in science than in theology'. It was Huxley or

Clifford or one of the nineteenth-century scientists, I think. Another good remark I read long ago in one of E. Nesbitt's fairy tales—'Grown ups know that children can believe almost anything: that's why they tell you that the earth is round and smooth like an orange when you can see perfectly well for yourself that it's flat and lumpy' . . .

I dined the other night at an Italian Professor's, who is a Fellow of Magdalen, and sat next to a Frenchwoman who has met Mussolini. She says he is a rhetorician, and escapes from questions he doesn't want to answer into a cloud of eloquence. I asked if she thought him a charlatan. She said no: he quite believes all his own gas, like a school boy, and is carried away by it himself. It interested me very much as being true to type—Cicero must have been just that sort of man . . .

I quite see that the hotel in Donegal is in some ways unattractive. But temperance and plain diet are to be had everywhere. May I suggest that nothing hinders—indeed the Lenten season encourages—you and the Colonel to make Leeborough during the coming week into a *temperance hotel* with *plain but plentiful food*. Dumb bells and 'Instant Postum' you know.

[Jack and Warren were anxious about their father's health although it was not clear what was wrong. Mr Lewis was delighted when Warren suddenly showed up at 'Little Lea' on 26 March and, using one of his son's nicknames, he wrote in his diary: 'Badge arrived on a flying visit after finishing his course of Economics at London University. Well and cheerful, and good company.'

Warren reported to Woolwich on 2 April and two days later he learned that he was ordered to Aldershot on 7 April in preparation for sailing to Shanghai. On Wednesday the 6th he took his books and other belongings to Oxford and he spent the night with Jack. He arrived in Southampton on 11 April and he sent Mr Lewis a postcard of the troopship *Derbyshire* on which he was sailing. On it he wrote: 'Just off (2.30). Double berth outside cabin to myself. Good bye, Warren.' He feared that he might not see his father again.]

TO HIS BROTHER: from 'Hillsboro'

26 April 1927

I arrived back from my travels at lunch time yesterday and found your letter, posted at Gib. [Gibraltar], awaiting me. It had come in fact the day after I left. It left me with a fine impression of boundless leisure and sea air, that is particularly tantalizing in view of the recollection that term begins on Friday. The arrival of income tax forms this morning drives home my irritation with this hanky-panky which keeps a few hundreds of self-indulgent fellows like you fooling about in the Mediterranean on my money in order to fill the pockets of the 'China Merchants'. However, you may be in less pleasant circumstances by the time this reaches you, so I must suppress the note of envy. Still, provided that you don't meet with a war in China, every ordinary boredom and discomfort which may await you is a price almost worth paying for a free trip half round the world, well fed, unworked, and in tolerably congenial society. (You must be putting on flesh at a desperate rate.)

I thought we had mentioned Squire Western's choice of table talk before [in Fielding's *Tom Jones*]. It goes to the root of the matter, doesn't it? By the way I have never been able to share that popular feeling about Western as a fine type of bluff, honest, genial Englishman: he seems to me one of the four or five most intolerable people in fiction (I mean to meet: of course he is excellent in a book). *Tom Jones* goes far to explain why Johnson and his set didn't like the country. I can quite imagine that a countryside of highwaymen and the rural jokes of the period, inhabited by Westerns and Blifils would have led him to 'abstract his mind and think of Tom Thumb':[126] for one can hardly imagine him knocking them down with folios. At least, if he had made the attempt, he would have liked the country even less after it than before it. He would have dismissed Mr Square as a infidel dog, and I don't feel that he would have got on with Thwackum. Sophia is good. She comes during that lucid interval when good heroines were possible in novels written by men, when the restoration tradition by which a heroine must be a whore was dead, and the Victorian tradition by which she must be a fool had not been born.

Now for my own adventures. I was joined [on 19 April] at Oxford station by two others and we proceeded together to Goring.[127] One of them was new to the game and turned up

---

[126] Percival Merritt, *The True Story of the So-Called Love Letters of Mrs Piozzi* (1927), p. 70.

[127] The friends who met Jack in Oxford for a walk on the Berkshire Downs were Owen Barfield and Cecil Harwood. They were joined at Goring by Walter Ogilvie 'Wof' Field (1893–1957) who came up to Trinity College, Oxford, from Marlborough College in 1912. He left to

carrying a Tommies pack filled square like a tommy's pack, for inspection. On the way we extracted from it a large overcoat, a sponge, four shirts, a heavy tin mug holding about a pint, two strong metal cigarette cases of pudaita proportions, and a number of those insane engines which some people associate with holidays. You know—the adaptable clasp knife which secrets a fork at one end and a spoon at the other, but in such a way that you could never really use the fork and the spoon together—and all those sort of things. Having recovered from our delighted laughter and explained that we were going to walk in an English county and not in Alaska, we made up the condemned articles into a parcel wh. we compelled him to post home from Goring. It weighed about seven pounds. Our fourth met us at Goring station.

After tea in the garden of the lock keeper at Goring lock—we ate it sitting just beside the weir, dipping our hands into the water and enjoying the rush and the noise—we set out N.N.W. In half an hour the suburbanity of Goring was out of sight. We soaked for a long time in a winding valley with all the bigness of downs opening behind and the richer Chiltern country towards Henley rising in the distance. We were on the broad grass track of the Icknield Way, the grass very short and fine and perfectly dry, as it is nearly all the year round in these chalk hills. It was an afternoon of lovely sunshine with a pleasant light wind, and a lark overhead

---

join the Warwickshire Rifle Regiment in 1914, and in 1916, having continued his studies, he took a war degree from Trinity College. He was promoted to Captain in 1916 and after seeing action in France and Italy he was wounded and forced to retire in 1919. In 1926 he became a teacher at the Rudolf Steiner School in Forest Row, Sussex.

displayed all its accomplishments. That night we slept at East Ilsley which (I think) you and I went through on our way to Salisbury.

We spent nearly the whole of Wednesday [20 April] following the Icknield Way along the northern edge of the downs, overlooking the Wantage valley on our right. Around us, and to our left, the country had all the same character: close smooth grass, very pale in colour, deliciously springy to the foot: chalk showing through here and there and making the few ploughed pieces almost cream colour: and, about three to a mile, clumps of fir, whose darkness made them stand out very strikingly from the low tones of the ground. The extent of prospect was (or seemed to be) larger than any I have seen, even from the highest hills I have been on—just wave after wave of down, and then more of them, for ever. The air is very clear here and one sometimes sees a hay stack or a farm on a ridge, so distinct and at the same time so remote that it is like something seen through the wrong end of a telescope. We had tea at Lambourn and slept at Aldbourne.

Thursday [21 April] opened with discussions. A survey of the maps showed a lamentable discrepancy between the route we wanted to follow and the possible places for lunch. Then emerged the dark and hideous prospect of 'taking' lunch. Perfectly simple you know. Buy some bread and cheese before we start and have lunch where we like. Makes you independant you know. Drinks? Oh, get a few oranges if you don't feel inclined to carry a bottle of beer in your pack for the first ten miles. I need hardly say that our novice—the Knight of the Adaptable Jack Knife—was entirely in favour of a scheme which promised to restore his original conception. I of course, who had seen days spoiled this way before, was the head of the opposition. The wrong party won. We stuffed our packs with bread, butter, cheese and oranges. The only thing I look back on with satisfaction was that the butter, at any rate, was not in my pack. Then we set off.

The first mile made us thoroughly aware of the fact that the wind (wh. had been in our faces since Goring) had risen to a gale. The next three miles left no one in any doubt of the fact that when a strong wind blows in your face all day, it parches your throat and chaps your lips without cooling your body. We were now in sight of 'Barberry Castle', a Roman Camp, for the sake of seeing which all this folly had started. The exponents of the 'carry your lunch' school had now reached the stage of indulging in a quite unusual degree of praise of the scenery and the pleasures of walking tours, on the 'this is fine' lines. But long before we had reached the top of that disastrous camp they slunk in silence, and only the malcontents (Barfield and myself) felt inclined to talk. In fact we talked quite a lot.

When we reached the top we found ourselves in one of those places where you can neither speak for the hurricane nor open your eyes for the sun. Beyond the suggestion (mine) of performing on the wind (and the Romans) a certain physiological operation disallowed by English law and by polite conversation, we were silent here. Turning up our collars and pulling our hats down hard on our heads, we couched under a scrannel gorse bush wherever prickles and sheep dung left a space, and produced our scanty and squalid meal. The appearance of the butter faintly cheered us (all of us except the man among whose socks and pyjamas it had travelled), but it was a sight that moved mirth, not appetite. The last straw was the oranges, wh. proved to be of the tough, acrid, unjuicy type, which is useless for thirst and revolting to taste.

The midday siesta (that great essential of a day's walking) was out of the question in that abominable camp, and we set off gloomily S. W. Barfield and I dropped behind and began composing in Pope-ian couplets a satire on the people who arrange walking tours. Nothing cd have been happier. At a stroke every source of irritation was magically changed into a precious fragment of 'copy'. By the time we had walked three miles we were once more in a position to enjoy the glorious country all round us. Five o'clock found us descending a slope full of druidical stones, where we started three hares successively so close that we had nearly trodden on them, into the village of Avebury.

Avebury overwhelmed me and put me into that dreamlike state which is sometimes the reward of being very tired. Imagine a green ancient earthwork with four openings to the four points of the compass, almost perfectly circular, the wall of a British city, large enough to contain broad fields and spinneys inside its circuit, and, in the middle of them, dwarfed by its context, a modern village. Obviously here was the capital of a great king before the Roman times. We had been passing British things all day—stones, mounds, camps etc. But it was extraordinary to find a Berkshire village inside one. Here we had tea gloriously, in the orchard of an inn: and took off our shoes, and ordered a fresh pot and more hot water, and fair copied the satire and lay on our backs and talked Oxford reminiscences and smoked pipes.

Then Wof—he's the jack knife man—did a sensible thing by returning after a moment's absence and saying 'If you're not very keen on *walking* to Marlborough there's a man here with a milk cart who will take us in'. So we sat among milk cans (which are just the right angle to lean against) and bumped and rattled along the Bath road (of Pickwickian and coaching memories) into Marlborough. Field is an old Marlburian but we were too tired to let him show us the sights. He told us however (what will interest you) that the fine old Georgian building which faces you as you enter the school precincts was an inn on the Bath road in the old days. Pleasant days they must have been.

Next day [22 April] we walked about four miles into Savernake Forest. It is not to be compared with the Forest of Dean, but well worth an hour or so. It is the typically English kind of wood—nearly all big oaks with broad mossy spaces between them and deer flitting about in the distance. Leaving the forest we struck westward into the vale of Pewsey, and were threading about little woods and field-paths for an hour or so. After our windy days on the Downs this was a pleasant change: the richness of the colours, the soft burring of the wind (now harmless) in the little trees, and the flowers everywhere were specially delightful by contrast. We crossed a fine rise called Hansell Hill: a thing rising so abruptly on both sides that it was like a gigantic tumulus. From the top of this we had one of the finest views in England. Northward, the Berkshire Downs, huge even in their apparent extent, and huger to our minds because we had spent two whole days walking on them. Southward, across the valley, rose the edge of the Salisbury plain.

We came down the side of that hill over a big spur called the Giant's Grave and lunched admirably in the village of Ocue—beer and bread and cheese followed by a pot of tea, and then a game of darts: you know the apparatus for that game which one finds in pubs. Shortly after lunch we had the best 'soak'[128] I've ever had in a walk, by turning out of a little grassy lane into a wood where the grass grew soft and mossy, and there were solid clumps of primroses the size of dinner plates: not to mention a powdering of those little white flowers—wood anemones. We laid ourself flat on our back with packs under our head for pillows (for it is in the beauty of a pack that it can thus convert into a regular bed a flat ground otherwise useless for soaking): some rash attempts at conversation were ignored and we spent an hour with half shut eyes listening to the burring of the wind in the branches, and an occasional early bumble bee. The remainder of the day brought forth a bad bit of wrong map reading: but this also is among the delights of a journey: for it found us ambling into our tea stopping place along the grassy tow-path of an all but obsolete canal where we had never meant to go and which was all the better for that. We lay at Devizes: a poor inn.

Next day [23 April] we struck south across the vale of Pewsey. We expected to be bored in this low ground which divides the Berkshire Downs from Salisbury Plain: but it turned out a pleasant morning's tramp through roads with very fine beech trees and a tangle of footpaths. Even if it had been dull, who would not make sacrifices to pass through a

---

[128] 'Soak' was coined by Jack to mean sitting idle or sleepily doing nothing. By a 'soaking machine' he meant a place for these operations.

place called Cuckold's Green. (We passed Shapley Bottom two days before.) I myself was for tossing a pot of beer at Cuckold's Green, which we might have done by going two hundred yards out of our course, but the other two being both married, ruled that this was no place to rest a moment longer than we need. So did literary associations render possible a joke that the illiterate would hardly venture on. (In passing, if one had lived in the 17th century, what a horrible fate it would have been to live at Cuckold's Green. 'Your servant sir. Your wife tells me that you are carrying her to the country in a few days. Pray sir where do you live?' 'Cuckold's Green.' By the age of forty one wd be quite definitely tired of the joke.)

We lunched this side of the climb on to the Plain, and crawled up on to that old favourite afterwards. It pleased me as much as ever: more than all, after being given tea by a postmistress, with boiled eggs and bread and jam at lib., for which she wanted to take only 6d. Oddly enough, up there in the chalk of the plain, that village was almost completely under water. Our evening walk, up and down mile and mile of unfenced chalk road with smooth grey grass all round and sheep and young lambs (so numerous that in places they were deafening), and a mild setting sun in our faces, was heavenly.

But what no one can describe is the delight of coming (as we came—) to a sudden drop and looking down into a rich wooded valley where you see the roofs of a place where you're going to have supper and bed: specially if the sunset lies on the ridge beyond the valley. There is so much mixed in it: the mere physical anticipations as of a horse nearing its stable, the sense of accomplishment and the feeling of 'one more town', one further away into the country you don't

know, and the old never hackneyed romance of travelling
(not of 'travel' wh. is what you are doing and wh. no doubt
has its own different pains and pleasures). It always seems
to sum up the whole day that is behind you—give it a sort
of climax and then stow it away with the faintly melancholy
(but not unpleasant) feeling of things going past. This town I
am gassing about was Warminster . . .

Next day [24 April] we walked all morning through the
estates of the Marquis of Bath, in a very old and fine forest
on a hillside. About a mile and a half below us on the hillside
we saw the house—a rather tiresome place on the lines of
Blenheim, with three lakes—and we emerged at one o'clock
into a village just outside one of the park gates. The atmosphere here is feudal, for the hostess of our *Mittagessen* pub
would talk about nothing but His Lordship, who apparently lives here all the year round and knows everyone in
the village. We asked how old he was. 'O, we don't think
'im old', she replied, which stumped me. The rest of that day
was so intensively complex in route and so varied in scenery
(also we were so embroiled in conversation) that I give no
account of it . . . Next day we all returned home by train . . .

And now for Lamb's final division of a letter—'puns'.
I think I have only two. (1). The story of a man who was
up with me, and who was the only genuine maker of mala-
propisms I ever met: but this one I never heard till the other
day. It appears that while having tea with the 'dear Master
of University' he conducted a long conversation with the
ladies, chiefly re places to stay for one's holidays, under the
impression that the word 'salacious' meant 'salubrious'. You
can imagine the result. But what you can't imagine is that

when the Mugger himself, whose brow had been steadily darkening for some minutes (during which he had heard his daughters told that they wouldn't like Devonshire very much because it wasn't very salacious) finally decided to cut it short and broke in with 'Well Mr Robson-Scott, how do you like Oxford?' Robson-Scott turned to him with imperturbable good humour and said 'Well to tell you the truth sir, it isn't so salacious as I had hoped.'[129]

This fellow Robson indulged also—as I well remember—in a kind of complicated misfire of meaning: rather like a rarefied or quintessential p'daitaism. Two I can vouch for. When arriving with me late somewhere he observed panting, 'We might have known that it wd take us longer than it did.' Another time, in a debate, he said, 'I quite agree with Mr So-and-So's point *as far as it goes* but it goes much too far.' You will see how easily this sort of thing wd pass for sense in the heat of the moment.

(2). I don't know if this can rank as a pun, but I'll put it down. When S. P. B. Mais (whose *Diary of a Schoolmaster* we have both read) got a 3rd in English here, the examiners told him they were very sorry, but added by way of consolation that he 'was the very best Third they had ever examined'. On which Raleigh remarked 'It is bad enough for a man to get a Third: but to be pointed out as the most brilliant Third of your year is damnable.'

---

[129] William Douglas Robson-Scott (1900–80) matriculated at Univ. in 1919, and in 1923 he took a First in English Literature. He became the Professor of German Language and Literature at Birkbeck College, University of London.

TO HIS FATHER: from Magdalen College

[28 May 1927]

Your wire, which arrived this morning, contributed more to my grandeur than to my peace of mind. It contributed to my grandeur because it happened to be the third communication of an urgent nature which I had received during that hour, and the pupil who was with me, seeing me inundated with these messages and telegrams, must doubtless have supposed that I was the hub of some mighty academical, or even national intrigue. I am sorry you were bothered. I had not thought my silence had been long enough to give you serious anxiety, though it was longer than I wished. If I had written before I could only have given you a line, for the summer term is always the busiest and my days are very full . . .

Now for a more important matter. W and I both agreed that heaven and earth must be moved to get you out of Ireland this summer—preferably to some place where rheumatics are cured. The Colonel's parting instructions were given with characteristic emphasis 'Take him to Droitwich and just get him *boiled in mud* or whatever it is they do to people there.' And I agreed, and promised to do my best. I don't insist on the boiling and the mud: but I do frankly think that it would be absurd for a man who has otherwise a very tolerable constitution to sit down with 'close lipped patience, sister of despair' under rheumatism while all the natural cures (muds, waters etc.) and all the modern electrical cures remain untried. Confess that the man who could be induced to wearing zinc in his boots and drinking (what was it you were advised to drink—an onion soaked in gin, or port or mustard?) but who could not be induced to try what has cured hundreds, is in an indefensible position.

I therefore propose that part or all of my annual holiday should be spent in some such places as I have suggested with perhaps a few days here in Oxford—as our jam after our powder. I know there are difficulties. What have you ever done in which there was not? A man of your age and in your position cannot really be the slave of business engagements. I know too that the thought of an hotel in a 'spa' does not fill you with rapture: but even a troglodyte can't find the presence of strangers as painful as sciatica. And after all, once the plunge is made, would there not be a sort of holiday spirit that would descend on us in such a place and make us no unpleased spectators of the 'stir'. The change of diet alone, and of hours and of way of life is I think a pick-me-up. I know I have always found it so. Monotony is no better for the body than for the mind. Now the first essential of this scheme is to concert our movements. August would be impossible for me. That leaves September and the early part of October. Whether you have time or inclination to write me a long letter or not, please let me have a line soon giving me at least the outline of a scheme possible for you. I have really set my heart on the plan and very earnestly hope that an indulgence of my wishes and a reasonable care for yourself will combine to persuade you to the effort (it cannot really be a very great one) of making arrangements and removing obstacles. If you will fix a time for getting away I will start finding out details at once (I wish W. were here, he'd do it far better and serve you up five alternative operation orders worked out to a half minute at every station, while you waited. But alas—!)

Yes. There is no good balking the fact that this China journey is a bad business, a piece of rotten luck. I confess that when he sailed I was horribly uneasy. By this time (if I can judge at all from the papers) the chance of a war in China is greatly lessened and I am more cheerful. If the trouble clears up I don't see why he might not be home again in eighteen months or so . . .

His letters are of the greatest interest and very good. How the travels of anyone we know suddenly light up the waste places of the Atlas. I suppose the Red Sea coast is described in hundreds of books: but we had to wait till Warnie went East before we ever heard about it. (I always imagined it flat and sandy myself.)

There is no need to bother about my health, and, even when busiest, I usually get my daily walk. I work as a rule from 9 till 1, from 5 till 7.15 (when we dine) and then after dinner till about 11 or 12. This you see gives me time for a good long tramp every afternoon. Nightmares I am afraid are hereditary in more senses than the one you meant. The thing, or what is stands [for] is in the blood of not one family but of the creature called Man . . .

TO HIS BROTHER (now in China): **from 'Hillsboro'**
9 July 1927

The Term has now been over some weeks, for which I am not sorry. It produced one public event of good omen—the carrying in Congregation of a Statute limiting the number of wimmen at Oxford. The appalling danger of our degenerating into a woman's university (nay worse still, into *the* women's university, in contradistinction to Cambridge, *the* men's university) has thus been staved off. There was fierce opposition of course, our female antagonists being much more expert than we in the practice of 'whipping' in the parliamentary sense.

Since the victory the papers have been full of comment from such people as Sybil Thorndike, Lady Astor, Daisy Devoteau, Fanny Adams and other such notable educational authorities. They mostly deplore (especially in the *Daily Mirror* and the Little Ha'penny Sketch) one more instance of the unprogressiveness of those 'aged Professors'. The word 'academic' is also worked hard: tho' how the politics of an academy could, or why they should, cease to be 'academic', 'might admit of a wide conjecture'.

But the question of the age of the anti-feminists is an interesting one: and the voting (we have no secret franchise) revealed very consolatory facts. First came the very old guard, the octogenarians and the centurions, the full fed patriarchs of Corpus, the last survivors of the days when 'women's rights' were still new fangled crankery. They were against the women. Then came the very-nearly-as-old who date from the palmy days of J. S. Mill, when feminism was the new, exciting, enlightened thing: people representing, as someone said, 'the progressiveness of the "eighties".' They voted for the women. Then came the young and the post-war (I need not say I trust that I did my duty) who voted solid *against*. The arrangement is quite natural when you think it out. The first belong to the age of innocence when women had not yet been noticed: the second, to the age when they had been noticed but not yet found out: the third to us. Ignorance, romance, realism . . .

I have just read Smollet's *Roderick Random* which, as
you probably know, is our chief literary document for the
life of the navy in the 18th century ... By the way, can you
suggest why it is that when you read Boswell, Walpole's
letters, or Fanny Burney's diary you find the 18th century
a very delightful period, differing from ours chiefly by a
greater formality and 'elegance' of manners, whereas when
you turn to the novel (including *Evelina*), you suddenly
step into a world full of full-blooded, bawdy, brutal, stri-
dent, pull-away-the-chair barbarity? The sea captain in
Evelina who supplies the comic element does so by playing a series of tricks on an elderly French lady, whom he
addresses as 'Madam Frog', throws into ditches, and trips
up in the mud. What is the common denominator between
this and Johnson's circle? And what is true? Perhaps both
are and one sees what the Doctor meant when he said that
in a jail the society was commonly better than at sea.

But I mustn't spend too long on books for I have *the* ludicrous adventure of my own to tell. Unfortunately it needs
a good deal of introduction to render it intelligible, but I
think it is worth it. Mme Studer is the widow of M. Studer
who died recently under distressing circumstances. She had
been temporarily insane once during his lifetime: and tho'
there was no serious fear of a relapse, her state of mind after
his death, together with some traces of hysteria and more
depression than even the death of a husband seemed to justify, led most of her friends to keep an eye on her. Minto
[Mrs Moore] went to see her pretty regularly. So did (the
heroine of my story) a Mrs Wilbraham. She is what is called
'a brave little woman' (tho' it is not known what dangers she

ever had to encounter) and is never idle. She brings up her daughter in the light of lectures on child psychology delivered by professors whose own children never get born at all or are notable puppies. She is a spiritualist: a psychoanalyst, but does not believe in the theories of Freud because they are so horrid: she weighs the babies of poor women: her business in fact is universal benevolence. 'If only one feels that one can be of some use in the world . . .' as she often says.

Well, the other night I was just settling down to translate a chapter of the Edda, when suddenly Minto called me out of the dining room and said 'Mrs Wilbraham is here. She says Mrs Studer has twice tried to commit suicide today. She's got a taxi here and wants me to go and see the doctor at the Warneford [Asylum]. We shall have to get a nurse for Mrs Studer.' I said I'd come along, because Minto has been rather poorly and I didn't know what she might be let in for. So Mrs W., Minto and I drove off to the Warneford. I remained in the taxi while the two ladies went in to see the Doctor. It was about half past nine, dusk and raining. At an unlighted window just opposite stood a very pale man with a long beard who fixed his eyes on the taxi with insane steadiness for half an hour without ever blinking or moving as far as I could see: to complete the picture (you'll hardly believe it) a large black cat sat on the window sill beneath him. (I always imagined they kept the patients in back rooms or something, or at any rate had bars on the window.) I liked this so little that in desperation I tried to start a conversation with Griffin the taximan (also your garager when you are at Headington). 'This is an unpleasant place, Griffin', said I. He replied promptly 'You know sir you can't put her in without a doctor and a magistrate.' I then realized that he thought we were there for the purpose of 'putting in' either Minto or Mrs W. In my dismay, not quite decided what I meant, I blurted out 'Oh I hope that won't be necessary' and when he replied 'Well it was the last time I got one put in 'ere' I realized that I had hardly improved matters.

The others emerged at last with a Nurse Jones and we started off for the Studer's. But now the question was what to do? Madame would certainly refuse to have a strange young woman thrust upon her for the night for no apparent reason: as her husband was dead and her relatives abroad, no one had any authority over her. And even if we wished, no doctor would certify her as insane on the evidence of a child—the only person who ever claimed to have seen the attempt at suicide. Mrs Wilbraham said it was all perfectly simple. She would stay hidden in Mme Studer's garden all night. Nurse would be put up in the bungalow of a stranger opposite Madame's house. She must herself stay in the garden. It was no good arguing. It was her duty. If only her nephew was here! If only she could have a *man* with her, she confessed, she would feel less nervous about it. I began to wish I'd stayed at home: but in the end of course I had to offer.

No one raised the question as to why the Nurse had been prevented from going to bed at the Warneford in order to be carried half a mile in a taxi and immediately put to bed in another house totally unconnected with the scene of action, where she could not possibly be of the slightest use. The girl herself, who was possibly in some doubt as to who the supposed lunatic might be, remained in a stupefied silence.

I now suggested as a last line of defence that nothing wd be more likely to upset Mme Studer than to find dim figures walking about her garden all night: to which Mrs W. replied brightly that we must keep out of sight and go very quietly. 'We could put our stockings on outside our boots you know.' At that moment (we were all whispering just outside a house further down in the same street as Madame's, and it was now about eleven o'clock) a window opened overhead and someone asked me rather curtly whether we wanted anything, and if not, would we kindly go away. This restored me to some of the sanity I was rapidly losing, and I determined that whatever else happened, four o'clock should not find me 'with my stockings over my boots' explaining to the police that I was (v. naturally) spending the night in some one else's garden for fear the owner might commit suicide.

I therefore ruled that we must keep our watch in the road, where, if we sat down, we wd be hidden from the window by the paling (and, I added mentally, wd be open to arrest for vagabondage, not for burglary). Several neighbours had now turned up (all women, and nearly all vulgar) to revel in excitement and Mrs W. (while insisting on the absolute necessity of letting no one know—'it would be dreadful if it got about poor thing') gave each newcomer, including the total strangers, a full account of the situation.

I came home with Minto, drank a cup of tea, put on my great coat, took some biscuits, smokes, a couple [of] apples, a rug, a waterproof sheet and two cushions, and returned to the fatal road. It was now twelve o'clock. The crowd of neighbours had now melted away: but one (neither vulgar nor a stranger) had had the rare good sense to leave some sandwiches and three thermos flasks. I found the brave little woman actually eating and drinking when I arrived. Hastily deciding that if I were to lie under the obligations of a *man* I wd assume his authority, I explained that we should be really hungry and cold later on and authoritatively put a stop to that nonsense. My next step was to provide for my calls of nature (no unimportant matter in an all night *tête-à-tête* with a fool of an elderly woman who has had nothing to do with men since her husband had the good fortune to die several years ago) by observing that the striking of a match in that stillness wd easily be heard in the Studer's house and that I wd tiptoe to the other end of the road to light my pipe.

Having thus established my right to disappear into the darkness as often as I chose—she conceded it with some reluctance—I settled down. There had been some attempt at moonlight earlier, but it had clouded over and a fine rain began to fall. Mrs Wilbraham's feminine and civilian vision of night watches had apparently not included this. She was really surprised at it. She was also surprised at its getting really cold: and most surprised of all to find that she became sleepy, for she (after the first ten minutes) had answered to my warning on that score with a scornful 'I don't think there's much danger of *that*!' However all these hardships gave her the opportunity of being 'bright' and 'plucky' as far as one can be in sibilant whispers.

If I could have been quit of her society I wd have found my watch just tolerable—despite the misfortune of finding my greatcoat pockets stuffed with camphor balls (Minto is very careful about moths) which I flung out angrily on the road and then some hours later forgetting this and trying to eat one of the apples that had lain in those pockets. The taste of camphor is exactly like the smell. During the course of the night my companion showed signs of becoming rather windy and I insisted on playing with her the old guessing game called 'Animal, Vegetable, or Mineral'. (Incidentally I thought I would find it more interesting than her conversation.) After assuring me that she was thinking of an animal, a live animal, an animal we had seen that night, she had the impudence to announce in the end that 'it' was the 'voice of an owl we had heard'—which shows the working of her mind. However my story is over now, and when I have added that the crows had been 'tuning up their unseasonable matins' a full half hour before any other bird squeaked (a fact of natural history which I never knew before) I may dismiss Mrs-Ruddy-Wilbraham from my mind . . .

TO HIS FATHER: from Magdalen College

29 July [1927]

I am a little surprised at your response to the programme of being 'boiled in mud'. Neither of us of course would choose Harrogate or any similar place for pleasure: that may be taken as a starting point to any discussion on the subject—tho', I repeat, the unpleasantness must not be exaggerated. (Damme Sir, are we to be frightened of some retired colonels and rich old maids?) I suggested it purely and simply on medical grounds and your reply strikes me rather as if I had said to a man with toothache 'Why not go to a dentist?' and he had answered 'You're quite right—I will go out. But I won't go to a dentist. I'll go and get fitted for a new pair of boots.' However, I am so pleased at your agreement on the main issue, that of going away, that I must not press the other too hard . . .

I am just in the few days lull between my two 'fittes' of summer examining. I have finished reading the boy's answers in Oxford, and next week I go to Cambridge for the pleasanter (and more profitable) business of awarding. I had rather a heavy dose of it this time, and the strain took the form of giving me neuralgia. At least my dentist, after striking probes into me, punching me in the face, and knocking my teeth with small hammers—accompanied with the blatantly impertinent question 'Does that hurt?' (to which the proper reply seems to be a sharp return blow at *his* jaw with the words 'Yes, just like that')—my dentist I say, assured me that there was nothing wrong with my teeth and therefore it must be neuralgia . . .

My labours were rewarded by some good things from the candidates (who are school boys under sixteen). The definition of a *Genie* as 'an oriental spirit inhabiting bottles and buttons and rings' is a rather rare example of a correct answer which is funny. 'A *Censer* is one who incenses people' is more of the familiar type. In answer to a question from a paper on *Guy Mannering* 'Would you have liked Colonel Mannering as a father? Support your answer by an account of his behaviour to Julia', one youth sagely replied that he would. It is true that Mannering was cold, suspicious, autocratic etc., 'but he was very rich and I think he would have made an excellent father'. That boy should be sent to the City at once: he has the single eye . . .

My only other recent adventure was a purely literary one—that of quite accidentally picking up *The Woman in White* and reading it: a book of course now practically unknown to anyone under forty. I thought it extremely good of its kind, and not a bad kind. But what spacious days those were! The characters, or at least all the wicked ones, flame in jewels and the hero is so poor in one place that he actually travels *second class* on the railway. I have decided to model my behaviour for the future (socially I mean, not morally) on that of Count Fosco, but without the canaries and the white mice.

Another curious thing is the elaborate descriptions of male beauty, which I hardly remember to have seen since Elizabethan poetry: or do the 'noble brow', the 'silky beard' and the 'Manly beauty' still flourish in fiction which I don't happen to have read? Of course only third rate people write that kind of novel now, whereas Wilkie Collins was clearly a man of genius: and there is a good deal to be said for his point of view (expressed in the preface) that the first business of a novel is to tell a story, and that characters etc. come second . . .

TO HIS BROTHER: from Perranporth, Cornwall
3 September [1927]

I returned from Cambridge and almost immediately set out with Minto, Maureen, Florence de Forest and Baron Papworth [a dog] for Perranporth (Cornwall) where I am now writing. On Sunday (it is now Friday) I set out for P'daitaheim: whether to spend my days interminably strolling in the cemetry-like walks of a hydro garden or drinking two o'clock buckets of sherry in the study, I don't yet know: for of course it is still quite uncertain whether he can be got to move or not . . .

The only Cornish city I have been to is Truro. The town is an ordinary little market town, much less pleasing than any in the 'homely' counties between Morlockheim and the West Country: in fact so true is the Co. Down element in my Cornish recipe that Truro has more than a flavour of Newtownards about it. The Cathedral is the poorest, almost, that I have ever seen . . . The main object of my visit was to get a book, having finished *Martin Chuzzlewit* which I brought down.

And here let me digress for a moment to advise you v. strongly to make one more effort with Dickens and make it on *Martin Chuzzlewit,* if only for the sake of an account of 19th century America . . . Of course to enjoy it, or any other Dickens you must get rid of all idea of realism—as much as in approaching William Morris or the music hall. In fact I should say he is the good thing of which the grand Xmas panto. is the degeneration and abuse: broadly typical sentiment, only rarely intolerable if taken in a jolly after dinner pantomime mood, and broadly effective 'comics': only all done by a genius, so that they become mythological . . .

But this is all by the way. I had assumed that as Truro was a cathedral city, it must have at least a clerical intelligentsia: and if that, a decent bookshop. If appeared to have only a Smith's and a faded looking place that seemed half a news agents. At the door of this I stopped an elderly parson and asked him whether this and Smith were the only two booksellers. He said they were: then a few moments later came back walking on tip toes as some parsons do, and buzzed softly in my ear (he had a beard) 'There is an S.P.C.K. depot further down this street'. This almost adds a new character to my world: henceforth among my terms of abuse none shall rank lower than 'he's the sort of man who'd call an S.P.C.K. depot a bookshop'.

I discovered however that my unpromising book-shop had a second hand quarter upstairs. This at first was depressing as it appeared to consist entirely of two sections: one labelled 'books on Cornwall', the other 'Second hand rewards'. That also is a valuable new idea . . . However in the end I discovered an upper garret where there were at last some *books*. I had v. little money and the selection was poor. I got inter alia the poetical work of 'Armstrong, Dyer, and Green' . . . As for my poets, Dyer you will remember as the author of *The Fleece*, perhaps the best example of that curious 18th century growth, the commercial epic—cf. Also *Cyder* and *The Sugar Cane*. Armstrong wrote a similar poem in Miltonic blank verse on *The Art of Preserving Health*. I have read it with huge enjoyment. It is beyond all parody as the specimen of the noble art of making poetry by *translating* ordinary sentences into 'Miltonic' diction. Thus 'some people can't eat eggs' is rendered,

> *Some even the generous nutriment detest*
> *Which, in the shell, the sleeping embryo rears.*

(Where 'rears' I suspect is a misprint for 'bears.') If one eats too much fat,

The irresoluable oil
So gentle late and blandishing, in floods
Of rancid bile o'erflows: what tumults hence
What horrors rise, were nauseous to relate.[130] . . .

I enclose some photos and good wishes from all.

TO HIS BROTHER: **aboard the S.S. Patriotic, about
to leave Belfast** (where he had been with his father from
6 September to 5 October)

5 October 1927
[posted with letter of 12 December]
Tho' I am uncertain when my next proper letter to you will
be written, I should be unpardonable if I failed to salute
you on an occasion over which your spirit so emphatically
presides . . . The cry of 'Any more for the shore' has gone
round. Arthur, who saw me off and drank with me (nay!
at *his* expence) has just gone. The 'flip, flip' of the boots of
Belfastians on the rubber floor of the saloon deck is heard
on all sides. In a moment we shall shove off. I gave the
P'daytabird *four* solid weeks and a day: tomorrow I shall
be in Oxford. Of course it proved impossible to get him
away . . . So the attempt to get him boiled in mud, which
I made sincerely and even importunately, was a complete
failure. A usual P'daytaborough holiday took its place, with
an inordinate number of P'dayta Days. It is cruellest of all

---

[130] *The Poetical Works of Armstrong, Dyer and Green,* with Memoirs and
Critical Dissertations by the Rev. George Gilfillan (1858), pp. 15, 16.

when he comes home on Monday at 11.30. To be given just enough time to decant the brisk liquour of Monday morning and then to have the cup dashed from your hand.

It was specially annoying this time because I wanted to be very busy putting into action my project of an Encyclopedia Boxoniana. I have worked through the texts down to The Locked Door and at Christmas hope to be able to begin the actual encyclopedia . . . I find the work fascinating: the consistency between the very early texts and the ones we usually read is much greater than I dared to hope for: and an odd sentence in the Locked Door or the Life of Big will fit into a narrative written in Wynyard or pre-Wynyard days in the most startling way. I suppose it is only accident, but it is hard to resist the conviction that one is dealing with a sort of reality. At least so it seems to me, alone in the little end room. How it will appear tomorrow in Magdalen Common Room or a month hence to you in How Kow is another matter. We're off. The screw turns. I had stewed steak for lunch today and boiled mutton for supper dinner. I am going to eat some supper. Can you forget the flavour of one's first non-P'dayta meal. (I was mistaken. The screw has stopped again.)

TO HIS FATHER: from Magdalen College
[29? November 1927]

They had great fun at the Union last week. Birkenhead [F. E. Smith] came to speak. The first thing that worried him was the private business in which two gentlemen got up and discussed the library list—additions to the library of the Union being a subject which naturally comes up in private business. On this occasion the merits of *Psmith Journalist* by P. G. Woodhouse, *That Ass Psmith* by the same author, and *The Wreck of the Birkenhead* were hotly canvassed. The noble lord was understood to make some observations to those around him in which the word 'schoolboys' figured.

Then the debate began. The first speaker produced the good old ancient Wadham story of how Smith and Simon had decided what parties they were to follow in their political careers by the toss of a coin the night before they took schools. You will hardly believe me when I tell you that Smith jumped up: 'baseless fabrication'—'silly, stale story'—'hoped that even the home of lost causes had abandoned that chestnut, etc. etc.'—and allowed himself to be sidetracked and leg pulled to such an extent that he never reached his real subject at all. It seems to me impossible that a man of his experience could fall to such frivolous tactics: unless we accept the accompanying story that he was drunk at the time, or the even subtler explanation that he was *not* ...

TO HIS BROTHER: from Magdalen College

12 December [1927]

I enclose a fragment written when and how, you will see. I had hoped to continue it in reasonable time: but the monthly letter has proved an impossibility during the term. My evenings for the fortnight in term run thus. *Mon.* Play reading with undergraduates (till Midnight). *Tue.* Mermaid club. *Wedn.* Anglo-Saxon with undergraduates. *Thurs.*— *Frid.*—*Sat.*—*Sunday.* Common room till late. *Mon.* Play reading. *Tue.* Icelandic Society. *Wedn.* Anglo-Saxon. *Thurs.* Philosophical supper. *Fri. — Sat. — Sunday.*

As you will see this gives at the very best only three free evenings in the even weeks, and two in the odd. And into these two everything in the way of casual entertaining, correspondence and what we used to call 'A-h-h-h!' has to be crammed . . .

I have done very little reading outside my work these last months. In Oman's *Dark Ages* I have come up against a thing I had almost forgotten since my school days — the boundless self assurance of the pure text book. 'The four brothers were all worthy sons of their wicked father — destitute of natural affection, cruel, lustful, and treacherous.' Lewis the Pious was 'a man of blameless and virtuous habits' — tho' every other sentence in the chapter makes it plain that he was a sh*t. 'Charles had one lamentable failing — he was too careless of the teaching of Christianity about the relations of the sexes.' It is so nice too, to be told without a hint of doubt who was in the right and who was in the wrong in every controversy, and exactly why every one did what he did. Yet Oman is quite right: that is the way — I suppose — to write an *introduction* to a subject . . . I am almost coming to the conclusion that all histories are bad. Whenever one turns from the historian to the writings of the people he deals with, there is always such a difference . . .

By the way, what a wonderful conceit of Thomas Brown's referring to the age of the long lived antediluvians — 'an age when living men might be antiquities'. Query: *Would* a living man a thousand years old give you the same feeling that an old building does? I think there is a good deal to be said for Alice Meynell's theory that one's idea of antiquity and the standard one measures it by, is derived entirely from one's own life. Certainly 'Balbec and Tadmor' (whoever they may be) could hardly give one a more weird sense of 'ages and ages ago' than some early relic discovered in the drawers of the little end room often does. One has one's own 'dark ages'. But I daresay this is not so for everyone: it may be that you and I have a specially historical sense of our own lives. Are you often struck, when you become sufficiently intimate with other people to know something of their development, how *late* their lives begin so to speak? . . .

TO HIS FATHER: **from Magdalen College** (after spending Christmas with his father)

25 February 1928

I have had one letter from Warnie since I left, but it largely duplicated his last to you. I cannot help envying him the richness of his subject matter. My own life is hard to turn into matters for letters. You make the same complaint I know of yours: but at least you have the advantage, that you can write trifles to me because I know the people and places concerned. If you tell me you had a very jolly evening's chat with John Greeves or went and had a slap-up dinner with excellent champagne at Uncle Hamilton's, that is of interest because I know who John Greeves and Uncle Hamilton are. If I, on the other hand, were to tell you how I enjoyed Bircham's brilliant and original views on Hamlet last night, or what a pleasant talk I had the other day with Nicholl Smith (statements by the way as probable as those I have put in your mouth), it would convey nothing.

However, I see that the main thing is to go on talking: for this wheeze brings into my head the fact that I did really have a very good evening the night before last when I exercised for the first time my newly acquired right of dining at Univ.—an exercise which must be rare because it is so damned expensive. Poynton, the Fark, Carritt and Stevenson, as luck would have it, were all in that evening, and it was delightful to revisit the whimsical stateliness of that particular common room. There's no getting away from the fact that we at Magdalen are terribly 'ordinary' beside it. We are just like anyone else: there, every single one of them is a character part that could be found nowhere outside their own walls.

I wonder is there some influence abroad now-a-days that prevents the growth of rich, strongly marked personal peculiarities. Are any of our contemporaries 'characters' as Queen Victoria or Dizzy or Carlyle were 'characters'? I am not asking the ordinary question whether we produce greater or smaller men. 'To be a character' in this sense is not the same thing as 'to have character'. For instance, I suppose Abraham 'had character', but no one ever thought of calling him 'a character': your friend in the Rocket, on the contrary, was lacking in character, but he distinctly *was* 'a character'. There seems to be no doubt that the thing is growing rarer. Or is it that you need to be at least elderly to be a character? In that case, each generation, seeing the characters all among its elders, would naturally conclude that the phenomenon was passing away. Or perhaps it goes further yet. Perhaps the secret of being a character in the very highest degree is to be dead, for then the anecdotes cluster and improve unchecked.

But all this is from the purpose. What I began on was the difficulties of letter writing. I fear

The fault, dear Brutus, is not in our stars
But in ourselves.[131]

for the born letter writer is quite independent of material. Have you ever read the letters of the poet Cowper? He had nothing—literally nothing—to tell any one about: private life in a sleepy country town where Evangelical distrust of 'the world' denied him even such miserable society as the place would have afforded. And yet one reads a whole volume of his correspondence with unfailing interest. How his tooth came loose at dinner, how he made a hutch for a tame hare, what he is doing about his cucumbers—all this he makes one follow as if the fate of empires hung on it . . .

TO HIS FATHER: from Magdalen College

31 March [1928]

My studies in the XVIth Century—you will remember my idea of a book about Erasmus—has carried me much further back than I anticipated. Indeed it is the curse and the fascination of literary history that there are no real beginnings. Take what point you will for the start of some new chapter in the mind and imagination of man, and you will invariably find that it has always begun a bit earlier: or rather, it

---

[131] Shakespeare, *Julius Caesar*, I, ii, 139–40.

branches so imperceptibly out of something else that you are forced to go back to the something else. The only satisfactory opening for any study is the first chapter of Genesis.

The upshot of all this is that the book will be a very different one from what I imagined, and I hope to try a preliminary canter in a course of lectures sometime next year. In the mean time I spend all my mornings in the Bodleian: and the evenings in trying, for the hundredth time, to get a real working knowledge of the German language, since in my present occupation I find my ignorance of it up against me at every turn. For example, the only history of mediaeval Latin literature is in German. The authoritative edition of an old French poem I shall have to read is in German. And so on. But I am making progress.

If only you could smoke, and if only there were upholstered chairs, the Bodleian would be one of the most delightful places in the world. I sit in 'Duke Humphrey's Library', the oldest part, a Fifteenth-Century building with a very beautiful painted wooden ceiling above me and a little mullioned window at my left hand through which I look down on the garden of Exeter where, these mornings, I see the sudden squalls of wind and rain driving the first blossoms off the fruit trees and snowing the lawn with them. At the bottom of the room the gilt bust of Charles I presented by Laud, faces the gilt bust of Strafford — poor Strafford.

The library itself — I mean the books — is mostly in a labyrinth of cellars under the neighbouring squares. This room however is full of books (duplicate copies I suppose, or overflows) which stand in little cases at right angles to the wall, so that between each pair there is a kind of little 'box'—in the public house sense of the word—and in these boxes one sits and reads. By a merciful provision, however many books you may send for, they will all be left on your chosen table at night for you to resume work next morning: so that one gradually accumulates a pile as comfortably as in ones own room. There is not, as in modern libraries, a forbidding framed notice to shriek 'Silence': on the contrary a more moderate request 'Talk little and tread lightly'. There is indeed always a faint murmur going on of semi-whispered conversations in neighbouring boxes. It disturbs no one. I rather like to hear the hum of the hive, and it is pleasant when someone steps into your box and says 'Hello, are *you* here?'

As you may imagine one sees many oddities among one's fellow readers—people whom I have never met elsewhere and who look as if they were shut up with the other proper-ties every night. Positively the only drawback to the place is that beauty, antiquity and over-heating weave a spell very much more suited to dreaming than to working. But I resist to the best of my abilities and trust in time to become innoc-ulated. (The practice of opening the window in one's box is not, I need hardly say, encouraged.) In such a life as this, what news should there be?

By the time this reaches you, you will probably have heard the result of the boat race—with the same very moderated grief as myself. Perhaps you will also have heard that there is a religious revival going on among our undergraduates. Which is true. It is run by a German-American called Dr [Frank] Buchman. He gets a number of young men together (some reports say women too, but I believe not) and they confess their sins to one another. Jolly, ain't it? But what can one do?

If you try to supress it (I am assuming that you agree with me that the thing is unhealthy) you only make martyrs . . .

TO HIS BROTHER: from 'Hillsboro'

1 April 1928

My last letter, if I remember rightly, was ironically begun on the return from the summer visit to P'daytaheim and finished only on the eve of the Christmas visit. I have thus a new 'holiday' period to record, which is almost barren in events. The p'dayta crop was singularly poor. The only item worth remembering was his curious contribution to the problem of venereal disease, to the effect that obviously it must have begun with women and spread thence to men. Being asked why, he replied 'Sure how could a man have given it to a woman if he hadn't got it from a woman herself?' This is unanswerable.

Another illuminating remark was made in answer to some casual remark of mine as to the control of one's imagination—I was talking, I think, about not letting one's mind brood on grievances or fears. He replied 'What on earth do you mean by controlling the imagination? One controls ones appetites.' That is the whole psychology of his generation in a nutshell, isn't it? A man sits thinking of negus and making 'iron rules' not to drink any, with much contortion of the face and muttered 'Oh Lords' until the inevitable moment when he finds some excellent reason for breaking the iron rules. The idea of a simpler method—that of applying his mind to something else and using a little concentration—would never occur.

The discussion ended (of course) with the infuriating statement that we were not 'ad idem' on the 'connotation' of the word control. Which reminds me of the splendid definition of an egoist which he read to me out of *Punch* in happy unconsciousness of its application. 'An egoist is a man who thinks that all the words he doesn't understand are misprints' . . .

Apart from these there is little to record. We had the usual regrets that you were in the army and the usual astonishment that you didn't appear to be nearly as unhappy as a man of your income ought by all reason to be. We had the usual discussions on theology, drifting off into something else as soon as one had cleared one's ground to begin. His health was tolerable, I thought . . .

TO OWEN BARFIELD: from Magdalen College

[7? June 1928]

Come on Tuesday next and let your lady wife come and lie at Headington while you stay in College, for both will be very welcome. I haven't read Aeschylus this long time but I don't mind having a shot. The *Prometheus* is a bit easier than the *Agamemnon*.

You cd hardly expect the man in the T.L.S. to know the esoteric doctrine of myths.[132]

By the bye, we now need a new word for the 'science

---

[132] Mr Barfield was probably referring to the review of Hermann Gunkel's *What Remains of the Old Testament and Other Essays* in *The Times Literary Supplement* (26 April 1928), p. 302.

of the nature of myths' since 'mythology' has been appropriated to the myths themselves. Would 'mythonomy' do? I am quite serious. If your views are not a complete error this subject will become more important and it's worth while trying to get a good word before they invent a beastly one. 'Mytho-logic' (noun) wouldn't be bad, but people wd read it as an adjective. I have also thought of 'mythopoeics' (cf. 'Metaphysics') but that leads to 'a mythopoeician' wh. is frightful: whereas 'a mythonomer' (better still 'The Mythonomer Royal') is nice. Or shall we just invent a new word—like 'gas'. (Nay Sir, I meant nothing.)

I am writing a great new poem—also a Mnemonic rime on English sound changes in octosyllabic verse

> (*Thus Æ to Ĕ they soon were fetchin',*
> *Cf. such forms as ÞÆC and ÞECCEAN.*)

which will be about as long as the Cursor Mundi, & great fun.

Arrive about 3 o'clock on Tuesday, if that suits you.

P.S. Wd 'Mythologics' do?

TO HIS FATHER: **from Magdalen College** (with an early reference to the book which became *The Allegory of Love*)

10 July [1928]

I have actually begun the first chapter of my book. This perhaps sounds rather odd since I was working on it all last vac., but you will understand that in a thing of this sort the collection of the material is three quarters of the battle. Of course, like a child who wants to get to the painting before it has really finished drawing the outline, I have been itching to do some actual *writing* for a long time. Indeed—you can imagine it as well as I—the most delightful sentences would come into one's head: and now half of them can't be used because, knowing a little more about the subject, I find they aren't true. That's the worst of facts—they do cramp a fellow's style. If I can get it—the first chapter—to the stage of being typed, I shall bring a copy home for your amusement.

I should warn you, by the by, that Erasmus and all that has had to be postponed to a later book. The actual book is going to be about mediaeval love poetry and the mediaeval idea of love which is a very paradoxical business indeed when you go into it: for on the one hand it is extremely super-sensual and refined and on the other it is an absolute point of honour that the lady should be some one else's wife, as Dante and Beatrice, Lancelot and Guinevere etc. The best introduction is the passage in Burke about 'the unbought grace of life'.

I am intending by the way to pay you my summer visit in *August* this year instead of at the usual time. This is because the whole of the later part of the Long [Vacation] will be occupied with the preliminary stages of the Presidential election, specially the informal conversations which matter most. I am particularly anxious to be there, with one or two others, at the early parts and see what is going on: for—I am almost ashamed to tell you—I am beginning to be rather disillusioned about my colleagues. There is a good deal more intrigue and mutual back-scratching and even direct lying than I ever supposed possible: and what worries me most of all, I have good reason to believe that it is not the same in other colleges.

Of course it may simply be that, being rather an innocent in practical matters myself, and having been deceived once or twice, I have rushed too hastily to conclusions: as they say a simple man becomes too knowing by half when he once becomes knowing at all. Let us hope so. But the bad thing is that the decent men seem to me to be all the old ones (who will die) and the rotters seem to be all the young ones (who will last my time) . . .

TO HIS BROTHER: from 'Hillsboro'

'Begun Aug. 2nd' [1928]

I am glad you like the *Lives of the Poets*. There is no subject on which more nonsense has been talked than the style of Johnson. For me his best sentences in writing have the same feeling as his best conversation—'pop! it was so sudden'. I don't know anyone who can settle a thing so well in half a dozen words. I have read a good deal of the *Rambler* last term, which is supposed to be more Johnsonian than the *Lives*. But he does the dagger business—or no, it's more like a mace, but a mace properly used is not a cumbersome weapon—what is there clumsy about choosing an infinitesimal point of time in which quietly to break a man's head with a perfectly directed tap of a sledge hammer?—he does it again and again.

You know that the *Rambler* is a mass of moral platitudes—and infuriates the French critics who say that they haven't come to their time of life to be told that life is short and that wasted time can never be recovered. Johnson, anticipating that kind of objection, simply remarks 'People more frequently require to be reminded, than to be instructed'. What more is there to say? or again 'The natural process of the mind is not from enjoyment to enjoyment but from hope to hope'. That would be a page of whining and snivelling in Thackery—ah, which of us, dear reader, has his hearts desire etc., etc.

Better still, this on marriage: 'Marriage is not otherwise unhappy than as life is unhappy.' I can't say that would be a whole novel with the moderns because the whole novel would not get as far as that. The author would make a great fuss about how Pamela got on Alan's nerves and how in the end they decided that life was a failure, and would be praised for his fearless criticism of the institution of marriage, without ever getting one glimpse of the fact that he was merely describing the *general* irritatingness of daily life, as it happens in the case of married people. Johnson just knocks a whole silly literature aside. He has been through all that (Ibsen and Wells and such) before it was written. But the Lives are the best—specially Savage, Dryden and Pope. I can imagine that the atmosphere, the Englishness, is specially delightful to you in 'furrin parts'. To me, the queerest thing about Johnson is that he is by no means an enthusiastic critic and yet he always makes me want to read the people he talks of even when I know that I shall dislike them . . .

Earlier in the year—just before term began—I had a delightful week end at a farm house in the Forest of Dean. As you know, I have walked in those parts before, but never stayed there. It is, I think, the most glorious *inland* place I know . . . almost untouched by trippers, and excellently solitary: almost uncannily so on an all day walk if one gets into the fir districts where birds don't sing and happens to be for a moment out of the sound of a stream (Mr Papworth by the way decided at once that the whole forest was a dangerous place, and always kept close to heel). Here and there in the wood you come on a little old farm house with a few acres of clearing, surrounded by a hedge and approached by a road so desolate that it is hardly different from the green 'rides' that pierce the wood in every direction. In these 'islands' of farms—in one of which we stayed—there is the most comfortable sense of being tucked away miles deep from the world, of being snugged down in a blanket, of having found a lee shore. We lived in a world of country butter and fresh eggs and boiled fowl, of early hours and hens lazily squawking (*not* crowing, just making that long drawling sound that they make). The nights were noisy with the sounds that keep no right thinking man awake—owls, a very good nightingale, and once the barking of a fox. 'A pleasant land of drowsyhead it was . . .' But as a matter of fact it isn't the drowsiness that really counts, its the sense of being 'well away' . . .

It sounds astonishing but English poetry is one of the things that you can come to the end of. I don't mean of course that I shall ever have read everything worth reading that was ever said in verse in the English language. But I do mean that there is no longer any chance of discovering a new long poem in English which will turn out to be just what I want and which can be added to the *Faerie Queene, The Prelude, Paradise Lost, The Ring and the Book,* the *Earthly Paradise,* and a few others—because they aren't any more. I mean, in the case of poems one hasn't read, one knows now pretty well what they're like, and knows too that tho' they may be worth reading, they will not become part of ones permanent stock.

In that sense I have come to the end of English poetry—as you may be said to have come to the end of a wood, not where you have actually walked every inch of it, but when you have walked about in it enough to know where all the boundaries are and to feel the end near even when you can't see it: when there is no longer any hope (as there was for the first few days) that the next turn of the path might bring you to an unsuspected lake or cave or clearing on the edge of a new valley—when it can no longer conceal anything . . .

TO HIS FATHER: **from Magdalen College** (as the College prepared to elect a new President)

[3 November 1928]

Thank heavens our electioneering troubles are nearly over. This day fortnight we shall all be locked into chapel like so many Cardinals and proceed to make a President and then goodbye to the endless talk and agreements and disagreements and personalities that I have lived in since term began. A subject of this sort hanging in the air manifests itself chiefly by a plethora of informal meetings which naturally spring up on those few hours and days when the ordinary routine has left one a little freedom. As I have anyway a rather heavy time table this term—chiefly, alas, those philosophy pupils whom I share with Weldon and whom he regards as his if they turn out well and mine if they turn out ill—I am now heartily sick of the whole business.[133]

---

[133] On 17 November Magdalen College elected George Stuart Gordon its President.

At the same time I have added to my occupations in other and I hope more hopeful ways. Two or three of us who are agreed as to what a College ought to be, have been endeavouring to stimulate the undergraduates into forming some sort of literary society. In any other Colleges the idea that undergraduates should require, or endure, stimulus in that direction from the dons, would be laughable. But this is a very curious place. All College societies whatever were forbidden early in the reign of the late President—an act which was then necessitated by the savagely exclusive clubs of rich dipsomaniacs which really dominated the whole life of the place. This prohibition succeeded in producing decency, but at the cost of all intellectual life. When I came I found that any Magdalen undergraduate who had interests beyond rowing, drinking, motoring and fornication, sought his friends outside the College, and indeed kept out of the place as much as he could. They certainly seldom discovered one another, and never collaborated so as to resist the prevailing tone. This is what we wish to remedy: but it had to be done with endless delicacy, which means, as you know, endless waste of time.

First of all we had to make sure that our colleagues would agree to the relaxation of the rule against societies. Then we had to pick our men amongst the undergraduates very carefully. Luckily I had been endeavouring already for a term or two to get a few intelligent men to meet one another in my rooms under the pretext of play reading or what not, and that gave us a lead. Then we had to try to push those chosen men v. gently so that the scheme should not appear too obviously to be managed by the dons. At present we are at the stage of holding a preparatory meeting 'at which to discuss the foundation of a society' next Monday—so the whole show may yet be a dismal failure. I hope not: for I am quite sure that this College will never be anything more than a country club for all the idlest 'bloods' of Eton and Charterhouse as long as undergraduates retain the schoolboy's idea that it would be bad form to discuss among themselves the sort of subjects on which they write essays for their tutors. Ours at present are all absolute babies and terrific men of the world—the two characters I think nearly always go together. Old hearts and young heads, as Henry James says: the cynicism of forty and the mental crudeness and confusion of fourteen.

I sometimes wonder if this country will kill the public schools before they kill it. My experience goes on confirming the ideas about them which were first suggested to me by Malvern long ago. The best scholars, the best men, and (properly understood) the best gentlemen, seem now to come from places like Dulwich, or to be wafted up on country scholarships from secondary schools. Except for pure classics (and that only at Winchester, and only a few boys even there) I really don't know what gifts the public schools bestow on their nurslings, beyond the mere surface of good manners: unless contempt of the things of the intellect, extravagance, insolence, self-sufficiency, and sexual perversion are to be called gifts . . .

The first chapter of my book is finished and typed and the only two people who have seen it approve. The unfortunate thing is that nobody in Oxford really knows anything about the subject I have chosen. I may have made some elementary blunder which the French people—who have so far mainly studied the matter—would pounce on in a moment. However, my translation of some Old French into contemporary English (forgery is great fun) has passed Onions who knows more than anyone else about the English of that period . . .

TO HIS FATHER: from Magdalen College (after spending Christmas at 'Little Lea')

[3 February 1929]

I look in vain for any item of news fit to be extracted from the uneventful routine . . . The new President and his family have not yet moved into the Lodgings, where the work of putting in bathrooms which is now going forwards, throws a new light on the venerable domestic economy of the previous regime.

My current lecture (on Elyot, Ascham, Hooker and Bacon) has attracted as a distinguished member of its audience the Mother Superior of the local hostel for papish undergraduettees—I suppose because I fired off by an attack on Calvin. If you hear indirectly that the Church of Rome is hoping for a distinguished convert among the young Oxford dons, you will know how to interpret it.

The undergraduates have just brought off a good rag by getting a copy of the university seal and circularizing all the garages in Oxford with a notice purporting to come from the Vice Chancellor and Proctors and rescinding an order made last term by which all these places were compelled to shut for undergraduate use at eleven. Unfortunately this excellent joke was disclosed before it had had any time to run its course . . .

TO HIS BROTHER (in Shanghai): **from 'Hillsboro'**

Postmark: 13 April 1929

I am ashamed of my long idleness, though indeed the gap between my last and your last was almost as long as the gap between your last and this. I must admit too, that I am moved to write at this moment by the selfish consideration that I heard last night a thing which you of all people ought to hear—you know how one classifies jokes according to the people one wants to tell them to—and am therefore uneasy till I have unloaded it.

The other night an undergraduate, presumably drunk, at dinner in the George covered the face of his neighbour with potatoes, his neighbour being a total stranger. Whether this means simply that he flung the contents of the potato dish at him or (as I prefer to think) that he seized him firmly by the short hairs and systematically lathered him with warm mash, my informant could not say. But that is not the point of the story. The point is, that being haled before the Proctors and asked why he had done so, the culprit, very gravely and with many expressions of regret, pleaded in so many words 'I couldn't think of anything else to do!'

I am sure you will share my delight at this transference of the outrage from the class of *positive* to that of *negative* faults: as though it proceeds entirely from a failure of the inventive faculty or a mere poverty of the imagination. One ought to be careful of sitting near one of these *unimaginative* men. The novel idea can be worked equally well from either end: whether one thinks of the mohawk bashing your hat over your eyes with the words 'Sorry old chap, I know its a bit hackneyed, but I can't think of anything better'—or of some elderly P'dayta exclaiming testily 'Ah what all these young men lack now-a-days is initiative' as he springs into the air from the hindward pressure of a pin . . .

By the by, I thoroughly agree with you about Scott: in fact I think that even his most fanatical admirers have 'given up' his heroines (with the exception of Die Vernon and Jeanie Deans) and his love scenes. But then one gives *that* up in all XIX Century novels: certainly in Dickens and Thackeray. And when you have ruled that out, what remains is pure delight. Isn't it nice to find a person who knows history almost entirely by tradition? History to Scott means *the stories remembered in the old families,* or sometimes the stories remembered by sects and villages. I should say he was almost the last person in modern Europe who did know it that way: and that, don't you think, is at the back of all his best work. Claverhouse, say, was to Scott not 'a character out of Macaulay' (or Hume or Robertson) but the man about whom old Lady so and so tells one story and about whom some antediluvian local minister's father told another. Printed and documented history probably kills a lot of this traditional local history and what is finally left over is put in guide books. (When nothing else can be said about an old church you can always say that Cromwell stabled his horses in it.)

Scott was only just in time to catch it still living. This (so historians tell me) has had one unforseen result, that Scotch history has ever since been more neglected than that of any other civilized country: the tradition, once stamped by Scott's imagination, has so satisfied curiosity that science has hardly ventured to show its head. It is a pity that no one similarly caught the tradition in England—tho' probably there was less to catch.

I suppose the Scotch were a people unusually tenacious of old memories, as for example Mr Oldbuck. I am not sure that *The Antiquary* is not the best. Do you remember his efforts to get the hero to write an epic on the battle of ? in order to work in his excursus on castramentation? . . . Nothing militates so much against Scott as his popularity in Scotland. The Scotch have a curious way of rendering wearisome to the outside world whatever they admire. I daresay Burns is quite a good poet—really: if only he could ever escape from the stench of that unmerciful haggis and the lugubrious jollities of *Auld Lang Syne*. What a world it opens upon—the 'kail yard' school—beside the bonny briar bush—Mansie Wauch.

I have just suddenly (as I write) seen what is the trouble about all this Scotchness. When you want to be typically English you pretend to be very hospitable and honest and hearty. When you want to be typically Irish you try to be very witty and dashing and fanciful. That is to say, the typical English or Irish mode consists in the assumption of certain qualities which are in themselves quite pleasant. But the typically Scotch consists not in being loud or quiet, or merry or sad, or in any recognizable quality, but just in being *Scotch* . . .

TO HIS FATHER: from Magdalen College

[19 May 1929]

I hope your recovery from the winter 'flu has been permanent. My own prolonged cold, having lasted out the term, worked up into a sore throat and temperature and a few days in bed about Easter time. This finally got rid of the trouble and was not unpleasant. It gave me the excuse to be idle and the chance to re-read some old favourites—including *The Antiquary*. Read the *Antiquary*. I think it contains the cream of Scott's humour and very nearly the cream of his tragedy.

I also re-read *Pickwick*, but this, as you know, I can hardly call an old favourite. Indeed I have only read it once before. This time I hoped I had at last got the secret and become a real convert: but my second reading has broken the spell, I am a relapsed heretic. It won't do. I like the Wellers, both father and son, and I like the trial: but Eatanswill and Mrs Leo Hunter and Bill Stumps, his Mark, seem to me laboured and artificial, and I can't forgive him for showing us poor Jingle in prison and repentance. The whole spirit in which we enjoy a comic rogue depends on leaving out the consideration of the consequences which his character would have in real life: bring that in, and every such character (say Falstaff) becomes tragic. To invite us to treat Jingle as a comic character and then spring the tragic side on us, is a mere act of bad faith. No doubt that is how Jingle wd end in real life. But then in real life it would have been our fault if we had originally treated him as a comic character. In the book you are forced to do so and are therefore unjustly punished when the tragedy comes . . .

I have a capital story which is quite new to me. The hero is a certain Professor Alexander, a philosopher, at Leeds, but I have no doubt that the story is older than he. He is said to have entered a railway carriage with a large perforated cardboard box which he placed on his knees. The only other occupant was an inquisitive woman. She stood it as long as she could, and at last, having forced him into conversation and worked the talk round (you can fill in that part of the story yourself) ventured to ask him directly what was in the box. 'A mongoose madam.' The poor woman counted the telegraph posts going past for a while and again could bear her curiosity no further. 'And what are you going to do with the mongoose?' she asked. 'I am talking it to a friend who is unfortunately suffering fom delirium tremens.' 'And what use will a mongoose be to him?' 'Why, Madam, as you know, the people who suffer from that disease find themselves surrounded with snakes: and of course a mongoose eats snakes.' 'Good Heavens!' cried the lady, 'but you don't mean that the snakes are real?' 'Oh dear me, no' said the Professor with imperturbable gravity. 'But then *neither is the mongoose!*' ...

TO HIS FATHER: **from Magdalen College**

17 July [1929]

This week a curious thing has happened. I have had a letter from Malvern stating that 'Malvern College Ltd' has been wound up and the school has now been put under a board of governors, and asking me to allow my name to be put up for election as one of them. As they are to number over a hundred the honour is not so overwhelming as at first appears. In my first heat I composed a very fine letter declining on the ground of my 'limited knowledge of public school life and, still more, my imperfect sympathy with the aims and ideals of public schools'. This I enjoyed doing: but then alas 'the native hue of resolution was sickled o'er with the pale cast of thought'. I reflected that this would get about and that the great junta of masters and old boys of various schools would pass from one to the other the word—'If you have a boy going to Oxford, I shouldn't recommend Magdalen. Lot of queer fish there now. Cranks etc. etc.' So I funked it, tore up my first letter, and wrote an acceptance. I hope I should have been able to hold out against the purely pruden-tial considerations ('funk' is the simpler word) if I had not been supported by the feeling, as soon as I had cooled, that membership of such a huge board would be purely nominal, except for the ring of 'insiders', and that therefore if I refused I should be only making a storm in a teacup. But won't Warnie be tickled?—if I remember you and I discussed this situation purely as a joke when I was last at home.

Try to let me have a line when you feel like it. Don't be put off writing altogether because you feel unequal to an essay—just a note to say that you have made up your mind where we are going. I should also be glad to hear some news of the Colonel, and of when he is coming back. He is badly in my epistolatory debt.

[For some time Jack had been trying to take his father on a holiday away from Belfast. But this time Mr Lewis was avoiding a holiday because he felt too ill to go any-where. One of the doctors attending him was his brother Joseph's son, Dr Joseph 'Joey' Lewis (1898–1969), who had known Jack and Warren all his life. 'Joey' was a distinguished blood specialist in the Belfast Infirmary and he persuaded his uncle to have some X-rays made on 26 July. That evening Mr Lewis wrote in his diary: 'Xrayed. Results rather disquieting.' Jack had already heard from Mr Lewis's brother, Richard Lewis, who had visited Albert 4–9 July, that his father was not well. He learned from 'Joey' about the results of the X-rays.]

TO HIS FATHER: **from Magdalen College**
Postmark: 5 August 1929

My dear, dear Papy,

I am very glad you have written. I had heard the news and was anxious to write, but hardly knew how to do so. I will, of course, come home at the first moment. Unfortunately I have to go to Cambridge on the 8th for this examining, but will cross to Ireland on the 12th. Don't bother to write yourself if you are not up to it, but see that I am informed.

I gather from what I heard that there is much that is hopeful in the first photo. It would be silly to pretend that this can set worries at rest for either of us; there is surer ground—at least for you—in the wonderful spirit, as shown in your letter, with which you are taking it. I wish I could convey to you one tithe of the respect and affection which I felt in reading it. For the rest, what can I say to you that is not already understood? What can any of us do for one another except give a handshake and a good wish, and hope to do as well when our own time comes to be under fire. It has been a bit of a strain this last week to keep my mind on examination papers for nine hours a day, and I am specially glad that you have written. I was told everything in confidence, I didn't know that you knew I knew, and I could do nothing. I wish I could come straight away but I can hardly get out of Cambridge now. I know what hospitals and nursing homes are like—there at any rate I can sympathize with some experience.

Whatever the next few days brings forth I hope you will make no decision about your treatment without letting me know. I don't of course mean to postpone such decision (necessarily) till next week: but see that I am told. Of course if there is serious trouble, you will have other advice than that of the Belfast crowd.

With all my love and my best wishes—I wish there was anything more useful I could offer—your loving son . . .

TO HIS BROTHER: from 'Little Lea'

25 August 1929
In the study, 8.30 P.M.

This is a line to let you know that P. is rather seriously ill. The first I heard of it was from Uncle Dick about a month ago when I was still in Oxford, and then, in answer to my enquiry, from Joey who is attending him. The trouble is abdominal. The first fear was of course cancer. Xray photos cannot apparently disprove this with certainty, but their evidence, I'm glad to say, is all against it and according to Joey the other features of the case render it very improbable. We must not of course kid ourselves by saying impossible. The present diagnosis is that he is suffering from a narrowing of the passage in one of the bowels. The ordinary cure for this is the operation known as short circuiting: but they had hoped that if he would go on a light diet he would manage to get along, not in perfect health but in tolerable comfort, without being operated upon—or at any rate that the operation would be indefinitely postponed.

I came home immediately after my Cambridge examining and found things at this point. He was up and pretty well. About a week ago however he had an attack in the night of a sort of convulsion and shivering—they call it *rigor*—of which I only learnt next morning. This was not regarded as a very serious symptom by either Joey or Squeaky, but they kept him in bed. Next night when I took his temperature about nine I found it 103 and got the surgeon McConnell (a colleague of Joey's in the case from the start) out to see him about midnight. He was light headed but the temperature fell in the morning. Since then he has been monkeying up and down and of couse he has been in bed. This evening they have told him that it is pretty certain that he will have to have the operation. They are to consult again in a few days and we shall then know for sure. He is taking it extraordinarily well. I shall of course stay until the operation is over, unless they postpone it till Christmas. *As for you,* I suppose it would be (a) Impossible, (b) Useless for you to get special leave as the affair is pretty sure to be settled before you could get home.

I have a great many things on other subjects to say—on Liverpool Cathedral and the new Liverpool boat and so forth—but this is only a note for necessity. I have been up the most of a good many nights with the P'daitabird and can't leave the house long enough to get decent walks, so am rather tired and do not feel in form for a letter. This is from the little end room at about 10. P.M. What a pity you're not here. In spite of the worrying situation we should find redeeming features about Leeborough under the present regime. When one is alone it is by no means so pleasant. Thanks for your last letter and excuse me for this scrawl. Remember I have the Leeborough demoralization on me as well as the cures of a patient. And by Gum, both ones *morals* and ones morale are hard put to it.

Of course the present emergency does not cancel immemorial rules. If your letter arrives P. may be—lets hope to goodness he will be—up again, and you must write therefore only what can be shown. When I am creeping about at night at present, or looking at his fire, I often derive a sort of whimsical pleasure from thinking of the long training in stealth for quite different purposes of which he is now the object in a new sense. I'm sorry that you have had an envelope in my handwriting, of which the contents will disappoint you so much as this. I am just going to creep on tiptoe to the cellar—the key being very sensibly in my charge—to get a mouthful of the whiskey.

TO HIS BROTHER: from 'Little Lea'

29 August 1929

To be frank, you owe this second letter to a typically Leeburian situation. I had mentioned to the P'daitabird that I was writing to you, and this has provoked such a hailstorm of advice and warning—I must write on the thinnest paper and I must go to Condlin [his managing clerk] to get the right sort of envelope—and of questions—how am I getting on with my letter to the Colonel—that there is nothing for it. Sooner or later I must satisfy him with the touch and sight of a letter that by its size will not [be] too obviously a notification of his illness and therefore a cause of alarm to him. And I think it would be really too unkind to send you a wad of toilet paper.

Things are no better since I last wrote, and I am really very despondent about him. Yet it would be an offence against Pigiebotian ethics to seal ourselves up therefore in perpetual solemnity: and, however you may feel in China, I on the spot can only get through my days and nights by allowing myself an enjoyment of the old humours, which, needless to say, show through even this situation. If only it did not always raise anxiety, the daily visit of the Doctor would be irresistably funny. The patient's utter refusal to answer to the point, his hazy accounts (on the familiar 'mouthful' principle) of what he has eaten, and his habit of replying to some such question as 'Have you noticed any change in yourself?' with a sudden 'Doctor! I'm perfectly satisfied in my own mind that the root of all this trouble etc. etc.' and his subsequent belief that the doctor has propounded to him the grossly improbable theory which he had in fact propounded to the doctor—all this you will be able to imagine on the slightest of hints from me. It was very alarming the night he was a little delirious. But (I cannot refrain from telling you) do you know the form it took? The watercloset element in his conversation rose from its usual 30% to something nearly like 100% . . .

However, perhaps all this water closet world is appropriate to me at the moment as I have just finished the formidable task of reading the whole of the works of Rabelais . . . I had to read him for the light he throws on the Renaissance in general and his particular influence on our own Elizabethans.

Would I advise you to do the same? I hardly know. He is very long, very incoherent, and very, very stercoraceous. But you must base no opinion of him on what you hear from uneducated people who have never read any other comic book written before the reign of Queen Victoria and are therefore so blinded by a few familiar words when they first see them in print that they never go on seeing the drift of a page, much less a chapter, as a whole.

The first surprise is that about a quarter of the book is perfectly serious propaganda in favour of humanist education. The comic parts are mostly satires on the papacy, monasticism, and scholastic learning. The free farce of the Miller's Tale-cum-Decameron type is really only about a third of the whole. There is a great deal of quite sincere piety and humanity of a pleasant Shandeyian, Montaignesque type. Some of the aphorisms must be added to our stock at once. 'The greatest loss of time that I know is to count the hours'—'Drunkards live longer than physicians' ... Some of the satire—tho' satire tends always to bore me—is very 'sly', to use a good old word which we moderns have dropped or degraded without finding a better to fill its place.

31 August 1929

I have been continuously on the run since I got up—going to the McNeills to fetch the various jellies and confections with which they daily supply us—their decency to the O.A.B. all along has been extraordinary—helped your father to shave, giving him cheques to sign and endorse. If I start to work now I shall be interrupted by the doctor before I have well got my head into it, so I may as well put in ten minutes conversation with you.

After finishing your letter-portion last night and wiped up the deluge occasioned by opening one of those remarkable soda water bottles, I read a few pages of Macaulay's letters. My reading them pleased the patient and as I have to do them some time or other I may as well do it now when it provides a common topic for our conversations. They are not uninteresting. Do you know that Macaulay developed his full manner as a schoolboy and wrote letters home from school which read exactly like pages out of the Essays? This is very illuminating. He was talking about the nature of government, the principles of human prosperity, the force of the domestic affections and all that (you know the junk) at the age of fourteen. He could not at that age have *known* anything about them: least of all could he have known enough for the flowing generalizations which he makes. One can see quite clearly that having so early acquired the *talk* he found he could go on quite comfortably for the rest of his life without bothering to notice the *things.* He was from the first clever enough to produce a readable and convincing slab of claptrap on any subject whether he understood it or not, and hence he never to his dying day discovered that there was such a thing as understanding. Don't you think the last word on him is Southey's statement—'Macaulay's a clever lad, and a clever lad he'll remain'—? . . .

This is Saturday night. The patient is rather better . . . The great consolation about Leeborough at present is my control of the meals. As soon as I came home and found P. on light diet I said I would make things easier for him by giving up my own meat for lunch. I substituted bread and cheese, cream crackers and butter, and fruit. This may not appeal to you: but the glory is that I can have it when I choose. There has not been a day for the last fortnight on which one o'clock has not seen me sitting down to my cheese, fruit and wine in a dining room with the windows open. A little effort of imagination will enable you to realize what a comfort this is. I maintain the same arrangement during the week end. Fancy a Leeboro *Saturday* with light lunch at *one* instead of a gorge at half past two, and then high tea (cold roast chicken and ham tonight) at seven! . . .

If only I wasn't constantly bothered about the P'daitabird (for one never knows really what the next temperature may bring forth), if only I could get decent walks, and if only I could get some more work done, it wouldn't be a bad life. A formidable list of exceptions! Its like the poacher in *Punch* 'If I get three more after the one I'm after now, I shall have caught four.' . . . I break off here and drink my drop of spirits.

By the way we had tonight the old stunt about whiskey being an unpalatable drink. Incidentally all the doctors without exception say that he has done and is doing himself harm with it. Joey says that when he mentions this to the patient, the patient simply laughs at him—and has ruled that there's no good trying to stop it as the good which cd now be done by cessation would be less than the psychological irritation. He gave me a real fright as I was going out of the gate the other day, having left him as comfortably settled up for the afternoon as I could. He suddenly appeared at his window shouting at me in a voice that made me think some terrible crisis had come. I [went] tearing upstairs to find the real tragedy: he had suddenly discovered that I was going out with the cellar key in my pocket—and apparently the 'odd dregs' in the *two* bottles which he keeps in the wardrobe were not enough to last him the afternoon. There is a very serious side to all this, but I agree with Joey: and I'd go a long way before I'd be leagued with the doctors to deprive the poor old chap of what is about his only pleasure. Let us hope Rabelais is right . . .

Sept. 3rd. The surgeon and Squeaky and Joey have all consulted today and decided on an operation. He is taking it like a hero. By the time this reaches you all will be settled for good or ill. It has been the devil of a day as you may imagine, infernally nerve racking and painful and I'm dead sleepy. I shall post this tomorrow. I had meant to write more, but I'm too tired. As to *facts* theres nothing more to add. Anyway this can't reach you in time to give any information.

TO OWEN BARFIELD: from 'Little Lea'

9 September 1929

Many thanks for your letter. I am not sure that the distinction between 'intimacy' and 'familiarity' is really very profound. It seems to be largely a matter of accident that you know so little of my previous history. I knew more of yours because we meet in England: if we had met in Ireland the position would be reversed. Again, we do not much narrate our past lives, but this is because we have so much else to talk about. Any day might have started a topic to which such narrative would have been relevant, and out it would have come. Consider how many bores whose history you know well after a short acquaintance, not because familiarity has in their case replaced intimacy but because they had nothing to say and would not be silent.

I am not saying that there is nothing in the distinction. When the parties are of different sexes it may be more important. I suppose a good Greek was familiar with his wife and intimate with his ἑταίρα. But between men I suspect that intimacy includes familiarity potentially. Now with a woman, of course, no degree of intimacy includes any familiarity at all; for that there must be στόργη or ἔρωσ or both.

The test really is this. When you have talked to a man about his soul, you will be able, whenever the necessity arises, say, to assist him in using a catheter or nurse him through an attack of dysentry, or help him (if it should so happen) in a domestic problem. This is not so in the case of a woman.

As for my present situation, it frightens me for what it implies. I argue thus: 1. I am attending at the almost painless sickbed of one for whom I have little affection and whose society has for many years given me much discomfort and no pleasure. 2. Nevertheless I find it almost unendurable. 3. Then what in heavens name must it be like to fill the same place at the sickbed, perhaps agonized, of someone really loved, and someone whose loss will be irreparable? A formidable argument *a fortiori*. No doubt under 1. it is proper to include the fact that if lack of real affection spares some pains, it introduces others. Where every kind word and forbearance is the result of calculated duty, and where all we do leaves us still rather ashamed, there is, I suppose, a particular *kind* of strain which would be absent from the other situation. There is also, in this present case, though no spiritual sympathy, a deep and terrible physiological sympathy.

My father and I are physical counterparts: and during these days more than ever I notice his resemblance to me. If I were nursing you I should look forward to your possible death as a loss lifelong and irremediable: but I don't think I should shrink from the knife with the sub-rational sym-pathy (in the etymological sense) that I feel at present.

Having said all this I must proceed to correct the exaggeration which seems to be inherent in the mere act of writing. Who was it said that disease has its own pleasures of which health knows nothing? I have my good moments to which I look forward, and perhaps, though the whole tone of the picture is lowered, there is as much chiaroscuro as ever. When my patient is settled up for the night I go out and walk in the garden. I enjoy enormously the cool air after the atmosphere of the sick room. I also enjoy the frogs in the field at the bottom of the garden, and the mountains and the moon. I often get an afternoon walk when things are going well, and my friend Arthur Greeves—the 'friend' of It you know, who mentioned the beech tree in his letter—sees me every day, and often twice a day. Some of my consolations are very childish and may seem brutal. When Arthur and I talk late into the night there is, even now, a magical feeling of successful conspiracy; it is such a breach, not of course of the formal rules but of the immemorial custom of a house where I have hardly ever known freedom. There is pleasure of the same kind in sitting with open windows in rooms where I have suffocated ever since childhood: and in substituting a few biscuits and fruit for the Gargantuan mid-day meal which was hitherto compulsory. I hope this is not so uncharitable as it sounds.

At any rate, I have never been able to resist the retrogressive influence of this house which always plunges me back into the pleasures and pains of a boy. That, by the bye, is one of the worst things about my present life. Every room is soaked with the bogeys of childhood, the awful 'rows' with my father, the awful returnings to school: and also with the old pleasures of an unusually ignoble adolescence.

By the way, that is just the point about intimacy *containing* familiarity. If it ever became really relevant to some truth that we were exploring in common I could and would expand the last sentence into detail: on the other hand I have not the slightest inclination to do so. i.e. what would be an *end* for familiars is only an instrument for intimates. I enclose a few epigrams on which I would like your opinion. With many thanks . . .

[Warren did not receive the last two letters from Jack until some forty days after they were posted. He was, in fact, unaware that there was anything wrong with his father until he received a cable from Jack on 27 September which read: 'Sorry report father died painless twenty-fifth September. Jack.']

TO HIS BROTHER: from 'Hillsboro'

29 September 1929

By this [time] you will have had my cable and the two letters written from Leeboro. As there is a good deal of business I will only give you the bare facts. The operation, in spite of what they prophesied, discovered cancer. They said he might live a few years. I remained at home, visiting him in the Nursing Home, for ten days. There were ups and downs and some bad spasms of pain from flatulence (apparently the usual sequence to abdominal operations) going over the wound: but nothing really dreadful. Quite often he was himself and telling wheezes, tho' of course he was often wandering from the dopes. By this time I had been at home since Aug. 11th and my work for next term was getting really desperate, and, as Joey said, I might easily wait several weeks more and still be in the same position— i.e. not really making the progress he should, but not likely to take a sudden turn for the worse. I therefore crossed to Oxford on Saturday Sept. 22. On Tuesday 24 I got a wire saying that he was worse, caught the train an hour later, and arrived to find that he had died on Tuesday afternoon. The immediate cause seems to have been some blood moving on to the brain: at least that is how they interpreted it. The facts were that he never woke on Tuesday, and remained all that day in a state of unconsciousness with a rising temperature . . . [134]

TO HIS BROTHER: from 'Hillsboro'

27 October [1929]

What you say in your letter is v. much what I am finding myself. I always before condemned as sentimentalists and

---

[134] The dates in this letter are confused. As Jack informed Warren by cable, Mr Lewis died on Wednesday 25 September. He was born on 22 August 1863 and, so, was a little over 66 years old.

hypocrites the people whose view of the dead was so different from the view they held of the same people living. Now one finds out that it is a natural process. Of course, on the spot, ones feelings were in some ways different. I think the mere pity for the poor old chap and for the life he had led really surmounted everything else. It was also (in the midst of home surroundings) almost impossible to believe. A dozen times while I was making the funeral arrangements I found myself mentally jotting down some episode or other to tell him: and what simply got me between wind and water was going into Robinson and Cleaver's to get a black tie and suddenly realizing 'You can never put anything down to his account again'.

By the way, a great deal of his jollities and wheezes remained to the end. One of the best things he ever said was the day before I left—four days before his death. As I came in the day nurse said 'I've just been telling Mr Lewis that he's exactly like my father.' P. 'And how am I like your father?' N. 'Why he's a pessimist.' P. (after a pause) 'I suppose he has several daughters.'

As time goes on the thing that emerges is that, whatever else he was, he was a terrific *personality*. You remember 'Johnson is dead. Let us go to the next. There is none. No man can be said to put you in mind of Johnson.'[135] How he filled a room! How hard it was to realize that physically he was not a very big man. Our whole world, the whole Pigiebotian world, is either direct or indirect testimony

---

[135] James Boswell, *The Life of Samuel Johnson* (1791) after Dr Johnson's death in 1784.

to the same effect. Take away from our conversation all that is imitation or parody (sincerest witness in the world) of his, and how little is left. The way we enjoyed going to Leeborough and the way we hated it, and the way we enjoyed hating it: as you say, one can't grasp that *that* is over. And now you could do anything on earth you cared to in the study at midday or on Sunday, and it is beastly.

I sympathize with you in the strange experience of returning to a British Isles which no longer contains a P'daitaheim. I hope that when all your books are set up (presumably in the non-glassed little end room bookcase) in Magdalen, where you can always have an empty sitting room to which you can repair at all hours, I hope that a leave at Hillsboro will be able to pass not unpalatably. Its no good pretending that its the old thing, but there you are . . . [136]

TO HIS BROTHER: from 'Hillsboro'

21 December 1929

One of the pities of the present state of affairs seems to be that it is impossible for either of us to write the other a real letter. I will try to break the spell by giving you some account of my adventures since you last heard from me before the great divide. The chief adventure is the quite new light thrown on

---

[136] Mrs Moore wrote to Warren on 27 October 1929 saying, 'I hope you will spend your leaves with us or wherever we are. We hope some day to get a larger house, when things would be more comfortable for you, so please do think of our home as your home, and be assured always of a very hearty welcome.'

P. by a closer knowledge of his two brothers.[137] One of his failings—his fussily directed manner 'Have you got your keys etc.'—takes on a new air when one discovers that in his generation the brothers all habitually treated one another in exactly the same way.

On the morning of the funeral Uncle Dick arrived before breakfast and came to Uncle Bill who was sleeping in the spare room. I drifted in. After a few greetings, it was with a shock of mild surprise that I heard Limpopo [Bill] suddenly cut short a remark of Uncle Dick's with the words 'Now Dick, you'd better go and take off your collar, huh, (gesture) and wash yourself and that sort of thing, eh, and have a bit of a shave.' To which his brother, with perfect seriousness replied 'Now how had we better handle the thing, eh Jacks? You'd better go to the bathroom first and I'll go downstairs and get a cup of tea. Bill, you'd better lie down (gesture) and cover yourself up and I'll come and tell you . . .' *Limpopo* (cutting in) 'Well Dick, get along downstairs, huh, and Jacks will go and tell you, wouldn't that be best, eh?'

Later in the day we had a session of the wardrobe committee quite in the old manner: and in the afternoon I was told 'Jacks, show Mrs Hamilton that coat you found. Isn't it a splendid fit, huh, might have been made for him, wha'?'

Another light came to me during the visit to the undertakers: the whole scene had such an insane air of diaboli-

---

[137] Albert Lewis was the youngest of four sons. His brother Joseph had died in 1908. The other two, William and Richard, had moved to Scotland in 1883 and entered into a partnership selling rope and felt. Their business was located in Glasgow, but they lived some fifteen miles away at Helensburgh.

cal farce that I cannot help recording it. After a man with a dusty face had approached me with the assurance that he had buried my grandfather, my mother, and my uncle, a superior person led us into an inner room and enquired if we wanted 'a suite of coffins'. Before I had recovered from this—and it sounded like the offer of some scaley booking clerk at an hotel in hell—the brute suddenly jerked out of the wall a series of enormous vertical doors, each one of which when lowered revealed on its inner side a specimen coffin. We were quite surrounded by them. Slapping one of them like a drum with his resonant hand he remarked 'That's a coffin I'm always very fond of' and it was then that the 'light' came.

Limpopo—and even Limpopo came as a relief in such an atmosphere—put an end to this vulgarity by saying in his deepest bass 'What's been used before, huh? There must be some tradition about the thing. What has the custom been in the family, eh?' And then I suddenly saw, what I'd never seen before: that to them family traditions—the square sheet, the two thirty dinner, the gigantic overcoat—were what school traditions and college traditions are, I don't say to me, but to most of our generation. It is so simple once you know it. How could it be otherwise in those large Victorian families with their intense vitality, when they had not been to public schools and when the family was actually the solidest institution they experienced? It puts a great many things in a more sympathetic light than I ever saw them in before.

But apart from these two lights, what I carried away from those few days was the feeling (perhaps I mentioned it before) that all the other members of that family were only fragments of our own P'daitabird. Uncle Dick has the wheezes, but only the crudest of them and none of the culture. In Joey you see the wheeze side of the character gone to seed—the man whose conversation is nothing but giggles. In Limpopo, of course you see simply all the bad points without any of the good: with the additional property of being an outrageous bore, which is the one thing P. never was at any time.

His idea of conversation is almost unbelievable. On the evening of the day of his arrival, after dinner, having been supplied with whiskey, he drew up the little wooden seated study chair to the fire, and having placed his little tubby body in it and crossed his flaccid hands on his belly, proceeded to enunciate the following propositions. 'I usually leave town about quarter to six, huh, and then I get out to Helensburgh about quarter past and walk up to me house, eh, and then I (Jacks I'll have another drop of that whiskey) put on an old coat, huh, then I come down and have something to drink and a bit of a chat with your Aunt Minnie, huh, and then . . .' Without any exaggeration, he kept me up till 1.30 with this drivel. The last night, when the Hamiltonians were there, was much better. Limpopo explained that he had given up dealing with Hogg. 'The last suit he sent me . . . the trousers came up to my chin (gesture) . . . I was very nearly going to law with him.' *Uncle Gussie:* 'I think you should. You should have gone into court wearing that suit.' *Limpopo* (with profound gravity): 'Oh, I wouldn't like to have done that, huh' . . .

TO HIS BROTHER: from 'Hillsboro'

12 January 1930

Do you find that the present state of affairs produces a permanent condition of—so to speak—comfortless excitement? Every thing is unsettled: all the old *structure* of things has collapsed and the complete liberty of making plans exactly as we choose, which one would once have sighed for, turns out to be in practice merely a bewildering impossibility of envisaging the future at all.

For the moment however, you will be most anxious to hear about the present, or, as it will be for you, the past. Well up to date Leeboro has not been sold. It will become very anxious as the time draws nearer your return. If a really good offer, *plus* a demand for immediate possession turns up, say, a fortnight before you are due at Liverpool, I really think I shall go out of my mind . . . It is not 'Can we afford to keep it three—or ten—months longer before selling it' but 'Can we afford to refuse any good offer for a thing that may turn out to be unsaleable?' Can we afford to gamble on the off chance of there being a second good offer *at all*? (Remember, there hasn't been *one* yet.) That is, we are not in the position of an impoverished Victorian Colonel wondering whether he can afford to go on hunting for one season more, but rather in that of a middle aged Victorian spinster wondering if she can safely refuse *any* proposal.

This infernal 'two presents' system—which began by being a joke and has ended by being an incubus—has naturally reduced most of your logical divisions and subdivisions of alternative possibilities to matchwood. To take the points that survive . . .

The trunk in the attic [containing the Boxen toys]. I entirely agree with you. Our only model for dealing with our world is the heavenly P'daita's method of dealing with this: and as he has long since announced his intention of ending the universe with a general conflagration, we will follow suit . . . I should not like to make an exception even in favour of Benjamin. After all these characters (like all others) can, in the long run, live only in 'the literature of the period': and I fancy that when we look at the actual *toys* again (a process from which I anticipate no pleasure at all), we shall find the discrepancy between the symbol (remember the outwards and visible form of *Hedges, the Beetle* — or *Bar* or even *Hawki*) and the character, rather acute. No, Brother. The toys in the trunk are quite plainly corpses. We will resolve them into their elements, as nature will do to us . . .

The New little end room. The most jarring comment on this proposal reached me before the proposal itself, in the form of a rather offensive letter from that old harridan Aunt Mary, to the following effect — that she had heard that 'Little Lea' was going to be sold: that she supposed I knew about the two book cases of Uncle Joe's that P. has 'stored' for him: that she very much wanted to have them: could she send and have them taken away at once: she had expected to see me at Christmas etc. etc. The minute I read it I knew in my bones that it was our little end room bookcases . . . Well that is the first and great comment on your plan of a new little end room.

The second is that to my mind the question largely turns on another: if we can succeed in getting another and larger house than Hillsboro, and you (as I hope—but this comes in a later paragraph) are with us, should such a room be there or in College. Thirdly, apart from these questions, your proposal is one that I partly agree with and partly disagree with. It runs in your letter 'A place where we can always meet on the common ground of the past and *ipso facto* a museum of the Leeborough we want to preserve.' Now my view would run 'A place where we can always meet on the common ground of the past and present and *ipso facto* a continuation and development of the Leeborough etc.' You see, Pigiebuddie, a *museum* is preciously like a *mausoleum*. An attempt at exact reconstruction (supposing it could succeed—wh. it can't in a room of quite different size and shape—) would fix the externals of a certain period for ever. But if you and I had gone home and lived at Leeborough, that is precisely what wouldn't have happened. Sooner or later we should have substituted good prints for the groups. As our library grew, new bookcases would have come. In the mere course of time the long thin table would have finished the process which it had already made a good start on, of falling to pieces. A thing fixed in imitation of the little end room as it is, can only be a perpetual reminder that that whole life is not *going on.* If it were going on, it would gradually change . . . I [think] that an attempt to imitate the little end room in detail would be a mistake. A mistake in sentiment, for it could only mean that we were embalming the corpse of something that isn't really dead, and needn't die at all. An aesthetic mistake—because we don't really want to have the taste of our schooldays established as a boundary for our whole lives . . .

What I am chiefly talking against in all this is the faint implication that *the past* is the only 'common ground' on which we can meet. I think, perhaps this is an occasion for frankness—a virtue which should be very sparingly used, but not never. I have no doubt that there have been times when you have felt that, shall we call it, Pigiebotianism was in danger of being swallowed up by, shall we say, Hillsborovianism: at such moments you may even have felt that the past was the only common ground—that wearing the national costume had become, as in Wales, an archaic revival. I am very sorry to have been the cause of such a period (this is not an apology but a statement)—but isn't that period itself passed? We have both changed since the real old days, but, on the whole, we have changed in the same direction. We are really much nearer together now than in the days when I was writing ridiculous epic poems at Cherbourg and you were wearing scarcely less ridiculous patent leathers at the Coll.

Now, as to your own plans. If you decide to become a full and permanent member of the household, you will be very welcome to all of us: and I must confess that it doesn't seem good enough that the two Piggiebudda should spend so much of their life divided by the whole breadth of the planet. Having laid this down as a starting pont, you won't I hope think that I am trying to dissuade you if I put up certain signposts. e.g. I suppose you do realize that to exchange an institutional for a domestic life is a pretty big change. (I take it for granted obviously that as a permanent member you neither could nor would wish to have, even remotely, the guest status.) Both kinds of life have their discomforts: and *all* discomforts are in a sense intolerable.

The great thing is to choose with one's eyes open. Can you stand as a permanency our cuisine—Maureen's practising—Maureen's sulks—Minto's burnettodesmondism—Minto's mare's nests—the perpetual interruptions of family life—the partial loss of liberty? This sounds as if I were either sick of it myself or else trying to make you sick of it: but neither is the case. I have definitely chosen and don't regret the choice. What I hope—very much hope—is that you, after consideration, may make the same choice, and not regret it: what I can't risk is your just floating in on the swell of a mood and then feeling trapped and fed up. Of course to weigh it fairly one must compare the best of this sort of life with the best of the other, and the worst of this with the worst of the other. What one is tempted to do is just the opposite—when one is exasperated in a home, to compare it with one of those splendid evenings one had in a mess or common room. Of course what one ought to do is to weigh it against the evening with the mess bore. On the whole my judgement would be that domestic life denies me a great many pleasures and saves me a great many pains.

There is also this further point. I spoke above of Pigiebotianism and Hillsborovianism. I presume that if you join us you are prepared for a certain amount of compromise in this matter. I shall never be prepared to abandon Pigiebotianism to Hillsborovianism. On the other hand there are the others to whom I have given the right to expect that I shall not abandon Hillsborovianism to Pigiebotianism. Whether I was right or wrong, wise or foolish, to have done so originally, is now only an historical question: once having created expectations, one naturally fulfills them . . .

TO OWEN BARFIELD: from Magdalen College

[3? February 1930]

Terrible things are happening to me. The 'Spirit' or 'Real I' is showing an alarming tendency to become much more personal and is taking the offensive, and behaving just like God. You'd better come on Monday at the latest or I may have entered a monastery ...

[Warren arrived back in England on 16 April 1930, having been away a little over three years. On the 17th he met Jack in London and they took a holiday with Mrs Moore and Maureen in Southbourne, Dorset. On 22 April the brothers set off for Belfast, arriving there on the 23rd. After visiting their father's grave they went to 'Little Lea' for their last stay there together. On the afternoon of the 23rd they carried the tin trunk containing the Boxen toys into the garden and, by mutual consent, buried it unopened. On 24 April they returned to Oxford and Warren stayed at 'Hillsboro' until he reported for duty at Bulford in Wiltshire on 15 May. Warren paid one last visit to 'Little Lea', 1–3 June, before it was sold.]

TO OWEN BARFIELD: from Magdalen College

10 June 1930

I have just finished the *Angel in the House*. Amazing poet![138] How all of a piece it is—how the rivetted metre both ex-

---

[138] Coventry Patmore (1823–96).

presses and illustrates his almost fanatical love of incarnation. What particularly impressed me was his taking—what one expects to find mentioned only in anti-feminists—the Lilithian desire to be admired and making it his chief point—the lover as primarily the mechanism by wh. the woman's beauty apprehends itself.

I see now why Janet saw female breasts on the dog collars, and have at last brought into consciousness the important truth: Venus is a female deity, not 'because men invented the mythology' but because she is. The idea of female beauty is the erotic stimulus for women as well as men . . . i.e. a lascivious man thinks about women's bodies, a lascivious woman thinks about her own. What a world we live in! . . .

TO A PUPIL: **from Magdalen College** (This is an early example of the innumerable painstaking and courteous letters Jack wrote to pupils and ex-pupils.)

18 June 1931

Now as to work. If you are staying up over the week-end and could call on me on Saturday morning we could discuss this. If this is impossible, my present advice is this:

Doing Chaucer and Shakespeare in the same term seems to me a hazardous experiment, unless there is some special reason which I don't know yet. Our usual plan here is to spend a term on Chaucer and his contemporaries. As regards reading for the Vac., my general view is that the Vac. should be given chiefly to reading the actual literary texts, without much attention to problems, getting thoroughly familiar with stories, situation, and style, and so having all the data for *aesthetic* judgement ready; then the term can be kept for more scholarly reading. Thus, if you were doing Chaucer and contemporaries next term, I shd advise you to read Chaucer himself, Langland (if you can get Skeat's edtn, the selection is not much good), Gower (again Macaulay's big edtn if possible, not so that you may read every word of the *Confessio* but so that you may select yourself—not forgetting the end which is one of the best bits), Gawain (Tolkien and Gordon's edtn), Sisam's XIV century prose and verse (all the pieces of any literary significance). If you can borrow Ritson's *Metrical Romance* so much the better.

But perhaps you have read all these before. If so, and if there are other special circumstances, we must try to meet. If Saturday is impossible, ring me up on Friday and I will squeeze in a time somehow or other.

[Warren discovered almost as soon as he arrived back in England that Jack and Mrs Moore were thinking of building their own home. On 25 May 1930 he covered in his diary the reasons why he chose to become a member of their household. Then, on 6 June they went to see a house called The Kilns in Headington Quarry which was coming up for sale. They liked the house, with its eight acres of woodlands, so much that in the end Jack, Warren and Mrs Moore bought it together. They moved there on 11 October 1930.

The following Autumn Warren was posted for the second time to Shanghai. He sailed from Southampton on 9 October 1931.]

TO ARTHUR GREEVES: from The Kilns, Kiln Lane, Headington Quarry

22 September 1931

I couldn't write to you last Sunday because I had a week-end guest—a man called Dyson who teaches English at Reading University.[139] I meet him I suppose about four or five times a year and am beginning to regard him as one of my friends of the 2nd class—i.e. Not in the same rank as yourself or Barfield, but on a level with Tolkien[140] or Macfarlane.[141]

He stayed the night with me in College—I sleeping in in order to be able to talk far into the night as one cd hardly do out here. Tolkien came too, and did not leave till 3 in the morning: and after seeing him out by the little postern on Magdalen bridge Dyson and I found still more to say to one another, strolling up and down the cloister of New Building, so that we did not get to bed till 4. It was really a memorable talk. We began (in Addison's walk just after dinner) on metaphor and myth—interrupted by a rush of

---

[139] Henry Victor Dyson ('Hugo') Dyson (1896–1975) was an undergraduate at Exeter College and took his B.A. in 1921. He was a Lecturer and Tutor in English Literature at the University of Reading 1921–45, and a Fellow and Tutor of Merton College 1945–63. For more about this charming member of 'The Inklings' see *Surprised by Joy* and Humphrey Carpenter's *The Inklings* (1978).

[140] John Ronald Reuel Tolkien (1892–1973) is as famous as he deserves to be. However, it may not be amiss to mention that when he and Jack met in 1926 he was already the Rawlinson and Bosworth Professor of Anglo-Saxon at Oxford. He 'changed chairs' to become the Merton Professor of English Language and Literature in 1945. See *Surprised by Joy* and Humphrey Carpenter's *J. R. R. Tolkien: A Biography* (1977).

[141] Kenneth Bruce McFarlane (1903–66) took his B.A. from Exeter College in 1925 and was Tutor in Modern History at Magdalen College 1927–66.

wind which came so suddenly on the still, warm evening and sent so many leaves pattering down that we thought it was raining. We all held our breath, the other two appreciating the ecstasy of such a thing almost as you would. We continued (in my room) on Christianity: a good long satisfying talk in which I learned a lot . . .

I am so glad you have really enjoyed a Morris again. I had the same feeling about it as you, in a way, with this proviso—that I don't think Morris was conscious of the meaning either here or in any of his works, except *Love Is Enough* where the flame actually breaks through the smoke so to speak. I feel more and more that Morris has taught me things he did not understand himself. These hauntingly beautiful lands which somehow never satisfy—this passion to escape from death *plus* the certainty that life owes all its charm to mortality—these push you on to the real thing because they fill you with desire and yet prove absolutely clearly that in Morris's world that desire cannot be satisfied.

The Macdonald conception of death—or, to speak more correctly, St Paul's—is really the answer to Morris: but I don't think I should have understood it without going through Morris. He is an unwilling witness to the truth. He shows you *just how far* you can go without knowing God, and that is far enough to force you (tho' not poor Morris himself) to go further. If ever you feel inclined to relapse into the mundane point of view—to feel that your book and pipe and chair are enough for happiness—it only needs a page or two of Morris to sting you wide awake into uncontrollable longing and to make you feel that everything is worthless except the hope of finding one of his countries. But if you read any of his romances through you will find the country dull before the end. All he has done is to rouse the desire: but so strongly that you *must* find the real satisfaction. And then you realise that *death* is at the root of the whole matter, and why he chose the subject of the Earthly Paradise, and how the true solution is one he never saw . . .

TO ARTHUR GREEVES: **from The Kilns** (on his conversion to Christianity)

18 October 1931

What has been holding me back (at any rate for the last year or so) has not been so much a difficulty in believing as a difficulty in knowing what the doctrine *meant:* you can't believe a thing while you are ignorant *what* the thing is. My puzzle was the whole doctrine of Redemption: in what sense the life and death of Christ 'saved' or 'opened salvation to' the world. I could see how miraculous salvation might be necessary: one could see from ordinary experience how sin (e.g. the case of a drunkard) could get a man to such a point that he was bound to reach Hell (i.e. complete degradation and misery) in this life unless something quite beyond mere natural help or effort stepped in. And I could well imagine a whole world being in the same state and similarly in need of miracle. What I couldn't see was how the life and death of Someone Else (whoever he was) two thousand years ago could help us here and now — except in so far as his *example* helped us. And the example business, tho' true and important, is not Christianity: right in the centre of Christianity, in the Gospels and St Paul, you keep on getting something quite different and very mysterious expressed in those phrases I have so often ridiculed ('propitiation'—'sacrifice'—'the blood of the Lamb')—expressions wh. I cd only interpret in senses that seemed to me either silly or shocking.

Now what Dyson and Tolkien showed me was this: that if I met the idea of sacrifice in a Pagan story I didn't mind it at all: again, that if I met the idea of a god sacrificing himself to himself (cf. the quotation opposite the title page of *Dymer*) I liked it very much and was mysteriously moved by it: again, that the idea of the dying and reviving god (Balder, Adonis, Bacchus) similarly moved me provided I met it anywhere *except* in the Gospels. The reason was that in Pagan stories I was prepared to feel the myth as profound and suggestive of meanings beyond my grasp even tho' I could not say in cold prose 'what it meant'.

Now the story of Christ is simply a true myth: a myth working on us in the same way as the others, but with this tremendous difference that *it really happened:* and one must be content to accept it in the same way, remembering that it is God's myth where the others are men's myths: i.e. the Pagan stories are God expressing Himself through the minds of poets, using such images as He found there, while Christianity is God expressing Himself through what we call 'real things'. Therefore it is *true,* not in the sense of being a 'description' of God (that no finite mind could take in) but in the sense of being the way in which God chooses to (or can) appear to our faculties. The 'doctrines' we get *out of* the true myth are of course *less* true: they are translations into our *concepts* and *ideas* of that wh. God has already expressed in a language more adequate, namely the actual incarnation, crucifixion, and resurrection. Does this amount to a belief in Christianity? At any rate I am now certain (a) That this Christian story is to be approached, in a sense, as I approach the other myths. (b) That it is the most important and full of meaning. I am also *nearly* certain that it really happened . . .

TO HIS BROTHER: from Magdalen College
24 October 1931
I hasten to tell you of a stroke of good luck for us both—I now have the 15 volume in Jeremy Taylor, in *perfect* condition, and have paid the same price of 20/-. My old pupil Griffiths spent a night with me last Monday and told me that Saunders the bookseller, who is a friend of his, had a copy.[142] He went round next day, got the book reserved and arranged the price . . .

On the same visit Griffiths presented me with a poorly bound but otherwise delightful copy (1742) of Law's An Appeal/ To all that doubt, or disbelieve/ The Truths of the Gospel/ Whether they be *Deists, Arians/ Socinians* or *Nominal Christians/*. It bears the book plate of Lord Rivers. I like it much better than the same author's *Serious Call,* and indeed like it as well as any religious work I have ever read. The *prose* of the *Serious Call* has here all been melted away, and the book is saturated with delight, and the sense

---

[142] Alan Richard Griffiths (now Dom Bede Griffiths, O.S.B.) was born in 1906 and read English under Jack at Magdalen. In *Surprised by Joy* (ch. XV) Jack speaks of him as his 'chief companion' on the road to Christianity. Dom Bede has told his own story of their friendship in *The Golden String* (1954).

of wonder: one of those rare works which make you say of Christianity 'Here is the very thing you like in poetry and the romances, only this time it's true' . . .

I am glad you liked Browne as far as you got when your letter was written. Your query 'Was there anything he didn't love?' hits the nail on the head. It seems to me that his peculiar strength lies in liking everything *both* in the serious sense (Christian charity and so forth) *and* in the Lambian sense of natural gusto: he is thus at once sane and whimsical, and sweet and pungent in the same sentence—as indeed Lamb is. I imagine that I get a sort of double pleasure out of Thomas Browne, one from the author himself and one reflected from Lamb. I always feel Lamb, as it were, reading the book over my shoulder. A lot of nonsense is talked about the society of books, but 'theres more in it than you boys think' in a case of this sort: it *is* almost like getting into a club . . .

Yes, indeed: how many essays I have heard read to me on Descartes' proofs (there are more than one) of the existence of God. (It was a remark of Harwood's first suggested to me that God might be defined as 'a being who spends his time having his existence proved and disproved'.) The particular one you quote ('I have the idea of a perfect being') seems to me to be valid or invalid according to the meaning you give the words 'have an idea of'. I used to work it out by the analogy of a machine. If I have the idea of a machine which I, being unmechanical, couldn't have invented on my own, does this prove that I have received the idea from some really mechanical source—e.g. a talk with the real inventor? To which I answer 'Yes, if you mean a really detailed idea': but of course there is another sense in which e.g. a lady novelist 'has an idea' of a new airship invented by her hero—in the sense that she attaches *some* vague meaning to her words, which proves nothing of the sort. So that if anyone asks me whether the idea of God in human minds proves His existence, I can only ask '*Whose* idea?' The Thistle-Bird's idea, for instance, clearly not, for it contains nothing whereof his own pride, fear, and malevolence could not easily provide the materials . . .

On the other hand it is arguable that the 'idea of God' in *some* minds does contain, not a mere abstract definition, but a real imaginative perception of goodness and beauty, beyond their own resources: and this not only in minds which already believe in God. It certainly seems to me that the 'vague something' which has been suggested to ones mind as desirable, all ones life, in experiences of nature and music and poetry, even in such ostensibly irreligious forms as 'The land East of the Sun and West of the Moon' in Morris, and which rouses desires that no finite object even pretends to satisfy, can be argued *not* to be any product of our own minds. Of course I am not suggesting that these vague ideas of something we want and haven't got, wh. occur in the Pagan period of individuals and of races (hence mythology) are anything more than the first and most rudimentary forms of the 'idea of God' . . .

TO HIS BROTHER: **from The Kilns**

22 November 1931

I am sorry I have not been able to write for some weeks. During the week it is out of the question. My ordinary day is as follows. Called (with tea) 7.15. After bath and shave I usually have time for a dozen paces or so in Addison's walk (at this time of year my stroll exactly hits the sunrise) before chapel at 8. 'Dean's Prayers' — which I have before described to you — lasts about quarter of an hour. I then breakfast in common room with the Dean's Prayers party (i.e. Adam Fox, the chaplain, Benecke and Christie)[143] which is joined punctually by J. A. Smith at about 8.25. I have usually left the room at about 8.40, and then saunter . . . answer notes etc till 9. From 9 till 1 is all pupils — an unconscionable long stretch for a man to act the gramaphone in. At one Lyddiatt or Maureen is waiting for me with the car and I am carried home.

My afternoons you know. Almost every afternoon as I set out hillwards with my spade, this place gives me all the thrill of novelty. The scurry of the waterfowl as you pass the pond, and the rich smell of autumnal litter as you leave the drive and strike into the little path, are always just as good as new. At 4.45 I am usually driven into College again, to be a gramaphone for two more hours, 5 till 7. At 7.15 comes dinner.

On Tuesday, which is my really shocking day, pupils come to me to read Beowulf at 8.30 and usually stay till about 11, so that when they have gone and I have glanced round the empty glasses and coffee cups and the chairs in the wrong

---

[143] The Rev. Adam Fox (1883–1977) took his B.A. from University College in 1906 and was ordained a priest in 1911. He was Dean of Divinity at Magdalen College 1929–42, Professor of Poetry 1938–43, and a Canon of Westminster 1942–63.

John Traill Christie (1899–1980) was a Fellow and Classical Tutor of Magdalen 1928–32, Headmaster of Repton School 1932–37, Headmaster of Westminster School 1937–49, and Principal of Jesus College, Oxford, 1950–67.

places, I am glad enough to crawl to bed. Other standing engagements are on Thursday when a man called Horwood (another English don)[144] comes and reads Dante with me, every second Monday when the College literary society meets. When you have thrown in the usual irregular dinner engagements you will see that I am lucky when I have two evenings free after dinner.

The only exception to this programme (except of course Saturday when I have no pupils after tea) is Monday when I have no pupils at all. I have to employ a good deal of it in correcting transcripts done by B. Litt. pupils, and other odd jobs. It has also become a regular custom that Tolkien should drop in on me of a Monday morning and drink a glass. This is one of the pleasantest spots in the week. Sometimes we talk English school politics: sometimes we criticise one another's poems: other days we drift into theology or 'the state of the nation': rarely we fly no higher than bawdy and 'puns'.

What began as an excuse for not writing has developed into a typical diary or hebdomadal compendium. As to the last two week ends, they have both been occupied. The one before last I went to spend a night at Reading with a man called Hugo Dyson—now that I come to think of it, you heard all about him before you left. We had a grand evening. Rare luck to stay with a friend whose wife is so nice that one *almost* (I can't say quite) *almost* regrets the change when he takes you up to his study for serious smoking and

---

[144] Frederick Chesney Horwood (1904–) matriculated at St Catherine's College in 1922 and took his B.A. in 1925. He was a Fellow and Tutor in English at St Catherine's College 1930–70.

for the real midnight talking. You would enjoy Dyson very much for his special period is the late 17th century: he was much intrigued by your library when he was last in our room. He is a most fastidious bookman and made me (that same ocasion) take out one of the big folios from the bottom shelf of the Leeboro bookcase because they were too tightly packed . . .

At the same time he is far from being a dilettante as anyone can be: a burly man, both in mind and body, with the stamp of the war on him, which begins to be a pleasing rarity, at any rate in civilian life. Lest anything should be lacking, he is a Christian and a lover of cats. The Dyson cat is called Mirralls, and is a Viscount . . .

Tutorial necessities have spurred me into reading another Carlyle *Past and Present* which I recommend: specially the central part about Abbot Samson. Like all Carlyle it gets a little wearisome before the end—as all listening to these *shouting* authors does. But the pungency and humour and frequent sublimity is tip-top. It is very amusing to read the 19th century editor's preface (in our Leeborough edition), obviously by a P'daita: pointing out that, of course, the matter of the book is out of date, but it 'lives by its style'. 'We can afford to smile at the pessimism with which the sage approached problems that have since vanished like a dream before the onward march etc. etc.' Actually the book is an indictment of the industrial revolution pointing out precisely the problems we have *not* solved and prophesying most of the things that *have* happened since.

I get rather annoyed at this endless talk about books 'living by the style'. Jeremy Taylor 'lives by the style in spite of his obsolete theology'; Thos. Browne does the same, in spite of 'the obsolete cast of his mind': Ruskin and Carlyle do the same in spite of their 'obsolete social and political philosophy'. To read histories of literature, one would suppose that the great authors of the past were a sort of chorus of melodious idiots who said, in beautifully cadenced language that black was white and that two and two made five. When one turns to the books themselves—well I, at any rate, find nothing obsolete. The silly things these great men say, were as silly then as they are now: the wise ones are as wise now as they were then . . .

I had to set a paper for School Certificate the other day on the Clarendon Press selections from Cowper—a ridiculous book for schoolboys. It includes a large chunk of Bagehot's Essay on Cowper which makes me think I must read all Bagehot. We have him, haven't we? Not that I 'hold with him', he is too much of a pudaita by half: but he has great fun . . . How delicious Cowper himself is—the letters even more than the poetry. Under every disadvantage—presented to me as raw material for a paper and filling with a job an evening wh. I had hoped to have free—even so he charmed me. He is the very essence of what Arthur calls 'the homely' which is Arthur's favourite genre. All these cucumbers, books, parcels, tea-parties, parish affairs. It is wonderful what he makes of them.

I suppose we may expect a Colombo letter from you soon. I will vary the usual 'must stop now' by saying 'I am going to stop now'. I am writing in the common room (Kilns) at 8.30 of a Sunday evening: a moon shining through a fog outside and a bitter cold night.

TO HIS BROTHER: from The Kilns

Christmas Day 1931

I also heard at the same binge a very interesting piece of literary history from an unexceptionable source—that the hackneyed 'A German officer crossed the Rhine' was being sung at undergraduate blinds in 1912. What do you make of that? Can it date from the Franco Prussian war? Or is it a German student song made in anticipation of *Der Tag* about 1910? The latter would be an interesting fact for the historian. I never heard the ballad as a whole, but think it is poor—in fact, nasty. Bawdy ought to be outrageous and extravagant . . . must have nothing cruel about it . . . it must not approach anywhere near the pornographic . . .

We had a poorish discourse from Thomas at Matins, but otherwise he has been keeping his end up very well.[145] In one sermon on foreign missions lately he gave an ingenious turn to an old objection. 'Many of us' he said 'have friends who used to live abroad, and had a native Christian as a cook who was unsatisfactory. Well, after all there are a great many unsatisfactory Christians in England too. In fact I'm one myself.' Another interesting point (in a different sermon) was that we should be glad that the early Christians expected the second coming and the end of the world quite soon: for if they had known that they were founding an

---

[145] The Rev. Wilfrid Savage Thomas (1879–1959) was the Vicar of the Church of the Holy and Undivided Trinity, Headington Quarry, which is about half a mile from The Kilns. Father Thomas took a B.A. from Pembroke College, Cambridge, in 1900. Following his ordination in 1903 he held a number of livings in England and Australia. He was the Vicar of Headington Quarry 1924–35.

organisation for centuries they would certainly have organised it to death: believing that they were merely making provisional arrangements for a year or so, they left it free to live.

How odd it is to turn from Thomas to F. K.[146] He really surpassed himself the other day when he said that he objected to the early chapters of St Luke (the Annunciation particularly) on the ground that they were—*indelicate*. This leaves one gasping. One goes on re-acting against the conventional modern re-action against nineteenth century prudery, and then suddenly one is held up by a thing like this, and almost pardons all the followers of Lytton Strachey. If you turn up the passage in St Luke the thing becomes even more grotesque. The Middle Ages had a different way with these things. Did I tell you that in one of the Miracle Plays, Joseph is introduced as a typical comic jealous husband, and enters saying 'This is what comes of marrying a young woman' . . .

I have bought *The Brothers Karamazov* but not yet read it with the exception of some special detachable pieces (of which there are many). Thus read it is certainly a great religious and poetical work: whether, as a whole, it will turn out a good, or even a tolerable novel I don't know. I have not forgotten your admirable Russian novel 'Alexey Poldorovna lived on a hill. He cried a great deal' . . .

---

[146] The Rev. Edward Foord-Kelcey (1859–1934) took a B.A. from Pembroke College, Oxford, in 1887 and was ordained in 1888. His last living was as Rector of Kimble 1906–26, after which he retired to a house in Northfield Road, Headington. He came to know Jack and the Moores when they were living in 28 Warneford Road. There is a delightful portrait of him by Jack in the *Lewis Papers*, vol. XI, pp. 24–25 which ends 'He was the worst preacher I ever sat under: and one of the most lovable—though by no means the least irritating—men I have ever known.'

TO HIS BROTHER: from Magdalen College

17 January 1932

It is one of the 'painful mysteries' of history that all languages progress from being very particular to being very general. In the first stage they are bursting with meaning, but very cryptic because they are not general enough to show the common element in different things: e.g. you can talk (and therefore think) about all the different kinds of trees but not about *Trees*. In fact you can't really reason at all. In their final stage they are admirably clear but are so far away from real things that they really say nothing. As we learn to talk we forget what we have to say. Humanity, from this point of view, is rather like a man coming gradually awake and trying to describe his dreams: as soon as his mind is sufficiently awake for clear description, the thing which was to be described is gone. You see the origin of journalese and of the style in which you write army letters.

Religion and poetry are about the only language in modern Europe—if you can regard them as 'languages'—which still have traces of the dream in them, still have something to say. Compare 'Our Father which art in Heaven' with 'The supreme being transcends space and time'. The first goes to pieces if you begin to apply the literal meaning to it. How can anything but a sexual animal really be a father? How can it be in the sky? The second falls into no such traps. On the other hand the first really *means* something, really represents a concrete experience in the minds of those who use it: the second is mere dexterous playing with counters, and once a man has learned the rule he can go on that way for two volumes without really using the words to refer to any concrete *fact* at all...

Most of my recent reading, before term, has been of rather a simple and boyish kind. I re-read *The People of the Mist*—a tip-top yarn of the sort. If someone would start re-issuing all Rider Haggard at 1/- a volume I would get them all, as a permanent fall-back for purely recreational reading. Then I read *The Wood Beyond the World*—with some regret that this leaves me no more Wm Morris prose romances to read (except *Child Christopher* wh. is an adaptation of a mediae-val poem already known to me and therefore hardly counts). I wish he had written a hundred of them! I should like to have the knowledge of a new romance always waiting for me the next time I am sick or sorry and want a real treat . . .

While at Cambridge (staying, as I foretold you in a posh hotel, at the expense of the Board. Four of us had to hold an examiners meeting one evening, and accordingly, just like the heroes of a romance, called for fire, lights, and a bottle of claret in a private room. All that was lacking was to have prefaced the order by tweaking the landlord's nose with a 'Hark'ee, rascal!' This was in the University Arms which perhaps you know)—while in Cambridge, or rather on my long, slow, solitary, first class journey there and back through fields white with frost—I read Pater's *Marius the Epicurean*. This is the best specimen extant of the Epicurean-aesthetic business: which one wrongs by reading it in its inferior practitioners such as George Moore and Oscar Wilde. As you probably know it is a novel—or, since the story is so slight, a faintly narrative *causerie*—laid in the reign of Marcus Aurelius. The interest-ing thing is, that being a really consistent aesthete, he has to bring in the early Christians favourably because the *flavour* of the early Church—the new music, the humility, the chastity, the sense of order and quiet decorum—appeal to him aesthetically. It is doubtful if he sees that he can only have it in by blowing to bits the whole Epicurean basis of his outlook—so that aestheticism, honestly followed, refutes itself by leading him to something that will put aestheticism in its place—and Pater's position is therefore, in the long run, all nonsense. But it is [a] very beautiful book . . . I should try it if it is in your library. Gad! How it would have bowled one over at eighteen. One would be only just beginning to recover now . . .

If your idea of reading Descartes holds, begin with the *Discourse on Method.* This is in biographical form and is on the border-land between philosophy proper and what might be called the 'history of intellectual manners'. But I'm not at all sure that a man so steeped in the XVIIth century as you would not find his natural starting point in Boethius—I suppose 'Boece' is as common in France at that time as he was in England? As he was translated about once a century into every civilised language, you would have no difficulty in finding a well flavoured version . . .

How ones range of interests grows! Do you find a sort of double process going on with relation to books—that while the number of subjects one wants to read is increasing, the number of books on each which you find worth reading steadily decreases. Already in your own corner of French history you have reached the point at which you know that most of the books published will be merely re-hashes, but in revenge you are reading Vaughan and thinking of reading Taylor. Ten years ago you would have read eight books on your period (getting only what the *one* book behind those eight would have given you) and left Vaughan and Taylor out of account . . .

TO HIS BROTHER: **from Magdalen College** (Warren was in Shanghai and possibly in danger from the Japanese attack on the Chinese part of that city.)

21 February 1932

I have had your cheering letter of Jan 14th—'cheering' for giving one some conversation with you, though of course it bears not at all on the source of anxiety. I must confess I have imbibed enough of that rather specially shabby super-stition which cries 'Touch wood' etc, to shudder when I read your proposals about walks in Ulster etc. In fact I have two unpleasantly contrasted pictures in my mind. One 'features' the two Pigibudda with packs and sticks de-training into the sudden stillness of the moors at Parkmore: the other is of you progressing from the Bund to Gt Western Rd with an eye cocked skyward, just in the old French manner, curse it, and ducking at the old *Who-o-o-o-p—Bang!*

Like Boswell, on that perilous crossing in the Hebrides, I 'at last took refuge in piety: but was much embarrassed by the various objections which have been raised against the doctrine of special providences'. Unfortunately I have not at hand the work of Dr Ogden in which Boswell found this difficulty solved.

I suppose the solution lies in pointing out that the effi-cacy of prayer is, at any rate *no more* of a problem then the efficacy of *all* human acts. i.e. if you say 'It is useless to pray because Providence already knows what is best and will certainly do it', then why is it not equally useless (and for the same reason) to try to alter the course of events in any way whatever—to ask for the salt or book your seat in a train? . . .

TO HIS BROTHER: from The Kilns

20 March 1932

Next to the good news from China, the best thing that has happened to me lately is to have assisted at such a scene in the Magdalen smoking room as rarely falls one's way. The Senior Parrot—that perfectly ape-faced man whom I have probably pointed out to you—was seated on the padded fender with his back to the fire, bending down to read a paper, and thus leaving a tunnel shaped aperture between his collar and the nape of his neck [designated 'P' in a drawing of the man]. A few yards in front of him stood MacFarlane. Let MacFarlane now light a cigarette and wave the match to and fro in the air to extinguish it. And let the match be either not wholly extinguished or so recently extinguished that no fall of temperature in the wood has occurred. Let M. then fling the match towards the fire in such a way that it follows the dotted line and enters the aperture at P with the most unerring accuracy. For a space of time which must have been infinitesimal, but which seemed long to us as we watched in the perfect silence which this very interesting experiment so naturally demanded, the Senior Parrot, alone ignorant of his fate, continued absorbed in the football results. His body then rose in a vertical line from the fender, without apparent muscular effort, as though propelled by a powerful spring under his bottom. Re-alighting on his feet he betook himself to a rapid movement of the hands with the apparent intention of applying them to every part of his back and buttock in the quickest possible succession: accompanying this exercise with the distention of the cheeks and a blowing noise. After which, exclaiming (to me) in a very heightened voice 'It isn't so bloody funny' he darted from the room.

The learned Dr Hope (that little dark, mentally dull, but very decent demi-butty who breakfasted with you and me)[147] who alone had watched the experiment with perfect gravity, at this stage, remarked placidly to the company in general, 'Well, well, the match will have gone out by now', and returned to his periodical—But the luck of it! How many shots would a man have taken before he succeeded in throwing a match into that tiny aperture if he had been trying?

You asked Minto in a recent letter about this Kenchew man. As a suitor he shows deplorable tendency to hang fire, and I fancy the whole thing will come to nothing. (Ah there won't *be* any proposal): as a character, however, he is worth describing, or seems so to me because I had to go for a walk with him. He is a ladylike little man of about fifty, and is to-a-tee that 'sensible, well-informed man' with whom Lamb dreaded to be left alone.

My troubles began at once. It seemed good to him to take a bus to the Station and start our walk along a sort of scrubby path between a factory and a greasy strip of water—a walk, in fact, which was as good a reproduction as Oxford could afford of our old Sunday morning 'around the river bank'. I blundered at once by referring to the water as a canal. 'Oh—could it be possible that I didn't know it

---

[147] Edward Hope (1866–1953) took a Sc.D. from Manchester and in 1919 he was elected Fellow and Tutor in Natural Science at Magdalen and Lecturer in Chemistry.

was the Thames? I must be joking. Perhaps I was not a walker?' I foolishly said that I was. He gave me an account of his favourite walks; with a liberal use of the word 'picturesque'. He then called my attention to the fact that the river was unusually low (how the devil did he know that?) and would like to know how *I* explained it. I scored a complete Plough, and was told how *he* explained it.

By this time we were out in Port Meadow, and a wide prospect opened before him. A number of hills and church spires required to be identified, together with their 'picturesque', mineral, or chronological details. A good many problems arose, and again I did very badly. As his map, though constantly brought out, was a *geological* map, it did not help us much. A conversation on weather followed, and seemed to offer an escape from unmitigated fact. The escape, however, was quite illusory, and my claim to be rather fond of nearly all sorts of weather was received with the stunning information that psychologists detected the same trait in children and lunatics.

Anxious to turn my attention from this unpleasing fact, he begged my opinion of various changes which had recently been made in the river: indeed every single lock, bridge, and stile for three mortal miles had apparently been radically altered in the last few months. As I had never seen *any* of the places before ('But I thought you said you were a walker . . .') this bowled me middle stump again. The removal of a weir gave us particular trouble. He could not conceive how it had been done. What did I think? And then, just as I was recovering from this fresh disgrace, and hoping that the infernal weir was done with, I found that the problem of *how* it had been removed was being raised only as the preliminary to the still more intricate problem of *why* it had been removed. (My feelings were those expressed by Macfarlane at dinner one night last term, in an answer to someone's question. 'Yes. He is studying the rhythms of mediaeval Latin prose, and it is a very curious and interesting subject, but it doesn't interest me.') For a mile or so after the weir we got on famously, for Kenchew began 'I was once passing this very spot or, no, let me see—perhaps it was a little further on—no! It was exactly here—I remember that very tree—when a very remarkable experience, really remarkable in a small way, happened to me.' The experience remarkable in a small way, with the aid of a judicious question or two on my part, was bidding fair to last out the length of the walk, when we had the horrible misfortune of passing a paper mill (You see, by the bye, what a jolly walk it was even apart from the company!). Not only *a* paper mill but *the* paper mill of the Clarendon Press. 'Of course I had been over it. No? Really etc.' (The great attraction was that you could get an electric shock.)

But I must stop my account of this deplorable walk somewhere. It was the same all through—sheer information. Time after time I attempted to get away from the torrent of isolated, particular facts: but anything tending to opinion, or discussion, to fancy, to ideas, even to putting some of his infernal facts together and making something out of them— anything like that was received in blank silence. Once, while he was telling me the legendary foundation of a church, I had a faint hope that we might get onto history: but it turned out that his knowledge was derived from an Edwardian Oxford *pageant*. Need I add that he is a scientist? A geographer, to be exact. And now that I come to think of it he is exactly what one would have expected a geographer to be. But I mustn't give you too black an impression of him. He is kind, and *really* courteous (you know the rare quality I mean) and a gentleman. I imagine he is what women call '*Such* an interesting man. And *so* clever' . . .

TO HIS BROTHER: from Magdalen College

8 April 1932

I wonder can you imagine how reassuring your bit about Spenser is to me who spend my time trying to get unwilling hobble-de-hoys to read poetry at all? One begins to wonder whether literature is not, after all, a failure. Then comes your account of the *Faerie Queene* on your office table, and one remembers that all the professed 'students of literature' don't matter a rap, and that the whole thing goes on, unconcerned by the fluctuations of the kind of 'taste' that gets itself printed, living from generation to generation in the minds of the few disinterested people who sit down alone and read what they like and find that it turns out to be just the thing that every one has liked since they were written. I agree with all you say about it, except about the distinctions of characters. The next time I dip in it I shall keep my weather eye on them. It would be quite in accord with all ones experience to find out one day that the usual critical view (i.e. that Spenser has no characters) was all nonsense . . .

By the way, I most fully agree with you about 'the lips being invited to share the banquet' in poetry, and always 'mouth' it while I read, though not in a way that would be audible to other people in the room. (Hence the excellent habit which I once formed but have since lost, of not smoking while reading a poem.) I look upon this 'mouthing' as an infallible mark of those who really like poetry. Depend upon it, the man who reads verses in any other way, is after 'noble thoughts' or 'philosophy' (in the revolting sense given to that word by Browning societies and Aunt Lily) or social history, or something of the kind, not poetry.

To go back to Spenser—the battles *are* a bore . . .

The whole puzzle about Christianity in non-European countries is very difficult . . . Sometimes, relying on his remark 'Other sheep I have that are not of this fold' I have played with the idea that Christianity was never intended for Asia—even that Buddha is the form in which Christ appears to the Eastern mind. But I don't think this will really work. When I have tried to rule out all my prejudices I still can't help thinking that the Christian world is (partially) 'saved' in a sense in which the East is not. We may be hypocrites, but there is a sort of unashamed and *reigning* iniquity of temple prostitution and infanticide and torture and political corruption and obscene imagination in the East, which really does suggest that they are off the rails—that some necessary part of the human machine, restored to us, is still missing with them . . . For some reason which we cannot find out they are still living in the B.C. period (as there are African tribes still living in the stone-age) and it is apparently not intended that they should yet emerge from it . . .

TO OWEN BARFIELD: from Magdalen College

[April? 1932]

As regards our argument about Gethsemane, I quite see that it sounds odd to attribute to perfect man a fear which imperfect men have often overcome. But one must beware of interpreting 'perfect man' in a sense which would nullify the temptation in the wilderness: a scene on which, at first, one would be tempted to comment (a) As regards the stone and bread 'Imperfect men have voluntarily starved' (b) As regards Satan's demand for worship 'Most men have never sunk so low as to feel this temptation at all'.

If we are to accept the Gospels however, we must interpret Christ's perfection in a sense which admits of his feeling *both* the commonest and most animal temptations (hunger and the fear of death) and those temptations which usually occur only to the worst of men (devil worship for the sake of power). I am assuming that the stones and bread represents hunger: but if you prefer to regard it as primarily a temptation to *thaumaturgy* ('If thou be the Son of God, command these stones') then it falls into my second class.

The consideration of this second class at once raises the question 'Are there not temptations proper to the very best and the very worst, which the middle sort of men do not feel?': or, again 'Do not common temptations attack most fiercely the best and the worst?' I should answer Yes, and say that fear of death was one of these: and in respect of that fear I wd divide men into three classes.

A. The very bad to whom death represents the final defeat of the systematic self-regarding caution and egoism which has been the sole occupation of life. (False freedom defeated)

B. The virtuous. These in fact do not conquer fear of death without the support of any or all of the following

(1) Pride . . .

(2) Fear (Charge, charge, 'tis too late to retreat!)

(3) *Taedium vitae* (My baby at my breast, that lulls the nurse asleep.)

(4) Abandonment of the exhausting attempt at real freedom wh. makes the Necessary appear as a *relief* (The ship glides under the green arch of peace).

C. The Perfect. He cannot resort to any of the aids wh. class B. have, for they all depend on defect. His position is thus closely parallel to class A: death for Him also is the final defeat, but the time of *real* Freedom. (I am taking it for granted that the spiritual essence of death is 'the opposite of Freedom': hence the most *mortal* images are rigidity, suffocation etc.)

No doubt, He also knows the answer—that voluntary death (really voluntary, not the anodynes and dutch courages) makes unfreedom itself the assertion of freedom. But voluntary submission does not mean that there is nothing to submit to.

What is it to an ordinary man to die, if once he can set his teeth to bear the merely animal fear? To give in—he has been doing that nine times out of ten all his life. To see the lower in him conquer the higher, his animal body turning into lower animals and these finally into the mineral—he has been letting this happen since he was born. To relinquish control—easy for him as slipping on a well worn shoe. But in Gethsemane it is essential Freedom that is asked to be bound, unwearied control to throw up the sponge, Life itself to die. Ordinary men have not been so much in love with life as is usually supposed: small as their share of it is they have found it too much to bear without reducing a large portion of it as nearly to non-life as they can: we have drugs, sleep, irresponsibility, amusement, are more than half in love with easeful death—if only we could be sure it wouldn't hurt! Only He who really lived a human life (and I presume that only one did) can fully taste the horror of death. I am sure that if the thing were presented to you in a myth you wd be the first to cry out upon the prosaic critic who complained that the Sun was discredited because it fled from the Wolves.

Your idea of Christ as *suffering* from the mere fact of being in the body, and therefore tempted, if at all, to hasten rather than postpone his death, seems to imply that he was not (as the Christian mystery runs) 'perfect God and perfect man' but a kind of composite being, a δαιμων or archangel imprisoned in a vehicle unsuitable to it (like Ariel in the oak) and in constant revolt against that vehicle. This is mythological in the bad sense. The Son was certainly not incarnated in such a sense as not also to remain God (if He had been, the universe wd have disappeared).

I don't pretend to have an explanation: but I take it that the precise *differentia* of the Christian doctrine is that 'Something wh. eternally *is* in the Noumenal world (and is impassible, blessed, omniscient, omnipotent etc) nevertheless once *was* in the phenomenal world (and was suffering etc).' You can't regard the earthly life of Jesus as an episode in the eternal life of the Son: as the slavery to Admetus was an episode in the immortal life of Apollo.

I need not say that on my view, the doctrine (do you hold it) that what was incarnated was 'One of the hierarchies' (or 'one of' the 'anythings') appears to me quite incompatible with the position given to Christ by his own words and by his followers. *Aut deus aut malus angelus* is as true as the old *aut deus aut malus homo.*

TO HIS BROTHER: **from Schools** (where he was invigilating)

14 June 1932

I have just read your letter of May 15th, but not as you supposed in College. 'Schools' has arrived and I am invigilating and although your letter arrived before lunch I deliberately brought it here unopened so that the reading it might occupy at least part of the arid waste of talk-less, smoke-less, exercise-less time between 2 P.M. and 5 P.M. Theoretically of course there ought to be no greater blessing than three hours absolutely safe from interruption and free from reading: but somehow or other—everyone has made the discovery—reading is quite impossible in the Schools. There is a sort of atmosphere at once restless and soporific which always ends in that stage which (for me) is a signal to stop reading:—the stage I mean at which you blink and ask yourself 'Now what *was* the last page about' . . .

I have read, or rather re-read, one novel namely *Pendennis*. How pleased the Pdaitabird would have been—why hadn't I the grace to read it a few years ago. Why I re-read it now I don't quite know—I suppose some vague idea that it was time I gave Thackeray another trial. The experiment, on the whole, has been a failure. I can just see, mind you, why they use words like 'great' and 'genius' in talking of him which we don't use of Trollope. There are indications, or breakings in, all the time of something beyond Trollope's range. The scenery for one thing (tho' to be sure there is only one scene in Thackeray—always summer evening—English garden—rooks cawing) has a sort of depth (I mean in the painting sense) wh. Trollope hasn't got. Still more there are the sudden 'depths' in a very different sense in Thackeray. There is one v. subordinate scene in *Pendennis* where you meet the Marquis of Steyne and a few of his led captains and pimps in a box at a theatre. It only lasts a page or so—but the sort of rank, salt, urinous stench from the nether pit nearly knocks you down and clearly has a kind of power that is quite out of Trollope's range. I don't think these bits really improve Thackeray's books: they do, I suppose, indicate whatever we mean by 'genius'. And if you are the kind of reader who values genius you rate Thackeray highly.

My own secret is—let rude ears be absent—that to tell you the truth, brother, *I don't like genius.* I like enormously some *things* that only genius can do: such as *Paradise Lost* and the *Divine Comedy*. But it is the results I like. What I don't care twopence about is the sense (apparently dear to so many) of being in the hands of 'a great man'—you know: his dazzling personality, his lightening energy, the strange force of his mind—and all that. So that I quite definitely prefer Trollope—or rather this re-reading of *Pen.* confirms my long standing preference. No doubt Thackeray was the genius: but Trollope wrote the better books. All the old things I objected to in Thackeray I object to still.

Do you remember saying of Thomas Browne in one of your letters 'Was there anything he didn't love?' One can ask just the opposite of Thackeray. He is wrongly accused of making his virtuous women too virtuous: the truth is he does not make them virtuous enough. If he makes a character what he wd call 'good' he always gets his own back by making her (its always a female character) a bigot and a blockhead. Do you think Sir, pray, that there are many slum parishes which could not produce half a dozen old women quite as chaste and affectionate as Helen Pendennis and ten times more charitable and more sensible? Now Phippy is a much better woman than most of Thackeray's 'good' women. Still—the Major deserves his place in ones memory. So does Foker—surely the most *balanced* picture of the kindly vulgar young fop that there is. I'm not sure about Costigan. There's a good deal too much of Thackeray's habit of laughing at things like poverty and mispronunciation in the Costigan parts. Then, of course theres 'the style'—Who the deuce wd begin talking about the style in a novel till all else was given up.

I have had another visit to Whipsnade [Zoo]—Foord Kelcie motored Arthur and me over on a fine Monday when Arthur was staying here. This was not the best company in the world with whom to revisit Whipsnade as F. K. combines extreme speed of tongue with a very slow walk, which is reduced to a stop when he has a good thing to say ... Perhaps however it was just as well that A. drew me out of my course, for the place has been so increased and altered that I should have missed a good deal. The novelties include lions, tigers, polar bears, beavers etc. Bultitude [a bear] was still in his old place. Wallaby wood, owing to the different season, was improved by masses of bluebells: the graceful faun-like creatures hopping out of one pool of sunshine into another over English wildflowers—and so much tamer now than when you saw them that it is really no difficulty to stroke them—and English wildbirds singing deafeningly all round, came nearer to ones idea of the world before the Fall than anything I ever hoped to see . . .

TO HIS BROTHER: from The Kilns

12 December 1932

A thousand welcomes to Harve (of hated memory.) We have had so many alarms about you that I shall hardly believe it till I see you with my own eyes. But on that score, and on all your last six months' adventures there is so much to be said that it is absurd to begin. You would be amused to hear the various hypotheses that were entertained during your long summer silence—that you had been captured by bandits—were in jail—had gone mad—had married— had married a Chinese woman. My own view of course was 'Indeed he's such a fellow etc', but I found it hard to maintain this against the riot of rival theories . . .

It all seems too good to be true. I can hardly believe that when you take your shoes off a week or so hence, please God, you will be able to say 'This will do me—for life' . . .

[In July 1932 Warren applied to be placed on retired pay. He left Shanghai by cargo ship on 22 October and reached Liverpool on 14 December. Upon reaching The Kilns he was delighted to find that the new wing of the house, containing a study and bedroom, had been built specially for him. His retirement from the Royal Army Service Corps after eighteen years became official on 21 December 1932.

The letter which follows reveals something of the interests which led Jack to write *The Allegory of Love* and to begin his 'Prolegomena' lectures which led ultimately to his book *The Discarded Image: An Introduction to Medieval and Renaissance Literature* (1964). These twice-weekly lectures began on 18 January 1932 and were entitled 'Prolegomena to Medieval Poetry'. They were continued during Trinity Term of 1932 and the final two lectures, devoted to Chaucer, were given in Trinity Term of 1933 — 24 and 26 April. These lectures were repeated a number of times. In Trinity Term of 1937 he began his other well-known series entitled 'Prolegomena to Renaissance Poetry'.]

TO SISTER MADELEVA C. S. C. of Notre Dame, Indiana: **from Magdalen College** (Sister Madeleva was living in Oxford at the time and attending the 'Prolegomena' lectures.)

7 June 1934
In answer to your first question, there are probably such printed bibliographies as you mention, but I have no knowledge of them. The history of my lecture is this. After having worked for some years on my own subject (which is the medieval allegory) I found that I had accumulated a

certain amount of general information which, tho' far from being very recondite, was more than the ordinary student in the school could gather for himself. I then conceived the idea of my 'prolegomena'. There were however several gaps in the general knowledge which I had accidentally got. To fill these up I adopted the simple method of going through Skeats notes on Chaucer and Langland, and other similar things, and following these up to their sources when they touched on matters that seemed to me important. This led me sometimes to books I already knew, often to new ones. This process explains why I inevitably appear more learned than I am. E.g. my quotations from Vincent of Beauvais don't mean that I turned from a long reading of Vincent to illustrate Chaucer, but that I turned from Chaucer to find explanations in Vincent. In fine, the process is inductive for the most part of my lecture: tho' on allegory, courtly love, and (sometimes) on philosophy, it is deductive—i.e. I *start* from the authors I quote. I elaborate this point because, if you are thinking of doing the same kind of thing (i.e. telling people what they ought to know as the *prius* of a study of medieval vernacular poetry) I think you would be wise to work in the same way—starting *from* the texts you want to explain. You will soon find of course that you are working the other way at the same time, that you can correct current explanations, or see things to explain where the ordinary editors see nothing. I suppose I need not remind you to cultivate the wisdom of the serpent: there will be misquotations, and misunderstood quotations in the best books, and you must always hunt up all quotations for yourself and find what they are really like *in situ.*

But, of course, I do not know what it is you propose to do. I have therefore mentioned all the more important 'sources' in my note-book without any attempt at selection. You will see at once that this is the bibliography of a man who was following a particular subject (the love-allegory), and this doubtless renders the list much less useful to you, who are hardly likely to be after the same quarry. In the second part, texts, I have been more selective, and have omitted a certain amount of low or low-ish Latin love poetry which is useful only for my own special purpose. You will observe that I begin with classical authors. This is a point I would press on anyone dealing with the middle ages, that the first essential is to read the relevant classics over and over: the key to everything—allegory, courtly love etc—is there. After that the two things to know really well are the *Divine Comedy* and the *Romance of the Rose*. The student who has really digested these (I don't claim to be such a person myself!), with good commentaries, and who also knows the Classics and the Bible (including the *apocryphal* New Testament) has the game in his hands, and can defeat over and over again those who have simply burrowed in obscure parts of the actual middle ages.

Of scholastic philosophy and theology you probably know much more than I do. If by any chance you don't, stick to Gilson as a guide and beware of the people (Maritain in your Church, and T. S. Eliot in mine) who are at present running what they call 'neo-scholasticism' as a fad.

Of periodicals you will find *Romania, Speculum,* and *Medium Aevum* useful.

Remember (this has been all important to me) that what

you want to know about the Middle Ages will often not be in a book on the Middle Ages, but in the early chapters of some history of general philosophy or science. The accounts of your period in such books will, of course, usually be patronising and ill-informed, but it will mention dates and authors whom you can follow up and thus put you in the way of writing a *true* account for yourself.

If there is any way in which I can assist you, or if you would care to call and discuss anything with me, do not hesitate to let me know . . .

P. S. I shd warn you that I am very bad at German and this has doubtless influenced my choice of reading.

I suppose you will have access to a complete Aristotle wherever you are working? He is often useful.

TO OWEN BARFIELD: **from Magdalen College** (while reading the proofs of *The Allegory of Love* which was published on 21 May 1936)

[December 1935]

The Diary of an Old Soul is magnificent. You placed the moment of giving it to me admirably. I remember with horror the absurdity of my last criticism on it, and with shame the vulgarity of the form in which I expressed it. He knows all about the interplay between the religious and metaphysical aspects of the One. I see now (since I began this letter) that these two are opposite only with the fruitful opposition of male & female (how deep the old erotic metaphor of the *proelia Veneris* is) and what they beget is the solution.

Incidentally, since I have begun to pray, I find my extreme view of personality changing. My own empirical self is becoming more important and this is exactly the opposite of self love. You don't teach a seed how to die into treehood by throwing it into the fire: and it has to become a good seed before its worth burying.

As to my own book—the question whether notes shd come at the end of the chapter or the bottom of the page is partly for publisher & printer. Personally I loathe a book where they come at the end—and I am writing mainly for people who will want to know where they must look to verify my facts . . .

TO MRS JOAN BENNETT (of Cambridge): **from Magdalen College**

13 January 1937

A foul copy of an essay (which now that I re-read it doesn't seem as good as I had hoped) is a poor return for the delightful, the champagne holiday you gave me. But you asked for it and here it is.

What splendid talk goes on in your house!—and what a wonderful thing . . . your English Faculty is. If only we and you could combine into a single teaching body (leaving out your freaks and our nonentities) we could make 'English' into an education that would not have to fear any rivalries. In the meantime we have lots to exchange. I am sure you practise more 'judgement'; I suspect we have more 'blood'. What we want is to be well commingled.

The Lucas book proves disappointing as you go on. His attack on [I. A.] Richards for splitting up poetic effects which we receive as a unity, is silly; that is what analysis *means* and R. never suggested that the products of analysis were the same as the living unity. Again, he doesn't seem to see that Richards is on his side in bringing poetry to an ethical test in the long run; and his own ethical standard is so half-hearted—he's so afraid of being thought a moralist that he tries to blunt it by gas about 'health' and 'survival'. As if survival can have any value apart from the prior value of what survives. To me especially it is an annoying book; he attacks *my* enemies in the wrong way . . . and a good deal of mere 'superiority' too . . .

TO MRS JOAN BENNETT: from Magdalen College

[February? 1937]

I also have been having 'flu or you should have heard from me sooner. I enclose the article; pray make whatever use you please of it[148] . . . It is a question (for your sake and that of the *Festschrift,* not mine) whether a general pro-Donne paper called *Donne and his critics*—a glance at Dryden and Johnson and then some contemporaries including me—wouldn't be better than a direct answer. C.S.L. as professional controversialist and itinerant prize-fighter is, I suspect, becoming already rather a bore to our small pub-

---

[148] He is referring to his essay 'Donne and Love Poetry in the Seventeenth Century' which appeared in *Seventeenth Century Studies Presented to Sir Herbert Grierson* (1938).

lic, and might in that way infect you.[149] Also, if you really refute me, you raise for the editor the awkward question, 'Then why print the other article?' However, do just as you like . . . and good luck with it whatever you do.

I've had a grand week in bed — *Northanger Abbey, The Moonstone, The Vision of Judgement, Modern Painters* (Vol. 3), *Our Mutual Friend,* and *The Egoist.* Of the latter I decided this time that it's a rare instance of the conception being so good that even the fantastic faults can't kill it. There's a good deal of the ass about Meredith — that dreadful first chapter — Carlyle in icing sugar. And isn't the supposedly witty conversation much poorer than much we have heard in real life? Mrs Mountstuart is a greater bore than Miss Bates — only he didn't mean her to be. The Byron was not so good as I remembered; the Ruskin, despite much nonsense, glorious.

TO A FORMER PUPIL: from Magdalen College

8 March 1937

I haven't yet got Grierson's new book *Milton and Wordsworth,* but I'm going to: it ought to kill two of your birds

---

[149] He means the debate going on between himself and Dr E. M. W. Tillyard of Jesus College, Cambridge. It began with Jack's essay 'The Personal Heresy in Criticism' in *Essays and Studies by Members of the English Association,* Vol. XIX (1934). This was answered by Dr Tillyard's 'The Personal Heresy in Criticism: A Rejoinder' in Vol. XX of *Essays and Studies* (1935), to which Jack wrote a response entitled an 'Open Letter to Dr Tillyard', Vol. XXI of *Essays and Studies* (1936). These essays, with two more from Dr Tillyard and one from Jack, were published as *The Personal Heresy: A Controversy* (1939).

with one stone. Have you read F. L. Lucas' *Decline and Fall of the Romantic Ideal*? Hideously over-written in parts, but well worth reading: he has grasped what seems to be a hard idea to modern minds, that a certain degree of a thing might be good and a further degree of the same thing bad. Elementary, you will say—yet a realisation of it would have forbidden the writing of many books.

These are new. A few years old—but you may not have read it—is E. K. Chambers' *Sir Thomas Wyatt and Other Studies.* Some of the essays are medieval, but most of it is 16th century. I can't think of anything much on 'general tendencies of the 17th century' since one you almost certainly read when you were up, Grierson's *Cross Currents of XVIIth c. Lit,* very good indeed. By the bye a *festschrift* to Grierson shortly appearing (Tillyard, Nichol Smith, Joan Bennett and myself are among the contributors) might contain something of what you want. The book on the 17th c. by Willey (I have forgotten the title) is more on the thought background than the poets, rather doing for that century, what my Prolegomena tried to do for the middle ages. I don't know of anything general on the 18th century. Sherburn's *Early Life of Pope* tho' good is hardly what you want . . .

TO OWEN BARFIELD: from The Kilns

2 September 1937

'Curiously comfortless stuff in the background' is the criticism of a sensible man just emerging from the popular errors about Morris. Not so curiously, not quite in the background—that particular *discomfort* is the main theme of all his best work, the thing he was born to say. The formula is 'Returning to what seems an ideal world to find yourself all the more face to face with gravest reality without ever drawing a pessimistic conclusion but fully maintaining that heroic action in, or amelioration of, a temporal life is an absolute duty though the disease of temporality is incurable.'

Not quite what you expected, but just what the essential Morris is. 'Defeat and victory are the same in the sense that victory will open your eyes only to a deeper defeat: so fight on.' In fact he is the final statement of *good* Paganism: a faithful account of what things are and always must be to the *natural* man. Cf. what are in comparison the ravings of Hardy on the one hand and optimistic Communists on t'other.

But the *Earthly Paradise* after that first story is inferior work. Try *Jason, House of the Wolfings, Roots of the Mts, Well at the World's End.*

The thriller is finished and called *Out of the Silent Planet*[150] ...

TO OWEN BARFIELD: from Magdalen College

10 June 1938

Think not the doom of man reversed for thee. Apropos of Johnson, isn't this good, from the Rambler, from a man who decided not to marry a blue-stocking on finding her an athe-

---

[150] *Out of the Silent Planet,* the first of Jack's three interplanetary novels, was published in the Autumn of 1938.

ist and a determinist: 'It was not difficult to discover the danger of committing myself forever to one who might at any time mistake the dictates of passion, or the calls of appetite, for the decree of fate; or consider cuckoldom as necessary to the general system, as a link in the everlasting chain of successive causes.'

And, in another way, isn't this splendid 'Whenever, after the shortest relaxation of vigilance, reason and caution return to their charge, they find hope again in possession.'

What is the betting I forget to put that lyric in after all? — They keep sheep in Magdalen grove now and I hear the fleecy care bleating all day long; I am shocked to find that none of my pupils, though they are all acquainted with pastoral poetry, regards them as anything but a nuisance: and one of my colleagues has been heard to ask why sheep have their wool cut off. (Fact)

It frightens me almost. And so it did the other night when I heard two undergrads. giving a list of pleasures which were (a) Nazi. (b) Leading to homosexuality. They were, feeling the wind in your hair, walking with bare feet in the grass, and bathing in the rain. Think it over: it gets worse the longer you look at it.

More cheering is the true report from Cambridge of a conversation:

A. What is this *Ablaut* that K. keeps on talking about in his lectures?

B. Oh don't you know, he was in love with Eloise . . .

TO OWEN BARFIELD: **from Magdalen College** (at the
time of Munich and the approach of the next war)

12 September 1938

What awful quantities of this sort of thing seem necessary to break us in, or, more correctly, to break us off. One
thinks one has made some progress towards detachment,
some μελετὴ, Θανάτου and begin to realise, and to acquiesce
in, the rightly precarious hold we have on all our natural
loves, interests, and comforts: then when they are really
shaken, at the very first breath of that wind, it turns out to
have been all a sham, a field-day, blank cartridges.

This is how I was thinking last night about the war danger. I had so often told myself that my friends and books
and even brains were not given me to keep: that I must teach
myself at bottom to care for something else more (and also
of course to care for them more, but in a different way), and
I was horrified to find how *cold* the idea of really losing them
struck.

An awful symptom is that part of oneself still regards
troubles as 'interruptions'—as if (ludicrous idea) the happy
bustle of our personal interests was our real ἔπνον, instead of
the opposite. I did in the end see (I dare not say 'feel') that
since nothing but these forcible shakings will cure us of our
worldliness, we might have at bottom reason to be thankful for them. We *force* God to surgical treatment: we won't
(mentally) diet . . .

Of course, our whole joint world may be blown up before
the end of the week. I can't feel in my bones that it will, but
my bones know damn-all about it. If we are separated, God

bless you, and thanks for a hundred good things I owe to you, more than I can count or weigh. In some ways we've had a corking time these twenty years.

Be thankful you have nothing to reproach yourself about in your relations with your father (I had lots) and that it is not some worse disease. The horror of a stroke must be felt almost entirely by the spectators . . .

TO OWEN BARFIELD: from Magdalen College

8 February [1939]

Two week ends of Feb. fall in term: the 5th–8th and the 12th–15th. If you choose the former you will be able to hear Tillyard and me finishing our controversy *viva voce,* but as I have to give him a bed perhaps the 12th wd be better. No doubt I shall be defeated in the controversy.[151]

I don't know if Plato *did* write the *Phaedo:* the canon of these ancient writers, under the surface, is still quite chaotic. It is also a very corrupt text. Bring it along by all means, but don't pitch your hopes too high. We are both

---

[151] One of Jack's pupils at this time, John Lawlor, saw the debate with Dr E. M. W. Tillyard. In his essay 'The Tutor and the Scholar', in *Light on C. S. Lewis,* ed. Jocelyn Gibb (1965), Professor Lawlor wrote: '[Lewis] was the dialectician all his life; and one must only add that he was superb . . . There was a memorable occasion when in the Hall at Magdalen Dr Tillyard met him to round off in debate the controversy begun with the publication of Lewis's indictment of "the Personal Heresy". I am afraid there was no debate. Lewis made rings round Tillyard; in, out, up, down, around, back again—like some piratical Plymouth bark against a high-built galleon of Spain.'

getting so rusty that we shall make very little of it—and my distrust of all lexicons and translations is increasing. Also of Plato—and of the human mind.

I suppose for the sake of the others we must do something about arranging a walk. Those maps are so unrealiable by now that it is rather a farce—but still 'Try lad, try! No harm in trying'. Of course hardly any districts in England are unspoiled enough to make walking worth while: and with two new members—I have very little doubt it will be a ghastly failure.

I haven't seen C. W.'s play: it is not like to be at all good.[152]

As for *Orpheus*—again it's no harm trying. If you can't write it console yourself by reflecting that if you did you wd have been v. unlikely to get a publisher.[153] I am more and more convinced that there is no future for poetry.

Nearly everyone has been ill here: I try to prevent them all croaking and grumbling but it is hard being the only optimist. Let me know which week end: whichever you choose something will doubtless prevent it. I hear the income-tax is going up again. The weather is bad and looks like getting worse. I suppose war is certain now. I don't believe language *is* a perpetual Orphic song . . .

P.S. Even my braces are in a frightful condition. 'Damn braces' said Blake.

---

[152] Charles Williams's *Judgement at Chelmsford* (1939).
[153] Owen Barfield's *Orpheus* was performed on the stage in 1948. It was published as *Orpheus: A Poetic Drama*, ed. John C. Ulreich, by The Lindisfarne Press in 1983.

TO MRS JOAN BENNETT: **from Magdalen College**
(Mrs Bennett had probably taken exception to the chapter
entitled 'Limbo' in Lewis's book *The Pilgrim's Regress*
[1933].)

5 April 1939

I'm sorry about the Athanasian Creed—the passage illustrates how important it is in writing to say what you mean
and not to say anything you don't mean. As the context
suggests, I was thinking purely of the Trinitarian doctrine
and had quite forgotten the damnatory clauses. There are
however several palliatives. Residence in Limbo I am told is
compatible with 'perishing everlastingly' and you'll find it
quite jolly, for whereas Heaven is an acquired taste, Limbo
is a place of 'perfect *natural* happiness'. In fact you may
be able to realise your wish 'of attending with one's whole
mind to the history of the human spirit'. There are grand
libraries in Limbo, endless discussions, and no colds. There
will be a faint melancholy because you'll all know that you
have missed the bus, but that will provide a subject for
poetry. The scenery is pleasant though tame. The climate
endless autumn.

Seriously, I don't pretend to have any information on the
fate of the virtuous unbeliever. I don't suppose this question provided the solitary exception to the principle that
actions on a false hypothesis lead to some less satisfactory
result than actions on a true. That's as far as I would go—
beyond feeling that the believer is playing for higher stakes
and incurring danger of something really nasty . . .

TO DOM BEDE GRIFFITHS, O.S B.: **from Magdalen College**

8 May 1939

It was nice to hear from you again. I think I said before that I have no contribution to make about re-union. It was never more needed. A united Christendom should be the answer to the new Paganism. But how reconciliation of the Churches, as opposed to conversions of individuals from a church to another, is to come about, I confess I cannot see. I am inclined to think that the immediate task is vigorous co-operation on the basis of what even now is common— combined, of course, with full admission of the differences. An *experienced* unity on some things might then prove the prelude to a confessional unity on all things. Nothing wd give such strong support to the Papal claims as the spectacle of a Pope actually functioning as head of Christendom. But it is not, I feel sure, my vocation to discuss reunion.

Yes, I do like George Eliot. *Romola* is a most purgative work on the *facilis descensus,* because the final state of the character is so different from his original state and yet all the transitions are so dreadfully natural. Mind you, I think George Eliot *labours* her morality a bit: it has something of the ungraceful ponderousness of all heathen ethics. (I recently read all Seneca's epistles and think I like the Stoics better than George Eliot.) The best of all her books as far as I have read is *Middlemarch.* It shows such an extraordinary understanding of different kinds of life—different classes, ages, and sexes. Her humour is nearly always admirable.

I thought we had talked of Patmore. I think him really great within his own limited sphere. To be sure he pushes the parallel between Divine and human love as far as it can sanely or decently go, and perhaps at times a little further. One can imagine his work being most pernicious to a devout person who read it at the wrong age. But a superb poet. Do you remember the comparison of the naturally virtuous person who receives grace at conversion to a man walking along and suddenly hearing a band playing, and then 'His step unchanged, he steps in time'. Or on the poignancy of spring, 'With it the blackbird breaks the young day's heart'. Or the lightening during a storm at sea which reveals 'The deeps/ *Standing* about in stony heaps'. That is sheer genius. And the *tightness* (if you know what I mean) of all his work. The prose one (*Rod, Root & Flower*) contains much you might like.

No, I haven't joined the Territorials. I am too old. It wd be hypocrisy to say that I regret this. My memories of the last war haunted my dreams for years. Military service, to be plain, includes the threat of *every* temporal evil; pain and death wh. is what we fear from sickness: isolation from those we love wh. is what we fear from exile: toil under arbitrary masters, injustices and humiliation, wh. is what we fear from slavery: hunger, thirst, cold and exposure wh. is what we fear from poverty. I'm not a pacifist. If its got to be, its got to be. But the flesh is weak and selfish and I think death wd be much better than to live through another war.

Thank God, He has not allowed my faith to be greatly tempted by the present horrors. I do not doubt that whatever misery He permits will be for our ultimate good unless, by rebellious will, we convert it to evil. But I get no further than Gethsemane: and am daily thankful that that scene, of all others in Our Lord's life, did not go unrecorded. But what state of affairs in this world can we view with satisfaction?

If we are unhappy, then we are unhappy. If we are happy, then we remember than the crown is not promised without the cross and tremble. In fact, one comes to realize, what one always admitted theoretically, that there is nothing here that will do us good: the sooner we are safely out of this world the better. But 'would it were evening, Hal, and all well'. I have even, I'm afraid, caught myself wishing that I have never been born, wh. is sinful. Also, meaningless if you try to think it out.

The process of living seems to consist in coming to realize truths so ancient and simple that, if stated, they sound like barren platitudes. They cannot sound otherwise to those who have not had the relevant experience: that is why there is no real teaching of such truths possible and every generation starts from scratch . . .

TO SISTER PENELOPE, C.S.M.V. (who had written to him about *Out of the Silent Planet*): **from Magdalen College**

9 July [August] 1939

The letter at the end is pure fiction and the 'circumstances wh. put the book out of date' are merely a way of preparing for a sequel. But the danger of 'Westonism' I meant to be real.

What set me about writing the book was the discovery that a pupil of mine took all that dream of interplanetary colonisation quite seriously, and the realisation that thousands of people, in one form or another depend on some hope of perpetuating and improving the human species for the whole meaning of the universe—that a 'scientific' hope of defeating death is a real rival to Christianity. At present, of course, the prospect of a war has rather damped them: which shows that whatever evil Satan sets on foot God will always do some good or other by it. I don't think even 'for believers only' I could describe Ransom's revelation to Oyarsa: the fact that you want me to really proves how well advised I was merely to *suggest* it.

You will be both grieved and amused to learn that out of about sixty reviews, only two showed any knowledge that my idea of the fall of the Bent One was anything but a private invention of my own! But if only there were someone with a richer talent and more leisure, I believe this great ignorance might be a help to the evangelization of England: any amount of theology can now be smuggled into people's minds under cover of romance without their knowing it.

I have given your *God Persists* a first reading with great pleasure. I value it particularly for its frank emphasis on those elements in the faith which too many modern apologists try to keep out of sight for fear they will be called mythical. I am sure this weakens our case. I like very much your treatment of Heathenism (my own debts to it are enormous—it was through *almost* believing in the gods that I came to believe in God) on p. 31. Also p. 33 on the seedling for special culture and the danger of reverting to 'common' weed. That continual narrowing out, selecting from a selection, does seem to be so very characteristic of God's method. Can you tell me anything more about the 'crossing' of the nomadic and agricultural religions on p. 36? On p. 43 'God sat again for His portrait' is a most successful audacity.

I think your task of finding suitable fiction for the convalescents must be interesting. Do you know George Macdonald's fantasies for grown-ups (his tales for children you probably know already): *Phantastes* & *Lilith* I found endlessly attractive, and full of what I felt to be holiness before I really knew that it was. One of his novels, *Sir Gibbie* (Everyman), though often, like all his novels, amateurish, is worth reading. And do you know the works of Charles Williams? Rather wild, but full of love and excelling in the creation of convincing *good* characters. (The reason these are rare in fiction is that to imagine a man worse than yourself you've only got to stop doing something, while to imagine one better you've got to do something.)

Though I'm forty years old as a man I'm only about twelve as a Christian, so it would be a maternal act if you found time sometimes to mention me in your prayers.

[Following Germany's invasion of Czechoslovakia in March 1939 Neville Chamberlain announced that England would support Poland should it be invaded. It was clear that war was inevitable. Warren, who was on the Army Reserve List, learned that he would be called back into active service. Men between the ages of eighteen and forty-one were liable for military service and for a while it looked as if Jack might have to go back into the Army as he would not be forty-two until 29 November. It had been announced that New Building would be required for government use and, as it seemed there would be no one to teach in any case, Jack and Warren had to move all their books into the cellar. Unfortunately, Jack had to lecture on Shakespeare at Stratford on 31 August and 1 September, and he arrived back home on 1 September to find that Warren had just left for an Army base at Catterick in Yorkshire. That same day Germany invaded Poland, and on 3 September England declared war on Germany. Children were being evacuated from London and, like many families, Jack and the Moores offered to look after those sent to them.]

TO HIS BROTHER: from Magdalen College

2 September 1939

Apparently I arrived at Oxford station yesterday very shortly before you left from it—however, this is perhaps a good thing for though a farewell tankard can just be carried off, a farewell cup of camp coffee is almost unbearable.

Our schoolgirls have arrived and all seem to me—and, what's more important, to Minto—to be very nice, unaffected creatures and all most flatteringly delighted with their new surroundings. They're fond of animals which is a good thing (for them as well as for us) . . .

My second lecture at Stratford was cancelled and my first went down very well. It was fully reported (the irony!) in the *Times* yesterday. I had a pretty ghastly time—a smart, nearly empty hotel in a strange town with a wireless blaring away all the time and hours and hours to get through without work compose perhaps the worst possible background to a crisis . . . The brightest spot was *Right-Ho Jeeves* which, in opposition to you, I think one of the funniest books I've ever read. Fink-Nottle's speech at the speech-day made me laugh aloud in an empty lounge.

I've just been to see the President who laughs to scorn the alarms raised in my breast by the announcement of liability to service up to 41. I hope he's right . . .

Did you see that the enemy planes retreated from Warsaw(?) before Polish fighters & went to bomb a holiday resort in the neighbourhood instead!

God save you, brother.

TO HIS BROTHER: from The Kilns

10 September 1939

One of the most reminiscent features of the last war has already appeared—i.e. the information which always comes too late to prevent you doing an unnecessary job. We have just been informed that New Building will not be used by Govt. and that fellows' rooms in particular will be inviolable: also that we *are* going to have a term and quite a lot of undergraduates up. So you see—I had pictured myself either never seeing those books again or else, with you, and in great joy, unearthing them after the war. To-morrow, I suppose, I must start on the never envisaged task of bringing them up single-handed during a war. I daresay it's the sort of thing you'd think funny!

Another quite unexpected blow is Bleiben's announcement this morning that though 'some of us would know' he had been intending to leave the Parish, 'in the present circumstances he feels it his duty' to stay on.[154] A *non sequitur* in my opinion. In the Litany this morning we had some extra petitions, one of which was 'Prosper, oh Lord, our righteous cause'. Assuming that it was the work of the Bishop or someone higher up, when I met Bleiben in the porch, I ventured to protest against the audacity of informing God that our cause was righteous—a point on which He may have His own view.* But it turned out to be Bleiben's own. However, he took the criticism very well.

Along with these not very pleasant indirect results of the war, there is one pure gift—the London branch of the University Press has moved to Oxford so that Charles Williams is living here.[155] I lunched with him on Thursday and hope to do so again on Monday.

Life at The Kilns is going on at least as well as I expected. We had our first air raid warning at 7.45 the other morning when I expect you had yours too. Everyone got to the dug-out quite quickly and I must say they all behaved well, and though v. hungry and thirsty before the all clear went, we

---

[154] The Rev. Thomas Eric Bleiben (1903–47) succeeded Father Thomas as the Vicar of Headington Quarry. While Father Thomas had been exactly right for the Anglo-Catholic church in this parish, Jack found Father Bleiben, Vicar 1935–47, too much of a modernist.

[155] Charles Walter Stansby Williams (1886–1945), an employee of the Oxford University Press since 1908, had published a number of what Jack called 'theological thrillers' before they met in 1936. Upon his arrival in Oxford he was quickly absorbed into 'The Inklings'. Jack paid tribute to his friend in his Preface to *Essays Presented to Charles Williams*, ed. C. S. Lewis (1947). The best biography of Williams is probably Alice Mary Hadfield's *Charles Williams: An Exploration of His Life and Works* (1983).

quite enjoyed the most perfect late summer morning I have
ever seen. The main trouble of life at present is the blacking
out which is done (as you may imagine) with a most complicated Arthur Rackham system of odd rags—quite effectively but at the cost of much labour. Luckily I do most of
the rooms myself, so it doesn't take me nearly so long as if I
were assisted . . .

    * I hope it's quite like ours, of course: but you never know
with Him.

TO HIS BROTHER: from The Kilns

                18 September 1939
For the moment dons are a reserved occupation: and as long
as they stick to their present plans of not calling up boys
between 18 and 20 there will, of course, be a full generation
of freshmen each year who must do something between
leaving school and joining the army . . .

    I am about two-thirds of the way through the job of
restoring the books to the shelves [in Magdalen]. Your
bookcase by the window is now almost full again and looks,
to my unskilled eye, very nearly its old self, though *you* will
doubtless perceive a most perverse disorder, suggesting a
positive determination to separate natural neighbours . . .

    I have said that the [evacuated] children are 'nice', and so
they are. But modern children are poor creatures. They keep
on coming to Maureen and asking 'What shall we do now?'
She tells them to play tennis, or mend their stockings, or
write home: and when that is done they come and ask again.
Shades of our own childhood! . . .

I quite agree that one of the worst features of this war is the spectral feeling of all having happened before. As Dyson said 'When you read the headlines (French advance—British steamship sunk) you feel as if you'd had a delightful dream during the last war and woken up to find it still going on.' But perhaps the better view is the Frenchman's 'Well, that was a good armistice!' If one could only hibernate. More and more sleep seems to me the best thing—short of waking up and finding yourself safely dead and not quite damned . . .

TO HIS BROTHER: **from The Kilns** (In October Warren was posted to the Base Supply Depot at Le Havre.)

5 November 1939

I was glad to hear that your journey had proved so much pleasanter than we both expected. The account of the moonlight ride in [the] black-out train was, for some reason, curiously vivid and I almost have the sense of having done it myself. I suppose I shall hear a definite address from you soon . . .

I had a pleasant evening on Thursday with Williams, Tolkien, and Wrenn, during which Wrenn *almost* seriously expressed a strong wish to burn Williams, or at least maintained that conversation with Williams enabled him to understand how inquisitors had felt it right to burn people.[156]

---

[156] Charles Wrenn (1895–1969) was educated at Queen's College, Oxford. After lecturing in a number of universities he returned to Oxford in 1930 as University Lecturer in Anglo-Saxon. In 1939 he was elected to a professorship at King's College, London. In 1946 he once again returned to Oxford, this time to succeed J. R. R. Tolkien as Professor of Anglo-Saxon.

Tolkien and I agreed afterwards that we *just* knew what he meant: that as some people . . . are eminently kickable, so Williams is eminently combustible.

The occasion was a discussion of the most distressing text in the Bible ('narrow is the way and few they be that find it') and whether one really could believe in a universe where the majority were damned and also in the goodness of God. Wrenn, of course, took the view that it mattered precisely nothing whether it conformed to your ideas of goodness or not, and it was at that stage that the combustible possibilities of Williams revealed themselves to him in an attractive light. The general sense of the meeting was in favour of a view on the lines taken in *Pastor Pastorum* — that Our Lord's replies are never straight answers and never gratify curiosity, and that whatever this one meant its purpose was certainly not statistical . . .

TO SISTER PENELOPE, C.S.M.V.: from Magdalen College

8 November 1939

The Tableland [in *The Pilgrim's Regress*] represents *all* high and dry states of mind, of which High Anglicanism then seemed to me to be one — most of the representatives of it whom I had then met being v. harsh people who called themselves scholastics and appeared to be inspired more by hatred of their fathers' religion than anything else. I wd modify that view now: but I'm still not what you'd call high. To me the real distinction is not between high and low but between religion with real supernaturalism & salvationism on the one hand and all watered-down and modernist versions on the other. I think St Paul has really told us what to do about the divisions within the Ch. of England: i.e. I don't care twopence what I eat on Friday but when I am at table with High Anglicans I abstain in order not 'to offend my weak brother' ...

TO HIS BROTHER: from The Kilns

11 November [1939]

On Thursday we had a meeting of the Inklings—you and Coghill both absented unfortunately. We dined at the Eastgate. I have never in my life seen Dyson so exuberant—'a roaring cataract of nonsense'. The bill of fare afterwards consisted of a section of the new Hobbit book from Tolkien, a nativity play from Williams (unusually intelligible for him, and approved by all) and a chapter out of the book on *The Problem of Pain* from me. It so happened—it would take too long to explain why—that the subject matter of the three readings formed almost a logical sequence, and produced a really first rate evening's talk of the usual wide-ranging kind—'from grave to gay, from lively to severe'. I wished very much we could have had you with us ...

Yes—I too enjoyed our short time together in College enormously, until the shadow of the end began to fall over it: not that one has lost the art (our boyhood was well trained in it) of dealing with such shadows, but that one so *resents* having to start putting it into practice again after so many years. Pox on the whole business.

TO HIS BROTHER: from **The Kilns**

24 November 1939

I am almost ashamed to describe my leisurely days to one leading such a gruelling life as you—by the way, there is a curious irony about your present job, because, thirty years ago, bustling about between ships and trains would have seemed to you *the* ideal occupation. Do you remember what a triumph a bit of 'unforced traffic' was in the attic days? Well, my son, you have it now! No, I hadn't thought of it's being a crime to keep an engine waiting, though it's fairly obvious when you come to think of it: I *had* known already, I suppose from notices half consciously read in goods stations that 'an engine in steam' is a venerable object, almost like a mare in foal.

A few hours ago while waiting for the bus outside Magdalen I saw a sight I bet you've never seen—an undergraduate whom I know approaching with what I took to be a dead pheasant in his hand but what turned out to be a live falcon on his wrist. It was hooded with a little leather hood and is quite a gaily coloured bird, provided on the lower leg with natural spots of a kind of yellow varnish. Blessings on the man who while waiting to be called up for a first class European war is exclusively intent on restoring the ancient sport of hawking...

I suppose a French novel is the very last thing you want to read at present, but I can't refrain from telling you that in the French library (where the exam was held) I picked up Balzac's *Curé de Tours* quite carelessly and was immediately enchanted—just as I was by his *Père Goriot* in 1917. It is so very *unlike* most French things—the Cure and the whole cathedral surroundings in Tours are almost Trollopian: so provincial, loveable, prosaic, unobstrusive ...

The day is wet—an outside world of dripping branches and hens in the mud and cold which I am glad to have shut out (tea is just finished) but which, no doubt, is very much pleasanter than your sugar-floored sheds. How nasty the sugar cottage in Hansel and Grettel must have been in wet weather. I gave your greetings to those of the Inklings who were present on Thursday which were received with gratification.

TO HIS BROTHER: from The Kilns

3 December 1939

This has been a beautiful week. It began to clear up last Sunday (you remember my letter was written on Saturday) and that afternoon I had the first really enjoyable walk I've had this many a day ... Later, I had the odd experience of leaving home for college at about 6, as Harwood had announced his intention of coming for the night. The journey in by bus was delightful because it was now bright moonlight and the lights inside the bus were so dimmed as to make no difference, so that I had the quite unusual experience of seeing Magdalen bridge and tower by moonlight from the height and speed of a bus-top: a *short* thing compared with the train journey you described, but of course the elevation gave it an advantage.

Harwood, owing to train difficulties, didn't turn up till about 10.30, but we sat up lateish and had a good talk. I may have mentioned to you that he has evacuated to Minehead—

nicely placed for country but with bad prospects financially, as the splitting up of their pupils' London homes has led to their losing a good many. His son John is not with them but billeted in the neighbourhood—with the local M.F.H. [Master of Foxhounds]! and already has acquired a new language and says that his father ought to get his hair cut!

I hardly know which to pity more—a father like Harwood who watches his son being thus 'translated' or a son in process of such translation who has the embarrassment of a father like Harwood. I think, the son: for as some author whom I've forgotten says the anxiety that parents have about children 'being a credit to them' is a mere milk and water affair beside the anxiety of children that their parents should not be an absolute disgrace. Certainly it wd not be pleasant to have to explain to a M.F.H. that one's father was an Anthroposophist—except that the only impression left on the M.F.H.'s mind wd probably be that your father was some kind of chemist. (If the M.F.H. was a P'daita it might, of course, lead to almost anything—'Sort of fellow who comes to the door offering to feel your bumps'.) . . .

Talking of books, I have been looking rapidly through St François de Sales this week end to find a passage I wanted to quote, and have derived much 'social pleasure' from your pencillings: as I have experienced before, to read a book marked by you in your absence is almost the nearest thing to a conversation. When I read that hares turn white in winter because they eat nothing but snow (used as an argument for frequent communion) and see your mark it is almost as if one of us was pointing the passage out to the other here in the study . . .

The usual Thursday evening party did not meet as Williams & Hopkins were both away,[157] so I went up to Tolkien's . . . We had a very pleasant evening drinking gin and lime juice (wh. sounds chilly, but I was quite in a sweat by the time I got to Northmoor Rd) and reading our recent chapters to each other—his from the new Hobbit and mine from *The Problem of Pain*. (N.B. If you are writing a book about pain and then get some actual pain as I did from my rib, it does *not* either, as the cynic wd expect, blow the doctrine to bits, nor, as a Christian wd hope, turn into practice, but remains quite unconnected and irrelevant, just as any other bit of actual life does when you are reading or writing) . . .

TO HIS BROTHER: from The Kilns

18 December 1939

Yes, I know well what you mean by the *materialistic* gains of being a Christian. It more often presents itself to me the other way round—how on earth did we manage to enjoy all these books so much as we did in the days when we had really no conception of what was at the centre of them? Sir, he who embraces the Christian revelation rejoins the main tide of human existence! And I quite agree about Johnson. If one had not experienced it, it wd be hard to understand how a dead man out of a book can be almost a member of one's

---

[157] Gerard Walter Sturgis Hopkins (1892–1961), a translator and critic, served the Oxford University Press 1920–57, first as Publicity Manager and later as Editorial Adviser. He and Charles Williams had rooms in 9 South Parks Road, Oxford.

family circle — still harder to realise, even now, that you and I have a chance of someday really meeting him . . .

We had a very pleasant 'cave' in Balliol last Wednesday. Everyone remarked that it was more frolic and youthful than any we have had for years — quite one of the old caves in fact — a curious result, if it is a result, of war conditions. During the evening Ridley read to us a Swinburne ballad and, immediately after it, that ballad of Kipling's which ends up 'You've finished with the flesh, my Lord'.[158] Nobody except me knew who the second one was by, and everyone agreed that it just *killed* the Swinburne as a real thing kills a sham. I then made him read 'Iron, cold iron' with the same result and later he drifted into McAndrew's Hymn. Surely Kipling must come back? When people have had time to forget 'If' and the inferior *Barrack Room Ballads,* all this other stuff must come into its own. I know hardly any poet who can deliver such a *hammer stroke.* The stories, of course, are another matter and are, I suppose, even now admitted to be good by all except a handful of Left idiots . . .

TO HIS BROTHER: from The Kilns

31 December 1939

Minto has probably told you of the 'ludicrous edisode' on the Wednesday in which Havard had to come up with a

---

[158] Maurice Rey Ridley (1890–1969), who had been an undergraduate at Balliol College, was a Fellow and Tutor in English Literature at Balliol 1920–45. From there he went on to become a Lecturer at Bedford College in London 1948–67.

hack-saw and saw my ring off my finger.[159] To you, I expect, the most interesting feature of this event will be the extreme P'daytaishness of my act in forcing the damned thing into such a position originally: it being a marked trait in the character of a P'dayta that tho' being physically rather feeble for any useful purpose such as cranking a car or lifting a log, he is subject to fits of demoniac strength when it is a question of jamming, twisting, bursting or crushing anything into ruin—e.g. a lobster or a door. Havard performed his operation with great skill and delicacy, beguiling the time with interesting and edifying conversation.

I couldn't help contrasting him with B. E. C. Davies, a professor of London, whom I went on to see in Old Headington the same morning. Here is a man of my own age, who knew Barfield when he was up: of my own profession, who has written on Spenser. You'd have thought these were all the materials for a good meeting. But no. One got through all the preliminary stuff about how his London she-students were getting on in Oxford, thinking that the real conversation would then begin. But every single time I tried to turn it to books, or life, or friends (as such) I was completely frustrated. i.e. about friends, he'd talk of their jobs, marriages, houses, incomes, arrangements, but

---

[159] Robert Emlyn Havard (1901–85) read Chemistry at Keble College before he studied medicine and became a doctor. He had a surgery in St Giles, a few steps from 'The Eagle and Child' pub, and another in Headington. He became the doctor to Jack and the other occupants of The Kilns in about 1934, and in 1940 he became one of 'The Inklings'. Jack gave him the nickname 'Humphrey', and 'Humphrey' he was to The Inklings and other friends for the rest of his life.

not of them. Books—oh yes, editions, prices, suitability for exams—not their contents. In fact hardly since the days of 'How are things at the yard, Gussie?' have I had to endure so much irredeemably 'grown-up conversation'. Unless I misjudge him, he is one of those dreadful fellows who never refers to literature except during the hours he's paid for talking about it. Just as one meets clergymen—indeed we are told the Archdeacon was one of them—who resent the intrusion of Christianity into the conversation. How small a nucleus there is in each liberal profession of people who care about the thing they are supposed to be doing: yet I suppose the percentage of garage-hands and motor-touts who are really interested in motoring is about 95! . . .

TO HIS BROTHER: from **The Kilns**

9 January 1940

It seems almost brutal to describe a January walk taken without you in a letter *to* you, but I suppose 'concealment is in vain' . . . When I reached Taunton [by train] it was definitely a warm evening. God send us to be soon together again, for here came that moment in a holiday which you would so have appreciated and wh. cannot be fully enjoyed alone—the moment when, at the last of the *big* stations, you find, far from the other traffic, in a remote silent bay, the little, dark, non-corridor train of two coaches—usually, for some reason, exuding steam from all the compartments— which is going to jerk and bump you to your real destination. And then those stops at unheard-of halts with wooden platforms, and the gleam of an oil lantern in a porter's hand.

It wd have been partly spoiled for you, however, by the presence of a young man of undergraduate type and age who turned out to be a student training to be a mining engineer, and who, having tackled me on politics, the English character, propaganda, improvements in the Everymans series, Hindu theology and so forth, exclaimed 'You must be a man of very wide interests!' and, do you know, I never realised before the naivete with which we all *think* this, even if we do not say it, in such circumstances—i.e. the bland inference 'By gum! His interests are as wide as *mine*!'

This brought me to Minehead, at about 6.30. I dined that evening with the Harwoods, and being 'carried' back to my hotel by him at about 10.30 had the very unpleasant surprise of finding it locked up and silent as the grave. It was about 10 minutes' work of banging and shouting and ringing before I was let in—and during the time I had, as you may suppose, some 'very uneasy sensations'.

Next morning, leaving my greatcoat and suitcase at this hotel, and retaining rucksack and mack, I climbed the steep hill to Harwood's billet and collected him. His children are now so numerous that one ceases to notice them individually, any more than a scuffle of piglets in a field or a waddle of ducks. A few platoons of them accompanied us for about the first mile of the walk, but returned, like tugs, when we were out of harbour.

The idea had been to cross Dunkery Beacon and lie at Exford, but the day was so misty that we decided to hug the valleys where one wd have those near-at-hand beauties which mist rather enhances than destroys. It wouldn't be much good trying to describe the route without a map—but it consisted in reaching Porlock by a very wide detour up one valley and down another. I was 'very angry' with Harwood when, though professing to know the country, he brought us at 1 o'clock to a village without a pub! (Luccombe). We succeeded (a sort of success, by the bye, which *never* happens to you and me when we are on our own) in finding a cottage that gave us tea and bread and cheese and jam—in one of those slippery, oil-clothy, frosty best parlours, with an oil stove that created an intolerable stench and a small library of *reference* works—you know, *Plain Man's Encyclopedia, Inquire within about everything*—monuments, doubtless, to the success of those advertisements which promise you a rise in salary and endless occupation for the long winter evenings if you will buy such works. One that specially intrigued us was 'Every Man his own Lawyer—*Illustrated*'. We looked in vain however for a portrait of a tort or a south aspect of Habeas Corpus—the pictures consisting entirely of photos of court-houses and famous judges. Can you imagine anything more infuriating than, on turning to such a book to try to extricate yourself from an income tax muddle or an injudicious betrothal (and for what other purpose wd you ever open it?) to be met by the bland features of Lord Darling? . . .

TO DOM BEDE GRIFFITHS, O.S.B.: from Magdalen College

17 January 1940

Thanks for letter and article. I believe I found myself in agreement with every point you made in the latter. The Platonic and neo-Platonic stuff has, no doubt, been reinforced (a) By the fact that people not very morally sensitive or instructed by trying to do their best recognise temptations of appetite as temptations but easily mistake all the spiritual (and worse) sins for harmless or even virtuous states of mind: hence the illusion that the 'bad part' of oneself is the body. (b) By a misunderstanding of the Pauline use of σάρξ, wh in reality cannot mean the body (since envy, witchcraft, and other spiritual sins are attributed to it) but, I suppose, means the unregenerate manhood as a whole. (You have no doubt noticed that σῶμα is nearly always used by St Paul in a good sense.) (c) By equating 'matter' in the ordinary sense with ὕλη or *materia* in the scholastic and Aristotelian sense, i.e. equating the concrete corporeality of flesh, grass, earth or water with 'pure potentiality'. The latter, being nearest to not-being and furthest from the Prime Reality can, I suppose, be called the 'least good' of things. But I fear Plato thought the concrete flesh and grass bad, and have no doubt he was wrong. (Besides these two senses of 'matter' there is also a third—the thing studied in physics. But who would dare to vilify such a miracle of unceasing energy as *that*?—its more like pure form than pure potentiality.)

Yes, I've read the *Scale of Perfection* with much admiration. I think of sending the anonymous translator a list of passages that he might reconsider for the next edition. I've also read the work of R. W. Chambers which you mention.[160] It is first class as an essay on the continuity of the devotional tradition, but not, what it professes, the continuity of prose style. At least I think some of the passages he

---

[160] *The Continuity of English Prose* (1932).

quotes as similar in style are really similar only in matter. I doubt if he recognises that More's style is greatly inferior to Hilton's. But Chambers is a very good man. If you have his *Man's Unconquerable Mind,* read the essay on *Measure for Measure.* He simply treats it as an ordinary Christian story and all the old stuff about 'Shakespeare's dark period' vanishes into thin air. I see what you mean by calling G. Eliot's Dorothea a saint *manquée:* nothing is more pathetic than the potential holiness in [the] quality of the devotion which actually wrecks itself on Casaubon. If you like such leisurely novels, let me recommend John Galt: specially the *Entail.*

About active service—I think my account was true in what it said, but false in what it excluded. I quite agree that the obedience and comradeship are very good things: and I have no sympathy with the modern view that killing or being killed is *simpliciter* a great evil. But perhaps the truths are rather odious on the lips of a civilian, unless some pastoral or civil office absolutely obliges him to utter them.

Fascism and Communism, like all other evils, are potent because of the good they contain or imitate. *Diabolus simius Dei.* And, of course, their occasion is the failure of those who left humanity starved of that particular good. This does not for me alter the conviction that they are very bad indeed. One of the things we must guard against is the penetration of both into Christianity—availing themselves of that very truth you have suggested and I have admitted. Mark my words: you will frequently see both a Leftist and a Rightist pseudo-theology developing—the abomination will stand where it ought not . . .

TO HIS BROTHER: from The Kilns

3 February 1940

This has been an interesting week in some ways. On Monday Williams began his lectures in the beautiful carved Divinity School.[161] A good audience. I attended with Tolkien and Hopkins and afterwards repaired to the Mitre Bar, joined by Williams, to drink sherry. I think he will retain most of his audience.

That afternoon I had the coldest dawdle round the estate with old Taylor [a neighbour] that I have yet had. In spite of the bitter wind we had to stop to examine every track and speculate what kind of animal it was—but indeed I am rather ashamed that a man of over seventy should have so much more gust for natural philosophy and so much less shrinking from the wind than I. (Between ourselves, too, I have a sort of faint hope that what I can put in with such as F. K. [Foord-Kelcey] and old Taylor may be accepted as a kind of penance for my many sins against the P'daitabird: the blackest chapter in my life.) . . .

We had the usual pleasant party on Thursday evening in college with the welcome addition of Havard, who has been bidden all along but has hitherto been prevented from attending by various accidents. He read us a short paper on his clinical experience of the effects of pain, wh. he had written in order that I might use all or part of it as an appendix

---

[161] Jack arranged for Charles Williams to give a series of lectures during Hilary Term on 'Milton'. They were delivered on Mondays at 11 A.M., the first one (referred to above) occuring on 29 January in the Divinity School of the Bodleian Library. His second lecture on 5 February, which Jack wrote to Warren about on 11 February, was on *Comus*.

to my book. We had an evening almost equally compounded of merriment, piety, and literature. Rum this time again. The Inklings is now really v. well provided, with Fox as chaplain, you as army, Barfield as lawyer, Havard as doctor—almost all the estates!—except, of course, anyone who could actually produce a single necessity of life, a loaf, a boot, or a hut . . .

[On 27 January Warren was promoted to the rank of Major. Not long after this he spent some time in a hospital with a 'high temperature'. It is not clear what caused him so much illness during his time in France.]

TO HIS BROTHER: from The Kilns

11 February 1940

We have your letter (with note enclosed for me) telling us that you are again in hospital. It is impossible, on your hint that you might be sent home, not to wish that this may happen, though I see your point of view about it too. But surely if you keep on returning to bed with these high temperatures even the invincible army must decide in the end that keeping you in France *at all* is too costly? Anyone who knows your medical history for the last ten years must realise that active service even at the base is for you 'an impossible pleasure'. Let us, while you are ill, have short notes at pretty frequent intervals, will you? . . .

On Monday C. W. lectured nominally on *Comus* but really on Chastity. Simply as criticism it was superb—because here was a man who really started from the same point of view as Milton and really cared with every fibre of his being about 'the sage and serious doctrine of virginity' which it would never occur to the ordinary modern critic to take seriously. But it was more important still as a sermon. It was a beautiful sight to see a whole room full of modern young men and women sitting in that absolute silence which can *not* be faked, very puzzled, but spell-bound: perhaps with something of the same feeling which a lecture on *un*chastity might have evoked in their grandparents—the forbidden subject broached at last. He forced them to lap it up and I think many, by the end, liked the taste more than they expected to. It was 'borne in upon me' that that beautiful carved room had probably not witnessed anything so important since some of the great medieval or Reformation lectures. I have at last, if only for once, seen a university doing what it was founded to do: teaching Wisdom. And what a wonderful power there is in the direct appeal which disregards the temporary climate of opinion—I wonder is it the case that the man who has the audacity to get up in any corrupt society and squarely preach justice or valour or the like *always* wins? . . .

TO HIS BROTHER: **from The Kilns**

18 February 1940

Barfield has been up to spend an evening with me: rather unfortunately it was Thursday, for, though he knows most of that set and harmonises with them very well, I should have preferred to have him to myself. He is going to take a part time job in—of all disgusting things—the Inland Revenue.

He is very much depressed having a greater faculty than you or I for feeling the miseries of the world in general—

which led to a good deal of argument, how far, as a man and a Christian, one *ought* to be vividly and continuously aware of, say, what it's like on the Mannerheim line at this moment. I took the line that the present rapidity of communication etc. imposed a burden on sympathy for which sympathy was never made: that the natural thing was to be distressed about what was happening to the poor Jones's in *your own village* and that the modern situation, in which journalism brings the Chinese, Russians, Finns, Poles and Turks to your notice each morning really *could not* be met in the same way. Of course I know the more obvious reply, that you can't do them any good by being miserable, but that is hardly the point, for in the case of the Jones's next door we should think ill of the man who felt nothing whether his feeling did them good or not.

I am afraid the truth is in this, as in nearly everything else I think about at present, that the world, as it is now becoming and has partly become, is simply *too much for* people of the old square-rigged type like you and me. I don't understand its economics, or its politics, or any dam' thing about it. Even its theology—for that is a most distressing discovery I have been making these last two terms as I have been getting to know more and more of the Christian element in Oxford.

Did you fondly believe—I did—that where you got among Christians, there, at least, you would escape (as behind a wall from a keen wind) from the horrible ferocity and grimness of modern thought? Not a bit of it. I blundered into it all, imagining that I was the upholder of the old, stern doctrines against modern quasi-Christian slush: only to find that *my* 'sterness' was *their* 'slush'. They've all been reading a dreadful man called Karl Barth, who seems the right opposite number to Karl Marx. 'Under judgement' is their great expression. They all talk like Covenanters or old Testament prophets. They don't think human reason or human conscience of any value at all: they maintain, as stoutly as Calvin, that there's no reason why God's dealings should appear just (let alone, merciful) to us: and they maintain the doctrine that *all* our righteousness is filthy rags with a fierceness and sincerity which is like a blow in the face . . .

But, in a private letter, one may, for a moment, bewail happier days—the old world when Politics meant Tariff Reform, and war, war with Zulus, and even religion meant (beautiful word) Piety. 'The *decent* church that crowns the neighbouring hill'—Sir Roger at Church—'Mr Arabin sent the farmers home to their baked mutton very well satisfied' . . .

TO HIS BROTHER: from The Kilns

25 February 1940

Plague on this nonsense of putting back the clock which has docked me of an hour's sleep and which for the next few weeks will give me darkness at shaving and dressing time when I want light and light after tea when it is an impertinence; and which also, by abolishing 3.30 Evensong has sent me back to Mattins and the old morning rush.

I am just back from it now. The change was aggravated by the fact that, as Bleiben announced 'We are now approaching that time of the year in which the Church revises her Electoral Roll'. We had the whole bag of tricks of course, followed by a full exposition of the Free Will Offering scheme. He preached a very good sermon, however, on Joseph, as the type of man who has an almost unique series of excuses for being 'embittered', 'disillusioned' and all the usual bunk but doesn't take them.

Reflection on the story raised in my mind a problem I never happen to have thought of before: why was Joseph imprisoned, and not killed, by Potiphar? Surely it seems extraordinarily mild treatment for attempted rape of a great lady by a slave? Or must one assume that Potiphar, tho' ignorant of the lady's intention to make him a cuckold, was aware in general (like Bishop Proudie and many other husbands) that her stories about the servants were to be taken with a grain of salt—that his real view was 'I don't suppose for a moment that Joseph did anything of the sort, but I foresee there'll be no peace till I get him out of the house'? One is tempted to begin to imagine the whole life of the Potiphar family: e.g. how often had he heard similar stories from her before? . . .

TO HIS BROTHER: from The Kilns

3 March 1940

One pleasant thing which happened this week was a visit from Dyson on Thursday which produced a meeting of all Inklings except yourself and Barfield. Fox read us his latest 'Paradisal' on Blenheim Park in winter. The only line I can quote (wh. seems to me very good) is 'Beeches have figures; oaks, anatomies'. It was in the *Troilus* stanza and full of his own 'cool, mellow flavour' as the tobacconists say. He has really in some respects a considerable similarity to Miss Sackville West. Dyson, according to Tolkien (you know how bad an observer of such things I am) was looking changed and ill, but he was in his usual form and, on being told of Williams' Milton lectures on 'the sage and serious doctrine of virginity', replied 'The fellow's becoming a common *chastitute*' ...

TO HIS BROTHER: from Magdalen College
(on Maundy Thursday)

[21 March] 1940

About Spain—after, first, Hitler's, and, now, Mussolini's, abandonment of anti-Communism I am prepared for almost anything. There are people in Europe quite depraved enough to stage that whole ceremony without having the slightest belief in Christianity or the slightest intention of treating it as anything more than a bait. Let us hope—and indeed pray—that France is not one of them. Even if he is not, he might be sincere in a sense which bodes very ill for us. I mean, his Christendom might be, on the Papist side, what Ulster Orangeism is on the Protestant side. One can imagine Condlin, if he were a Dictator, whipping up a kind of Protestant revival which wd be in a sense sincere, but which would be quite ready to ally itself with Germany or Russia or both for the destruction of Italy and Spain. I can never forget Tolkien's Spanish friend who, after having several colleges pointed out to him by name from the roof of the Radder, observed with surprise 'So this was once a Christian country?'

Mind you, I think the Pope is sound. Something might be done through him to persuade France to put the Christian-Totalitarian issue first, at any rate for the present, and the Papist-Protestant second. Of course I absolutely agree with you that Papistry even of the most obscurantist and persecuting kind would be better (I mean in terms of this world) than the great rebellion of the other force not only against Grace but against Nature.

Why should quiet ruminants as you and I have been born in such a ghastly age? Let me palliate the apparent selfishness of this complaint by asserting that there *are* people who, while not, of course, liking actual suffering when it falls to their own share, *do* really like the 'stir', the 'sense of great issues'. Lord!, how I loathe great issues. How I wish they were all adjourned *sine die*. 'Dynamic' I think is one of the words invented by this age which sums up what it likes and I abominate. Could one start a Stagnation party—which at General Elections would boast that during its term of office *no* event of the least importance had taken place . . .

TO A FORMER PUPIL: **from Magdalen College**

26 March 1940

(1) About obedience. Nearly everyone will find himself in the course of his life in positions where he ought to command and in positions where he ought to obey . . . Now each of them requires a certain training or habituation if it is to be done well; and indeed the habit of command or of obedience may often be more necessary than the most enlightened views on the ultimate moral grounds for doing

either. You can't begin training a child to command until it has reason and age enough to command someone or something without absurdity. You can at once begin training it to obey: that is teaching it the art of obedience *as such* — without prejudice to the views it will hold later on as to who should obey whom, or when, or how much . . . since it is perfectly obvious that every human being is going to spend a great deal of his life in obeying.

(2) Psychoanalysis. In talking to me you must beware, because I am conscious of a partly pathological hostility to what is fashionable. I may therefore have been betrayed into statements on this subject which I am not prepared to defend. No doubt, like every young science, it is full of errors, but so long as it remains a science and doesn't set up to be a philosophy, I have no quarrel with it, i.e. as long as people judge what it reveals by the best human logic and scheme of values they've got and do not try to derive logic and values from it. In practice no doubt, as you say, the patient is always influenced by the analyst's own values. And further, in so far as it attempts to *heal,* i.e. to make better, every treatment involves a value-judgement. This could be avoided if the analyst said, 'Tell me what sort of a chap you want to be and I'll see how near I can make you': but of course he really has his own idea of what goodness and happiness consist in and works to that. And his idea is derived, not from his science (it couldn't) but from his age, sex, class, culture, religion and heredity, and is just as much in need of criticism as the patients's . . .

Another way in which *any* therapeutic art may have bad philosophical results is this. It must, for the sake of method, take perfection as the norm and treat every departure from it as disease: hence there is always a danger that those who practise it may come to treat a perfectly ideal perfection as 'normal' in the popular sense and consequently waste their lives in crying for the moon . . .

I see no reason why a Christian shd not be an analyst. Psychoanalysis after all merely defines what was always admitted, that the moral choices of the human soul operate inside a complex non-moral situation . . . The Christian view would be that every psychological situation, just like every degree of wealth or poverty, had its own peculiar temptations and peculiar advantages: that the worst could always be turned to a good use and the best could always be abused, to one's spiritual ruin . . . This doesn't mean that it wd be wrong to try to cure a complex any more than a stiff leg: but it does mean that if you can't, then so far from the game being up, life with a complex or a stiff leg, is precisely the game you have been set . . . We must play the parts we find ourselves given . . . Once make the medical norm our idea of the 'normal' and we shall never lack an excuse for throwing up the sponge. But these are all illegitimate abuses of analysis.

(3) Christianity. My own experience in reading the Gospels was at one stage even more depressing than yours. Everyone told me that there I should find a figure whom I couldn't help loving. Well, I could. They told me I would final moral perfection—but one sees so very little of Him in ordinary situations that I couldn't make much of that either. Indeed some of His behaviour seemed to me open to criticism, e.g. accepting an invitation to dine with a Pharisee and then loading him with torrents of abuse.

Now the truth is, I think, that the sweetly-attractive-human-Jesus is a product of 19th century scepticism, produced by people who were ceasing to believe in His divinity but wanted to keep as much Christianity as they could. It is not what an unbeliever coming to the records with an open mind will (at first) find there. The first thing you find is that we are simply not *invited* to speak, to pass any moral judgement on Him, however favourable: it is only too clear that He is going to do whatever judging there is: it is *we* who are *being* judged, sometimes tenderly, sometimes with stunning severity, but always *de haut en bas.* (Have you ever noticed that your imagination can hardly be forced to picture Him as shorter than yourself?)

The first real work of the Gospels on a fresh reader is, and ought to be, to raise very acutely the question, 'Who or What is this?' For there is a good deal in the character which, unless He really is what He says He is, is not lovable or even tolerable. If He *is,* then of course it is another matter: nor will it then be surprising if much remains puzzling to the end. For if there is anything in Christianity, we are now approaching something which will never be fully comprehensible.

On this whole aspect of the subject I should go on . . . to Chesterton's *Everlasting Man.* You might also find Mauriac's *Vie de Jesus* useful . . . If childish associations are too intrusive, in reading the New Testament it's a good idea to try it in some other language, or Moffat's translation.

As for theology proper: a good many misunderstandings are cleared away by Edwyn Bevan's *Symbolism and Belief.* A book of composite authorship and of varying merit, but on the whole good, is *Essays Catholic and Critical* ed. E. G. Selwyn (S.P.C.K.). Gore's *The Philosophy of the Good Life* (Everyman) is rather wordy, but taught me a lot. If you can stand serious faults of style (and if you can get them, they are long out of print) Geo. Macdonald's 3 vols of *Unspoken Sermons* go to the very heart of the matter. I think you would also find it most illuminating to re-read now many things you once read in 'Eng. Lit.' without knowing their real importance—Herbert, Traherne, *Religio Medici.*

As for a person 'with whom to discuss', choice is more ticklish. L. W. Grensted is very interested in psychoanalysis and wrote a book on its relations to Christianity: would that be an advantage or the reverse? O. C. Quick whom I know and like. Milford, the present rector of St Mary's, some like and some don't. Let me know what, or what sort you want, and I'll see what can be done.

Come and see me when you're better and bring the gudeman.

TO DOM BEDE GRIFFITHS, O.S.B.: from Magdalen College

16 April 1940

Congratulations (if that is the right word) on becoming a Priest, and thanks for the pleasing woodcut. Yes: Melchisedech is a figure who might have been intended (nay, *was* intended, since God provides not for an abstraction called Man but for individual souls) for people who were being led to the truth by the peculiar route that you and I know.

I do most thoroughly agree with what you say about Art and Literature. To my mind they are only healthy when they are either (a) Definitely the handmaids of religious, or at least moral, truth—or (b) Admittedly aiming at nothing but innocent recreation or entertainment. Dante's alright, and *Pickwith* is alright. But the great *serious irreligious* art—art for art's sake—is all balderdash; and, incidentally, never exists when art is really flourishing. In fact one can say of Art as an author I recently read says of Love (sensual love, I mean) 'It ceases to be a devil when it ceases to be a god'. Isn't that well put? So many things—nay, every real *thing*—is good if only it will be humble and ordinate.

One thing we want to do is to kill the word 'spiritual' in the sense in which it is used by writers like Arnold and Croce. Last term I had to make the following remark to a room full of Christian undergraduates 'A man who is eating or lying with his wife or preparing to go to sleep, in humility, thankfulness, and temperance, is, by Christian standards, in an infinitely *higher* state than one who is listening to Bach or reading Plato in a state of pride'—obvious to you, but I could see it was quite a new light to them.

I don't know what to think about the present state of the world. The sins on the side of the democracies are very great. I suppose they differ from those on the other side by being less deliberately blasphemous, fulfilling less the condition of a *perfectly* mortal sin. Anyway, the question 'Who is in the right' (in a given quarrel) is quite distinct from the question 'Who is righteous?'—for the worse of two disputants may always be in the right on one particular issue. It is therefore *not* self righteous to claim that we are in the right now. But I am chary of doing what my emotions prompt me to do every hour; i.e. identifying the enemy with the forces of evil. Surely one of the things we learn from history is that God never allows a human conflict to become unambiguously one between simple good and simple evil?

The practical problem about charity (in our prayers) is very hard work, isn't it? When you pray for Hitler & Stalin, how do you actually teach yourself to make the prayer real? The two things that help me are (a) A continual grasp of the idea that one is only joining one's feeble little voice to the perpetual intercession of Christ, who died for those very men (b) A recollection, as firm as one can make it, of all one's own cruelty wh. might have blossomed, under different conditions, into something terrible. You and I are not, at bottom, so different from these ghastly creatures.

I have been reading Lady Julian of Norwich. What do you make of her? A dangerous book, clearly, and I'm glad I didn't read it much earlier. (Have you noticed how God so often sends us books at just the right time?) One thing in her pleased me immensely. *Contemptus mundi* is dangerous and may lead to Manicheeism. Love of the creature is also dangerous. How the good of each is won, and the danger rejected, in her vision of 'all that is made' as a little thing like a hazel nut 'so small I thought it could hardly endure'. Not bad, you see: just very, very small.

I'm enclosing a book in which you might like the last essay. I've been busy this winter on a book called *The Problem of Pain* wh. I was asked to write for a thing called The Christian Challenge Series. I have hopes you may like it . . .

TO A FORMER PUPIL: from Magdalen College

18 April 1940

On the marriage service. The three 'reasons' for marrying, in modern English are (a) To have children, (b) Because you are very unlikely to succeed in leading a life of total sexual abstinence, and marriage is the only innocent outlet, (c) To be in a partnership. What is there to object to in the order in which they are put?

The modern tradition is that the proper reason for marrying is the state described as 'being in love'. Now I have nothing to say against 'being in love': but the idea that this is or ought to be the exclusive reason or that it can ever be by itself an *adequate* basis seems to me simply moonshine. In the first place, many ages, many cultures, and many individuals don't experience it—and Christianity is for all men, not simply for modern Western Europeans. Secondly, it often unites most unsuitable people. Thirdly, is it not usually transitory? Doesn't the modern emphasis on 'love' lead people either into divorce or into misery, because when that emotion dies down they conclude that their marriage is a 'failure', tho' in fact they have just reached the point at wh. *real* marriage begins. Fourthly, it wd be undesirable, even if it were possible, for people to be 'in love' all their lives. What a world it wd be if most of the people we met were perpetually in this trance! The Prayer Book therefore begins with something universal and solid—the biological aspect. No one is going to deny that the *biological* end of the sexual functions is offspring. And this is, on any sane view, of more importance than the *feelings* of the parents. Your descendants may be alive a million years hence and may number tens of thousands. In this regard marriages are the fountains of *History*. Surely to put the mere emotional aspects first would be sheer sentimentalism.

Then the second reason. Forgive me: but it is simply no good trying to explain this to a woman. The *emotional* temptations may be worse for women than for men: but the pressure of mere *appetite* on the male, they simply don't understand. In this second reason, the Prayer Book is saying 'If you can't be chaste (and most of you can't) the alternative is marriage'. This may be brutal sense, but, to a man, it is *sense*, and that's that.

The third reason gives the thing that matters far more than 'being in love' and will last and increase, between good people, long after 'love' in the popular sense is only as a memory of childhood—the partnership, the loyalty to 'the firm', the composite creature. (Remember it is not a *cynic* but a devoted husband and inconsolable widower, Dr Johnson, who said that a man who has been happy with one woman cd have been equally happy with any one of 'tens of thousands' of other women. i.e. the original attraction will turn out in the end to have been almost accidental: it is what is built up on that, or any other, basis wh. may have brought the people together that matters.)

Now the second reason involves the whole Christian view of sex. It is all contained in Christ's saying that two shall be 'one flesh'. He says nothing about two 'who married for love': the mere fact of marriage *at all*—however it came about—sets up the 'one flesh'. There is a terrible comment on this in I Cor. VI. 16 'he that is joined to a harlot is one flesh'. You see? Apparently, if Christianity is true, the mere fact of sexual intercourse sets up between human beings a relation wh. has, so to speak, transcendental repercussions — some *eternal* relation is established whether they like it or not. This sounds very odd. But is it? After all, if there *is* an eternal world and if our world is its manifestation, then you would expect bits of it to 'stick through' into ours. We are like children pulling the levers of a vast machine of which *most* is concealed. We see a few little wheels that buzz round on *this* side when we start it up — but what glorious or frightful processes we are initiating *in there*, we don't know. That's why it is so important to do what we're told. (Cf.— what does the Holy Communion imply about the real significance of *eating*?)

From this all the rest flows. (1) The seriousness of sexual sin and the importance of marriage as 'a remedy against sin'. (I don't mean, of course, that sins of that sort will not, like others, be forgiven if they are repented, nor that the 'eternal relations' wh. they have set up will not be redeemed. We believe that God will use all repented evil as fuel for fresh good in the end.) (2) The *permanence* of marriage wh. means that the intention of fidelity matters more than 'being in love'. (3) The *Headship* of the Man.

I'm sorry about this — and I feel that my defence of it wd be more convincing if I were a woman. You see, of course, that if marriage is a permanent relation, intended to produce a kind of new organism ('the one flesh') there must be a Head. It's only so long as you make it a temporary arrangement dependent on 'being in love' and changeable by frequent divorce, that it can be strictly democratic — for, on that view, when they really differ, they part. But if they are not to part, if the thing is like a nation not a club, like an organism not a heap of stones, then, in the long run, one party or other must have the casting vote. That being so, do you really *want* the Head to be the woman? In a particular instance, no doubt you may. But do you really want a matriarchal world? Do you really like women in authority? When you seek authority yourself, do you naturally seek it in a woman?

Your phrase about the 'slave-wife' is mere rhetoric, because it assumes servile subordination to be the only kind of subordination. Aristotle cd have taught you better. 'The householder governs his slave despotically. He governs his wife and children as being both *free*—but he governs the children as a constitutional monarch, and the wife politically' (i.e. as a democratic magistrate governs a democratic citizen).

My own feeling is that the Headship of the husband is necessary to protect the outer world against the family. The female has a strong instinct to fight for its cubs. What do nine women out of ten care about justice to the outer world when the health, or career, or happiness of their own children is at stake? That is why I want the 'foreign policy' of the family, so to speak, to be determined by the man; I expect more mercy from him! Yet this fierce maternal instinct must be preserved, otherwise the enormous sacrifices involved in motherhood wd never be borne. The Christian scheme, therefore, does not suppress it but protects us defenceless bachelors from its worst ravages! This, however, is only my own idea. The Headship doctrine is that of Christianity. I take it to be chiefly about man *as* man and woman *as* woman, and therefore about husbands and wives, since it is only in marriage that they lawfully meet *as* epitomes of their sex. Notice that in I Cor. XI just after the bit about the man being the Head, St Paul goes on to add the baffling reservation (v. 11) that the sexes 'in the Lord' don't have any separate existence. I have no idea what this means: but I take it it must imply that the existence of a man or woman is not exhausted by the fact of being male or female, but that they exist in many other modes.

I mean, you may be a citizen, a musician, a teacher etc. as well as a woman, and you needn't transfer to all these personalities everything that is said about you as wife *qua* wife. I think that is the answer to your view that the Headship doctrine wd prevent women going in for education. St Paul is not a *system* maker, you know. As a Jew, he must, for instance, have believed that a man ought to honour and obey his Mother: but he doesn't stop and put that in when talking about the man being Head in marriage. As for Martha & Mary, either Christ and St Paul are inconsistent here, or they are not. If they're not, then, whether you can see how or not, St Paul's doctrine can't have the sense you give it. If they *are* inconsistent, then the authority of Christ of course completely over-rides that of St Paul. In either event, you needn't bother.

I very strongly agree that it's no use trying to create a 'feeling'. But what feeling do you want to have? Isn't your problem one of thought, not feeling? The question is 'Is Christianity true—or even, is there some truth mixed up in it?' The thing in reading Macdonald is not to try to have the feelings he has, but to notice whether the whole thing does or does not agree with such *perceptions* (I mean, about good &

evil etc.) as you already have—and, where it doesn't, whether it or you are right.

Term begins on Saturday next. If you and the gudeman cd come and lunch with me on the following Saturday (27th) it wd suit admirably. Let me know (address to College). Thank you for taking my mind off the war for an hour or so!

P.S. I don't think the Marriage Service is ascetic, and I think your real objection to it may be that it's not *prudish* enough! The service is *not* for celebrating the flesh, but for making a solemn *agreement* in the presence of God and of society—an agreement which involves a good many other things besides the flesh . . . 'Sober and godly matrons' may be a stickler, if you haven't read the English Schools: but *you* ought to know that all the associations you are putting into it are modern and accidental. It *means* 'Married women (matrons) who are religious (godly) and have something better and happier to think about than jazz and lipstick (sober).' But you must know that as well as I do!

TO HIS BROTHER: from The Kilns

21 April 1940

I never told you a curious thing—I have meant to include it in several letters—wh. provides a new instance of the malignity of the Little People. I was going into town one day and had got as far as the gate when I realized that I had odd shoes on, and one of them clean and the other dirty. There was no time to go back. As it was impossible to clean the dirty one, I decided that the only way of making myself look less ridiculous was to *dirty* the clean one. Now wd you have believed that this is an impossible operation? You can of course get some mud on it—but it remains obviously a clean shoe that has had an accident and won't look in the least like a shoe that you have been for a walk in. One discovers new catches and snags in life every day . . .

TO OWEN BARFIELD: from The Kilns

2 June 1940

Mrs Moore told me yesterday about your loss of your mother. I cannot imagine myself, in similar circumstances, not feeling very strongly *felix opportunitate mortis,* but I daresay, when it comes to the point, that is very far from being the predominant emotion; I have always remembered what you told me of the dream in which you were condemned to death and of the part your mother played in it. I am very sorry you should have this particular desolation added to the general one in which we are. It is like the first act of *Prometheus* 'Peace is in the grave, the grave hides all things beautiful and good'. He was near, however, to his release when he said that, and I accept the omen—that you and I and our friends will soon be past the worst, if not in one way, then in the other. For I am very thankful to say that while my θρεπτική often plays tricks I am ashamed of, I retain my faith, as I have no doubt you do yours. 'All shall be well, and all shall be well, and all manner of thing shall be well'—This is from Lady Julian of Norwich whom I have been reading lately and who seems, in the Fifteenth century, to have rivalled Thomas Aquinas' reconciliation of Aristotle and Christianity by nearly reconciling Christianity with Kant.

The real difficulty is, isn't it, to adapt ones steady beliefs about tribulation to this *particular* tribulation; for the particular, when it arrives, always *seems* so peculiarly intolerable. I find it helpful to keep it very particular—to stop thinking about the ruin of the world etc., for no one is going to experience *that,* and to see it as each individual's personal sufferings, which never can be more than those of one man, or more than one man, if he were very unlucky, might have suffered in peacetime.

Do you get sudden lucid intervals? islands of profound peace? I do: and though they don't last, I think one brings something away from them.

I wish we could meet more, but I can hardly reckon on any one evening at present. But make no mistake: if you ever feel inclined to doubt whether (to talk in our old style!) language really *is* a P.O.S., you needn't. All is well still—except ones stomach.

And oddly enough, I notice that since things got really bad, everyone I meet is less dismayed. Macdonald observes somewhere that 'the approach of any fate is usually also the preparation for it'. I began to hope he is right. Even at this present moment I don't feel nearly so bad as I should have done if anyone had prophesied it to me eighteen months ago.

But I am merely doling out what you know as well as I and are better qualified to say to me that I to you. Blessings on you for everything in our common life these twenty years.

TO HIS BROTHER: **from The Kilns** (In May Warren
had been evacuated with his unit from Dunkirk and sent to
Wenvoe Camp in Cardiff.)

12 July 1940

I've been up for some days now, still feeling rather weak,
and shall be embroiled in examiners' meetings all the
week end. Before the illness was over I read your copy of
Southey's letters from end to end with great enjoyment:—a
bad poet, but a delightful man. I also found things in it that
were very consoling; as (a) The daily fear of invasion. (b)
The haunting fear of traitors on the home front. (c) The
repeated statement that 'even now' we might pull through
if only we had a decent government. (d) The settled conviction that 'even if' we defeated Buonaparte we should still
have to face revolution at home. God send it's a true omen.

Other impressions were (a) How much *nicer people,*
tho' worse writers, the Tory romantics were than the other
crew—the Shelleys and L. Hunts and even Keats. (b) What a
happy life he had on the whole, and yet what a grim business
even a happy human life is when you read it rapidly through
to the inevitable end . . .

TO DOM BEDE GRIFFITHS, O.S.B.: **from Magdalen
College**

16 July 1940

A lot of work and an illness have kept me from answering
your letter, but I have been intending ever since I got it to let
you know that I think your criticisms on my Aristotelian idea
of leisure are largely right. I wouldn't write that essay now.

In fact I have recently come to the conclusion that a besetting sin of mine all my life has been one which I never suspected — laziness — and that a good deal of the high sounding doctrine of leisure is only a defence of *that*. The Greek error was a punishment for their sin in owning slaves and their consequent contempt for labour. There was a good element in it — the recognition, badly needed by modern commercialism, that the economic activities are not the *end* of man: beyond that, they were probably wrong. If I still wanted to defend my old view I shd ask you why *toil* appears in Genesis not as one of the things God originally created and pronounced 'very good', but as a punishment for sin, like death. I suppose one wd point out in reply that Adam was a gardener before he was a sinner, and that we must distinguish two degrees and kinds of work — the one wholly good and necessary to the animal side of the *animal rationale,* the other a punitive deterioration of the former due to the Fall.

My enjoyment of the Psalms has been greatly increased lately. The point has been made before, but let me make it again: what an admirable thing it is in the Divine economy that the sacred literature of the world shd have been entrusted to a people whose poetry, depending largely on parallelism, shd remain poetry in any language you translate it into ...

TO HIS BROTHER: **from The Kilns** (in which he records the conception of *The Screwtape Letters*)

20 July 1940

Humphrey [Havard] came up to see me last night (not in his medical capacity) and we listened to Hitler's speech together. I don't know if I'm weaker than other people: but it is a positive revelation to me how *while the speech lasts* it is impossible not to waver just a little. I should be useless as a schoolmaster or a policeman. Statements which I *know* to be untrue all but convince me, at any rate for the moment, if only the man says them unflinchingly. The same weakness is why I am a slow examiner: if a candidate with a bold, mature handwriting attributed *Paradise Lost* to Wordsworth, I shd feel a tendency to go and look it up for fear he might be right after all . . .

I resume [21 July] at coffee-time on Sunday morning. I have been to Church for the first time for many weeks owing to the illness, and considered myself invalid enough to make a mid-day communion . . . Before the service was over—one cd wish these things came more seasonably—I was struck by an idea for a book wh. I think might be both useful and entertaining. It wd be called *As One Devil to Another* and would consist of letters from an elderly retired devil to a young devil who has just started work on his first 'patient'. The idea wd be to give all the psychology of temptation from the *other* point of view. e.g. 'About undermining his faith in prayer, I don't think you need have any difficulty with his intellect, provided you never say the wrong thing at the wrong moment. After all, the Enemy will either answer his prayers or not. If he does *not*, then that's simple—it shows prayers are no good. If he *does*— I've always found that, oddly enough, this can be just as easily utilised. It needs only a word from you to make him believe that the very fact of feeling more patient after he's prayed for patience will be taken as a proof that prayer is a kind of self hypnosis. Or if it is answered by some external event, then since that event will have causes which you can point to, he can be persuaded that it would have happened anyway. You see the idea? Prayer can always be discredited either because it works or because it doesn't.' Or again. 'In attacking faith, I should be chary of argument. Arguments only provoke answers. What you want to work away at is the mere unreasoning *feeling* that "that sort of thing can't really be true"' . . .

TO HIS BROTHER: **from The Kilns** (Jack has begun his duties with the Local Defence Volunteers, the name of which was soon changed to The Home Guard.)

11 August [1940]

I have commenced my L.D.V. Duties with the 1.30 A.M. patrol on what they call Saturday morning and mortals call Friday night. As it seemed no use going to bed to be raked out at 12.45 I asked Dyson and Humphrey to dine and the others to join us afterwards so as to make a 'wake' of it in the original sense . . .

We have a very good Inklings breaking up about ten to one, when the others went home and I set out for my rendez-vous at Lake St. — eating my sandwiches on the way, as I didn't feel I cd provide sandwiches for the whole party and hadn't the face to eat my own in their presence. I was with two men much younger than myself: one a bluecoat and the other, I think a burley — both very nice and intelligent and neither too talkative nor too silent. One is allowed to smoke and I was pleased to find that our tour of duty included a quite prolonged soak on the veranda of a college pavilion—a pleasant spot, looking out over broad playing fields in a mild but windy night of sufficient starlight and some light clouds—with the occasional interest of a train trundling past. Unfortunately our watch was not so well arranged as Dogberry's ('All sit in the church porch till two, and then every man to bed'); still, the three hours passed surprisingly quickly, and if it hadn't been for the bother of lugging a rifle about all the time I should have said that pleasure distinctly predominated. I had quite forgotten the weight of a 'tripe' [rifle]. We broke off at 4.30 and after a really beautiful walk back through an empty and twilight Oxford I was in bed by 5 . . .

[Warren's health had been unsatisfactory ever since he went to France, and in August he retired and was transferred to the Reserve List. On 27 August Maureen was married to Leonard Blake who had been the Director of Music at Worksop College since 1935. Jack's new book, *The Problem of Pain,* which was both read to The Inklings as it was written and dedicated to them was published on 18 October.]

TO A FORMER PUPIL: **from The Kilns**

4 January 1941

Congratulations . . . on your own decision. I don't think this decision comes either too late or too soon. One can't go on thinking it over for ever; and one can begin to try to be a disciple before one is a professed theologian. In fact they tell us, don't they, that in these matters to act on the light one has is almost the only way to more light. Don't be worried about feeling flat, or about feeling at all.

As to what to *do*, I suppose the normal next step, after self-examination, repentance and restitution, is to make your Communion; and then to continue as well as you can, praying as well as you can . . . and fulfilling your daily duties as well as you can. And remember always that religious *emotion* is only a servant . . . This, I say, would be the obvious course. If you want anything more e.g. Confession and Absolution which our church enjoins on no-one but leaves free to all—let me know and I'll find you a *directeur*. If you choose this way, remember it's not the psychoanalyst over again: the confessor is the representative of Our Lord and declares His forgiveness—his advice or 'understanding' tho' of real, is of secondary importance.

For daily reading I suggest (in small doses) Thomas à Kempis' *Imitation of Christ* and the *Theologia Germanica* (Golden Treasury series, Macmillan) and of course the Psalms and N.T. Don't worry if your heart won't respond: do the best you can. You are certainly under the guidance of the Holy Ghost, or you wouldn't have come where you now are: and the love that matters is His for you—yours for Him may at present exist only in the form of obedience. He will see to the rest.

This has been great news for me I need hardly say. You have all my prayers (not that mine are worth much).

TO THE SAME: from Magdalen College

29 January 1941

Thanks very much for your kind letter. My own progress is so very slow (indeed sometimes I seem to be going backwards) that the encouragement of having in any degree helped someone else is just what I wanted. *Of course* the idea of not relying on emotion carries no implication of not rejoicing in it when it comes: you may remember Donne's *Litanie* 'That our affections kill us not—nor die'. One of the minor rewards of conversion is to be able to see at last the real point of all the old literature which we are brought up to read with the point left out! ...

TO SISTER PENELOPE, C.S.M.V.: from Magdalen College

10 April 1941

Yes, I will come and address your Junior Sisters next Easter unless 'wife and oxen' have by that time taken the form of incarceration in a German Concentration camp, an English Labour Company, or (to pitch on a brighter idea) some sort of Borstal Institution on the lower foot-hills of the mountain of Purgatory. But (if one may say so *salva reverentia*) what odd tasks God sets us; if anyone had told me ten years ago that I should be lecturing in a convent—! Thanks for the offer of hospitality in the Gate House, which I accept gratefully, though the Protestant in me has just a little suspicion of an oubliette or a chained skeleton—the doors do open outwards as well, I trust.

Thank you very much for the book.[162] It has given me real help. What I particularly enjoy in all your work, specially this, is the avoidance of that curious *drabness* which characterises so many 'little books on religion'. Partly it is due to your Hebraic background which I envy you: partly, no doubt, to deeper causes . . . There are, in fact, a good many Gifford Lectures and other such weighty tomes out of which I've got less meat (and indeed less efficient cookery!)

You never told me how you got on with the WAFS. I have just started doing something of the same kind with R.A.F. officers and shd be interested to compare notes . . .

[One of the immediate results of *The Problem of Pain* was a great deal of 'war work' for Jack. In the Winter of 1941 the Chaplain-in-Chief of the RAF asked him to accept a kind of travelling lectureship, which meant going round to various RAF bases and lecturing on Theology. The first of these talks was given at the RAF base in Abingdon during April 1941. In February 1941 he had been asked to give a series of talks over the BBC, and it is this series which he told Sister Penelope about in the letter which follows. The series consisted of four fifteen-minute talks entitled *Right and Wrong: A Clue to the Meaning of the Universe?* and they were given during August. Although Sister Penelope did

---

[162] All of Sister Penelope's books were published during these years as by 'A Religious of C.S.M.V.'. The book she had sent to Jack was *Windows on Jerusalem* (1941)

not speak over the radio herself, she was writing some talks for someone else to deliver.]

TO SISTER PENELOPE, C.S.M.V.: **from Magdalen College**

15 May 1941

We ought to meet about B.B.C. talks if nothing else as I'm giving four in August. Mine are *praeparatio evangelica* rather than *evangelium,* an attempt to convince people that there is a moral law, that we disobey it, and that the existence of a Lawgiver is at least very probable and also (*unless* you add the Christian doctrine of the Atonement) imparts despair rather than comfort. You will come after to heal any wounds I may succeed in making. So each of us ought to know what the other is saying.

I've given some talks to the R.A.F. at Abingdon already and as far as I can judge they were a complete failure. I await instructions from the Chaplain in Chief about the Vacation.

Yes—jobs one dare neither refuse nor perform. One must take comfort in remembering that God used an *ass* to convert the prophet: perhaps if we do our poor best we shall be allowed a stall near it in the celestial stable—rather like this:

[The remainder of the sheet is filled with an amusing drawing of the ass, flanked by a nun and a figure in a mortarboard, seated outside a stable in the radiance of the heavenly city.]

TO SISTER PENELOPE, C.S.M.V.: from Magdalen College

9 October 1941

I am ashamed of having grumbled. And your act was not that of a brute—in operation it was more like that of an angel, for (as I said) you started me on a quite new realization of what is meant by being 'in Christ', and immediately after that 'the power which erring men call chance' put into my hands [E. L.] Mascall's two books in the *Signposts* series which continued the process. So I lived for a week end (at Aberystwyth) in one of those delightful *vernal* periods when doctrines that have hitherto been only buried seeds began actually to come up—like snowdrops or crocuses. I won't deny they've met a touch of frost since (if only things would *last*, or rather if only *we* would!) but I'm still very much, and gladly, in your debt. The only real evil of having read your scripts when I was tired is that it was hardly fair to them and not v. useful to you.

I have had to refuse a request from Sister Janet. Will you tell her that the 'wives and oxen' are quite real ones?

I enclose the MS. of *Screwtape*. If it is not a trouble I shd like you to keep it safe until the book is printed (in case the one the publisher has got blitzed)—after that it can be made into spills or used to stuff dolls or anything.

Thank you very much for the photo of the Shroud. It raises a whole question on which I shall have to straighten out my thoughts one of these days.

TO SISTER PENELOPE, C.S.M.V.: **from Magdalen College** (The book referred to is *Perelandra*.)

9 November 1941

I've got Ransom to Venus and through his first conversation with the 'Eve' of that world: a difficult chapter. I hadn't realised till I came to write it all the *Ave-Eva* business. I may have embarked on the impossible. This woman has got to combine characteristics which the Fall has put poles apart—she's got to be in some ways like a Pagan goddess and in other ways like the Blessed Virgin. But if one can get even a fraction of it into words it is worth doing.

Have you room for an extra prayer? Pray for *Jane* if you have. She is the old lady I call my mother and live with (she is really the mother of a friend)—an unbeliever, ill, old, frightened, full of charity in the sense of alms, but full of uncharity in several other senses. And I can do little for her.

TO SISTER PENELOPE, C.S.M.V.: **from Magdalen College**

19 November 1941

It is a curious fact that the advice we can give to others we cannot give to ourselves and truth is more effective through any life rather than our own. Chas. Williams in *Taliessin* is good on this 'No one can live in his own house. My house for my neighbour, his for me'.

I think what really worries me is the feeling (often on waking in the morning) that there's really nothing I so much *dislike* as religion—that it's all against the grain and I wonder if I can really stand it! Have you ever had this? Does one outgrow it? Of course there's no intellectual difficulty. If our faith is true then that is just what it ought to feel like, until the new man is full-grown. But it's a considerable bore. What you say about 'disappointed with oneself' is very true—and a tendency to mistake mere disappointment (in wh. there is much wounded pride and much of a mere sportsman's irritation at breaking a record) for true repentance. I ought to have devoted a Screwtape letter to this.

Please tell Mother Annie Louisa that I have booked April 20th–22nd. I shouldn't reach Wantage until (I suppose) mid-day or tea-time Monday, but after that will do as I'm told . . .

TO MISS PATRICIA THOMSON: from Magdalen College

8 December 1941

When I said it was 'no good' trying to regard Jesus as a human teacher I only meant that it was logically untenable—as you might say 'It's no good trying to maintain that the earth is flat'. I was saying nothing in that sermon about the destiny of the 'virtuous unbeliever'. The parable of the sheep & the goats suggests that they have a very pleasant surprise coming to them. But in the main, we are not told God's plans about them in any detail.

If the Church is Christ's body—the thing He works through—then the more worried one is about the people outside, the more reason to get *inside* oneself, where one can help—you are giving Him, as it were, a new finger. I assumed last night that I was talking to those who already believed. If I'd been speaking to those who didn't, of course everything I'd said wd be different.

Fear isn't repentance—but it's alright as a *beginning*—much better at that stage than *not* being afraid.

How interested are you? If you care to come and talk about it I expect we can arrange a date. Let me know.

TO DOM BEDE GRIFFITHS, O.S.B.: **from The Kilns**
(Jack had asked Dom Bede to read and criticize a second series of talks for the BBC on 'What Christians Believe'.)

21 December 1941

(1) I'm extremely glad you've got onto my friend Chas. Williams, tho' onto one of his worst books. He is living in Oxford during the war and we made him lecture on Milton to the faculty, so that (would you believe it, remembering the English lectures of your own period) we actually heard a lecture on *Comus* wh. put the importance where Milton had put it. In fact the lecture was a panegyric of chastity! Just fancy the incredulity with which (at first) an audience of undergraduates listened to something so unheard of. But he beat them in the end.

He is an ugly man with rather a cockney voice. But no one ever thinks of this for five minutes after he has begun speaking. His face becomes almost angelic. Both in public and private he is of nearly all the men I have met the one whose address most overflows with *love*. It is simply irresistible. Those young men and women were lapping up what he said about Chastity before the end of the hour. It's a big thing to have done. I have seen his impress on the work in the Milton papers when I examined. Fancy an Oxford student, and a girl, writing about Mammon's speech in Book II 'Mammon proposes an ordered state of sin with such majesty of pride that but for the words *live to ourselves* which startle our conscience, we should hardly recognise it as sin, so natural is it to man.' (Compare that with the sort of bilge you and I were proud to write in Schools!)

Williams, Dyson of Reading, & my brother (Anglicans) and Tolkien and my doctor, Havard (your church) are the 'Inklings' to whom my *Problem of Pain* was dedicated. We meet on Friday evenings in my rooms: theoretically to talk about literature, but in fact nearly always to talk about something better. What I owe to them all is incalculable. Dyson and Tolkien were the immediate human causes of my own conversion. Is any pleasure on earth as great as a circle of Christian friends by a good fire? His stories (I mean Williams) are his best work—*Descent into Hell* and *The Place of the Lion* are the best. I quite agree about what you call his 'affectations'—not that they are affectations, but honest defects of taste. He is largely a self-educated man, labouring under an almost oriental richness of imagination ('clotted glory from Charles' as Dyson called it) which could be saved from turning silly and even vulgar in print only by a severe early discipline which he has never had. But he is a lovely creature. I'm proud of being among his friends.

(2) Now about the scripts. (a) The claim to forgive sins is in S. Mark and all the Synoptics. (b) Yes—I think I gave the impression of going further than I intended, in saying that all theories of the Atonement were 'to be rejected if we don't find them helpful'. What I meant was 'need not be used'—a v.

different thing. Is there, on your view, a real difference here: that the Divinity of Our Lord *has to be* believed whether you find it a help or a 'scandal' (otherwise you're not a Xtian at all) but the Anselmic theory of Atonement is *not* in that position. Wd you admit that a man was a Xtian (and could be a member of your Church) who said 'I believe that Christ's death redeemed man from sin, but I can make nothing of any of the theories as to *how*'?

You see, what I wanted to do in these talks was to give simply what is still common to us all, and I've been trying to get a *nihil obstat* from friends in various communions. (The other dissentient besides you is a Methodist who says I've said nothing about justification by faith.) It therefore doesn't much matter what you think of my *own* theory because that is advanced only as my own. But I'd like to be able to meet you on the other point—how far *any* theory is *de fide*. The Council of Trent 'made satisfaction' seems to be the real hitch. What was the context? What error was it directed against? Still—don't bother, for I fear I shall have to give up my original hope. I think I could get something you and your friends wd pass, but not without making the talk either longer or shorter: but I'm on the Procrustes' bed of neither more nor less than fifteen minutes—you can imagine the difficulty.

What did you think of *In Memorian* on re-reading it? I re-read it (with Barfield) some months ago and thought (1) That the last quarter is a falling off—and can hardly help being since the poem represents a sorrow neither being transmuted, nor ending in tragedy, but just petering out (2) That the mere difficulty of *construing* some stanzas is

v. great. (3) That a great deal of the poetry is simply over-whelmingly good.

About the Son being subject to the Father (as God—of course, obviously subject as Man in the Incarnation)—yes, that's what I think: but was recently contradicted by a theo-logian. Can you back me up? What is the correct interpreta-tion of 'equal to His Father as touching His Godhead' in the Athanasian Creed?

The Talks will be at 4.40 P.M. on Jan. 11th, 4.45 Jan. 18th, Feb. 1st., 4.40 Feb. 8th, 4.45 Feb. 15th.

You look positively fat in the photo—you abbey-lubber!

TO A FORMER PUPIL: from Magdalen College

20 January 1942

Sorry you're in a trough. I'm just emerging (at least I hope I am) from a long one myself. As for the difficulty of believ-ing it is a trough, one wants to be careful about the word 'believing'. We too often mean by it 'having confidence or assurance as a psychological state'—as we have about the existence of furniture. But that comes and goes and by no means always accompanies intellectual assent, e.g. in learning to swim you believe, and even know intellectu-ally, that water will support you, long before you feel any real confidence in the fact. I suppose a perfection of faith would make this confidence invariably proportionate to the assent. In the meantime, as one has learnt to swim only by acting on the assent in the teeth of all instinctive convic-tion, so we shall proceed to faith only by acting as if we had it. Adapting a passage in the *Imitation* one can say 'What would I do now if I had a full assurance that this was only a temporary trough', and having got the answer, go and do it. I am a man, therefore lazy; you a woman, therefore probably a fidget. So it may be good advice to you (though it wd be bad to me) not even to try to do in the trough all you can do on the peak.

I know all about the despair of overcoming chronic temptations. It is not serious, provided self-offended petulance, annoyance at breaking records, impatience etc., don't get the upper hand. *No amount* of falls will really undo us if we keep on picking ourselves up each time. We shall of course be v. muddy and tattered children by the time we reach home. But the bathrooms are all ready, the towels put out, and the clean clothes in the airing cupboard. The only fatal thing is to lose one's temper and give it up. It is when we notice the dirt that God is most present in us: it is the v. sign of His presence . . .

TO MARTYN SKINNER: from Magdalen College

23 April [1942]

I hope you got through Sanders some time ago my great enjoyment of your *Letters to Malaya*. A really good poem. Not in the least a pastiche as the silly people will say but a real proof that the Popian manner is a real *lingua franca* wh. anyone who has anything to say can use for original work. In fact, it is already *less* 'archaic' than the manner of 'Georgian poetry'. The pother about 'originality' all comes from the people who have nothing to say: if they had they'd be original without noticing it . . .

TO SISTER PENELOPE, C.S.M.V.: **from Magdalen College** (Upon leaving the Mother House of the Community of St Mary the Virgin in Wantage on 22 April Jack went to London to read a paper entitled 'Hamlet: The Prince or the Poem?' to the British Academy.)

11 May 1942

The Venus book is just finished, except that I now find the two first chapters need re-writing. I will send you a typed MS as soon as it is typed and you can report on it to Reverend Mother for her consent to the dedication.[163]

The British Academy made a v. stupid audience compared with your young ladies! They were all the sort of people whom one often sees getting out of taxis and going into some big doorway and wonders who on earth they are—all those beards and double chins and fur collars and lorgnettes. Now I know . . .

TO SISTER PENELOPE, C.S.M.V.: **from Magdalen College** (Sister Penelope was engaged upon a translation of St Athanasius' *De Incarnatione*.)

29 July 1942

(1) The Rabbit [in Magdalen's deer park] and I have quarrelled. I don't know why, unless I gave him something that disagreed with him. At any rate, he has cut me dead several times lately—so fair and so fickle! Life is full of disappointments. 'The strong *hearts* of the conies' is prob. the true

---

[163] *Perelandra* is dedicated 'To some Ladies at Wantage'—the Community of St Mary the Virgin.

reading in that Psalm. (2) I'm glad to hear you are a little better, but wish you were better still.

(3) After having to abandon S. Athanasius for examining, I have now returned to the *De Incarnatione* and have just finished the long section on Jewish prophecies. If that is the bit you are omitting, I expect you are right. Though it crosses my mind that modern apologetics may have given up too completely the old 'proof of prophecy'. Each individual passage can be explained away as really meaning something else, or accidental: but could it still be argued that to apply this to the whole lot involves stretching the arm of coincidence rather far?

(4) Have you read Martin Buber's *I and Thou.* Tell me what I am to think of it? From Heaven, or (very subtly) from Hell? I'm by no means sure. And why does he limit all true 'meeting' to a Thou-situation? Is there no ye-situation? What happens when three friends are together or when a man meets his wife *and* child? (5) On Witches. I didn't really mean to deny them, tho' I see I have given that impression.[164] I was interested in them at the moment only as an illustration. I think my considered view wd be much the same as yours. But if a truth, it is not a truth I am at all anxious to spread.

---

[164] Since he began talking over the BBC Jack had been getting an enormous number of letters from listeners. The two series, 'Right and Wrong' and 'What Christians Believe', were published in July 1942 under the title *Broadcast Talks.* This led to even more letters about those talks. Jack was here answering a question Sister Penelope asked about ch. 11 of *Broadcast Talks* in which he said 'It may be a great advance in *knowledge* not to believe in witches: there's no moral advance in not executing them when you don't think they are there!'

(6) About 'became Man' *versus* 'a man'. There is you will admit, a v. obvious sense in which He became 'a man'—a man of a particular height and weight, the Son of a particular Mother, who was in one place and time and *not* (in that mode) elsewhere. The Fathers, writing in a language with no indefinite article didn't have to plump for one or the other. Are you correct in saying 'the Person, the Ego, of the incarnated Lord is God'? I had thought there was a human *soul* involved (when we speak of His humanity we don't mean simply His body) and that the human and divine natures together made one Person. Your way of putting it suggests that there was simply a human body with God *substituted* for the human soul one wd ordinarily have expected. Is this right? I thought not, but I don't know . . .

TO A FORMER PUPIL: **from Magdalen College**
(answering a question about the reference to G. B. Shaw in ch. IV of *Broadcast Talks*)

[August? 1942]

Of course Shaw is not a scientist and the attack is not on science as such. But there is a sort of creed which might be called 'scientific humanism', tho' many of its votaries know very little science (just as some people go to Church who know very little theology), and which *is* shared by people so different as Haldane, Shaw, Wells, and Olaf Stapleton . . . cf. Shaw's Lilith's 'Beyond' with Haldane p. 309: 'It is possible that under the conditions of life on the outer planets the human brain may alter in such a way as to open up possibilities inconceivable to our own minds.' (on p. 303 one of these alterations, the elimination of pity, had already occurred.)[165] All tarred with the same brush in fact . . .

TO DOM BEDE GRIFFITHS, O.S.B.: from Magdalen College (in reply to questions about parts of *Broadcast Talks*.)

13 October 1942

I shouldn't have written quite as I did if I had thought that there was a consensus of theologians in favour of the Anselmic theory. I believed that it was not to be found either in N. T. or most of the Fathers. If I'm wrong in this, it is a matter of plain historical ignorance.

War & Peace is in my opinion *the* best novel—the only one wh. makes a novel really comparable to epic. I have read it about three times. What we lose (I'm told) in our translations is the *humour* wh. is an important merit of the real book.

You wouldn't be surprised at the space I give to Dualism if you knew how attractive it is to some simple minds. As for retiring into 'private life', while feeling *very* strongly the evil of publicity, I don't see how one can. God is my witness I don't *look* for engagements . . .

---

[165] He is referring to the essay entitled 'The Last Judgement' in J. B. S. Haldane's *Possible Worlds and Other Essays*, the Phoenix Library edition (1930).

TO SISTER PENELOPE, C.S.M.V.: **from The Kilns**

22 December 1942

Perelandra will reach you, I hope, early in January: I have deterred the artist from putting his idea of Tinidril (you can imagine!) on the cover. I have been very busy with one thing and another: there aren't the days and the hours there used to be, are there? The minute hand used to go as the hour hand goes now!

How does one feel thankful? I am thinking of the improvement in the war news, and I don't mean (rhetorically) 'How can one be thankful enough?' but just what I say. It seems to be something which disappears or becomes a mere word the moment one recognises one *ought* to be feeling it. I always tell people not to bother about 'feelings' in their prayers, and above all, never to *try* to feel, but I'm a bit puzzled about Gratitude: for if it is not a feeling, what is it? A funny thing how merely formulating a question awakes the conscience! I hadn't a notion of the answer at the bottom of the last sheet, but now I know exactly what you are going to say: '*Act* your gratitude and let feelings look after themselves.' Thank you. (Do *all* theoretical problems conceal shirkings by the will?) . . .

I have 'sinitis' (it feels like toothache but isn't) but not very badly and it is, I think, going away. I have to sit for twenty min. every evening with my face in a jug of Friars Balsam, like a horse with a nose-bag, and the family say all sorts of things and I can't *answer*, tho' it is 'pain and grief to me'! God bless you all for Christmas: you are in my daily prayers as I know I am in yours.

TO A FORMER PUPIL: from **The Kilns**

31 January 1943

I'm the worst person in the world to write to someone who is feeling weak and listless . . . because I don't myself *dislike* it nearly as much as most people. To lie in bed—to find one's eyes filling with facile tears at the least hint of pathos in one's book—to let the book drop from one's hand as one sinks deeper and deeper into reverie—to forget what you were thinking about a moment ago and *not to mind*—and then be roused by the unexpected discovery that it is already tea-time—all this I do *not* find disagreeable.

Yes, it is funny what horrid young men one meets in Dickens and Thackeray. Of course the *descent* of David Copperfield is partly due to the fact that no later chapters *could* come up to the early ones. Have you noticed that nearly all writers describe childhood (when it is in the first person) well? *Jane Eyre* is also best at the beginning: and almost every biography. But it is also due to the convention whereby Victorian novelists are not allowed to attribute their hero's peccadilloes in respect of chastity? Hence the 'scrapes' of youth all have to be represented by other less probable and (to me) more repellent sins. You notice that Tom Jones does not similarly lose our regard as he grows up . . .

No. Bears seem to be very modest. No one seems to know anything about their love passages. Perhaps they neither marry nor are given in marriage, but gather their young from the flowers as Virgil thought the bees did. It would explain why the bear's whelp has to be 'licked into shape'.

I've re-read *The Ring and the Book* in trains lately with great enjoyment: but don't recommend it to you in your present state . . . Jane Austen, Scott, and Trollope are my favourite authors when ill . . .

TO SISTER PENELOPE, C.S.M.V.: from The Kilns

20 February [1943]

I have been putting off my answer to your first letter from day to day in the hope that I shd be able to send *Perelandra* with it: but tho' the publishers said it wd be out in Jan. there is no sign of it yet. No doubt there is some hitch with the binders for it has been printed some months ago . . .

'Creation' as applied to human authorship (I'm on your *first* letter now, you see) seems to me an entirely misleading term. We make ἐξ ὑποχειμενων. i.e. we re-arrange elements He has provided. There is not a *vestige* of real creativity *de novo* in us. Try to imagine a new primary colour, a third sex, a fourth dimension, or even a monster wh. does not consist of bits of existing animals stuck together. Nothing happens. And that surely is why our works (as you said) never mean to others quite what we intended: because we are re-combining elements made by Him and already containing *His* meanings. Because of those divine meanings in our materials it is impossible we shd ever know the whole meaning of our own works, and the meaning we never intended may be the best and truest one.

Writing a book is much less like creation than it is like planting a garden or begetting a child: in all three cases we are only entering as *one* cause into a causal stream which works, so to speak, in its own way. I wd not wish it to be otherwise. If one cd *really* create in the strict sense wd one not find we had created a sort of Hell? . . .

How dull all ones books are except the one you are waiting for at the moment!—wh. again has an analogical bearing on the parable of the lost sheep. I shd have more joy of *Perelandra* at the moment than of 99 books that have had no hitch about them . . .

TO SISTER PENELOPE, C.S.M.V.: from Magdalen College

10 August 1943

I *should* like a few days at Wantage, but things are so bad at home that I'm cancelling several of my R.A.F. engagements. Pray for me, Sister, and for poor Jane (*very* bad with her varicose ulcer) and for 'Muriel' (a kind of lady gardener & 'help' who is putting off an operation she ought to have, out of funk, and getting hysterical and going into rages, and losing her faith) and for poor dear Margaret (certified 'mental deficient' maid, at times the humblest, most affectionate, quaintest little person you can imagine, but subject to fits of inexplicable anger and misery).

There is never any time when *all* these three women are in a good temper. When A is in B is out: and when C has just got over her resentment at B's last rage and is ready to forgive, B is just ripe for the next, and so on!

But out of evil comes good. From praying anxiously for a little of God's peace to communicate to *them*, I have been given more of it myself than I think I ever had before. Which is interesting. You don't get it when you ask for yourself: want it for the sake of the others, you do . . .

TO THE SOCIETY FOR THE PREVENTION OF
PROGRESS, OF WALNUT CREEK, CALIFORNIA:
from Magdalen College (in reply to an offer of membership)

[May 1944]

While feeling that I was *born* a member of your Society, I am
nevertheless honoured to receive the outward seal of membership. I shall hope by continued orthodoxy and the unre-
mitting practice of Reaction, Obstruction, and Stagnation to
give you no reason for repenting your favour.

I humbly submit that in my Riddell Lectures entitled *The
Abolition of Man* you will find another work not all unwor-
thy of consideration for admission to the canon.

Yours regressively . . .

[Ever since Jack began making any money from his
religious writings, beginning with the serialisation
of *The Screwtape Letters* in the now defunct Church
newspaper *The Guardian,* he had it sent to destitute
widows and others in need. He directed the BBC to
send the fees paid for his broadcasts to a list of widows which he provided. Jack had no idea that he would
have to pay tax on all this income until the Inland
Revenue demanded it. At this time Owen Barfield was
running his own legal firm in London and Jack turned
to him for help. Mr Barfield set up a Charitable Trust,
the 'Agape Fund' or 'Agapany', into which Jack hereafter paid two-thirds of his income from royalties for
helping the poor.

During the summer of 1944 Jack had a piece of shell,
received in the last war, removed from his chest. He

thought it would be rather nice if the Inland Revenue paid for the operation.]

TO OWEN BARFIELD: from The Kilns

20 August [1944]

(1) Have you read *Esmond* lately? What a detestable woman is Lady Castlewood: and yet I believe Thackeray means us to like her on the ground that all her actions spring from 'love'. This love is, in his language 'pure' i.e. it is not promiscuous or sensual. It is none the less a wholly uncorrected natural passion, idolatrous and insatiable. Was that the great 19th century heresy—that 'pure' or 'noble' passions didn't need to be crucified & re-born but wd of themselves lead to happiness? Yet one sees it makes Lady C. disastrous both as a wife & a mother and is a source of misery to herself and all whom she meets. This is all irrelevant, but I've been reading *Esmond* all day and it rose to the surface.

(2) Yes: do come, you and Harwood, on Sept 1st. If we think College has had enough of the two we can dine at the Eastgate: less well, but perhaps more at our ease. (3) Thanks for dealing with Mrs Boshell and Mrs Askins [widows]. (4) Congratulations on recovering £237 for the Agapany. This is stupendous . . . (5) While Government is reeling under this blow, is it worth while trying to get them to pay for my operation on the ground that it was due to a wound?

(6) When you ask me to remember you in my prayers, it is like the *Punch* joke where the Doctor says to the patient (a colonel) 'And I think I should recommend a glass of good nourishing wine once a day.' *Patient* 'Oh well—I've taken a

bottle of port every night for twenty years, but I don't mind trying to manage an extra glass if you like.'

I am v. sorry you are blue as a whortle-berry within. I feel what people feel when they say 'I'd do anything to amend it': which on closer introspection means, alas, 'I dare to hope that, if the situation really arose, even my cowardice and selfishness wd not prevent me doing something.' Blessings on you.

TO CHARLES A. BRADY: **from Magdalen College** (Professor Brady of Canisius College, Buffalo, New York, had sent Jack two articles entitled 'Introduction to Lewis' and 'C. S. Lewis: II' published in *America,* vol. 71 (27 May and 10 June 1944.)

29 October 1944

Obviously one ought never to thank a critic for praise: but perhaps one can congratulate a fellow scholar on the thoroughness of his work even if the subject of his work happens to be oneself. You are the first of my critics so far who has really read and understood *all* my books and 'made up' the subject in a way that makes you an authority. The results interest me of course because they flatter my vanity as an author. But there's also an interest of another kind. Here is a man trying to do what all of our profession do, and by the same methods, in the one case where I happen to know already the answers to most of the questions: surely an ideal opportunity for learning something about the efficiency of the methods themselves! The result is encouraging. I have always been haunted by the fear that all our studies of the dead authors (who can't up and protest when we go wrong) may, in spite of careful documentation etc, be quite wide of the mark: on the whole you set that at rest. The *Quellenforschung* is good.

Morris and Macdonald were more or less given you (Morris is more important than you suggest, I think) I admit, but you are the first to stress them properly. On the Tir-na'n-Og element, you hit the bull and might even have deduced much reading of the early Yates (worth twenty of the reconditioned 1920 model) and of James Stephens.

Space-and-time fiction, yes: but oddly enough not Rice-Burroughs. But this is probably a mere chance and the guess was a sound one. The real father of my planet book is David Lindsay's *Voyage to Arcturus,* which you also will revel in if you don't yet know it. I had grown up on Wells's stories of that kind: it was Lindsay who first gave me the idea that the 'scientifiction' appeal could be combined with the 'supernatural' appeal—suggested the 'cross' (in biological sense). His own spiritual outlook is detestable, almost diabolist I think, and his style is crude: but he showed me what a bang you cd get from mixing these two elements.

R. H. Benson is wrong: at least I think the *Dawn of All* (the only one I can remember having read) never meant much to me. Chesterton, of course: but more, I think, on thought than on imagination. Rackham, yes: but having mentioned him you just missed tapping my whole Norse complex—Old Icelandic, Wagner's *Ring* and (again) Morris. The Wagner is important: you will also see, if you look, how *operatic* the whole building up of the climax is in *Perelandra.* Milton I think you possibly over-rate: it is difficult to distinguish him from Dante & St Augustine. (Tinidril at her second appearance owes something to Matilda at the end of *Purgatorio*.)

When you talk about meetings of human races in connexion with Ransom and the Hrossa you say something that was not in my mind at all. So much the better: a book's not worth writing unless it suggests more than the author intended.

The only place where, as it seems to me, your work contains a *warning* for us all is the bit based on the portrait. The whole thing depends upon the portrait's being a good one. In fact it was drawn from a photo by a man who never saw me and, I'm told, is only just recognizable. Memo: let us both remember this the next time we're writing about a 17th century or Elizabethan author and feel inclined to base anything on his portrait! It may not have been at all like him. (Why do we continue to assume that all portrait painters in the past were faithful tho' experience in the present tells us that it is the rarest thing for even a good painter to produce a real likeness?)

Tolkien (and Charles Williams, whom I wish you'd do, specially his novels) is most important. *The Hobbit* is merely the *adaptation to children* of part of a huge private mythology of a most serious kind: the whole cosmic struggle as he sees it but mediated through an imaginary world. *The Hobbit's* successor, which will soon be finished, will reveal this more clearly. Private worlds have hitherto been mainly the work of decadents or, at least, mere aesthetes. This is the private world of a Christian. He is a very great man. His published works (both imaginative & scholarly) ought to fill a shelf by now: but he's one of those people who is never satisfied with a MS. The mere suggestion of publication provokes the reply 'Yes. I'll just look through it and give it a few finishing touches'—wh. means that he really begins the whole thing over again.

I have now had an orgy of talking about myself. But let me congratulate you again on your very thorough and perceptive piece of work. I need not, perhaps, add that if you ever come here our own little circle will make a red letter day of it. (By the way, port is usually drunk in *common room*, whereas *oaks* are *sported* in one's own private rooms! But we'll arrange port behind a sported oak for you if you like—though indeed beer and/or tea is our usual fare.) Tell me about yourself if you reply: I'm quite ignorant of modern American letters.

TO OWEN BARFIELD: **from Magdalen College** (about the death of Charles Williams on the 15th May 1945)

18 May 1945

Thanks for writing. It has been a very *odd* experience. This, the first really severe loss I have suffered, has (a) Given a corroboration to my belief in immortality such as I never dreamed of. It is almost tangible now. (b) Swept away all my old feelings of mere horror and disgust at funerals, coffins, graves etc. If need had been I think I cd have handled *that* corpse with hardly any unpleasant sensations. (c) Greatly reduced my feelings about ghosts. I think (but who knows?) that I shd be, tho afraid, more pleased than afraid, if his turned up. In fact, all v. curious. Great pain but no mere depression.

Dyson said to me yesterday that he thought what was true

of Christ was, in its lower degree, true of all Christians—i.e. they go away to return in a closer form and it is expedient for us that they shd go away in order that they may do so. How foolish it is to imagine one can imaginatively foresee what any event will be like! 'Local unique sting' alright of course for I love him (I cannot say more) as much as you: and yet—a sort of brightness and tingling . . .

To put it in a nutshell—what the idea of death has done to him is nothing to what he has done to the idea of death. Hit it for six. Yet it used to rank as a fast bowler!

TO A FORMER PUPIL: from The Kilns

20 May 1945

I also have become much acquainted with grief now through the death of my great friend Charles Williams, my friend of friends, the comforter of all our little set, the most angelic man. The odd thing is that his death has made my faith stronger than it was a week ago. And I find that all that talk about 'feeling that he is closer to us than before' isn't just talk. It's just what it does feel like—I can't put it into words. One seems at moments to be living in a new world. Lots, lots of pain, but not a particle of depression or resentment . . .

TO SISTER PENELOPE, C.S.M.V.: from The Kilns

28 May 1945

I was intensely interested in the story of your healing of the little dog. I don't see why one shouldn't. Perhaps indeed those to whom God allows a gift in this way should confirm their own faith in it by practising on beasts for in one way they may be easier to heal than men. Although they cannot have faith in Him (I suppose) they certainly have faith in us, wh. is faith in Him at one remove: and there is no sin in them to impede or resist. I am glad it happened.

You will have heard of the death of my dearest friend, Charles Williams, and, no doubt, prayed for him. For me too, it has been, and is, a great loss. But not at all a dejecting one . . .

The title *Who Goes Home?* has had to be dropped because someone has used it already. The little book will be called *The Great Divorce* and will appear about August. *That Hideous Strength* is due in July. The Miracle book is finished but will not come out till next year.

Jane is up and down: very liable, I'm afraid, to fits of really bad jealousy—she can't bear to see other people doing the work. Pray for her, dear Sister . . .

TO CECIL AND DAPHNE HARWOOD: **from The Kilns** (Cecil and his wife had each written to him about *That Hideous Strength*.)

11 September 1945

About Merlin, I don't think it wd have made any difference if I did hold your views of the after-world. I mean, of course he wouldn't be *naif* if he returned from *my* world any more than if he returned from yours. Whatever the normal *status animarum post mortem* may be, it is feigned that this one man was exempted from it and returned just as he was. (I know they don't really: I was writing a story).

Re Jane, she wasn't meant to illustrate the problem of the married woman and her own career in general: rather the problem of everyone who follows an *imagined* vocation at the expense of the real one. Perhaps I shd have emphasized more the fact that her thesis on Donne was all derivative bilge. If I'd been tackling the problem wh. Cecil thinks I had in mind, of course I'd have taken a woman capable of making a real contribution to literature.

I'm uncomfortably afraid Cecil is right (with MacPhee) about St Anne's being rather like the House of Lords in *Iolanthe*. All reviewers so far (except *Punch*) have damned the book: comfortingly for different reasons—I mean it can hardly be bad in so many different ways as all that . . .

TO I. O. EVANS: **from Magdalen College** (about *That Hideous Strength*)

26 September 1945

I'm glad you recognized the N.I.C.E. as not being quite the fantastic absurdity some readers think. I hadn't myself thought that any of the people in contemporary rackets were *really* dabbling in Magic: I had supposed that to be a romantic addition of my own. But there you are. The trouble about writing satire is that the real world always anticipates you, and what were meant for exaggerations turn out to be nothing of the sort.

About Merlin: I don't know much more than you do. Apart from Malory (the Everyman edition and the Temple Classics are both complete) you will get something more in Geoffrey of Monmouth (Temple Classics), and Layamon (to be found in the Everyman volume entitled 'Arthurian Chronicles from Wace to Layamon'). For Arthur in general see 'Arthur of Britain' by E. K. Chambers, Collingwood in Vol. I of *Oxford History of England*, and Vinaver's 'Malory'. But the blessing about Merlin (for you and me) is that 'very little is known'—so we have a free hand!

TO MISS DOROTHY L. SAYERS: from Magdalen College

10 December 1945

Although you have so little time to write letters you are one of the great English letter writers. (Awful vision for you—'It is often forgotten that Miss Sayers was known in her own day as an Author. We who have been familiar from childhood with the Letters can hardly realise! . . .) But I'm not.

No, Hopkins is not contributing to the volume [*Essays Presented to Charles Williams*]. A dear creature, though.

I'm all for little books on other subjects with the Christianity latent. I propounded this in the S.C.R. at Campion Hall and was told that it was 'Jesuitical'. The Hall Porter at the 'Bull', Fairford, likes 'The Man Born to be King' (and of such is the kingdom). I've got to have a long talk with you about Socratic Clubs soon.[166] In great haste.

---

[166] Miss Sayers was impressed by the Oxford University Socratic Club, of which Jack was President, and she hoped to start one in London.

TO A FRIEND (who was troubled about a younger woman's unsuitable devotion): **from Magdalen College**

[1945?]

'Frown not!' . . . ? We frown when we see a child too near a puddle: do we *frown* when we see it on the edge of a precipice (skeletons white on the rocks a thousand feet below)? . . .

I suppose it *is* all right, is it? I wish Charles Williams were alive: this was just his pigeon. His solution was, in a peculiar way, to teach 'em the *ars amandi* and then bestow them on other (younger) men. *Sic vos non vobis.* He was not only a lover himself but the cause that love was in other men.

But it's a ticklish game. Perhaps I'm taking it all too seriously—but the world is growing chilly and I just couldn't stand any serious miscarriage in your life. ('Save yourself for my sake, Pickwick!' said Mr Tupman.) I burn to explain to this young woman that a good many people have a concern in your happiness and Gad! she'd better mind what she's about . . .

TO SISTER PENELOPE, C.S.M.V.: **from Magdalen College**

31 January 1946

I had meant to write to you before now, but life is very crowded. The rush of pupils returning from the forces makes Terms quite different from what they were in war time. By the way, the returning men are *nice:* far nicer than my generation were when we came out of the army—and a much higher percentage of Christians . . .

That Hideous Strength has been unanimously damned by all reviewers.

About Holst's *Planets,* I heard Mars and Jupiter long ago and greatly admired them but have heard the complete work only within the last six weeks. But his characters are rather different from mine, I think. Wasn't his Mars brutal and ferocious?—in mine I tried to get the *good* element in the martial spirit, the discipline and freedom from anxiety. On Jupiter I am closer to him: but I think his is more 'jovial' in the *modern* sense of the word. The folk tune on which he bases it is not regal enough for my conception. But of course there is a general similarity because we're both following the medieval astrologers. His is, anyway, a rich and marvellous work.

Jane is up and down: some days miserable and jealous, at other times gentle and even jolly. We have two nice maids at present. My writing gets worse and worse, partly from rheumatism and partly from haste . . .

TO MISS DOROTHY L. SAYERS: from The Kilns

2 August 1946

I don't think the difference between us comes where you think. Of course one mustn't do *dishonest* work. But you seem to take as the criterion of honest work the sensible *desire* to write, the 'itch'. That seems to me precious like making 'being in love' the only reason for going on with a marriage. In my experience the *desire* has no constant ratio to the value of the work done. My own frequent uneasiness comes from another source—the fact that apologetic work is so dangerous to one's own faith. A doctrine never seems dimmer to me than when I have just successfully defended it. Anyway, thanks for an intensely interesting letter.

TO SISTER PENELOPE, C.S.M.V.: **from Magdalen College** (in reference to early rumours of actual travel in space)

21 October 1946

Yes, it is only too true. I begin to be afraid that the villains will really contaminate the moon.

TO MRS FRANK L. JONES: **from Magdalen College**

23 February 1947

(1) The doctrine that Our Lord was God and man does *not* mean that He was a human body which had God instead of the normal human soul. It means that a real man (human body *and* human soul) was in Him so united with the 2nd Person of the Trinity as to make one Person: just as in you and me a complete anthropoid animal (animal body *and* animal 'soul' i.e. instincts, sensations etc.) is so united with an immortal rational soul as to be one person. In other words, if the Divine Son had been removed from Jesus what wd have been left wd have been not a corpse but a living man.

(2) This human soul in Him was unswervingly united to the God in Him in that which makes a personality one, namely Will. But it had the *feelings* of any normal man: hence could be tempted, cd fear etc. Because of these feelings it could pray 'If it be possible, let this cup pass from

me': because of its perfect union with His Divine Nature
it unwaveringly answered 'Nevertheless, not as I will but
as thou wilt'. The Matthew passage and the John passage
both make clear this unity of will. The Matthew one gives
in addition the human feelings.

(3) God cd, had He pleased, have been incarnate in a man
of iron nerves, the Stoic sort who lets no sigh escape him.
Of His great humility He chose to be incarnate in a man
of delicate sensibilities who wept at the grave of Lazarus
and sweated blood in Gethsemane. Otherwise we should
have missed the great lesson that it is by his *will* alone that
a man is good or bad, and that *feelings* are not, in themselves, of any importance. We should also have missed the
all important help of knowing that He has faced all that
the weakest of us face, has shared not only the strength of
our nature but every weakness of it except sin. If He had
been incarnate in a man of immense natural courage, that
wd have been for many of us almost the same as His not
being incarnate at all.

(4) The prayer recorded in Matthew is much too short to
be long enough for the disciples to go to sleep! They record
the bit they heard before they fell asleep.

(5) It is probable that all the Gospels are based on acts
and sayings wh. the disciples deliberately learned by heart:
a much surer method even now than transmission by writing: still more so among people whose memories were
uninfected by too many books and whose books were only
MSS. But this is guess work. With all good wishes.

[P.S.] Keep clear of psychiatrists unless you know that
they are also Christians. Otherwise they start with the

assumption that your religion is an illusion and try to 'cure' it: and this assumption they make not as professional psychologists but as amateur philosophers. Often they have never given the question any serious thought.

TO MARTYN SKINNER: from Magdalen College

15 October 1947

I have just finished your admirable *Letters* [*to Malaya*] V wh. you kindly sent me more months ago than I care to remember. I think it is the best yet and full of plums . . . The smaller stabs of pleasure are too numerous to mention and on some pages almost continuous. I pick out for special loveliness the 'open boat, the drifting grave' and 'each temple like a curl'. A beautiful book and terrible too for one, who shares (as I do) your apprehensions.

It wd be less terrifying if one cd really attribute the murder of beauty to any particular set of evil men; the trouble is that from man's first and wholly legitimate attempt to win safety and ease from Nature it seems, step by step, to lead on quite logically to universal suburbia . . .

TO OWEN BARFIELD: from Magdalen College

16 December 1947

Yes, I did read your letter. You must bear with me. Things were never worse at The Kilns. W[arren] is away, so correspondence was never heavier in College. 'Sleep hath forsook and giv'n me o'er.' I hadn't thought retirement at our age was quite like betrothal: nor how concrete the proposal was. It needs thinking of. In any case the professional job is in some degree a compulsory defence against, and alleviation of, the domestic. Take care. Where there is no office there may be no leisure at all . . .

Your essay is magnificent and I don't know why you are disappointed with it.[167] Tolkien thinks the same & has read it twice. His is v. good too. Mine *thin*. D. Sayers perhaps a trifle vulgar in places . . .

In haste—have wasted most of the morning (soon there will be no mornings) packing up a huge MS sent me unsolicited by a brutal stranger with a name like Van Tripe. Well, all's one . . .

P.S. Of course the real trouble is within. All things wd be bearable if I were delivered from this internal storm (*buffera infernal*) of self-pity, rage, envy, terror, horror and general bilge!

TO OWEN BARFIELD: **from The Kilns**

22 December 1947

(This absurd notepaper is a present from an American.)

I already regret my last letter except in so far as it has produced such a valuable one from you. It was 2/3 temper and melodrama. Thus 'Sleep has forsook and given me o'er' meant 'I have had one or two bad nights lately' *plus* 'Isn't *Samson Agonistes* fine?'

---

[167] Owen Barfield's essay 'Poetic Diction and Legal Fiction' in *Essays Presented to Charles Williams,* ed. C. S. Lewis (1947).

There is no problem about vocation. Quite obviously one can't leave an old semi-paralysed lady in a house alone for days or even hours: and the duty of looking after one's people rests on us all and is common form.

The rage comes from *impatientia* in the strict theological sense: because one treats as an interruption of one's (self-chosen) vocation the vocation actually imposed on one—regards the exam paper actually set as a distraction from the one you wd like to be doing. Anyway, Maureen is coming for Christmas and W. and I are going to Malvern . . .

Don't imagine I didn't pitch into C[harles] W[illiams] for all I was worth.

TO EDWARD A. ALLEN, OF WESTFIELD, MASSACHUSETTS: **from Magdalen College** (Mr Allen and his mother were two of the numerous Americans who sent Jack food and other gifts after the War.)

29 January 1948

I just don't know what to say in answer to your letter of 23rd January. One, two, perhaps even three parcels can be inadequately, but not entirely unsuitably acknowledged, but what is one to say when bombarded with a non-stop stream of kindnesses? Nothing has in my time made such a profound impression in this country as the amazing outburst of individual American generosity, which has followed on the disclosure of our economic situation. (I say nothing of *government* action, because naturally this strikes the 'man in the street' much less obviously.) The length of time which a parcel takes to cross the Atlantic is a significant indication of the volume of food which must be pouring into England.

As regards the 'Tuxedo'—'dinner jacket' here, 'le smoking' in Paris—if it doesn't fit me, it will certainly fit one of my friends, and will save some grateful man a year's clothing coupons: and at least £25 cash.[168]

As regards things to send—*don't* send any of that sixty-six million tons of snow, thanks very much! We still shudder when we think of last winter. A packet or two of envelopes are almost always welcome; a small thing, but the constant shortage of them becomes very irritating to a busy man after a time. With heartiest thanks for all your great kindness, and best good wishes.

TO MISS VERA MATHEWS: **from Magdalen College**
(another American benefactor)

7 February 1948

How lovely! Bacon, tea, shortening, what not—and again. A thousand thanks. Typing expert is away, as you see, and me hardly able to write legibly. But (if you *can* make it out) believe me our hearts are very warm and we enjoy the kindness and friendship as well as its tangible (and chew-able) results. I really hardly know how to say what I feel; thank you again and again.

---

[168] The dinner jacket fitted to perfection Professor Tolkien's son, Christopher.

TO EDWARD A. ALLEN: from Magdalen College

29 May 1948

So once more I have to send you my inadequate, but very sincere thanks, not only for the 'tuxedo', but for the impending food parcel . . . The extent to which your folk have come to our rescue is amazing, and moving; I knew in a general way of course that very large quantities of gift food, clothing etc. were coming into Britain, but I was none the less surprised to read in a recent debate in the House of Lords that every household in the kingdom benefits by American aid to the tune of £1–0–0 a week, and has done so for the past *two years.* You may well be proud of yourselves . . .

'Just what a Don does?' Like a woman, his work is never done. Taking 'tutorials' occupies the best part of his day, i.e. pupils come in pairs, read essays to him, then follows criticism, discussion etc: then he gives public lectures in his own subject; takes his share in the business of managing the College; prepares his lectures and writes books; and in his spare time stands in queues.

I trust our meeting will not be postponed until the hereafter; why not take a trip over here and distribute some dollars among our hard working and deserving innkeepers? . . .

TO JOHN WAIN: from Magdalen College

6 November 1948

I am wondering whether you have thought of applying for the tutorial fellowship in English at New College? I understand (this is of course strictly confidential) that they have a strong candidate who is an old New College man but they are not *settled* to elect him, i.e. if a definitely stronger candidate puts in they will elect that candidate. I know you are well thought of by D. C.,[169] it is therefore possible that you might be the stronger candidate if you applied. If you were out of a job of course it wd be obvious that you shd try for this. As things are, I don't know if you will wish to or not. I shall never be satisfied myself until you are at Oxford: and this job wd no doubt be better paid than your present one. On the other hand it wd probably mean more work and of course, house-hunting. I don't know that I cd add anything by writing at greater length. Think it over for twenty-four hours and let me know.[170]

TO OWEN BARFIELD: from Magdalen College

10 November 1948

I wonder whether what you say about depressions does not really mark an advance in self criticism and objectivity—i.e. that the very same experiences wh. wd once have led you to say 'How nasty everyone (or the weather, or the political situation) is at present' now leads you to say 'I am depressed'—a Copernican revolution revealing as motion in the self what in ones more naif period was mistaken for motion in the

---

[169] Lord David Cecil (1902–86) was educated at Eton and Christ Church. He was a Fellow and Lecturer in Modern History at Wadham College 1924–30, and a Fellow of New College from 1939 until he was elected Goldsmith's Professor of English at Oxford in 1948. Lord David was also a member of The Inklings.

[170] John Wain is one of Jack's pupils who became a member of The Inklings. He is such a good writer that the most pleasant way of learning more about him and his connection with The Inklings is through his *Sprightly Running: Part of an Autobiography* (1962).

Cosmos. (True, your last letter shows some decline in your critical powers: but we have all been warned that an inability to appreciate new poetry comes with years!) But I'm serious about the other suggestion.

I also will soon be fifty. Just the twenty years more now! A happy birthday to you. If the knowledge that for some twenty-five years you have been always food (and often physic as well) to my mind and heart can contribute to it, well it is so.

TO DR WARFIELD M. FIROR, OF BALTIMORE, MARYLAND: **from Magdalen College** (Dr Firor was particularly generous in sending Jack hams.)

22 January 1949

Your bounty (see *Anthony and Cleopatra*) 'an autumn is that grows the more by reaping'. Only yesterday I said to myself, How I should like to see America if only one could see the quiet parts of it, and not the cities—things which in every country interest me only if I want to hear an opera or buy a book! And you anticipated me.[171]

But it's all impossible. An old invalid ties me to home. Absence in the afternoon, even for one day, has to be carefully planned ahead. So a visit to another continent is as impossible to me as one to the Moon. Oh what a pity! To think that I might as your guest have seen bears, beavers, Indians, and mountains! How did you know what I wanted?

---

[171] Dr Firor practised medicine in Baltimore but had a ranch in Cody, Wyoming. He knew that Jack needed a rest but was unlikely to like American cities, and he invited him to the ranch.

Meanwhile, the only chance of meeting is that you should visit this island prison. To all my set you are by now an almost mythical person—Firor-of-the-Hams, a sort of Fertility god.

TO I. O. EVANS: from Magdalen College

28 February 1949

I'm with you on the main issue—that art can teach (and much great art deliberately set out to do so) without at all ceasing to be art. On the particular case of Wells I wd agree with Burke, because in Wells it seems to me that one had *first* class pure fantasy (*Time Machine, First Men in the Moon*) and *third* class didacticism: i.e. I object to his novels with a purpose not because they have a purpose but because I think them bad. Just as I object to the preaching passages in Thackeray not because I dislike sermons but because I dislike bad sermons. To me, therefore, Wells & Thackeray are instances that obscure the issue. It must be fought on books where the doctrine is as good on its own merits as the art—e.g. Bunyan, Chesterton (as you agree), Tolstoi, Charles Williams, Virgil.

TO SARAH (a goddaughter): from The Kilns

3 April 1949

I am sorry to say that I don't think I shall be able to be at your confirmation on Saturday. For most men Saturday afternoon is a free time, but I have an invalid lady to look after and the weekend is the time when I have no freedom at all, and have to try to be Nurse, Kennel-Maid, Wood-cutter,

Butler, House-maid and Secretary all in one. I had hoped
that if the old lady were a little better than usual and if all
the other people in the house were in good tempers I might
be able to get away next Saturday. But the old lady is a good
deal worse than usual and most of the people in the house are
in bad tempers. So I must 'stick to the ship'.

If I *had* come and we had met, I am afraid you might have
found me very shy and dull. (By the way, always remember that old people can be quite as shy with young people as
young people can be with old. This explains what must seem
to you the idiotic way in which so many grown-ups talk to
you.) But I will try to do what I can by a letter.

I think of myself as having to be two people for you.
(1) The real, serious, Christian godfather (2) The fairy godfather. As regards (2) I enclose a bit of the only magic (a
very dull kind) which I can work. Your mother will know
how to deal with the spell. I think it will mean one or two,
or even five, pounds for you *now*, to get things you want,
and the rest in the Bank for future use. As I say, it is a dull
kind of magic and a really good godfather (of type 2) would
do something much more interesting: but it is the best an
old bachelor can think of, and it is with my love.

As for No 1, the serious Christian godfather, I feel
very unfit for the work—just as you, I dare say, may feel
very unfit for being confirmed and for receiving the Holy
Communion. But then an angel would not be really fit and
we must all do the best we can. So I suppose I must try to
give you advice. And the bit of advice that comes into my
head is this: don't expect (I mean, don't *count on* and don't
demand) that when you are confirmed, or when you make

your first Communion, you will have all the *feelings* you would like to have. You may, of course: but also you may not. But don't worry if you don't get them. They aren't what matter. The things that are happening to you are quite real things whether you feel as you wd wish or not, just as a meal will do a hungry person good even if he has a cold in the head which will rather spoil the taste. Our Lord will give us right feelings if He wishes—and then we must say Thank you. If He doesn't, then we must say to ourselves (and Him) that He knows best. This, by the way, is one of the very few subjects on which I feel I do know something. For years after I had become a regular communicant I can't tell you how dull my feelings were and how my attention wandered at the most important moments. It is only in the last year or two that things have begun to come right—which just shows how important it is to keep on doing what you are told.

Oh—I'd nearly forgotten—I have *one* other piece of advice. Remember that there are only three kinds of things anyone need ever do. (1) Things we *ought* to do (2) Things we've *got* to do (3) Things we *like* doing. I say this because some people seem to spend so much of their time doing things for none of the three reasons, things like reading books they don't like because other people read them. Things you ought to do are things like doing one's school work or being nice to people. Things one has got to do are things like dressing and undressing, or household shopping. Things one likes doing—but of course I don't know what *you* like. Perhaps you'll write and tell me one day.

Of course I always mention you in my prayers and will most especially on Saturday. Do the same for me.

TO OWEN BARFIELD: **from The Kilns** (with allusion
to some very unpleasant characters in his science fiction
trilogy)

4 April 1949

Did I ever mention that Weston, Devine, Frost, Wither,
Curry, and Miss Hardcastle were all portraits of you? (If
I didn't, that may have been because it isn't true. By gum,
though, wait until I write another story.)

Plus aux bois? We will, Oscar, we will.

Henry 7th had some mastiffs hanged for fighting a Lion:
said, they were rebelling against their natural sovereigne.
That's the stuff. Also, had his own hawk decapitated for
fighting an eagle.

Talking of beasts and birds, have you ever noticed this
contrast: that when you read a scientific account of any
animal's life you get an impression of laborious, incessant,
almost rational economic activity (as if all animals were
Germans), but when you study any animal you know, what
at once strikes you is their cheerful fatuity, the pointless-
ness of nearly all they do. Say what you like, Barfield, the
world is sillier and better fun than they make out . . .

TO MISS BRECKENRIDGE: **from Magdalen College**

1 August 1949

Don't bother about the idea that God 'has known for millions of years exactly what you are about to pray'. That isn't
what it's like. God is hearing you *now*, just as simply as a
mother hears a child. The difference His timelessness makes
is that this *now* (which slips away from you even as you

say the word *now*) is for Him infinite. If you must think of His timelessness at all, don't think of Him *having* looked forward to this moment for millions of years: think that to Him you are always praying this prayer. But there's really no need to bring it in. You have gone into the Temple ('one day in Thy court is better than a thousand') and found Him, as always, there. That is all you need to bother about.

There is *no* relation of any importance between the Fall and Evolution. The doctrine of Evolution is that organisms have changed, sometimes for what we call (biologically) the better . . . quite often for what we call (biologically) the worse . . . The doctrine of the Fall is that at one particular point one species, Man, tumbled down a moral cliff. There is neither opposition nor support between the two doctrines . . . Evolution is not only not a doctrine of *moral* improvements, but of biological changes, some improvements, some deteriorations . . .

TO MRS EDWARD A. ALLEN: from Magdalen College
16 August 1949

I shd think I *do* like salt water and in all its forms; from a walk on the beach in winter when there is not a soul in sight, or seen washing past (rather like beaten copper) from the deck of a ship, or knocking one head over heels in great green, ginger-beer-coloured waves. I grew up close to it, but there's no chance of getting there now. On the other hand I have discovered the joys of shallow river bathing . . . It is like bathing in *light* rather than in water; and having walked for miles, you can *drink* it at the same time . . . We also are in a drought and heat wave . . .

P.S. C is for CLIVE—no connection with the iniquitous Anglo-Indian of that name.

TO 'MRS LOCKLEY': **from Magdalen College** ('Mrs Lockley's' husband had taken a mistress.)

2 September 1949

Apparently I was mistaken in thinking that to condone the infidelity and submit to the arrangement your husband suggests would be *wrong*. My adviser of course says that it is impossible to him to 'give a fair ruling without knowing more of the parties'. But with that reservation he suggests (1) Mrs A. shd refuse to have intercourse with her husband, otherwise carry on, completely ignoring the mistress. (2) Mr A. must never mention the mistress in his house nor when he has seen her, nor shd he let Mrs A. or anyone else have any suspicion when or where he meets the mistress. I can't myself quite see the point of No. 2, and I take it that anyway it is impracticable . . .

On the actual practical arrangements I don't feel that I—an elderly bachelor and the most amateurish of theologians—can be useful. Where I *might* help, on the internal and spiritual problems for yourself, you obviously do not need my help. All the things I would have said to most women in your position (about charity, submission to God's will, and the poisonous nature of indulged jealousy, however just the

you clearly know already. I don't think it can do you arm to know that you have these graces, provided you that they are *Graces*, gifts from the Holy Spirit, and ur own merits. God, who foresaw your tribulation, cially armed you to go through it, not without pain but without stain; not a case of 'tempering the wind to the shorn lamb' but of giving the lamb a coat proportional to the wind. On all *that* side you have only to go on as you are doing. And you certainly needn't worry at all about there being any material for psychotherapy in you . . .

One point in your story looms large in my mind—the fatal consequences of your husband's lack of faith in you when he did not get those letters. For this is just how *we* also might desert God. If nothing, or nothing we recognise comes through, we imagine He has let us down and reject Him, perhaps at the very moment when help was on its way. No doubt your husband may have been readier to desert you because a quite different temptation had already begun. But then that applies to the God-Man situation also . . .

TO 'MRS LOCKLEY': from Magdalen College

6 September 1949

Telling these things to someone you approach as a consultant is no more disloyalty than revealing one's body to a doctor is indecent exposure. With a trained confessor this, as it were, *disinfectant* situation would be even more so.

I don't think the arrangement the old man suggested is 'dishonest'. I think his advice turns on the fine but important distinction between *enduring* a situation which is some one else's fault and *sanctioning* it in a way wh. makes on accessory. After all, your husband has no right to have it ways and you have no duty (or right) to make him fee he had. It wd do him no harm to realise that this affair *as much* adultery as if it were 'furtive visits to a prostit

TO 'MRS LOCKLEY': from Magdalen College

12? September 1949

I don't think your objection to 'setting yourself up as a judge' is cowardly. It may spring from the fact that you are the injured party and have a v. proper conviction that the plaintiff cannot also be on the Bench. I also quite realise that he didn't feel the sin as a Christian wd: but he must, as a man, feel the dishonour of breaking a promise. After all constancy in love thunders at him from every love-song in the world, . quite apart from our mystical conception of marriage . . .

As you say, the thing is to rely *only* on God. The time will come when you will regard all this misery as a small price to pay for having been brought to the dependence. Meanwhile (don't I know) the trouble is that relying on God has to begin all over again every day as if nothing had yet been done . . .

The reason why I am saddled with many people's troubles is, I think, that I have no natural curiosity about private lives and am therefore a good subject. To anyone who (in *that* sense) enjoyed it, it wd be a dangerous poison.

TO 'MRS LOCKLEY': from Magdalen College

22 September 1949

The intellectual problem (why some children lose one or both parents in this way and other ways) is no harder than the problem why some women lose their husbands. In each case, no doubt what we regard as a mere hideous interruption and curtailment of life is really the *data*, the concrete situation on which life is to be built . . . When the *data* are of the kind we naturally like (wealth, health, good fathers or husbands) of course we tend not to notice that they are data or limitations at all. But we're told that they are: and what seem to us the easiest conditions may really be the hardest ('How hardly shall they that have riches' etc.) . . .

TO 'MRS LOCKLEY': from Magdalen College

27 September 1949

Yes, yes, I know. The moment one asks oneself 'Do I believe?' all belief seems to go. I think this is because one is trying to turn round and look *at* something which is there to be used and work *from*—trying to take out one's eyes instead of keeping them in the right place and seeing *with* them. I find that it happens about other matters as well as faith. In my experience only v. robust pleasures will stand the question, 'Am I really enjoying this?' Or attention—the moment I begin thinking about my attention (to a book or a lecture) I have *ipso facto* ceased attending. St Paul speaks of 'Faith actualized in Love'. And 'the heart is deceitful': you know better than I how very unreliable introspection is. I shd be much more alarmed about your progress if you wrote claiming to be overflowing with Faith, Hope and Charity.

TO DR WARFIELD M. FIROR: from Magdalen College

(Dr Firor had come over to visit Jack in the summer of 1949.)

15 October 1949

To-day the less pleasant side of Autumn has showed itself for the first time. Up till now it has been paradisal, the sort of weather which for some reason excites me much more than spring: cool, cobwebby mornings developing into the mildest sunlight, and exquisite colours in the woods. It always gives me *Wanderlust* & 'divine discontent' and all that. To-day we have had a low, dirty, smoke-coloured sky racing overhead and a steady down-pour. That, however, has no causal connection (chronology proves it) with the subject that is uppermost in my mind and has been for some days: Old Age.

You are a bit further on the road than I am and will probably smile at a man whose fifty-first birthday is still several weeks ahead starting his meditation *de senectute*. Yet why? The realisation must *begin* sometime. In one way, of course (no, in two) it began much earlier (1) With the growing realisation that there were a great many things one wd never have time to do. Those golden days when one could still think it possible that one might some time take up a quite new study: say Persian, or Geology, were now definitely over. (2) Harder to express. I mean, the end of that period when every goal, besides being itself, was an earnest or promise of much more to come. Like a pretty girl at her first dance: valued not chiefly for itself but as the prelude to a whole new world. Do you remember the time when every pleasure (say, the smell of a hayfield or a country walk, or a swim) was big with futurity and bore on its face the notice 'Lots more where I came from'? Well, there's a change from that to the period when they all begin to say 'Make the most of me: my predecessors outnumber my successors'.

Both these two feelings—the twitch of the tether and the loss of promise I have had for a long time. What has come lately is much harsher—the arctic wind of the future catching one, so to speak, at a corner. The particular corner was the sharp realisation that I shall be compulsorily 'retired' in 1959, and the infernal *nuisance* (to put it no higher) of patching up some new sort of life somewhere. You will not suppose I am putting these things as lamentations: that, to a man older than oneself, wd be very odd. They are merely the *data*. (Add, of course, among them, the probable loss of friends, especially if, like me, one has the imprudent habit of making more friends among one's seniors than among one's juniors.) And as usual, the result of all this (wd you agree?) is almost entirely good.

Have you ever thought what it wd be like if (all other things remaining as they are) old age and death had been made optional? *All other things remaining:* i.e. it wd still be true that our real destiny was elsewhere, that we have no abiding city here and no true happiness, *but* the un-hitching from this life was left to be accomplished by our own will as an act of obedience & faith. I suppose the percentage of *di-ers* wd be about the same as the percentage of Trappists is now.

I am therefore (with some help from the weather and rheumatism!) trying to profit by this new realisation of my mortality. To begin to die, to loosen a few of the tentacles which the octopus-world has fastened on one. But of course it is continuings, not beginnings, that are the point. A good night's sleep, a sunny morning, a success with my next book—any of these will, I know, alter the whole thing. Which alteration, by the bye, being in reality a relapse from partial waking into the old stupor, wd nevertheless be regarded by most people as a returning to health from a 'morbid' mood!

Well, it's certainly not that. But it is a *very* partial waking. One ought not to need the gloomy moments of life for beginning detachment, nor be re-entangled by the bright ones. One ought to be able to enjoy the bright ones to the full and at that very moment have the perfect readiness to leave them, confident that what calls one away is better . . .

TO SARAH (a goddaughter): **from Magdalen College**

[9 January 1950]

I'm just back from a weekend at Malvern and found an awful pile of letters awaiting me, so I am scribbling in haste. But I must tell you what I saw in a field—one young pig cross the field with a great big bundle of hay in its mouth and deliberately lay it down at the feet of an old pig. I could hardly believe my eyes. I'm sorry to say the old pig didn't take the slightest notice. Perhaps *it* couldn't believe *its* eyes either . . .

TO SISTER PENELOPE, C.S.M.V.: **from Magdalen College**

12 January 1950

All good wishes for *St Bernard.* My book with Professor Tolkien—any book in collaboration with that great but dilatory and unmethodical man—is dated, I fear, to appear on the Greek Kalends![172] . . .

Term begins on Sat. and there is a cruel mail to-day, so I must stop. And pray for me: I am suffering incessant temptations to uncharitable thoughts at present: one of those black moods in which nearly all one's friends seem to be selfish or even false. And how terrible that there shd be even a kind of *pleasure* in thinking evil. A 'mixed pleasure' as Plato wd say, like scratching!

TO SISTER MARY ROSE: from Magdalen College

[January 1950]

I am sorry if I misunderstood your letter: and I think that you misunderstood mine. What I meant was that if I replied to your original question (why I am not a member of the Roman Church) I shd have to write a v. long letter. It would of course be answerable: and your answer would be answerable by me . . . and so on. The resulting correspondence would certainly not, of course, be in excess of the importance of the subject: but haven't you and I both probably more pressing duties? For a real correspondence on such a subject wd be nearly a wholetime job. I thought we cd both discuss the matter more usefully with people nearer at

---

[172] In 1944 Professor Tolkien and Jack began talking about writing a book together on Language. By 1948 it got as far as the title 'Language and Human Nature' and was advertised by the S.P.C.K. as due in 1949. It was never written.

hand. Even the two letters which we have exchanged have already revealed the pitfalls of argument by letter. With all good wishes.

TO ARTHUR GREEVES: from Magdalen College

2 May 1950

Once again the axe has fallen. Minto was removed to a Nursing Home last Saturday and her Doctor thinks this arrangement will probably have to be permanent. In one way it will be an enormous liberation for me. The other side of the picture is the crushing expense—ten guineas a week wh. is well over £500 a year. (What on earth I shall do if poor Minto is still alive nine years hence when I have to retire, I can't imagine.) The order of the day thus becomes for me stringent economy and such things as a holiday in Ireland are fantastically out of the question. So cancel all. I hardly know how I *feel*—relief, pity, hope, terror, & bewilderment have me in a whirl. I have the jitters! God bless you. Pray for me.

[Jack's problems had been mounting for a long time. Mrs Moore had become, in the course of time, old and ill. On 29 April she was moved into 'Restholme' in 230 Woodstock Road, Oxford. Unfortunately, Jack had not always been able to count on Warren being around to help with Mrs Moore and his vast correspondence. For some time now Warren had been going on alcoholic binges, and he sometimes needed more vigilant nursing than Mrs Moore. The last time Jack had been able to see Arthur was in 1947 when he had to go to Ireland to see Warren who had become ill over there from alcoholic poisoning. Overworked and tired, Jack became so ill in the summer of 1949 that he had to spend a week in the hospital. Dr Havard ordered a month's rest, and Jack planned to spend it in Ireland with Arthur. Before he could escape Warren was drinking again and Jack could not leave. And so it went on.

Unbelievably—but yet it's true—Jack wrote what might be his most enduring books in 1949 and the three years that followed. Encouraged by his friend Roger Lancelyn Green, he wrote most of *The Lion, the Witch and the Wardrobe* (1950) in March–April 1949. *Prince Caspian* (1951) and *The Voyage of the Dawn Treader* (1952) were completed by the end of February 1950. Before the year was out he had written *The Silver Chair* (1953), *The Horse and His Boy* (1954) and made a start on *The Magician's Nephew* (1955). *The Last Battle* was written in 1953.]

TO MRS HALMBACHER: from Magdalen College

28 November 1950

I avoided the word 'Grace' because I thought it didn't carry much clear meaning to the uninstructed readers I had in view. I think the *thing* is dealt with in a rough and ready way in *Case for Christianity* and *Beyond Personality*. Any advanced or technical theology of Grace was quite beyond my scope. Naturally that does not mean that I thought the subject unimportant.

The other question, about the limits of faith and superstition, is also important. But my own mind is v. far from clear on it. I think you must seek counsel (if it is a practical problem for you) from a real theologian, not from an amateur like me. I am sorry to disappoint you: but it is better to refuse than to mislead.

TO 'MRS ARNOLD': from Magdalen College

7 December 1950

(1) To the best of my knowledge the Episcopalian Church in America is exactly the same as the Anglican Church.

(2) The only rite which we know to have been instituted by Our Lord Himself is the Holy Communion ('Do this in remembrance of me.' 'If ye do not eat the flesh of the Son of Man and drink His blood, ye have no life in you.') This is an order and must be obeyed. The other services are, I take it, traditional and might lawfully be altered. But the New Testament does not envisage solitary religion: some kind of regular assembly for worship and instruction is everywhere taken for granted in the Epistles. So we must be regular practising members of the Church.

Of course we differ in temperament. Some (like you—and me) find it more natural to approach God in solitude: but we must go to church as well. For the Church is not a human society of people united by their natural affinities but the Body of Christ, in which all members, however different (and He rejoices in their differences and by no means wishes to iron them out) must share the common life, complementing and helping one another precisely by their differences. (Re-read 1st Corinthians Chap. 12 and meditate on it. The word translated *members* wd perhaps be better translated *organs*.) If people like you and me find much that we don't naturally like in the public and corporate side of Christianity all the better for us: it will teach us humility and charity towards simple lowbrow people who may be better Christians than ourselves. I naturally *loathe* nearly all hymns: the face and life of the charwoman in the next pew who revels in them teach me that good taste in poetry or music are *not* necessary to salvation.

(3) I am not clear *what* question you are asking me about spiritual healing. That this gift was promised to the Church is certain from Scripture. Whether any instance of it is a real instance, or chance, or even (as might happen in this wicked world) fraud, is a question only to be decided by the evidence in that particular case. And unless one is a doctor one is not likely to be able to judge the evidence. V. often I expect, one is not called upon to do so. Anything like a sudden *furore* about it in one district, especially if accompanied by a publicity campaign on modern commercial lines, would be to me suspect: but even then I might be wrong. On the whole my attitude wd be that any claim *may* be true, and that it is not my duty to decide if it is.

(4) 'Regular but cool' in Church attendance is no bad symptom. Obedience is the key to all doors: *feelings* come (or don't come) and go as God pleases. We can't produce them at will, and mustn't try.

TO MRS EDWARD A. ALLEN: from Magdalen College

28 December 1950

In term time I have my meals in College, including a free dinner, which has from time immemorial been part of the stipend of a tutor. My brother takes a snack in town in the middle of the day—usually something he has bought on the way in—and has the rest of his meals out at the house; he keeps a very sharp eye on my, or perhaps I should say *your* parcels, and abstracts anything likely to be useful for his lunches, justifying his peculations by quoting that 'the labourer is worthy of his hire' . . .

The whole question of the atomic bomb is a very difficult one; the Sunday after the news of the dropping of the first one came through, our minister asked us all to join in prayer for forgiveness for the great crime of using it. But, *if* what we have since heard is true, i.e. that the first item on the Japanese anti-invasion programme was the killing of every European in Japan, the answer did not, to me, seem so simple as all that . . .

TO SISTER PENELOPE, C.S.M.V.: from Magdalen College

30 December 1950

Our state is thus: my 'mother' has had to retire permanently into a Nursing Home. She is in no pain but her mind has almost completely gone. What traces of it remain seem gentler and more placid than I have known it for years. Her *appetite* is, oddly, enormous. I visit her, normally, every day, and am divided between a (rational?) feeling that this process of gradual withdrawal is merciful and even beautiful, and a quite different feeling (it comes out in my dreams) of horror.

There is no denying—and I don't know why I should deny to you—that our domestic life is both more physically comfortable and more psychologically harmonious for her absence. The expense is of course v. severe and I have worries about that. But it wd be v. dangerous to have no worries—or rather, no *occasion* of worry. I have been feeling that v. much lately: that *cheerful insecurity* is what Our Lord asks of us. Thus one comes, late & surprised, to the simplest & earliest Christian lessons! . . .

TO 'MRS ARNOLD': from Magdalen College

5 January 1951

Whether any individual Christian who attempts Faith Healing is prompted by genuine faith and charity or by spiritual pride is I take it a question we cannot decide. That is between God and him. Whether the cure occurs in any given case is clearly a question for the doctors. I am speaking now of healing by some *act* such as anointing or laying on of hands. *Praying* for the sick, i.e. praying simply, without any overt act, is unquestionably right and indeed we are commanded to pray for all men. And *of course* your prayers can do real good. Needless to say they don't do it either as a medicine does or as magic is supposed to do, i.e. automatically. Prayer is a request . . . One cannot establish the efficacy of prayer by statistics . . . It remains a matter of faith and of God's personal action; it would become a matter of demonstration only if it were impersonal or mechanical. When I say 'personal' I do not mean private or individual. All our prayers are united with Christ's perpetual prayer and are part of the Church's prayer. (In praying for people one dislikes I find it helpful to remember that one is joining in *His* prayer for them.)

TO MISS RUTH PITTER: from Magdalen College

6 January 1951

What is the point of keeping in touch with the contemporary scene? Why should one read authors one doesn't like because they happen to be alive at the same time as oneself? One might as well read everyone who had the same job or the same coloured hair, or the same income, or the same chest measurements, as far as I can see. I whistle, and plunge into the tunnel of term.

[Mrs Moore died at 'Restholme' on 12 January.]

TO 'MRS ARNOLD': from Magdalen College

7 February 1951

If 'planning' is taken in the literal sense of thinking before one acts and acting on what one has thought out to the best of one's ability, then of course planning is simply the traditional virtue of Prudence and not only compatible with, but demanded by, Christian ethics. But if the word is used (as I think you use it) to mean some particular politico-social programme, then one cd only say after examining that programme in detail . . . Where benevolent planning, armed with political or economic power, becomes wicked is when it tramples on people's *rights* for the sake of their *good* . . .

TO 'MRS LOCKLEY': from Magdalen College

5 March 1951

How right you are: the great thing is to stop thinking about happiness. Indeed the best thing about happiness itself is that it liberates you from thinking about happiness — as the greatest pleasure that money can give us is to make it unnecessary to think about money. And one sees why we have to be taught the 'not thinking' when we lack as well as when we have. And I'm sure that, as you say, you will 'get through somehow in the end'. Here is one of the fruits of unhappiness: that it forces us to think of life as something to go *through*. And out at the other end. If only we could steadfastly do that while we are happy, I suppose we shd need no misfortunes. It is hard on God really. To how few of us He *dare* send happiness because He knows we will forget Him if He gave us any sort of nice things for the moment . . .

I *do* get that sudden feeling that the whole thing is hocus pocus and it now worries me hardly at all. Surely the mechanism is quite simple? Sceptical, incredulous, materialistic *ruts* have been deeply engraved in our thought, perhaps even in our physical brains by all of our earlier lives. At the slightest jerk our thought will flow down those old ruts. And notice when the jerks come. Usually at the precise moment when we might receive Grace. And if you were a devil would you not give the jerk just at those moments? I think that all Christians have found that he is v. active near the altar or on the eve of conversion: worldly anxieties, physical discomforts, lascivious fancies, doubt, are often poured in at such junctures . . . But the Grace is not frustrated. One gets *more* by pressing steadily on through these interruptions than on occasions when all goes smoothly . . .

I am glad you all liked 'The Lion' [the Witch and the Wardrobe]. A number of mothers, and still more, schoolmistresses, have decided that it is likely to frighten children, so it is not selling very well. But the real children like it, and I am astonished how some *very* young ones seem to understand it. I think it frightens some adults, but v. few children . . .

TO MRS HALMBACHER: from Magdalen College
[March 1951]
The question for me (naturally) is not 'Why should I not be a Roman Catholic?' but 'Why should I?' But I don't like discussing such matters, because it emphasises differences and endangers charity. By the time I had really explained my objection to certain doctrines which differentiate you from us (and also in my opinion from the Apostolic and even the Medieval Church), you would like me less.

TO MISS VERA MATHEWS: from Magdalen College
27 March 1951
I have just got your letter of the 22nd containing the sad news of your father's death. But, dear lady, I hope you and your mother are not really trying to pretend it didn't happen. It does happen, happens to all of us, and I have no patience with the high-minded people who make out that it

'doesn't matter'. It matters a great deal, and very solemnly. And for those who are left, the pain is not the whole thing. I feel v. strongly (and I am not alone in this) that some great good comes from the dead to the living in the months or weeks after the death. I think I was much helped by my own father after his death: as if Our Lord welcomed the newly dead with the gift of some power to bless those they have left behind . . . Certainly they often seem just at that time to be very near us . . .

TO SHELDON VANAUKEN: from Magdalen College
(after becoming a Christian)

17 April 1951

My prayers are answered. No: a glimpse is not a vision. But to a man on a mountain road by night, a glimpse of the next three feet of road may matter more than a vision of the horizon. And there must perhaps always be just enough lack of demonstrative certainty to make free choice possible; for what could we do but accept if the faith were like the multiplication table?

There will be a counter attack on you, you know, so don't be too alarmed when it comes. The enemy will not see you vanish into God's company without an effort to reclaim you. Be busy learning to pray and (if you have made up yr mind on the denominational question) get confirmed. Blessings on you and a hundred thousand welcomes. Make use of me in any way you please: and let us pray for each other always.

TO MISS BRECKENRIDGE: from Magdalen College

19 April 1951

I think that if God forgives us we must forgive ourselves. Otherwise it is almost like setting up ourselves as a higher tribunal than Him.

Many religious people, I'm told, have physical symptoms like the 'prickles' in the shoulder. But the best mystics set no value on that sort of thing, and do not set much on visions either. What they seek and get is, I believe, a kind of direct experience of God, immediate as a taste or colour. There is no *reasoning* in it, but many would say that it is an experience of the intellect—the reason resting in it's enjoyment of its object . . .

TO DOM BEDE GRIFFITHS, O.S.B.: from Magdalen College

23 April 1951

A succession of illnesses and a holiday in Ireland have so far kept me from tackling Lubac. The *Prelude* has accompanied me through all the stages of my pilgrimage: it and the *Aeneid* (which I never feel you value sufficiently) are the two long poems to wh. I most often return.

The tension you speak of (if it *is* a tension) between doing full & generous justice to the Natural while also paying unconditional & humble obedience to the Supernatural is to me an absolute key position. I have no use for mere *either-or* people (except, of course, in that last resort, when the choice, the plucking out the right eye, is upon us: as it is in some mode, every day. But even then a man needn't abuse & blackguard his right eye. It was a good creature: it is my fault, not its, that I have got myself into a state wh. necessitates jettisoning it).

The reason I doubt whether it is, in principle, even a tension is that, as it seems to me, the subordination of Nature is demanded if only in the interests of Nature herself. All the beauty of nature withers when we try to make it an absolute. Put first things first and we get second things thrown in: put second things first & we lose *both* first and second things. We never get, say, even the sensual pleasure of food at its best when we are being greedy.

As to Man being in 'evolution', I agree, tho' I wd rather say 'in process of being created'.

I am not nearer to your Church than I was but don't feel v. inclined to re-open a discussion. I think it only widens & sharpens differences. Also, I've had enough of it on the opposite flank lately, having fallen among—a new type to me—bigoted & proselytizing Quakers! I really think that in our days it is the 'undogmatic' & 'liberal' people who call themselves Christians that are most arrogant & intolerant. I expect justice & even courtesy from many Atheists and, much more, from your people: from Modernists, I have come to take bitterness and rancour as a matter of course . . .

TO 'MRS ARNOLD': from Magdalen College

25 May 1951

About loving one's country, you raise two different questions . . . About there seeming to be (now) no reason for loving it, I'm not at all bothered. As Macdonald says, 'No one loves because he sees reason, but because he loves.' Surely, where we love, the very faults and blemishes of the object are a spur to love more? Or say there are two kinds of love: we love wise and kind and beautiful people because we need them, but we love (or try to love) stupid and disagreeable people because they need us. This second kind is the more divine because that is how God loves us: not because we are loveable but because He is love, not because He needs to receive but because He delights to give.

But the other question (*what* one is loving in loving a country) I do find v. difficult. What I feel sure of is that the personifications used by journalists and politicians have v. little reality. A treaty between the govts of two countries is not like a friendship between two people: more like a transaction between two people's lawyers.

I think love for one's country means chiefly love for people who have a good deal in common with oneself (language, clothes, institutions) and in that is very like love of one's family or school: or like love (in a strange place) for anyone who once lived in one's home town. The familiar is in itself ground for affection. And it is good, because any *natural* help towards our spiritual duty of loving is good and God seems to build our higher loves round our merely natural impulses — sex, maternity, kinship, old acquaintance etc. And in a less degree there are similar grounds for loving other nations — historical links and debts for literature etc . . . But I would distinguish that from the talk in the papers . . .

TO SISTER PENELOPE, C.S.M.V.: **from Magdalen College**

5 June 1951

My love for G. MacDonald has not extended to most of his poetry, though I have naturally made several attempts to like it. Except for the *Diary of an Old Soul* it won't (so far as I'm concerned) do . . .

As for me I specially need your prayers because I am (like the pilgrim in Bunyan) travelling across 'a plain called Ease'. Everything without, and many things within, are marvellously well at present. Indeed (I do not know whether to be ashamed or joyful at confessing this) I realise that until about a month ago I never really believed (tho' I thought I did) in God's forgiveness. What an ass I have been both for not knowing and for thinking I knew. I now feel that one must never say one believes or understands anything: any moment a doctrine I thought I already possessed may blossom into this new reality. Selah! But pray for me always, as I do for you . . .

TO 'MRS SONIA GRAHAM' (daughter of 'Mrs Catherine Arnold'): **from Magdalen College**

13 June 1951

(1) I think you are confusing the Immaculate Conception with the Virgin Birth. The former is a doctrine peculiar to the Roman Catholics and asserts that the mother of Jesus was born free of original sin. It does not concern us at all.

(2) The Virgin Birth is a doctrine plainly stated in the

Apostle's Creed that Jesus had no physical father, and was not conceived as a result of sexual intercourse. It is not a doctrine on which there is any dispute between Presbyterians as such and Episcopalians as such. A few individual Modernists in both these churches have abandoned it. The exact details of such a miracle—an exact point at which a supernatural enters this world (whether by the creation of a new spermatazoon, or the fertilisation of an ovum without a spermatazoon or the development of a foetus without an ovum) are not part of the doctrine. These are matters in which no one is obliged and everyone is free, to speculate. *Your* starting point about this doctrine will not, I think, be to collect the opinions of individual clergymen, but to read Matthew and Luke I and II.

(3) Similarly, your question about the resurrection is answered in Luke XXIV. This makes it clear beyond any doubt that what is claimed is *physical* resurrection. (All Jews except Sadducees already believed in spiritual revival—there would have been nothing novel or exciting in that.)

(4) Thus the questions that you raise are not questions at issue between real P. and real Ep. at all for both these claim to agree with Scripture. Neither church by the way seems to be very intelligently represented by the people you have gone to for advice, which is bad luck. I find it very hard to advise in your choice. At any rate the programme, *until* you can make up your mind, is to read your New Testament (preferably a modern translation) intelligently. Pray for guidance, obey your conscience in small as well as in great matters, as strictly as you can.

(5) Don't bother much about your feelings. When they are humble, loving, brave, give thanks for them: when they are conceited, selfish, cowardly, ask to have them altered. In neither case are they *you*, but only a thing that happens to you. What matters is your intentions and your behaviour. (I hope all of this is not very dull and disappointing. Write freely again if I can be of any use to you.)

P.S. Of course God does not consider you hopeless. If He did He would not be moving you to seek Him (and He obviously is). What is going on in you at present is simply the beginning of the *treatment*. Continue seeking Him with seriousness. Unless He wanted you, you would not be wanting Him.

TO 'MRS ARNOLD': from Magdalen College

12 September 1951

I have not a word to say against the doctrine that Our Lord suffers in all the sufferings of His people (see Acts IX. 6) or that when we willingly accept what we suffer for others and offer it to God on their behalf, then it may be united with His sufferings and, in Him, may help to their redemption or even that of others whom we do not dream of. So that it is not in vain: tho' of course we must not count on seeing it work out exactly as we, in our present ignorance, might think best. The key text for this view is Colossians 1.24. Is it not, after all, one more application of the truth that we are all 'members one of another'? I wish I had known more when I wrote *The Problem of Pain* . . .

TO MISS VERA MATHEWS: **from Magdalen College**

12 September 1951

Since then I have been in really quiet and unearthly spots in my native Ireland.[173] I stayed for a fortnight in a bungalow which none of the peasants will approach at night because the desolate coast on which it stands is haunted by 'the good people'. There is also a ghost but (and this is interesting) they don't seem to mind *him:* the faeries are a more serious danger . . .

TO DR WENDELL W. WATTERS: **from Magdalen College**

25 October 1951

Yes. I'm not surprised that a man who agreed with me in *Screwtape* (ethics served with an imaginative seasoning) might disagree with me when I wrote about religion. We can hardly discuss the whole matter by post, can we? I'll only make one shot. When people object, as you do, that if Jesus was God as well as Man, then He had an unfair advantage which deprives Him for them of all value, it seems to me as if a man struggling in the water shd refuse a rope thrown to him by another who had one foot on the bank, saying 'Oh but you have an unfair advantage'. It is because of that advantage that He can help.

---

[173] Jack and Warren were in southern Ireland for a holiday 14–28 August, after which Jack spent a fortnight with Arthur Greeves at Crawfordsburn, Co. Down.

But all good wishes: we must just differ: in charity I hope. You must not be *angry* with me for believing you know: I'm not angry with you . . .

TO A CHARITABLE READER: from Magdalen College

October 1951

I feel sure you will not be offended if I tell you that I have—with great reluctance—sent your gift straight on to someone else, whose need is much greater than mine . . . an elderly lady who has always had a struggle to make both ends meet and who . . . is now on the verge of actual want . . . Amongst the elderly, living on dwindling investment income in a world of rising prices, there is already discomfort, hardship, and I fear in many cases, real suffering . . .

TO THE PRIME MINISTER'S SECRETARY: from Magdalen College (in reply to the offer of a C.B.E.)

3 December 1951

I feel greatly obliged to the Prime Minister, and so far as my personal feelings are concerned this honour would be highly agreeable. There are always however knaves who say, and fools who believe, that my religious writings are all covert anti-Leftist propaganda, and my appearance in the Honours List would of course strengthen their hands. It is therefore better that I should not appear there. I am sure the Prime Minister will understand my reason, and that my gratitude is and will be none the less cordial.

[As far back as 1935 Jack had promised the Delegates of Oxford University Press to write the volume on *English Literature in the Sixteenth Century* for their 'Oxford History of English Literature'. It reached what he called its 'embryonic state' as the Clark Lectures which he gave in Cambridge in 1944. However, he needed much more time than he had previously had if he were ever to complete it. Because of the importance of the undertaking Magdalen College gave him a year off, beginning Michaelmas Term of 1951, to finish the book. It was, as it turned out, completed by June of 1952. Remembering the great amount of work which went into it, Jack always referred to *English Literature in the Sixteenth Century, excluding Drama* (1954) — vol. III in the 'O.H.E.L.' series — as 'the O Hell!']

TO DR WARFIELD M. FIROR: from Magdalen College

20 December 1951

How the years flick past at our time of life, don't they: like telegraph posts seen from an express train: and how they crawled once, when the gulf between one Christmas and another was too wide almost for a child's eye to see across. If ever I write a story about a long-liver, like Haggard's *She* or the *Wandering Jew* (and I might) I shall make that point. The first century of his life will, to the end, seem to him longer than all that have followed it: the Norman Conquest, the discovery of America and the French Revolution will be all huddled up in his mind as recent events.

My year 'off' has been, as it was meant to be, so far a year of very hard work, but mostly congenial. The book really begins to look as if it might be finished in 1952 and I am, between ourselves, pleased with the manner of it—but afraid of hidden errors. In that way I rather envy you for being engaged in empirical inquiry where, I suppose, mistakes rise up in the laboratory and proclaim themselves. But a mistake in a history of literature walks in silence till the day it turns irrevocable in a printed book and the book goes for review to the only man in England who wd have known it for a mistake.

This, I suppose, is good for one's soul: and the *kind* of good I must learn to digest. I am going to be (if I live long enough) one of those men who *was* a famous writer in his forties and dies unknown—like Christian going down into the green valley of humiliation. Which is the most beautiful thing in Bunyan and can be the most beautiful thing in life if a man takes it *quite* rightly—a matter I think and pray about a good deal. One thing is certain: much better to begin (at least) learning humility on this side of the grave than to have it all as a fresh problem on the other. Anyway, the desire wh. has to be mortified is such a vulgar and silly one . . .

TO 'MRS ARNOLD': from Magdalen College

26 December 1951

I am v. glad you have discovered François de Sales. I would regard his prose and Geo. Herbert's verse as the *sweetest* of religious writings. And how remarkable it is that such a man's mere statement that anxiety is a great evil at once helps you to escape from that evil. That indeed seems to be one of the magical Laws of this very creation in which we live: that the thing we know already, the thing we have said to ourselves a hundred times, when said by *someone else* becomes suddenly operative. It is part of C. Williams' doctrine, isn't it? — that no one can paddle his own canoe but everyone can paddle someone else's . . .

TO 'MRS LOCKLEY': from Magdalen College

8 January 1952

'Whether it is any good praying for actual things' — the first question is what one means by 'any good'. Is it a good thing to do? Yes: however we explain it, we are *told* to ask for particular things such as our daily bread. Does it 'work'? Certainly not like a mechanical operation or a magical spell. It is a *request* which of course the Other Party may or may not, for His own good reasons, grant. But how can it change God's will? Well — but how v. odd it would be if God in His actions towards me were bound to ignore what I did (including my prayers). Surely He hasn't to forgive me for sins I didn't commit or to cure me of errors into which I have never fallen? In other words His will (however changeless in some ultimate metaphysical sense) must be related to what I am and do? And once grant that, and why should my asking or not asking not be *one* of the things He takes into account? At any rate He *said* He would — and He ought to know. (We often talk as if He were not very good at Theology!)

I certainly believe (now *really*, long since with a merely intellectual assent) that a sin once repented and forgiven, is gone, annihilated, burnt up in the fire of Divine Love, white as snow. There is no harm in continuing to 'bewail' it, i.e. to express one's sorrow, but not to ask for pardon, for that you already have—one's sorrow for being that sort of person. Your conscience need not be 'burdened' with it in the sense of feeling that you have an unsettled account, but you can still in a sense be *patiently* and (in a sense) *contentedly* humbled by it . . .

TO SISTER PENELOPE, C.S.M.V.: **from Magdalen College**

10 January 1952

I have, if not thought, yet imagined, a good deal about the other kinds of Men. My own idea was based on the old problem 'Who was Cain's wife?' If we follow Scripture it wd seem that she must have been no daughter of Adam's. I pictured the True Men descendants (in Genesis VI. 1–4, where I agree with you), interbreeding and thus producing the wicked Antediluvians.

Oddly enough I, like you, had pictured Adam as being, physically, the son of two anthropoids, on whom, after birth, God worked the miracle which made him Man: said, in fact, 'Come out—and forget thine own people and thy father's house'. The Call of Abraham wd be a far smaller instance of the same sort of thing, and regeneration in each one of us wd be an instance too, tho' not a smaller one. That all seems to me to fit in both historically and spiritually.

I don't quite feel we shd gain anything by the doctrine that Adam was a hermaphrodite. As for the (rudimentary) presence in each sex of organs proper to the other, does that not occur in other mammals as well as in humans? Surely pseudo-organs of lactation are externally visible in the male dog? If so there wd be no *more* ground for making men (I mean, humans) hermaphroditic than any other mammal. (By the way, what an inconvenience it is in English to have the same word for *Homo* and *Vir.*) No doubt these rudimentary organs have a spiritual significance: there ought spiritually to be a man in every woman and a woman in every man. And how horrid the ones who haven't got it are: I can't bear a 'man's man' or a 'woman's woman'.

I will order *They Shall Be My People* and look forward to it. Congratulations. For my own part, I have been given a year's leave from all teaching duties to enable me to finish my book on XVIth century literature, so I am plugging away at that as hard as I can. My hope is to kill some popular mythology about that fabulous monster called 'the Renaissance'. There are five fairy tales already written, of which the second has now appeared.

'Jane' died almost a year ago, after a long but, thank God, painless illness. I beg you will often pray for her. She was an unbeliever and, in later years, very jealous, exacting, and irascible, but always tender to the poor and to animals . . .

TO 'MRS ARNOLD': from Magdalen College

31 January 1952

That suffering is not *always* sent as a punishment is clearly established for believers by the book of Job and by John IX. 1–4. That it *sometimes* is, is suggested by parts of the

Old Testament and Revelation. It wd certainly be most dangerous to assume that any given pain was penal. I believe that all pain is contrary to God's will, absolutely but not relatively. When I am taking a thorn out of my finger (or a child's finger) the pain is 'absolutely' contrary to my will: i.e. if I could have chosen a situation without pain I would have done so. But I do will what caused the pain, relatively to the given situation: i.e. granted the thorn I prefer the pain to leaving the thorn where it is. A mother spanking a child would be in the same position: she would rather cause it this pain than let it go on pulling the cat's tail, but she would like it better if no situation which demands a smack had arisen.

On the heathen, see I Tim. IV. 10. Also in Matt, XXV. 31–46 the people don't sound as if they were believers. Also the doctrine of Christ's descending into Hell (i.e. Hades, the land of the dead: not Gehenna the land of the lost) and preaching to the dead: and that would be outside time and would include those who died long after Him as well as those who died before He was born as Man. I don't think we know the details: we must just stick to the view that (a) All justice and mercy will be done, (b) but that nevertheless it is our duty to do all we can to convert unbelievers.

TO 'MRS SONIA GRAHAM': from Magdalen College

29 February 1952

I learn from 'Mrs Arnold' that you are taking the plunge. As you have been now for so long in my prayers, I hope it will not seem intrusive to send my congratulations. For whatever people who have never undergone an adult conversion may say, it is a process not without its distresses. Indeed they are the very sign that it is a true initiation. Like learning to swim or to skate, or getting married, or taking up a profession. There are cold shudderings about all these processes. When one finds oneself learning to fly *without* trouble one soon discovers (usually—there *are* blessed exceptions where we are allowed to take a real step without that difficulty) by waking up, that it was only a dream. All blessings and good wishes.

TO 'MRS SONIA GRAHAM': from Magdalen College

18 March 1952

Don't bother at all about that question of a person being 'made a Christian' by baptism. It is only the usual trouble about words being used in more than one sense. Thus we might say a man 'became a soldier' the moment that he joined the army. But his instructors might say six months later 'I think we have made a soldier of him'. Both usages are quite definable, only one wants to know which is being used in a given sentence. The Bible itself gives us one short prayer which is suitable for all who are struggling with the beliefs and doctrines. It is: 'Lord I believe, help Thou my unbelief.'

Would something of this sort be any good?: Almighty God, who art the father of lights and who has promised by thy dear Son that all who do thy will shall know thy doctrine: give me grace so to live that by daily obedience I daily increase in faith and in the understanding of thy Holy Word, through Jesus Christ our Lord. Amen.

TO 'MRS ARNOLD': from Magdalen College

1 April 1952

The advantage of a fixed form of service is that we know what is coming. *Ex tempore* public prayer has this difficulty: we don't know whether we can mentally join in it until we've heard it—it might be phoney or heretical. We are therefore called upon to carry on a *critical* and a *devotional* activity at the same moment: two things hardly compatible. In a fixed form we ought to have 'gone through the motions' before in our private prayers: the rigid form really sets our devotions *free*. I also find the more rigid it is, the easier it is to keep one's thoughts from straying. Also it prevents getting too completely eaten up by whatever happens to be the preoccupation of the moment (i.e. War, an election, or what not). The *permanent* shape of Christianity shows through. I don't see how the *ex tempore* method can help becoming provincial and I think it has a great tendency to direct attention to the minister rather than to God.

Quakers—well I've been unlucky in mine. The ones I know are atrocious bigots whose religion seems to consist almost entirely in attacking other people's religions. But I'm sure there are good ones as well.

TO 'MRS LOCKLEY': from Magdalen College

13 May 1952

In Bp. Gore's 'Sermon on the mount' . . . I find the view that Christ forbade 'divorce in such a sense as allowed re-marriage'. The question is whether He made an exception by allowing divorce in such a sense as allowed re-marriage when the divorce was for adultery. In the Eastern Church re-marriage of the innocent party is allowed: not in the Roman. The Anglican Bps at Lambeth in 1888 denied re-marriage to the guilty party, and added that 'there has always been a dif-ference of opinion in the Ch. as to whether Our Lord meant to forbid re-marriage of the innocent party in a divorce'.

It wd seem then that the only question is whether you can divorce your husband in such a sense as wd make you free to re-marry. I imagine that nothing is further from your thoughts. I believe that you are free as a Christian woman to divorce him especially since the refusal to do so does harm to the innocent children of his mistress: but that you must (or should) regard yourself as no more free to marry another man than if you had not divorced him. But remem-ber I'm no authority on such matters, and I hope you will ask the advice of one or two sensible clergymen of our own Church.

Our own Vicar whom I have just rung up, says that there *are* Anglican theologians who say that you must not divorce him. His own view was that in doubtful cases the Law of Charity shd always be the over-riding consideration, and in a case such as yours charity directs you to divorce him . . .

TO 'MRS SONIA GRAHAM': from Magdalen College
15 May 1952

Thanks for your letter of the 9th. All our prayers are being answered and I thank God for it. The only (possibly, not necessarily) unfavourable symptom is that you are just a trifle too excited. It is quite right that you should feel that 'something terrific' has happened to you . . . Accept these sensations with thankfulness as birthday cards from God, but remember that they are only greetings, not the real gift. I mean that it is not the sensations that are the real thing. The real thing is the gift of the Holy Spirit which can't usually be—perhaps not ever—experienced as a sensation or emotion. The sensations are merely the response of your nervous system. Don't depend on them. Otherwise when they go and you are once more emotionally flat (as you certainly will be quite soon), you might think that the real thing had gone too. But it won't. It will be there when you can't feel it. May even be operative when you can feel it least.

Don't imagine it is all 'going to be an exciting adventure from now on'. It won't. Excitement of whatever sort, never lasts. This is the push to start you off on your first bicycle: you'll be left to [do] lots of dogged pedalling later on. And no need to feel depressed about it either. It will be good for your spiritual leg muscles. So enjoy the push while it lasts, but enjoy it as a treat, not as something normal.

Of course none of us have 'any right' at the altar. You might as well talk of a non-existent person 'having a right' to be created. It is not *our* right but God's free bounty. An English peer said, 'I like the order of the Garter because it has no dam' nonsense about merit'. Nor has Grace. And we must keep on remembering that as a cure for Pride. Yes, pride is a perpetual nagging temptation. Keep on knocking it on the head but don't be too worried about it. As long as one knows one is proud one is safe from the worst form of pride.

If S— answers your letter, then let the correspondence drop. He is not a great philosopher (and none of my scientific colleagues think much of him as a scientist) but he is strong enough to do some harm. You're not David and no one has told you to fight Goliath. You've only just enlisted. Don't go off challenging enemy champions. Learn your drill. I hope this doesn't sound all like cold water. I can't tell you how pleased I was with your letter. God bless you.

TO DOM BEDE GRIFFITHS, O.S.B.: from Magdalen College

28 May 1952

It isn't chiefly *men* I am kept in touch with by my huge mail: it is *women*. The female, happy or unhappy, agreeing or disagreeing, is by nature a much more *epistolary* animal than the male.

Yes, Pascal does directly contradict several passages in Scripture and must be wrong. What I ought to have said was that the Cosmological argument is, for some people at some times, ineffective. It always has been for me. (By the way do read K. Z. Lorenz *King Solomon's Ring* on animal— especially bird—behaviour. There are instincts I had never dreamed of: big with a promise of real morality. The wolf is a v. different creature from what we imagine.)

The stories you tell about two perverts belong to a terribly familiar pattern: the man of good will, saddled with an abnormal desire wh. he never chose, fighting hard and time after time defeated. But I question whether in such a life the successful operation of Grace is so tiny as we think. Is not this continued avoidance either of presumption or despair, this ever renewed struggle itself a great triumph of Grace? Perhaps more so than the (to human eyes) equable virtue of some who are psychologically sound.

I am glad you think J. Austen a sound moralist. I agree. And not platitudinous, but subtle as well as firm.

TO 'MISS HELEN HADOW': from Magdalen College
20 June 1952

I would prefer to combat the 'I'm special' feeling not by the thought 'I'm no more special than anyone else', but by the feeling 'Everyone is as special as me'. In one way there is no difference, I grant, for both remove the speciality. But there is a difference in another way. The first might lead you to think, 'I'm only one of the crowd like everyone else'. But the second leads to the truth that there isn't any crowd. No one is like anyone else. All are 'members' (organs) in the Body of Christ. All different and all necessary to the whole and to one another: each loved by God individually, as if it were the only creature in existence. Otherwise you might get the idea that God is like the government which can only deal with the people as the mass.

About confession, I take it that the view of our Church is that everyone may use it but none is obliged to. I don't doubt that the Holy Spirit guides your decisions from within when you make them with the intention of pleasing God. The error wd be to think that He speaks *only* within, whereas in reality He speaks also through Scripture, the Church, Christian friends, books etc . . .

TO 'MRS ARNOLD': **from Magdalen College**

20 June 1952

Incense and Hail Marys are in quite different categories. The one is merely a question of ritual: some find it helpful and others don't, and each must put up with its absence or presence in the church they are attending with cheerful and charitable humility.

But Hail Marys raise a doctrinal question: whether it is lawful to address devotions to any *creature,* however holy. My own view would be that a *salute* to any saint (or angel) cannot in itself be wrong any more than taking off one's hat to a friend: but that there is always some danger lest such practices start one on the road to a state (sometimes found in R.C.s) where the B.V.M. is treated really as a divinity and even becomes the centre of the religion. I therefore think such salutes are better avoided. And if the Blessed Virgin is as good as the best mothers I have known, she does not *want* any of the attention which might have gone to her Son diverted to herself . . .

TO ROGER LANCELYN GREEN: **from Magdalen College** (Jack needed his friend's advice in finding a suitable name for the Narnian story which eventually was given the title *The Silver Chair.* He had only just come to know Mrs Joy Davidman Gresham from New York.)

26 September 1952

We also have had visitors. For heaven's sake don't let June [Lancelyn Green] increase her toils by bothering to write to me. But let me have her and your advice on my immediate problem wh. is the title of the new story. Bles, like you, thinks *The Wild Waste Lands* bad, but he says *Night Under Narnia* is 'gloomy'. George Sayer & my brother say *Gnomes Under N* wd be equally gloomy, but *News Under Narnia* wd do. On the other hand my brother & the American writer Joy Davidman (who has been staying with us & is a great reader of fantasy & children's books) both say that *The Wild Waste Lands* is a splendid title. What's a chap to do?

TO CHARLES MOORMAN: from Magdalen College
2 October 1952

I am sure you are on a false scent. Certainly most, perhaps all the poems in [Charles Williams's] *Taliessin* volume were written before the last novel, *All Hallows Eve*, was even conceived, and there had been Arthurian poems (not of much value) in his earlier manner long before. I can't tell you when he first became interested in the Arthurian story, but the overwhelming probability is that, like so many English boys, he got via Tennyson into Malory in his 'teens. The whole way in which he talked of it implied a life-long familiarity. Much later (but even so, before I met him) came the link-up between his long-standing interest in *Arthuriana* and a new interest in Byzantium.

Everything he ever said implied that his prose fiction, his 'pot boilers', and his poetry all went on concurrently: there was no 'turning from' one to the other. He never said anything to suggest that he felt his themes 'would not fit with ease into tales of modern life'. What would have expressed the real chronological relation between the novels would have been the words (tho' I don't think he ever actually said them) 'I haven't got much further with my Arthurian poems this week because I've been temporarily occupied with the idea for a new story'.

The question when did he first come across the doctrine of 'Caritas' puzzled me. What doctrine do you mean? If you mean the ordinary Christian doctrine that there are three theological virtues and 'the greatest of these is charity' of course he would never remember a time when he had not known it. If you mean the doctrine of Coinherence and Substitution, then I don't know when he first met these. Nor do I know when he began the *Figure of A*.[174] His knowledge of the earlier Arthurian documents was not that of a real scholar: he knew none of the relevant languages except (a little) Latin.

The VII Bears and the Atlantean Circle [in *That Hideous Strength*] are pure inventions of my own, filling the same purpose in the narrative that 'noises off' wd in a stage play. Numinor is a mis-spelling of Numenor which, like the 'true West', is a fragment from a vast private mythology invented by Professor J. R. R. Tolkien. At the time we all hoped that a good deal of that mythology would soon become public through a romance which the Professor was then contemplating. Since then the hope has receded . . .

---

[174] This appeared in *Arthurian Torso; Containing the Posthumous Fragment of 'The Figure of Arthur' by Charles Williams and A Commentary on the Arthurian Poems of Charles Williams by C. S. Lewis* (1948).

TO 'MRS ARNOLD': from Magdalen College
20 October 1952

I think you are perfectly right to change your manner of prayer from time to time and I should suppose that all who pray seriously do thus change it. One's needs and capacities change and also, for creatures like us, excellent prayers may 'go dead' if we use them too long. Whether one shd use written prayers composed by other people, or one's own words, or wordless prayer, or in what proportion one should mix all three, seems entirely a question for each individual to answer from his own experience. I myself find prayers without words the best *when* I can manage it, but can do so only when least distracted and in the best spiritual and bodily health (or what I think best). But another person might find it quite otherwise.

Your question about old friendship where there is no longer spiritual communion is a hard one. Obviously it depends very much on what the other party wants. The great thing in friendship, as in all other forms of love is, as you know, to turn from the demand to *be* loved (or helped or amused) to the wish to love (or help or amuse). Perhaps in so far as one does this one also discovers how much time one shd spend on the sort of friends you mention. I don't think a decay in one's desire for mere 'society' or 'acquaintance' or 'the crowd' is a bad sign. (We mustn't take it as a sign of our increasing spirituality of course: isn't it merely a natural neutral development as one grows older?)

All that Calvanist question—Free-will and Predestination—is to my mind indiscussible, insoluble. Of course (we say) if a man repents God will accept him. Ah yes (they say), but the fact of his repenting shows that God has already moved him to do so. This at any rate leaves us with the fact that in *any concrete case* the question never arises as a practical one. But I suspect it is really a *meaningless* question. The difference between Freedom and Necessity is fairly clear on the bodily level: we know the difference between making our teeth chatter and just finding them chattering with the cold. It begins to be less clear when we talk about human love (leaving out the *erotic* kind). 'Do I like him because I choose or because I must?' There are cases where this has an answer, but others where it seems to me to mean nothing. When we carry it up to relations between God and Man, has the distinction become perhaps nonsensical? After all, when we are most free, it is only with a freedom God has given us: and when our will is most influenced by Grace, it is still *our will.* And if what *our will* does is not voluntary, and if 'voluntary' does not mean 'free', what are we talking about? I'd leave it alone.

TO ROGER LANCELYN GREEN: from Magdalen College

21 October 1952

Your letter was more than usually welcome: for tho' reason assured me that so busy a man might have 100 motives for not writing, I had also a lurking fear that you might be offended. Forgive me the suspicion. It arose not at all because I judge you to be that kind of ass, or any kind, but because, we being 'of one blood', the loss of you wd be a very raw gash in my life . . .

I have just finished Vol I of Henry James's letters. An interesting man, tho' a dreadful prig: but he did appreciate Stevenson. A *phantasmal* man, who had never known God, or earth, or war, never done a day's compelled work, never had to earn a living, had no home & no duties . . .

TO 'MRS ASHTON': from Magdalen College
8 November 1952

I am returning your letter with the questions in it numbered so that you'll know wh. I am answering.

(1) Some call me *Mr* and some *Dr.* And I not only don't care but usually don't know which.

(2) Distinguish (A) A second chance in the strict sense, i.e. a new earthly life in which you wd attempt afresh all the problems you failed at in the present one (as in religions of Re-Incarnation). (B) Purgatory: a process by which the work of redemption continues, and first perhaps begins to be noticeable after death. I think Charles Williams depicts (B) and not (A).

(3) We are never given any knowledge of 'What would have happened if . . .'

(4) I think that every prayer which is sincerely made even to a false god or to a very imperfectly conceived true God, is accepted by the true God and that Christ saves many who do not think they know Him. For He is (dimly) present in the *good* side of the inferior teachers they follow. In the parable of the Sheep and the Goats (Matt. XXV. 31 and following) those who are saved do not seem to know that they have served Christ. But of course our anxiety about

unbelievers is most usefully employed when it leads us, not to speculation but to earnest prayer for them and the attempt to be in our own lives such good advertisements for Christianity as will make it attractive.

(5) It is Christ Himself, not the Bible, who is the true word of God. The Bible, read in the right spirit and with the guidance of good teachers, will bring us to Him. When it becomes really necessary (i.e. for our spiritual life, not for controversy or curiosity) to know whether a particular passage is rightly translated or is myth (but of course myth specially chosen by God from among countless myths to carry a spiritual truth) or history, we shall no doubt be guided to the right answer. But we must not use the Bible (our fathers too often did) as a sort of Encyclopedia out of which texts (isolated from their context and not read with attention to the whole nature and purport of the books in which they occur) can be taken for use as weapons.

(6) *Kill* means *murder.* I don't know Hebrew: but when Our Lord quotes this commandment he uses the Greek Φονεύειν . . .

(7) The question of what you wd 'want' is off the point. Capital punishment might be wrong tho' the relations of the murdered man wanted him killed: it might be right tho' they did not want this. The question is whether a Xtian nation ought or ought not to put murderers to death: not what passions interested individuals may feel.

(8) There is no doubt at all that the natural impulse to 'hit back' must be fought against by the Xtian whenever it arises. If one I love is tortured or murdered my desire to avenge him must be given no quarter. So far as nothing but

this question of retaliation comes in 'turn the other cheek' *is* the Christian law. It is however quite another matter when the neutral public authority (*not* the aggrieved person) may order killing of either private murderers or public enemies in mass. It is quite clear that St Paul . . . approved of capital punishment—he says 'the magistrate bears the sword and should bear the sword'. It is recorded that the soldiers who came to St John Baptist asking, 'What shall we do?' were *not* told to leave the army. When Our Lord Himself praised the Centurion He never hinted that the military profession was in itself sinful. This has been the general view of Christendom. Pacificism is a v. recent and local variation. We must of course respect and tolerate Pacifists, but I think their view erroneous.

(9) The symbols under which Heaven is presented to us are (a) a dinner party, (b) a wedding, (c) a city, and (d) a concert. It would be grotesque to suppose that the guests or citizens or members of the choir didn't know one another. And how can love of one another be commanded in this life if it is to be cut short at death?

(10) When I have learnt to love God better than my earthly dearest, I shall love my earthly dearest better than I do now. In so far as I learn to love my earthly dearest at the expense of God and *instead* of God, I shall be moving towards the state in which I shall not love my earthly dearest at all. When first things are put first, second things are not suppressed but increased. If you and I ever come to love God perfectly, the answer to this tormenting question will then become clear and will be far more beautiful than we cd ever imagine. We can't have it now.

TO MRS EDWARD A. ALLEN: from Magdalen College

19 January 1953

I don't wonder that you got fogged in *Pilgrim's Regress*. It was my first religious book and I didn't then know how to make things easy. I was not even trying to very much, because in those days I never dreamed I would become a 'popular' author and hoped for no readers outside a small 'highbrow' circle. Don't waste your time over it any more. The *poetry* is my own . . .

TO 'MRS ARNOLD': from Magdalen College

6–7 April 1953

I don't think gratitude is a relevant motive for joining an Order. Gratitude might create a state of mind in which one became aware of a vocation: but the vocation would be the proper reason for joining. They themselves would surely not wish you to join *without* it? You can show your gratitude in lots of other ways. Is there in this Order, even for lay members such as you would be, not something like a noviciate or experimental period? If so, that would be the thing wouldn't it? If not, I think I can only repeat my previous suggestion of undergoing a sort of unofficial noviciate by living according to the Rule for six months or so and seeing how it works. Most of the things you probably do anyway and are things we ought to do. (The only one I'm doubtful about is the 'special intention' clause. I'm not quite sure what the theological implications are.) . . . Is the vow irrevocable or can you contract out again?

About putting one's Christian point of view to doctors

and other unpromising subjects I'm in great doubt myself. All I'm clear about is that one sins if one's real reasons for silence is simply the fear of looking a fool. I suppose one is right if one's reason is that the other party will be repelled still further and only confirmed in his belief that Christians are troublesome and embarrassing people, to be avoided whenever possible. But I find it a dreadfully worrying problem. (I am quite sure that an importunate bit of evangelisation from a comparative stranger would *not* have done me any good when I was an unbeliever.)

I think our official view of Confession can be seen in the form for the Visitation of the Sick where it says, 'Then shall the sick person be moved (i.e. advised, prompted) to make a . . . Confession . . . if he feel his conscience troubled with any weighty matters.' That is, where Rome makes Confession compulsory for all, we make it permissable for any: not 'generally necessary' but profitable. We do not doubt that there can be forgiveness without it. But, as your own experience shows, many people do not *feel* forgiveness, i.e. do not effectively believe in 'the forgiveness of sins' without it. The quite enormous advantage of coming *really* to believe in forgiveness is well worth the horrors (I agree that they *are* horrors) of a first Confession. Also, there is the gain in self-knowledge: most of us have never really faced the facts about ourselves until we uttered them aloud in plain words, calling a spade a spade. I certainly feel that I have profited enormously by the practice. At the same time I think we are quite right not to make it generally obligatory, which might force it on some who are not ready for it and might do harm . . .

TO 'MRS ASHTON': from Magdalen College

17 July 1953

I'm v. glad you've seen that Christianity is as hard as nails: i.e. hard *and* tender at the same time. It's the *blend* that does it: neither quality would be any good without the other. You needn't worry about not feeling brave. Our Lord didn't—see the scene in Gethsemane. How thankful I am that when God became Man He did not choose to become a man of iron nerves: that would not have helped weaklings like you and me nearly so much. Especially don't *worry* (you may of course pray) about being brave over merely possible evils in the future. In the old battles it was usually the reserve, who had to *watch* the carnage, not the troops who were in it, whose nerve broke first. Similarly I think you in America feel much more anxiety about atomic bombs than we do: because you are further from the danger. If and when a horror turns up, you will then be given Grace to help you. I don't think one is usually given it in advance. 'Give us our daily bread' (not an annuity for life) applies to spiritual gifts too: the little *daily* support for the *daily* trial. Life has to be taken day by day and hour by hour.

The writer you quote *was* very good at the stage at wh. you met him: Now, as is plain, you've got beyond him. Poor boob—he thought his mind was his own. Never his own until he makes it Christ's: up till then merely a result of heredity, environment, and the state of his digestion. I became my own only when I gave myself to Another.

'Does God seem real to me?' It varies: just as lots of other things I firmly believe in (my own death, the solar system) *feel* more or less real at different times. I have dreamed dreams but not seen visions: but don't think all that matters a hoot. And the saints say that visions are unimportant. If Our Lord *did* seem to appear to you at your prayer (bodily) what·after all could you do but go on with your prayers? How cd you know that it was not an hallucination? . . .

No, no, I'm not committed to a real belief in Aslan, all that comes in a *story*. I haven't the faintest idea whether there was a real Grail or not. Of course I believe that people are still healed by faith: whether that has happened in any particular case one can't of course say without getting a real doctor who is also a real Christian to go through the whole case-history . . .

TO MRS EMILY McLAY: from Magdalen College

3 August 1953

I take it as a first principle that we must not interpret any one part of Scripture so that it contradicts other parts, and specially we must not use an apostle's teaching to contradict that of Our Lord. Whatever St Paul may have meant, we must not reject the parable of the sheep and the goats (Matt. XXV. 30–46). There, you see there is nothing about Predestination or even about Faith—all depends on works. But how this is to be reconciled with St Paul's teaching, or with other sayings of Our Lord, I frankly confess I don't know. Even St Peter you know admits that he was stumped by the Pauline epistles (II Peter III. 16–17).

What I *think* is this. Everyone looking back on *his own* conversion must feel—and I am sure the feeling is in some sense true—'It is not I who have done this. I did not choose Christ: He chose me. It is all free grace, which I have done nothing to earn.' That is the Pauline account: and I am sure it is the only true account of every conversion *from the inside.* Very well. It then seems to us logical and natural to turn this personal experience into a general rule, 'All conversions depend on God's choice'.

But this I believe is exactly what we must not do: for generalisations are legitimate only when we are dealing with matters to which our faculties are adequate. Here, we are not. *How* our individual experiences are *in reality* consistent with (a) Our idea of Divine justice, (b) The parable I've just quoted, and lots of other passages, we don't and can't know: what is clear is that *we* can't find a consistent formula. I think we must take a leaf out of the scientist's book. They are quite familiar with the fact that, for example, Light has to be regarded *both* as a wave in the ether and as a stream of particles. No one can make these two views consistent. Of course reality must be self-consistent: but till (if ever) we can *see* the consistency it is better to hold two inconsistent views than to ignore one side of the evidence.

The real inter-relation between God's omnipotence and Man's freedom is something we can't find out. Looking at the Sheep & the Goats every man can be quite sure that every kind act he does will be accepted by Christ. Yet, equally, we all do feel sure that all the good in us comes from Grace. We have to leave it at that. I find the best plan is to take the Calvinist view of my own virtues and other people's vices: and the other view of my own vices and other people's virtues. But tho' there is much to be *puzzled* about there is nothing to be *worried* about. It is plain from Scripture that, in whatever sense the Pauline doctrine is true, it is not true in any sense which *excludes* its (apparent) opposite.

You know what Luther said: 'Do you doubt if you are chosen? Then say your prayers and you may conclude that you are.'

TO MRS EMILY McLAY: from Magdalen College

8 August 1953

Your experience in listening to those philosophers gives you the technique one needs for dealing with the dark places in the Bible. When one of the philosophers, one whom you know on other grounds to be a sane and decent man, said something you didn't understand, you did not at once conclude that he had gone off his head. You assumed you'd missed the point.

Same here. The two things one must *not* do are (a) To believe, on the strength of Scripture or on any other evidence, that God is in any way evil. (In Him is no *darkness* at all.) (b) To wipe off the slate any passage which seems to show that He is. Behind that apparently shocking passage, be sure, there lurks some great truth which you don't understand. If one ever *does* come to understand it, one will see that [it] is good and just and gracious in ways we never dreamed of. Till then, it must be just left on one side.

But why are baffling passages left in at all? Oh because God speaks not only for us little ones but also to great sages and mystics who *experience* what we only *read about* and to whom all the words have therefore different, richer contents. Would not a revelation which contained nothing that you and I did not understand be for that v. reason rather suspect? To a child it wd seem a contradiction to say both that his parents made him and that God made him, yet we see both can be true.

TO MRS EDWARD A. ALLEN: from Magdalen College

9 January 1954

Thank you for your nice woody and earthy (almost like Thoreau or Dorothy Wordsworth) letter of the 6th. I think I go with you in preferring trees to flowers in the sense that if I had to live in a world without one or the other I'd choose to keep the trees. I certainly prefer tree-like people to flower-like people—the staunch and knotty and storm-enduring to the frilly and fragrant and easily withered . . .

I think what makes even beautiful country (in the long run) so unsatisfactory when seen from a train or a car is that it whirls each tree, brook, or haystack close up into the foreground, *soliciting* individual attention but vanishing before you can give it . . . Didn't someone give a similar explanation of the weariness we feel in a crowd where we can't help seeing individual faces but can do no more than see them so that (he said) 'it is like being forced to read the first page, but no more, of a hundred books in succession'? . . .

TO DOM BEDE GRIFFITHS, O.S.B.: from Magdalen College (Dom Bede was concerning himself with the problems of Christian missionary work in India.)

16 January 1954

I suspect that a great going-to-meet-them is needed not only on the level of thought but in method. A man who had lived all his life in India said 'That country might be Christian now if there had been *no* Missions in our sense but many single missionaries walking the roads with their begging-bowls. For that is the sort of Holy Man India believes in and she will never believe in any other.' Of course we must beware of thinking of 'the East' as if it were homogeneous. I suppose the Indian and the Chinese *ethos* are as alien to each other as either is to us.

The article on Tolerance in that same issue made my flesh creep. What do they mean by 'Error has no rights'? Of course Error has no rights, because it is not a person: in the same sense Truth has no rights. But if they mean 'Erroneous persons have no rights', surely this is as contrary to the plain dictates of Natural Law as any proposition could be?

Quite a different question. Has any one composed prayers for children NOT on the sense of special prayers supposed suitable for their age (which easily leads to wish-wash) BUT simply in the sense of *translation* of ordinary prayers into the easiest language? And wd it be worth doing?

TO MISS PAULINE BAYNES: from Magdalen College
(Miss Baynes had been chosen to illustrate 'The Chronicles of Narnia'.)

21 January 1954

I lunched with Bles yesterday to see the drawings for *The Horse [and His Boy]* and feel I must write to tell you how very much we both enjoyed them. It is delightful to find (and not only for selfish reasons) that you do each book a little bit better than the last—it is nice to see an artist growing. (If only you cd take six months off and devote them to anatomy, there's no limit to your possibilities.)

Both the drawings of Lasaraleen in the litter were a rich feast of line & of fantastic-satiric imagination: my only regret was that we couldn't have both. Shasta among the tombs (in the new technique, wh. is lovely) was exactly what I wanted. The pictures of Rabadash hanging on the hook and just turning into an ass were the best comedy you've done yet. The Tisroc was superb: far beyond anything you were doing five years ago. I thought that your human faces—the boys, K. Lune etc.—were, this time, really good. The crowds are beautiful, realistic yet also lovely wavy compositions: but your crowds always were. How did you do Tashbaan? We only got its full wealth by using a magnifying glass! The result is exactly right. Thanks enormously for all the intense work you have put into them all. And more power to your elbow: congratulations . . .

TO DOM BEDE GRIFFITHS, O.S.B.: from Magdalen College

23 January 1954

I *have* a taste for Dickens but don't think it a low one. He is the great author on mere *affection* (στοργη): only he & Tolstoi (another great favourite of mine) really deal with it. Of course his error lies in thinking it will do instead of Agape. Scott, as D. Cecil said, has, not the civilised *mind*, but the civilised *heart*. Unforced nobility, generosity, liberality, flow from him. But Thackeray I positively dislike. He is the voice of 'the World'. And his supposedly 'good' women are revolting: jealous *pharisiennes*. The publicans and sinners will go in before Mrs Pendennis and La. Castlewood . . .

TO DOM BEDE GRIFFITHS, O.S.B.: **from Magdalen College**

30 January 1954

Yes, I'd certainly rule out Little Emily and Little Nell and all the 'littles'. The Marchioness is the real thing.

The trouble in Thackeray, is that he can hardly envisage goodness except as a kind of εὐήθεια: all his 'good' people are not only simple, but simpletons. That is a subtle poison wh. comes in with the Renaissance: the Machiavellian (intelligent) villain presently producing the idiot hero. The Middle Ages didn't make Herod clever and knew the devil was an ass. There is really an un-faith about Thackeray's ethics: as if goodness were somehow charming, & . . . infantile. No conception that the purification of the will (*ceteris paribus*) leads to the enlightenment of the intelligence.

TO 'MRS ASHTON': **from Magdalen College**

18 February 1954

Of course taking in the poor illegitimate child is 'charity'. *Charity* means love. It is called Agape in the New Testament to distinguish it from Eros (sexual love), Storge (family affection) and Philia (friendship). So there are four kinds of love, all good in their proper place, but Agape is the best because it is the kind God has for us and is good in all circumstances. There are people I mustn't feel Eros towards, and people I can't feel Storge or Philia for: but I can practise Agape to God, Angels, Man and Beast, to the good and the bad, the old and the young, the far and the near.

You see Agape is all giving, not getting. Read what St Paul says about it in First Corinthians Chap. 13. Then look at a picture of Agape in action in St Luke, Chap. 10. vv. 30–35. And then, better still, look at Matthew Ch. 25. vv. 31–46: from which you see that Christ counts all that you do for *this* baby exactly as if you had done it for Him when He was a baby in the manger at Bethlehem: you are in a sense sharing in the things His mother did for Him. Giving money is only *one* way of showing charity: to give time and toil is far better and (for most of us) harder. And notice, tho' it is all giving—you needn't expect any reward—how you *do* get rewarded almost at once.

Yes. I know one doesn't even *want* to be cured of one's pride because it gives pleasure. But the pleasure of pride is like the pleasure of scratching. If there is an itch one does want to scratch: but it is much nicer to have *neither* the itch nor the scratch. As long as we have the itch of self-regard we shall want the pleasure of self-approval: but the happiest moments are those when we forget our precious selves and have neither but have everything else (God, our fellow humans, animals, the garden and the sky) instead . . .

[After a good deal of effort, Cambridge University persuaded Jack to accept the newly-created Chair of Medieval and Renaissance English Literature—a position created with him in mind. Although he had to teach at Magdalen during the Michaelmas Term of 1954 (he finished his last tutorial at 12.50 P.M. on 3 December), he gave his Inaugural Lecture in

Cambridge on 29 November 1954. It was published under the title *De Descriptione Temporum*. He did not move to Magdalene College, Cambridge until 7 January 1955.]

TO SISTER PENELOPE, C.S.M.V.: **from Magdalen College**

30 July 1954

Yes, I have been made Professor of 'Medieval & Renaissance English' at Cambridge: the scope of the chair (a new one) suits me exactly. But it won't be as big a change as you might think. I shall still live at Oxford in the Vac. and on many week ends in term. My address will be Magdalen*e*, so I remain under the same Patroness. This is nice because it saves 'Admin' re-adjustments in Heaven: also I can't help feeling that the dear lady now understands my constitution better than a stranger would . . .

TO MRS URSULA ROBERTS: **from Magdalen College**

31 July 1954

I am certainly unfit to advise anyone else on the devotional life. My own rules are (1) To make sure that, wherever else they may be placed, the main prayers should *not* be put 'last thing at night'. (2) To avoid introspection in prayer—I mean not to watch one's own mind to see if it is in the right frame, but always to turn the attention outwards to God. (3) Never, never to try to generate an emotion by will power. (4) To pray without words when I am able, but to fall back on words when tired or otherwise below par. With renewed thanks. Perhaps *you* will sometimes pray for *me*?

TO MRS EDWARD A. ALLEN: from **Magdalen College**
1 November 1954

I think it would be dangerous to suppose that Satan had created all the creatures that are disagreeable or dangerous to us for (a) those creatures, if they could think, wd have just the same reason for thinking that *we* were created by Satan. (b) I don't think evil, in the strict sense, can *create*. It can spoil something that Another has created. Satan may have corrupted other creatures as well as us. Part of the corruption in us might be the unreasoning horror and disgust we feel at some creatures quite apart from any harm they can do us. (I can't abide a spider myself.) We have scriptural authority for Satan originating diseases — see Luke XIII.16.

Do you know, the suffering of the innocent is *less* of a problem to me v. often than that of the wicked. It sounds absurd: but I've met so many innocent sufferers who seem to be gladly offering their pain to God in Christ as part of the Atonement, so patient, so meek, even so at peace, and so unselfish that we can hardly doubt they are being, as St Paul says, 'made perfect by suffering'. On the other hand I meet selfish egoists in whom suffering seems to produce only resentment, hate, blasphemy, and more egoism. They are the real problem.

Christian Scientists seem to me to be altogether too simple. Granted that all the evils are illusions, still, the existence of that illusion wd be a real evil and presumably a real evil permitted by God. That brings us back to exactly the same point as we began from. We have gained nothing by the theory. We are still faced with the great mystery, not explained, but coloured, transmuted, all through the Cross. Faith, not wild over-simplifications, is what will help, don't you think? It is so v. difficult to believe that the travail of all creation which God Himself descended to share, at its most intense, may be necessary in the process of turning finite creatures (with free wills) into—well, Gods ...

TO DOM BEDE GRIFFITHS, O.S.B.: from Magdalen College

1 November 1954

Your book came at a moment of low spiritual temper, external worry, and (mild) physical pain. I had prayed v. hard a couple of nights before that my faith might be strengthened. The response was immediate and your book gave the finishing touch. It did me a great deal of good: apart, of course from its lower gains in the way of interest and enjoyment. That made an objective literary judgement v. difficult, but I think you have probably done it very well. It must have been a job to keep it so short without becoming perfunctory, and so subjective without being (and it is not in the least) mawkish or suffocating. Much that you said about the Sacraments was v. illuminating. One felt how Paganism does not merely survive but first becomes really itself in the v. heart of Christianity. By the way wd you agree that the un-Christening of Europe (much of it) is an even bigger change that its Christening? So that the gap between Professor

[Gilbert] Ryle and, say Dante, is *wider* than that between Dante and Virgil?

TO DOM BEDE GRIFFITHS, O.S.B.: **from Magdalen College**

5 November 1954

The best Dickens always seems to me to be the one I have read last! But in a cool hour I put *Bleak House* top for its sheer prodigality of invention.

About death, I go through different moods, but the times when I can *desire* it are never, I think, those when this world seems harshest. On the contrary, it is just when there seems to be most of Heaven already here that I come nearest to longing for the *patria.* It is the bright frontispiece [which] whets one to read the story itself. All joy (as distinct from mere pleasure, still more amusement) emphasises our pilgrim status: always reminds, beckons, awakes desire. Our best havings are wantings.

TO MRS VERA GEBBERT (NÉE MATHEWS): **from Magdalen College**

17 December 1954

Would you believe it: an American school girl has been expelled from her school for having in her possession a copy of my *Screwtape.* I asked my informant whether it was a Communist school, or a Fundamentalist school, or an RC school, and got the shattering answer, 'No, it was a *select* school'. That puts a chap in his place, doesn't it? . . .

TO JOCELYN GIBB: **from Magdalen College** (Mr
Gibb, who had been the partner of Geoffrey Bles for
a few years, took over the publishing firm of Geoffrey
Bles Ltd when Mr Bles retired in 1954. He had sent Jack
handsomely bound copies of *Surprised by Joy* and *Mere
Christianity*.)

22 December 1954

I never had a handsomer present (both in a bibliophile's and
in Mr Woodhouse's sense of the word *handsome*). Perhaps
these two charming volumes will teach me at last to have
for the bodies of my own books the same reverence I have
for the bodies of all other books. For it is a curious fact that
I never can regard them as being really *books;* the boards
and print, in however mint a condition, remain a mere pre-
tence behind which one sees the scratchy, inky old MS.
You might do a little research to find out if it is so with all
authors. Thank you so much. Who did them?

I am always glad to hear of anyone's taking up that
Cinderella, *The Great Divorce*.

With renewed thanks and all good wishes for Christmas
and the New Year.

TO I. O. EVANS: **from Magdalen College**

22 December 1954

About the word 'hiking' my own objection wd lie only
against its abuse for something so simple as taking an ordinary 'walk': i.e. to the passion for making specialised & self-
conscious stunts out of activities which have hitherto been
as ordinary as shaving or playing with the kitten. Kipling's

Janeites, where he makes a sort of secret-society-ritual out of (of all things!) reading Jane Austen is a specimen. Or professionals on the BBC playing to an audience the same games we used to play for ourselves at children's parties. I expect any day to find a book written on how to swing your stick when you walk or a club (with badges) formed for Singers in the Bath.

There was a grain of seriousness in my sally against the Civil Service.[175] I don't think you have worse taste or worse hearts than other men. But I do think that the State is increasingly tyrannical and you, inevitably, are among the instruments of that tyranny . . . This doesn't matter for you who did most of your service when the subject was still a freeman. For the rising generation it will become a real problem, at what point the policies you are ordered to carry out have become so iniquitous that a decent man must seek some other profession. I expect you really feel at least as strongly as I do about it. All good wishes.

[On 28 December 1954 the Society held 'A Milton Evening in honour of Douglas Bush and C. S. Lewis'. They published for the occasion a pamphlet containing tributes to both men and a facsimile of the following undated letter. William B. Hunter Jr was Secretary of the Society.]

---

[175] This appeared in *Arthurian Torso; Containing the Posthumous Fragment of 'The Figure of Arthur' by Charles Williams and A Commentary on the Arthurian Poems of Charles Williams by C. S. Lewis* (1948).

TO THE MILTON SOCIETY OF AMERICA: from Magdalen College

Mr Hunter informs me that your society has done me an honour above my deserts. I am deeply grateful to be chosen for it and also delighted by the very existence of such a society as yours. May it have a long and distinguished history!

The list of my books which I send in answer to Mr Hunter's request will, I fear, strike you as a very mixed bag. Since he encourages me to 'make a statement' about them, I may point out that there is a guiding thread. The imaginative man in me is older, more continuously operative, and in that sense more basic than either the religious writer or the critic. It was he who made me first attempt (with little success) to be a poet. It was he who, in response to the poetry of others, made me a critic, and, in defence of that response, sometimes a critical controversialist. It was he who, after my conversion led me to embody my religious belief in symbolical or mythopoeic forms, ranging from *Screwtape* to a kind of theologised science-fiction. And it was, of course, he who has brought me, in the last few years to write the series of Narnian stories for children; not asking what children want and then endeavouring to adapt myself (this was not needed) but because the fairy-tale was the *genre* best fitted for what I wanted to say. But you see already that it is dangerous to ask an author to talk about his own work. The difficulty is to make him stop: and I should ill repay your kindness if I did not sternly draw rein . . .

TO 'MRS ASHTON': from Magdalene College, Cambridge

1 January 1955

Few presents can ever have arrived so opportunely as this notepaper of yours ...

This will be my first night in my new home and there is lots of work to do before I go to bed. The books are all on the shelves, but must be put in the right order. I can't bear to look at them till they are ...

TO MRS EDWARD A. ALLEN: from The Kilns

17 January 1955

No, my change of address does not imply retirement—or at least retirement from academic life; what has happened is that Cambridge has given me a Professorship. In many ways I regretted leaving Magdalen, but after nearly thirty years of the tutorial grind, I shall appreciate the less strenuous life of a 'Chair' at Cambridge. I am now settling in there, and think I shall be happy: many of my colleagues are Christians, more than was the case in my old College: my rooms are comfortable, and Cambridge, unlike Oxford, is still a country town, with a farming atmosphere about it. I plan to come back here at intervals during the term, and of course to stop here all the vacations. My brother will live here, so the break with the old life is not as violent as you have pictured it ...

TO 'MRS ASHTON': **from Magdalene College**

2 February 1955

Thanks for your letter. The day before I got a letter from someone else asking me if the 'Silent Planet' was a true story. It's not the first I've had. So I'm beginning to think that some people (and if you don't look out I'll have to include you!) just don't understand what fiction is. When you say what is natural with the intention of making people believe it, that's lying. When you say it with no such intention, that's fiction. But it may be perfectly serious in the sense that people often express their deepest thoughts, speculations, desires etc in a story. Of course it would have been wrong for R. [ansom] to talk bout the land of the Pf. [ifltriggi] when he hadn't really been there, as if he had: because *inside the book* R. is supposed (or pretended) to be telling his story as true. Surely we can have a character in a story telling a lie, and distinguish it from what he ought to have said, although the v. things he is lying about are themselves (from *our* point of view who live outside the story) imaginary?

As for 'writing stories about God', it would be rather a tall order to have a story strictly about God (beginning 'One day God decided' . . .). But to imagine what God might be supposed to have done in other worlds does not seem to be wrong: and a story is only imagining out loud.

It is right and inevitable that we shd be much concerned about the salvation of those we love. But we must be careful not to expect or demand that their salvation shd conform to some ready-made pattern of our own. Some Protestant sects have gone very wrong about this. They have a whole programme of conversion etc. marked out, the same for everyone, and will not believe that anyone can be saved who doesn't go through it 'just so'. But (see the last chapter of my *Problem of Pain*) God has His own way with each soul. There is no evidence that St John underwent the same kind of 'conversion' as St Paul.

It's not essential to believe in the Devil: and I'm sure a man can get to Heaven without being accurate about Methuselah's age. Also, as Macdonald says 'the time for *saying* comes seldom, the time for *being* is always here'. What we practise, not (save at rare intervals) what we preach is usually our great contribution to the conversion of others . . .

TO MISS RUTHER PITTER: from Magdalene College

5 March 1955

I await the marmalade with the sweet-sharp anticipation proper to it. Might it be Hesperian rather than Hyperborean? The word comes thro' Portuguese from *Meli-mela*, 'honey-apples' which was what the benighted Greeks called oranges, and oranges might be the golden apples of the Western Garden. The maker of elder-flower wine is G. Sayer, Hamewith, Alexandra Rd., Malvern, a Roman Catholic, a master at Malvern, a former pupil of mine and the most unselfish man I have ever gone about with. Like Long John Silver he has 'a face as large as a ham'.

It is lovely here (even tho' I have had burst pipes four times this term): unlike Oxford, it still shows the country town just an inch beneath the academic surface. I am having an 'impact', whether 'joyous' or not. If you have seen the 'Cambridge Number' of *The XXth Century* you'll see that the Orthodox

Atheists are v. alarmed at this influx of Christians (Butterfield, Knowles, and C.S.L.). They don't call themselves atheists, though, but 'Humanists', tho' I doubt if they cd write very good Latin and I am sure that E. M. Forster (who is the silliest of the lot: disappointing, for I liked his novels) wd not really enjoy a meeting with Poggio or Scaliger.

Thanks for all the lovely things you say about my Great Fat Book (always scribble, scribble, scribble, Mr Gibbon!).[176] It is glorious *not to be doing* it any longer ...

TO 'MRS ASHTON': from Magdalene College

16 March 1955

I am afraid I am not going to be much help about all the religious bodies mentioned in your letter of March 2nd. I have always in my books been concerned simply to put forward 'mere' Christianity, and am no guide on these (most regrettable) 'interdenominational' questions. I do however strongly object to the tyrannic and unscriptural insolence of anything that calls itself a Church and makes teetotalism a condition of membership. Apart from the more serious objection (that Our Lord Himself turned water into wine and made wine the medium of the only rite He imposed on all His followers) it is so provincial (what I believe you people call 'small town'). Don't they realise that Christianity arose in the Mediterranean world where, then as now, wine was as much part of the normal diet as bread? It was the 17th Century Puritans who first made the universal into a rich man's luxury ...

---

[176] *English Literature in the Sixteenth Century.*

I think I can understand that feeling about a housewife's work being like that of Sisyphus (who was the stone rolling gentleman). But it is surely in reality the most important work in the world. What do ships, railways, mines, cars, government etc. exist for except that people may be fed, warmed, and safe in their own homes? As Dr Johnson said, 'To be happy at home is the end of all human endeavour'. (1st to be happy to prepare for being happy in our own real home hereafter: 2nd in the meantime to be happy in our houses.) We wage war in order to have peace, we work in order to have leisure, we produce food in order to eat it. So your job is the one for which all others exist . . .

TO 'MRS ASHTON': from The Kilns

14 May 1955

My own view about Elisha and the bears[177] (not that I haven't known small boys who'd be much improved by the same treatment!) and other such episodes is something like this. If you take the Bible as a whole, you see a process in which something which, in its eccentric levels (these aren't necessarily the ones that come first in the Book as now arranged) was hardly moral at all, and was in some ways not unlike the Pagan religions, is gradually purged and enlightened till it becomes the religion of the great prophets, and of Our Lord Himself. That whole process is the greatest revelation of God's true nature. At first hardly anything comes through except mere power. Then

---

[177] II Kings II.23.

(v. imperfect) the truth that He is One and there is no other God. Then justice, then mercy, last wisdom.

Of course Our Lord never drank *spirits* (they had no distilled liquors) but of course the wine of the Bible was real fermented wine and alcoholic. The repeated references to the sin of drunkenness in the Bible, from Noah's first discovery of wine down to the warnings in St Paul's epistles, make this perfectly plain. The other theory could be (honestly) held only by a v. ignorant person. One can understand the bitterness of some temperance fanatics if one had ever lived with a drunkard: what one finds it harder to excuse is any educated person telling such lies about history.

I think myself that the shocking reply to the Syrophenician woman[178] (it came alright in the end) is to remind all us Gentile Christians—who forget it easily enough and even flirt with anti-Semitism—that the Hebrews are spiritually *senior* to us, that God *did* entrust the descendants of Abraham with the first revelation of Himself . . .

TO MRS VERA GEBBERT: from The Kilns

25 June 1955

I'm all for a planet without aches or pains or financial worries, but I doubt if I'd care for one of pure intelligence. No senses (no relish of smells, tastes), no affection, no nonsense. I must have a little fooling. I want to tickle a cat's ears and sometimes have a slugging match with an impertinent squirrel . . .

---

[178] Mark VII.24–30.

My lecture has proved a best seller and I've no copies left.[179] . . . You've got it nearly right: the only error being that instead of saying the Great Divide came between the Middle Ages and the Renaissance, I said at great length and emphatically that it *didn't*. But of course 'not' is a very small word and one can't get every fine shade just right!

TO FATHER PETER MILWARD: from **The Kilns**

22 September 1955

What Malory meant, I have no idea. I doubt if he had any clear intention. To use an image I have used before, I think his work is like one of our old English cathedrals to which many generations have contributed in many different styles, so that the total effect was foreseen by no-one and must be regarded as something midway between a work of art and a work of nature. I therefore give up asking what M. meant: we can ask only what his book in fact *means*. And to me it means primarily neither the Grail story nor the Lancelot story but precisely the tension and interlocking between the two.

I know v. little about the Albigensians (except that Denis de Rougemont talks manifest nonsense!). If I undertook a study of the Grail, I shd begin by making up (you perhaps know it already) the history—with v. exact chronology—of the doctrine of Transubstantiation and of contemporary controversies and reactions. I suspect the story is closely connected with these.

---

[179] *De Descriptione Temporum* (1955).

It is certainly a remarkable fact (I hadn't noticed it before) that the post-medieval interest in Arthur has been almost exclusively Protestant. But one must beware of seeking causes too deep. Might it not be simply that the only nation wh. cd regard Arthur as a *national* hero was a Protestant nation.

No, I never read St Ignatius. I must do so one of these days.

This is a short, dry letter, but not thro' lack of interest: I have nearly three weeks' mail to get through, having returned from Ireland to day . . .

TO JOAN LANCASTER (a child in America):
from Magdalene College

16 October 1955

In this country we hardly ever have any snow worth talking about till January, or later. Once we had it at Easter after all the trees had their spring leaves on. So the snow could lie on the trees far heavier than if they had been bare, and there was great destruction in the way of broken branches. We had our first frost last night—this morning the lawns are all grey, with a pale, bright sunshine on them: wonderfully beautiful. And somehow *exciting*. The first beginning of the winter always excites me: it makes me want adventures. I expect our autumn has gentler colours than your fall and it goes far slower. The trees, especially beeches, keep their leaves for weeks & weeks after they have begun to change colour, turning from yellow to gold & from gold to flame-colour.

I never knew a guinea-pig that took any notice of humans (they take plenty of one another). Of those small animals I think Hamsters are the most amusing—and, to tell you the truth, I'm still fond of mice. But the guinea-pigs go well with your learning German. If they talked, I'm sure that is the language they'd speak.

TO EDWARD A. ALLEN: from The Kilns
5 December 1955

I now pronounce the move to Cambridge a great success. However it may be with my new university, my new college is a smaller, softer, more gracious place than my old. The mental and social atmosphere is like the sunny side of a wall in an old garden. The only danger is less I grow too comfortable and over-ripe. The town, after Nuffield-ruined and industrialised Oxford, is delightfully small and I can get a real country walk whenever I want. All my friends say I look younger.

Oddly enough the week-end journies are no trouble at all. I find myself perfectly content in a slow train that crawls thro' green fields stopping at every station. Just because the service is so slow and therefore, in most people's eyes *bad,* these trains are almost empty and I have the compartment (you know the funny little boxes into which an English train is divided?) to myself, where I get through a lot of reading and sometimes say my prayers. A solitary railway journey is, I find, quite excellent for this purpose . . .

TO FATHER PETER MILWARD: from The Kilns

17 December 1955

Thank you for yr letter of Nov. 17. The enclosed card was one of the v. few I have been pleased at getting. Christmas cards in general and the whole vast commercial drive called 'Xmas' are one of my pet abominations: I wish they could die away and leave the Christian feast unentangled. Not of course that even secular festivities are, on their own level, an evil: but the laboured and organised jollity of this—the spurious childlikeness—the half-hearted and sometimes rather profane attempts to keep up some superficial connection with the Nativity—are disgusting. But yr card is most interesting as an application of Japanese style to a Christian subject: and, *me judice*, extremely successful.

Albigensianism, and ancient Celtic Paganism, are both increasingly popular 'sources' for medieval story: but, I fear, they are an *asylum ignorantiae*, chosen because we know so v. little about either. The facts I'd try to hold onto are (1) The name Galahad (Gilead). (2) The resemblance of the Grail to Manna (see, I think, *Wisdom:* the reference is at Cambridge). (3) The (I think proved) Cistercian *provenance*.

Enthusiasm is Ronny Knox's worst book. And of course you won't be misled by de Rougement's nonsense in *L'Amour et l'Occident*. (Not that the ethics of the last chapter—*l'amour cesse d'etre un demon quand il cesse d'etre un dieu*—aren't excellent; but the historical parts are mildly speculative.)

One quite sees the *chilvalric* idea in St Ignatius, but of course the chivalry of *Amadis* (an excellent romance, by the way) is pretty different from that of Arthuriana in general, let alone Sangrealiana in particular.

Oremus pro invicem:[180] Give thanks for me, for a great family anxiety has been lifted and perhaps forever removed. No doubt you have found, like me, that if one regularly transfers people from one's urgent-petition-list to one's thanksgiving list, the mere statistics of the two lists are some corroboration of faith. (Not of course that the efficacy of prayer cd strictly be either proved or disproved by empirical evidence.)

[Dom Bede, who was now in India, had published his autobiography, *The Golden String,* in 1954. Jack's autobiography, *Surprised by Joy,* had been published in September 1955. It was dedicated to Dom Bede, and it was this book Jack was sending him.]

TO DOM BEDE GRIFFITHS, O.S.B.: from Magdalene College

8 February 1956

I have just got yr letter of Jan. 1st., wh. is full of interest. I am having a copy of the book sent you and wd have done so long ago, but I had lost your address.

Yes, I do feel the old Magdalen years to have been a v. important period in both our lives. More generally, I feel the whole of one's youth to be immensely important and even of immense length. The gradual *reading* of one's own life, seeing the pattern emerge, is a great illumination at our age. And partly, I hope, getting *freed from* the past as past by apprehending it as structure. If I ever write a story about someone

---

[180] 'Let us pray for each other.'

like *She* or the Wandering Jew who lived for millennia, I shd make a great point of this: he wd, after 10,000 years, still feel his first 50 years to be the biggest part of his life. I am glad you found a Chestertonian quality in the book. Actually, it seems to me that one can hardly say anything either bad enough or good enough about life.

The one picture that is utterly false is the supposedly real-istic fiction of the XIX century where all the real horrors & heavens are excluded. The reality is a queer mixture of idyll, tragedy, farce, hymn, melodrama: and the characters (even the same characters) far better *and* worse than one ever imagined.

I wd have preferred yr book on Mysticism to be a Penguin, for I think they reach a larger audience than anything else. I look forward to it v. much. I think it is just the thing for you to do.

You are (as you well know) on dangerous ground about Hinduism, but someone must go to dangerous places. One often wonders how different the content of our faith will look when we see it in the total context. Might it be as if one were living on an infinite earth? Further knowledge wd leave our map of, say, the Atlantic quite *correct,* but if it turned out to be the estuary of a great river—and the continent thro' wh. that river flowed turned out to be itself an island—off the shores of a still greater continent—and so on! You see what I mean? Not one jot of Revelation will be proved false: but so many new truths might be added.

By the way, that business of having to look up the same word ten times in one evening is no proof of failing powers. You have simply forgotten that it was exactly like that when we began Latin or even French.

Your Hindus certainly sound delightful. But what do they *deny*? That's always been my trouble with Indians—to find any proposition they wd pronounce false. But truth must surely involve exclusions?

I'm reading Runciman's *Hist. of the Crusades:* a terrible revelation—the old civilisation of the E. Mediterranean destroyed by Turkish barbarians from the East & Frankish barbarians from the West. *Oremus pro invicem.*

TO 'MRS ASHTON': **from Magdalene College**

13 March 1956

You'll find my views about drinks in 'Christian Behaviour' . . . Smoking is much harder to justify. I'd like to give it up but I'd find this v. hard, i.e. I can abstain, but I can't concentrate on anything else while abstaining—not smoking is a whole time job.

Birth control I won't give a view on: I'm certainly not prepared to say that it is always wrong. The doctrines about the Blessed Virgin which you mention are R.C. doctrines aren't they? And as I'm not an R.C. I don't think I need bother about them. But the habit (of various Protestant sects) of plastering the landscape with religious slogans about the Blood of the Lamb etc. is a different matter. There is no question here of doctrinal difference: we agree with the doctrines they are advertising. What we disagree with is their taste. Well, let's go on disagreeing but don't let us *judge*. What doesn't suit us may suit possible converts of a different type.

My model here is the behaviour of the congregation at a 'Russian Orthodox' service, where some sit, some lie on their faces, some stand, some kneel, some walk about, and *no one takes the slightest notice of what anyone else is doing.* That is good sense, good manners, and good Christianity. 'Mind one's own business' is a good rule in religion as in other things ...

TO MRS R. E. HALVORSON: from Magdalene College

[March 1956]

One must first distinguish the effect which music has on people like me who are musically illiterate and get only the emotional effect, and that which it has on real musical scholars who perceive the structure and get an intellectual satisfaction as well.

Either of these effects is, I think, ambivalent from the religious point of view: i.e. *each* can be a preparation for or even a medium for meeting God but can also be a distraction and impediment. In that respect music is not different from a good many other things, human relations, landscape, poetry, philosophy. The most relevant one is wine which can be used sacramentally or for getting drunk or neutrally.

I think every *natural* thing which is not in itself sinful can become the servant of the spiritual life, but none is automatically so. When it is not, it becomes either just trivial (as music is to millions of people) or a dangerous idol. The emotional effect of music may be not only a distraction (to some people at some times) but a delusion: i.e. feeling certain emotions in church they mistake them for religious emotions when they may be wholly natural. That means that even genuinely religious emotion is only a servant. No soul is saved by having it or damned by lacking it. The love we are commanded to have for God and our neighbour is a state of the *will*, not of the affections (though if they ever also play their part so much the better). So that the test of music or religion or even visions if one has them is always the same — do they make one more obedient, more God-centered, and neighbour-centered and *less self-centred*? 'Though I speak with the tongues of Bach and Palestrina and have not charity etc.!'

TO 'MRS ARNOLD': from The Kilns

2 April 1956

I'm a little, but unamusedly, surprised that my *Surprised by Joy* causes you envy. I doubt if you really would have enjoyed my life much better than your own. And the whole modern world ludicrously overvalues books and learning and what (I loathe the word) they call 'culture'. And of course culture itself is the greatest sufferer by this error: for second things are always corrupted when they are put first . . .

TO FATHER PETER MILWARD: from Magdalene College

9 May 1956

You need not be afraid of telling me 'only what I know already' about the Grail legend, for indeed I know v. little. If you think otherwise, you are perhaps confusing my interest in C. [harles] W. [illiams] with C. W.'s interest in the legend.

For my own part, I am v. puzzled as to what exactly we are doing when we study — not this or that work of art — but a myth in abstract. Supposing (*pontionis causa*) that what people mean when they say 'The Grail is the Caldron of the Dead' is true, *what* do they mean? More briefly, what does *is* mean in such a sentence? It is not the *is* of equality (2X6 is 3X4) nor of classification (a horse is a mammal) nor of allegory (this Rock is Christ). How can an imagined object in one story 'be' an imagined object in another story?

About my Inaugural—aren't you rather forgetting that I was trying to fix merely the *cultural* change? From my angle even the original conversion of Europe, you remember, had to be ranked as a minor change. After that, you cd hardly expect the Reformation to be v. prominent. To be sure, if my point of view had been different, it wd have become fundamental and you and I wd of course differ v. widely about its character.

TO JOAN LANCASTER: **from The Kilns**

26 June 1956

You describe your Wonderful Night v. well. That is, you describe the place & the people and the night and the feeling of it all, very well—but not the *thing* itself—the setting but not the jewel. And no wonder! Wordsworth often does just the same. His *Prelude* (you're bound to read it about ten years' hence. Don't try it now, or you'll only spoil it for later reading) is full of moments in which everything except the *thing* itself is described. If you become a writer you'll be trying to describe the *thing* all your life: and lucky if, out of dozens of books, one or two sentences, just for a moment, come near to getting it across.

About *amn't I, aren't I,* and *am I not,* of course there are no right and wrong answers about language in the sense in which there are right and wrong answers in Arithemetic. 'Good English' is whatever educated people talk: so that what is good in one place or time wd not be so in another. *Amn't* was good fifty years ago in the North of Ireland where I was brought up, but bad in Southern England. *Aren't I* wd have been hideously bad in Ireland but was good in England. And of course I just don't know which (if either) is good in modern Florida. Don't take any notice of teachers and text-books in such matters. Nor of logic. It is good to say 'More than one passenger was hurt' although *more than one* equals at least two and therefore logically the verb ought to be plural *were* not singular *was!* What really matters is:

(1) Always try to use the language so as to make quite clear what you mean and make sure yr sentence couldn't mean anything else.

(2) Always prefer the plain direct word to the long, vague one. Don't *implement* promises, but *keep* them.

(3) Never use abstract nouns when concrete ones will do. If you mean 'more people died' don't say 'mortality rose'.

(4) In writing. Don't use adjectives which merely tell us how you want us to *feel* about the thing you are describing. I mean, instead of telling us a thing was 'terrible', describe it so that we'll be terrified. Don't say it was 'delightful': make *us* say 'delightful' when we've read the description. You see, all those words (horrifying, wonderful, hideous, exquisite) are only like saying to your readers 'Please will you do my job for me'.

(5) Don't use words too big for the subject. Don't say 'infinitely' when you mean 'very'; otherwise you'll have no word left when you want to talk about something *really* infinite ...

TO CHRISTOPHER DERRICK: from The Kilns

2 August 1956

(I'd sooner you called me Lewis *tout court,* both for old acquaintance sake and because, as Brightman—was he before your time?—used to say, 'When I was a young man no one was *called* professor except conjurors.'[181])

All universities are now N.I.C.E.s when it comes to buildings: tho' I met a civilised American don once who claimed that his own university (I forgot which) had got over that malady and, looking at the Parks with their new laboratories ... observed, 'I see you are still in the Stone Age'.

You ought to have been spending (if you haven't already done so) on Tolkien's 3 vol. *Lord of the Rings* the time you spent on OHEL. *The Lord* is the book we have all been waiting for.[182] And it shows too, which cheers, that there are thousands left in Israel who have not bowed the knee to Leavis ...

---

[181] Frank Edward Brightman (1856–1932) had been dead some years before Christopher Derrick read English under Jack at Magdalen. Brightman had taken his degree in 1879 and become a priest in 1885. After serving as a Librarian of Pusey House 1884–1903, he was a Fellow of Magdalen College 1902–32.

[182] After what seemed a very long gestation to Jack, Professor Tolkien's *The Lord of the Rings* had been published in three volumes during 1954–55.

TO FATHER PETER MILWARD: **from The Kilns**

22 September 1956

Tolkien's book is not an allegory—a form he dislikes. You'll get nearest to his mind on such subjects by studying his essay on Fairy Tales in the *Essays Presented to Charles Williams*. His root idea of narrative art is 'sub-creation'—the making of a secondary world. What you wd call 'a pleasant story for the children' wd be to him *more serious* than an allegory. But for *his* views, read the essay, wh. is indispensible.

My view wd be that a good myth (i.e. a story out of which ever varying meanings will grow for different readers and in different ages) is a higher thing than an allegory (into which *one* meaning has been put). Into an allegory a man can put only what he already knows: in a myth he puts what he does not yet know and cd not come to know in any other way.

[Joy Davidman Gresham had been divorced from her husband, William Lindsay Gresham, in 1953 and in that year she took up residence in England with her sons David and Douglas. They lived in London until August 1955 when they moved to 10 Old High Street, Headington. When it became clear that the Home Office would not renew Joy's permit to remain in Great Britain, Jack entered into a civil marriage with her so that she could remain in England. This took place in the Oxford Registry Office on 23 April 1956. Joy had for a long while been suffering from what seemed rheumatism. However, after she was taken to the Wingfield-Morris Orthopaedic Hospital, Oxford, on 19 October 1956 she was found to be suffering from cancer.]

TO A FORMER PUPIL: from Magdalene College

14 November 1956

I wish you would pray very hard for a lady called Joy Gresham and me. I am like v. shortly to be both a bridegroom and widower, for she has cancer. You need not mention this till the marriage (which will be at a hospital bedside if it occurs) is announced. I'll tell you the whole story some day . . .

TO ARTHUR GREEVES: from The Kilns

25 November 1956

Joy is in hospital, suffering from cancer. The prospects are 1. A tiny 100th chance of ultimate cure. 2. A reasonable probability of some years more of (tolerable) life. 3. A real danger that she may die in a few months.

It will be a great tragedy for me to lose her. In the meantime, if she gets over this bout and emerges from hospital she will no longer be fit to live alone so she must come and live here. That means (in order to avoid scandal) that our marriage must shortly be published. W. has written to Janie and the Ewarts to tell them I am getting married, and I didn't want the news to take you by surprise. I know you will pray for her and for me: and for W., to whom also, the loss if we lose her, will be great.

TO MR LUCAS: from Magdalene College

6 December 1956

(1) I think there may be *some* humour [in the New Testament]. Matt. IX.12 (People who are well don't need doctors) could well be said in a way that wd be v. funny to everyone

present except the Pharisees. So might Matt. XVII.25. And in Mark X.30—quickly slipping in 'tribulations' among all the assets—that cd be funny too. And of course the Parable of the Unjust Steward (it's comic element is well brought out in Dorothy Sayers' excellent *Man Born to Be King*).

(2) If there were more humour, should we (modern Occidentals) *see* it? I've been much struck in conversation with a Jewess by the extent to which Jews see humour in the O.T. where we don't. Humour varies so much from culture to culture.

(3) How much wd be recorded? We know (John XXI.25) that we have only a tiny fraction of what Our Lord said. Wd the Evangelists, anxious to get across what was vitally necessary, *include* it? They told us nothing about His appearance, clothes, physical habits—none of what a modern biographer would put in.

TO FATHER PETER MILWARD: **from The Kilns**
10 December 1956

One *historical* point first. There cd not have been an allegory about the atomic bomb when Tolkien began his romance for he did so before it was invented. That, however, has little to do with the theoretical question: tho' it has much to do with the extreme danger, in individual cases, of applying allegorical interpretations. We shd. probably find that many particular allegories critics read into Langland or Spenser are impossible for just that sort of reason, if we knew all the facts. I am also convinced that the wit of man *cannot* devise a story in wh. the wit of some other man cannot find an allegory.

For the rest, I wd agree that the word can be used in wider or narrower senses. Indeed, in so far as the things unseen are manifested by the things seen, one might from one point of view call the whole material universe an allegory. The truth is it's one of those words which needs defining in each context where one uses it. It wd be disastrous if anyone took your statement that the Nativity is the greatest of all allegories to mean that the physical event was merely *feigned*!

Who is the man on your stamp? Looks like a tough to me. Thanks for pleasant card, and all good wishes.

[The following announcement appeared in *The Times* on 24 December 1956, p. 8: 'A marriage has taken place between Professor C. S. Lewis, of Magdalene College, Cambridge, and Mrs Joy Gresham, now a patient in the Churchill Hospital, Oxford. It is requested that no letters be sent.']

TO MISS DOROTHY L. SAYERS: from The Kilns

24 December 1956

Thanks for your kind card. You may see in *The Times* a notice of my marriage to Joy Gresham. She is in hospital (cancer) and not likely to live; but if she gets over this go she must be given a home here. You will not think that anything wrong is going to happen. Certain problems do not arise between a dying woman and an elderly man. What I am mainly acquiring is two (nice) stepsons. Pray for us all, and God bless you.

TO PROFESSOR CLYDE S. KILBY: **from Magdalene College** (about his novel *Till We Have Faces,* which was published in September 1956)

10 February 1957

An author doesn't necessarily understand the meaning of his own story better than anyone else, so I give you *my* account of the TWHF simply for what's it's worth. The 'levels' I am conscious of are these.

1. A work of (supposed) *historical* imagination. A guess at what it might have been like in a little barbarous state on the borders of the Hellenistic world with Greek culture just beginning to affect it. Hence the change from the old priest (of a very normal fertility mother-goddess) to Arnom: Stoic allegorisations of the myths standing to the original cult rather as Modernism to Christianity (but this is a parallel, not an allegory). Much that you take as allegory was intended solely as realistic detail. The Wagon men are Nomads from the steppes. The children made mud pies not for symbolic purposes but because children do. The Pillar Room is simply a room. The Fox is such an educated Greek slave as you might find at a barbarous court—and so on.

2. Psyche is an instance of the *anima naturaliter Christiana* making the best of the Pagan religion she is brought up in and thus being guided (but always 'under the cloud', always in terms of her own imagination or that of her people) towards the true God. She is in some ways like Christ not because she is a symbol of Him but because every good man or woman is like Christ. What else could they be like? But of course my interest is primarily in Orual.

3. Orual is (not a symbol but) an instance, a 'case', of human affection in its natural condition: true, tender, suffering, but in the long run, tyrannically possessive and ready to turn to hatred when the beloved ceases to be its possession. What such love particularly cannot stand is to see the beloved passing into a sphere where it cannot follow. All this, I hoped, would stand in a mere story in its own right. But—

4. Of course I had always in mind its close parallel to what is probably at this moment going on in at least five families in your own town at this moment. Someone becomes a Christian, or, in a family nominally Christian already, does something like becoming a missionary or entering a religious order. The others suffer a sense of outrage. What they love is being taken from them! The boy must be mad! And the conceit of him! Or is there something in it after all? Let's hope it is only a phase! If only he'd listen to his natural advisers! Oh come back, come back, be sensible, be the dear son we used to know. Now I, as a Christian, have a good deal of sympathy with these jealous, puzzled, suffering people (for they do suffer and out of their suffering much of the bitterness against religion arises). I believe the thing is common. There is very nearly a touch of it in Luke II, 48, 'Son, *why hast thou* so dealt with us?' And is the reply easy for a loving heart to bear?

TO SISTER PENELOPE, C.S.M.V.: from Magdalene College

Ash Wednesday [6 March 1957]

Yes, it is true. I married (knowingly) a very sick, save by near-miracle a dying, woman. She is the Joy Davidman whose *Smoke on the Mountain* I think you read. She is in the Wingfield Morris Hospital at Headington. When I see her each week end she is, to a layman's eyes (but not to a doctor's knowledge) in full convalescence, better every week. The disease is of course cancer: by which I lost my mother, my father, and my favourite aunt. She knows her own state of course: I wd allow no lies to be told to a grown-up and a Christian. As you can imagine new beauty and new tragedy have entered my life. You wd be surprised (or perhaps you would not?) to know how much of a strange sort of happiness and even gaiety there is between us . . .

I don't doubt that Joy and I (and David & Douglas, the two boys) will have your prayers. Douglas is an absolute charmer (11½). David, at first sight less engaging, is at any rate a comically appropriate stepson for me (13), being almost exactly what I was—bookworm, pedant, and a bit of a prig.

TO MRS EDWARD A. ALLEN: from The Kilns

16 March 1957

I think I haven't told you my news. I have lately married a lady who is very ill and probably dying: I shall be left with two stepsons. Thus, as you may guess, great beauty and great tragedy have come into my life. We need your prayers more than ever . . .

In my job one hardly works to a schedule of hours you know: nor, apart from lectures and committees, can one draw any hard and fast line between what is and what is not 'work'. I couldn't tell you which of the books I read are professional reading and which are for pleasure. In *writing* I do regard all non-academic works (all the ones you have read) as being leisure occupations. They have been done at odd moments: nothing unusual about that for better authors would have said the same—Caesar, Chaucer, Sidney, Fielding, Lamb, Jane Austen and Trollope (the last incredibly copious: he wrote most of his novels on railways journeys).

[Jack had hitherto been using the word 'marriage' to refer to the civil marriage of 23 April 1956 as well as a real marriage (see the letter to Arthur Greeves of 25 November 1956) which might take place. What he and Joy considered the real one—the Christian sacrament—was performed by Father Peter Bide in the Wingfield-Morris Hospital at 11 A.M. on 21 March 1957.]

TO SISTER MADALEVA, C.S.C.: **from Magdalene College**

8 May 1957

It is always nice to hear from you again. But alas, I was never less likely to come to America than now. I am newly married and to a dying woman. Every moment is spent at her bedside. I am sure we may both count on your prayers: and I, your prayers for help and guidance in the difficult responsibility of bringing up two orphan stepsons. I have only one qualification, if it is one: these two boys are now facing the very same calamity that befell my brother and me at about their age.

TO SISTER PENELOPE, C.S.M.V.: from **The Kilns**

12 May 1957

The idea of anyone seeking a 'sober, male opinion' from such a wretched man of business as I am! I would advise you to do as I have at last done: put yourself in the hands of a good Literary Agent (Curtis Brown, Henrietta St., Covent Garden, is probably the best) and never deal direct with publishers again. An agent will of course take his percentage off your royalties, but then he will probably get you better terms.

One of my publishers, on hearing that I was in touch with Brown, motored down to Cambridge at once and offered to raise the terms on all previous books if I wd promise not to! That is surely significant. Also, which may be no less important, it will save you a lot of work and thought and frustration of a sort that people like you and me are not good at. ('Study to be quiet—'!)

Joy is now home here, completely bed-ridden. Though the doctors hold out no ultimate hope, the progress of the disease does seem to be temporarily arrested, to a degree they never expected. There is little pain, often none, her strength increases, and she eats and sleeps well. This has the paradoxical (but, come to think of it, natural) result of giving her lower spirits and less peace. The more *general* health, of course the stronger is the instinctive will to live. Forbidden and torturing hopes *will* intrude (on us both). In short, a dungeon is never harder to bear than when the door is opened and the sunshine & birdsongs float in. It is the doom of Tantalus. Pray hard for us both, dear sister.

TO MISS DOROTHY L. SAYERS: from **The Kilns**

25 June 1957

I ought to tell you my own news. On examination it turned out that Joy's previous marriage, made in her pre-Christian days, was no marriage: the man had a wife still living. The Bishop of Oxford said it was not the present policy to approve re-marriage in such cases, but that his view did not bind the conscience of any individual priest. Then dear Father Bide (do you know him?) who had come to lay his hands on Joy—for he has on his record what looks v. like one miracle—without being asked and merely on being told the situation at once said he wd marry us. So we had a bedside marriage with a Nuptial Mass.

When I last wrote to you I would not even have wished this: you will gather (and may say 'guessed as much') that my feelings have changed. They say a rival often turns a friend into a lover. Thanatos, certainly (they say) approaching but at an uncertain speed, is a most efficient rival for this purpose. We soon learn to love what we know we must lose. I hope you give us your blessing: I know you'll give us your prayers.

She is home now, not because she is better (tho' in fact she *seems* amazingly better) but because they can do no more for her at the Wingfield: totally bed-ridden but—you'd be surprised—we have much gaiety and even some happiness. Indeed, the situation is not easy to describe. My heart is breaking and I was never so happy before: at any rate there is more in life than I knew about. My own physical pains lately (which were among the severest I've known) had an odd element of relief in them . . .

TO JOAN LANCASTER: from The Kilns

18 July 1957

They tell me that one shd never try to learn Spanish and Italian at the same time. The fact that they are so alike of course helps one a bit over the meanings of words (but Latin wd help you almost equally for both) but it makes a confusion in one's mind about grammar and idioms—in the end one makes a horrid soup out of both. I don't know Spanish, but I know there are lovely things in Italian to read. You'll like Boiardo, Ariosto, and Tasso. By the way good easy Latin reading to keep one's Latin up with is the New Testament in Latin. Any Roman Catholic bookshop will have one: say you want a copy of the 'Vulgate (VULGATE) New Testament'. *Acts* goes specially well in Latin.

I don't think being good *always* goes with having fun: a martyr being tortured by Nero, or a resistance movement man refusing to give away his friends when tortured by the Germans, were being good but not having fun. And even in ordinary life there are things that wd be fun to me but I mustn't do them because they wd spoil other people's fun.

But *of course* you are quite right if you mean that giving up fun for no reason except that you think it's 'good' to give it up, is all nonsense. Don't the ordinary old rules about telling the truth and doing as you'd be done by tell one pretty well which kinds of fun one may have and which not? But provided the thing is in itself right, the more one likes and the less one has to 'try to be good', the better. A *perfect* man wd never act from sense of duty; he'd always *want* the right thing more than the wrong one. Duty is only a substitute for love (of God and of other people), like a crutch which is a substitute for a leg. Most of us need the crutch at times: but of course it's idiotic to use the crutch when our own legs (our loves, tastes, habits etc) can do the journey on their own!

TO MISS JANE GASKELL: **from The Kilns** (Her first novel, *Strange Evil,* had just been published.)

2 September 1957

My wife and I have just been reading your book and I want to tell you that I think it a quite amazing achievement — incomparably beyond anything I could have done at that age. The story runs, on the whole, very well and there is some real imagination in it. The idea of the gigantic spoiled brat (had you a horrid baby brother once?) is really excellent: perhaps even profound. Unlike most modern fantasies your book also has a firm core of civilised ethics. On all these grounds, hearty congratulations.

On the other hand there is no reason at all why your next book should not be at least twice as good. I hope you will not think it impertinent if I mention (this is only one man's opinion of course) some mistakes you can avoid in future.

1. In all stories which take one to another world, the difficulty (as you and I know) is to make something happen when we've got there. In fact, one needs 'filling'. Yours is quite sufficient in *quantity* (almost too much) but not quite, I think, of the right sort. Aren't all these economic problems and religious differences too like the politics of our own world? Why go to faerie for what we already have? Surely the wars of faerie should be high, reckless, heroical, romantic wars — concerned with the possession of a beautiful queen or

an enchanted treasure? Surely the diplomatic phase of them should be represented not by conferences (which, on your own showing, are as dull as ours) but by ringing words of gay taunt, stern defiance, or Quixotic generosity, interchanged by great warriors with sword in hand before the battle joins?

2. This is closely connected with the preceding. In a fantasy every precaution must be taken never to break the spell, to do nothing which will wake the reader and bring him back with a bump to the common earth. But this is what you sometimes do. The moving van on which they travel is a dull invention at best, because we can't help conceiving it as mechanical. But when you add upholstered seats, lavatories, and restaurants, I can't go on believing in faerie for a moment. It has all turned into commonplace technological luxury! Similarly even a half-fairy *ought not* climb a fairyhill carrying a suitcase full of new nighties. All magic dies at this touch of the commonplace. (Notice, too, the disenchanting implication that the faeries can't make for themselves *lingerie* as good as they can get—not even in Paris, which wd be bad enough—but, of all places, in London.)

3. Never use adjectives or adverbs which are mere appeals to the reader to feel as you want him to feel. He won't do it just because you ask him: you've got to *make* him. No good *telling* us a battle was 'exciting'. If *you* succeeded in exciting us the adjective will be unnecessary: if you don't, it will be useless. Don't tell us the jewels had an 'emotional' glitter; make us feel the emotion. I can hardly tell you how important this is.

4. You are too fond of long adverbs like 'dignifiedly', which are not nice to pronounce. I hope, by the way, you

always write by ear not by eye. Every sentence shd be tested on the tongue, to make sure that the sound of it has the hardness or softness, the swiftness or languor, which the meaning of it calls for.

5. Far less about clothes, please! I mean, ordinary clothes. If you had given your fairies strange and beautiful clothes and described *them*, there might be something in it. But your heroine's tangerine skirt! For whom do you write? No *man* wants to hear how she was dressed, and the sort of women who does seldom reads fantasy: if she reads anything it is more like to be the Women's Magazines. By the way, these are a baneful influence on your mind and imagination. Beware! they may kill your talent. If you *can't* keep off them, at least, after each debauch, give your imagination a good mouth-wash by a reading (or wd it be a re-reading) of the *Odyssey,* Tolkien's *Lord of the Rings,* E. R. Eddison's *The Worm Ouroboros,* the romances of Stephens, and all the early mythical plays of W. B. Yeats. Perhaps a touch of Lord Dunsany too.

6. Names not too good. They ought to be beautiful and suggestive as well as strange: not merely odd like *Enaj* (wh. sounds as if it came out of Butler's *Erewhon*).

I hope all this does not enrage you. You'll get so much bad advice that I felt I must give you some of what I think good.

TO DOM BEDE GRIFFITHS, O.S.B.: **from The Kilns**

24 September 1957

My wife's condition, contrary to the expectation of the doctors, has improved, if not miraculously (but who knows?) at any rate wonderfully. (How wd one say that in Latin?) No one, least of all herself, encourages me to dream of a permanent recovery, but this is a wonderful reprieve. Tho' she is still a cripple, her *general* health is better than I have ever seen it, and she says she has never been happier.

It is nice to have arrived at all this by something which began in Agape, proceeded to Philia, then became Pity, and only after that, Eros. As if the highest of these, Agape, had successfully undergone the sweet humiliation of an incarnation.

My own trouble, after one terrible fortnight, has taken a turn for the better. No one suggests that the disease is *either* curable *or* fatal. It normally accompanies that fatal disease we call Senility! but no one knows why I have got it so early (comparatively) in life ...

TO SISTER PENELOPE, C.S.M.V.: from Magdalene College

6 November 1957

Whatever our state had been a letter from you wd always have cheered and comforted. In reality it is beyond all we dared to hope. When they sent Joy home from hospital last April, they sent her home to die. The experienced nurses expected her life to be a matter of weeks. She could not even be moved in bed without a lifting squad of three of us, and, with all our care, we nearly always hurt her.

Then it began to appear that the cancer had been arrested: the diseased spots in the bones were no longer spreading or multiplying. Then the tide began to turn—they were disappearing. New bone was being made. And so little by little till the woman who cd hardly be moved in bed can now walk about the house and into the garden—limping and with a stick, but walking. She even found herself getting up *unconsciously* to answer the telephone the other day. It is the unconsciousness that is the real triumph—the body wh. could not obey the most planned volition now begins to act on its own. General health and spirits excellent. *Of course the sword of Damocles still hangs over us: or, shd I say, we* are forced to be aware of the sword wh. really overhangs all mortals.

Did I tell you I also have a bone disease? It is neither mortal nor curable: a prematurely senile loss of calcium. I was v. crippled and had much pain all summer but am in a good spell now. I was losing calcium just about as fast as Joy was gaining it, and a bargain (if it were one) for wh. I'm v. thankful. So continue your prayers but now with fervent thanks. I am almost frightened by God's mercies: how can we ever be good enough?

I've been reading some of the books you mention. I was busy on Macrobius, Chalcidius, Boethius, & Pseudo-Dionysius for a book wh. will probably be called *Prolegomena to Medieval Poetry.*[183] That late antique period when a sort of synthesised high Paganism (mainly neo-Platonic) and Christian theology were both contending and influencing each other is fascinating . . .

---

[183] This is the book which eventually became *The Discarded Image: An Introduction to Medieval and Renaissance Literature* (1964).

TO ROGER LANCELYN GREEN: from The Kilns
(Green had sent Jack a copy of his book, *Into Other Worlds: Space-Flight in Fiction, from Lucian to Lewis*)

17 November 1957

Nicest of all was getting your new book, which I should still be reading if Joy, after the manner of wives (how I have 'dwindled into a husband'!) had not taken it out of my hands.

What a lot there is in it, and how much I didn't know! The Lunar Hoax interested me especially, not primarily as a hoax, tho' that is good fun too, but because some of it is really the best invention and description of extra-terrestrial *landscape* (the animals are less good) before *First Men in the Moon.*

I think you are hard on Wells. Obviously, he touches off something in you which he didn't in me. I still think that a v. good book indeed and don't dislike the Selenites themselves as much as you do. Bedford is of course a cad. I'm with you about the 'ghastly materialistic' tenacity of Stapledon's humans. And of course I enjoyed the kind things you say about myself: as also the moving inscription in my copy.

By the way, Douglas, when home for half term,[184] quite unsolicited, produced a testimonial to Shirard whom he described as 'very popular' and then (oh the delicious superiority of small fry over smaller) 'one of the most promising New-Boys he had known'. So strike the stars with your sub-

---

[184] David and Douglas Gresham were already in school at Dane Court in Pryford, Surrey, when Roger Lancelyn Green's eldest son, Scirard, arrived there.

lime head, for this, you know, is 'beyond all Greek, beyond all Roman fame'. We both send our love to June and you.

TO JOCELYN GIBB: **from The Kilns** (his publisher, who had sent him some honey)

Christmas Day 1957

Your parcel, as it happened, was opened before your letter, so you had a good joke *in absentia.* We did wonder a little whether there were any core or whether we were peeling an onion. But the golden treasures surpassed the wrappings in value more than they surpassed it in bulk: I had a stanza of this edible poem for breakfast to-day with much enjoyment. Thank you very much.

Marry gup! The hymn, which you miscall a psalm, truly hath in that place 'to pay the price of sinne', which paying the price of sinne I do suppose to be all one with redeeming.[185] Go to. You lie at the catch, neighbour. Nor is it unfit that I admonish printers concerning printing and publishers concerning publishing, the which if I now were to handle I might chance to recall that old sawe *ex sutore medicus* and scribble the ultracrepidations of cobblers. With what stomach, think you, would Tullie have borne the Salii going about to mende his periods?

Mid-day dinner with a generous burgandy is perhaps a mistake . . . *Vinum locutum est.* I wish you a merry Christmas retrospectively.

---

[185] He is talking about a passage in Ch. IV of his *Reflections on the Psalms* which was published in September 1958.

TO MRS EDWARD A. ALLEN: from The Kilns

1 February 1958

I quite agree with the Archbishop that no *sin,* simply as such, should be made a *crime.* Who the deuce are our rulers to enforce their opinions about sin on us?—a lot of professional politicians, often venal time-servers, whose opinion on a moral problem in one's life we shd attach very little value to. Of course many acts which are sins against God are also injuries to our fellow-citizens, and must on that account, but only on that account, be made crimes. But of all the sins in the world I shd have thought homosexuality was the one that least concerns the State. We hear too much of the State. Government is at its best a necessary evil. Let's keep it in its place.

TO MISS MURIEL BRADBROOK: from Magdalene College

18 April 1958

I am glad you raised this question. I was maintaining yesterday that when a bifurcation of meaning is sufficiently old and wide, the resulting senses often enter the linguistic consciousness of each new generation as mere homophones, and their reunion has the explosion of a pun. But on the other hand, when the bifurcation is less wide there may be a period during which the speakers really do not know in which sense they are using the word. When *we* speak of a 'simple meal' do we always know whether we mean (a) not complicated, (b) modest, not 'posh', or (c) easy to prepare? (Of course they needn't coincide. A haunch of venison is more 'posh' than a shepherd's pie, but *less* complicated, and helpings of caviare out of a jar are easier to prepare than either.) In the passage you quote, almost all of the senses of 'sad' (including that which would yield a tautology) seem to me possible, and I suggest that Webster may not have made up his mind between them. Cf. the passage in Boswell where Goldsmith lets Johnson tell him what he meant by 'slow' in the first line of the *Traveller*.

TO MRS JOHN WATT: **from The Kilns** (following a holiday he and Joy had in Ireland with Arthur Greeves)

28 August 1958

All goes amazing well with us. My wife walks up the wooded hill behind our house and shoots—or more stictly shoots *at*—pigeons, picks peas and beans, and heaven knows what.

We had a holiday—you might call it a belated honeymoon—in Ireland and were lucky enough to get that perfect fortnight at the beginning of July. We visited Louth, Down, and Donegal, and returned drunk with blue mountains, yellow beaches, dark fuchsia, breaking waves, braying donkeys, peat-smell, and the heather just then beginning to bloom.

We flew to Ireland, for, tho' both of us wd prefer ship to plane, her bones, and even mine, could not risk a sudden lurch. It was the first flight either of us had ever experienced and we found it, after one initial moment of terror, enchanting. The cloud-scape seen from above is a new world of beauty—and then the rifts in the clouds through which one sees (like Tennyson's Tithonus) 'a glimpse of that dark world where I was born'. We had clear weather over the Irish Sea and the first Irish headland, brightly sunlit, stood out from the dark sea (it's very dark when you're looking directly *down* on it) like a bit of enamel.

As for the picture in *The Observer,* even our most ribald friends don't pretend it has any resemblance to either of us.[186] As a spiritualist picture of the ectoplasms of a dyspeptic orangutan and an immature Sorn it may have merits, but not as a picture of us . . .

TO MRS JOHN WATT: from The Kilns

30 October 1958

I was much interested to hear of the 'Eye on research' programme on TV: myself, I'm glad to say I don't often see television, but my brother, who sometimes looks in on a friend's set, says he can well understand your feelings of 'horror and terror'. He adds that to him the most terrible part of the business is the implicit assumption that progress is an inevitable process like decay, and that the only important thing in life is to increase the comfort of homo sapiens, at whatever cost to posterity and to the other inhabitants of the planet. I can well imagine how a 'scientific' programme would jar after watching such a stately ceremony as the opening of Parliament.

---

[186] Jack's essay 'Willing Slaves of the Welfare State' appeared in *The Observer* (29 July 1958) p. 6. Accompanying it was a photograph of Jack and Joy by Michael Peto. Speaking of this ghastly photograph, Jack told me he thought it made him look 'at least 120 years old'.

TO MRS HOOK: from **The Kilns**

29 December 1958

By an allegory I mean a composition (whether pictorial or literary) in wh. immaterial realities are represented by feigned physical objects e.g. a pictured Cupid allegorically represents erotic love (which in reality is an experience, not an object occupying a given area of space) or, in Bunyan a giant represents Despair.

If Aslan represented the immaterial Deity in the same way in which Giant Despair represents Despair, he would be an allegorical figure. In reality however he is an invention giving an imaginary answer to the question, 'What might Christ become like if there really were a world like Narnia and He chose to be incarnate and die and rise again in *that* world as He actually has done in ours?' This is not allegory at all. So in *Perelandra*. This also works out a *supposition*. ('Suppose, even now, in some other planet there were a first couple undergoing the same that Adam and Eve underwent here, but successfully'.)

Allegory and such supposals differ because they mix the real and the unreal in different ways. Bunyan's picture of Giant Despair does not start from supposal at all. It is not a supposition but a *fact* that despair can capture and imprison a human soul. What is unreal (fictional) is the giant, the castle, and the dungeon. The Incarnation of Christ in another world is mere supposal: but *granted* the supposition, He would really have been a physical object in that world as He was in Palestine and His death on the Stone Table would have been a physical event no less than his death on Calvary. Similarly, *if* the angels (who I believe to be real beings in the actual universe) have that relation to the Pagan gods which they are assumed to have in *Perelandra*, they might *really* manifest themselves in real form as they did to Ransom. Again, Ransom (to some extent) plays the role of Christ not because he allegorically represents Him (as Cupid represents falling in love) but because in reality every real Christian is really called upon in some measure to *enact* Christ. Of course Ransom does this rather more spectacularly than most. But that does not mean that he does it allegorically. It only means that fiction (at any rate my kind of fiction) chooses extreme cases.

There is no conscious connection between any of the phonetic elements in my 'Old Solar' words and those of any actual language. I am always playing with syllables and fitting them together (purely by ear) to see if I can hatch up new words that please me. I want them to have an emotional, not intellectual, suggestiveness: the heaviness of *glund* for as huge a planet as Jupiter, the vibrating, tintillating quality of *viritrilbia* for the subtlety of Mercury, the liquidity . . . of Maleldil. The only exception I am aware of is *hnau* which *may* (but I don't know) have been influenced by Greek *nous*.

TO PROFESSOR CLYDE S. KILBY: from Magdalene College

20 January 1959

As to Professor Van Til's point it is certainly scriptural to say that 'to as many as believed He gave power to become the sons of God', and the statement 'God became Man that men might become gods' is Patristic. Of course Van Til's wording 'that man must *seek* to *ascend* in the *scale* of life' with its suggestions (a) That we could do this by our own efforts, (b) That the difference between God and Man is a difference of position on a 'scale of life' like the difference between a (biologically) 'higher' and a (biologically) 'lower' creature, is wholly foreign to my thought.

I think an anthology of extracts from a living writer would make both him and the collector look rather ridiculous and I'm sure publishers would not agree to the plan. I am sorry to reply so ungraciously to a proposal which does me so much honour. But I'm convinced it would not do.

TO FATHER PETER BIDE: **from Magdalene College**
(Father Bide is the priest who married Jack and Joy, and now his wife was dying from cancer.)

29 April 1959

Indeed, indeed we both will. I don't see how any degree of faith can exclude the dismay, since Christ's faith did not save Him from dismay in Gethsemane. We are not necessarily doubting that God will do the best for us: we are wondering how painful the best will turn out to be. In a case like the one you refer to, where the growth is detected in its primary state and in the most operable part, there are of course solid grounds for an entirely optimistic view. But then *one* of your fears and her's, is of all the fears you *will* have to suffer before you are out of the wood. The monotony of anxiety—the circular movement of the mind—is horrible. As far as possible I think it is best to treat one's own anxiety as being also an illness. I wish I could help. Can I? You did so much for me.

As to the 'frightening monotony' I think this disease now ranks as a *plague* and we live in a plague-striken population.

God bless you both. I shall have no need to 'remind' myself to remember you. Let us have news as soon as there is any.

If you find (some do) that mental anguish produces an inclination to eat more—paradoxical but it can—I should jolly well do so.

TO DOM BEDE GRIFFITHS, O.S.B.: from Magdalene College

30 April 1959

First, in answer to your question. My wife has continuously gone on from strength to strength. Except that one leg will always be shorter than the other so that she walks with a stick and a limp, she now leads a normal, and active, life. My own bone-trouble, tho' not completely cured, is so much better as to be now merely a trivial inconvenience.

Thanks for *Christ and India*. It confirms what I had, less clearly, thought already—that the difficulty of preaching Christ in India is that there is no difficulty. One is up against true Paganism—the best sort of it as well as the worst—hospitable to all gods, naturally 'religious', ready to take any shape but able to retain none. Δεισιδαιμονία [fear of the gods] is harder to convert than materialism as a fog is harder to remove than a tree.

About the Semitic genius, my wife, who is a Jewess by blood, holds two views which wd interest you.

1. That the only living Judaism is Christianity. Where her own people still have any religion it is archaic, pedantic, and—so to speak—sectarian, so that being a devout Jew is rather like being a Plymouth Brother.

2. That we Goyim misread much of the O.T. because we start with the assumption that its sacred character excludes *humour*. That no one who knew the Jewish *ethos* from inside could fail to see the fully accepted comic element in Abraham's dialogue with God (Genesis XVIII) or in *Jonah*.

While we are on exegesis, am I right in thinking that the key to the parable of the Unjust Steward is to grasp that the Master in it is *The World*? (= this Aion). The dismissal is the notice—apparently now being served on you and long since served on me—that our present tabernacle will soon be taken down. The moral is 'Cheat your master'. If he gives us wealth, talent, beauty, power etc. use them for your own (eternal) purposes—spoil the Egyptian! If you can't do that with his kind of property, who will trust you with the true kind? Of course ὁ κύριοσ who praised the Steward is not the Master *in* the parable but Our Lord, the Master who is telling the story. And telling it not without paradoxical humour.

It would be very nice to meet when you are in Europe, if this should be at all possible.

The man (Peter Bide) who laid his hands on my wife and she recovered, writes to me that his own wife is now struck down with the same disease. Would you mention him in your prayers?

TO PROFESSOR CLYDE S. KILBY: **from Magdalene College** (Professor Kilby says of the following letter, 'Written after I had sent him a copy of the Wheaton College statement concerning inspiration of the Bible and asked for his opinion'.)

7 May 1959

I enclose what, at such short notice, I feel able to say on this question. If it is at all likely to upset anyone, throw it in the waste paper basket. Remember too that it is pretty tentative, much less an attempt to establish a view than a statement of the issue on which, whether rightly or wrongly, I have come to work. To me the curious thing is that neither in my own Bible-reading nor in my religious life as a whole does the question *in fact* ever assume that importance which it always gets in theological controversy. The difference between reading the story of Ruth and that of Antigone — both first class as literature — is to me unmistakable and even overwhelming. But the question 'Is Ruth historical?' (I've no reason to suppose it is *not*) doesn't really seem to arise till afterwards. It can still act on me as the Word of God if it weren't, so far as I can see. All Holy Scripture is written for our learning. But learning *of what*? I should have thought the value of some things (e.g. The Resurrection) depended on whether they really happened, but the value of others (e.g. the fate of Lot's wife) hardly at all. And the ones whose historicity matters are, as God's will, those where it is plain . . .

Whatever view we hold on the divine authority of Scripture must make room for the following facts.

1. The distinction which St Paul makes in I Cor vii between οὐκ ἐγὼ ἀλλ ὁ Κύριοσ (v. 10) and ἐγὼ λέγω, οὐΧ ὁ Κύριοσ (v. 12).[187]

2. The apparent inconsistencies between the genealogies in Matt i and Luke iii: with the accounts of the death of Judas in Matt xxvii 5 and Acts i. 18–19.

3. St Luke's own account of how he obtained his matter (i. 1–4).

4. The universally admitted unhistoricity (I do not say, of course, falsity) of at least some narratives in Scripture (the parables), which may well extend also to Jonah and Job.

5. If every good and perfect gift comes from the Father of Lights then all true and edifying writings, whether in Scripture or not, must be *in some sense* inspired.

6. John xi. 49–52. Inspiration may operate in a wicked man without his knowing it, and he can then utter the untruth he intends (propriety of making an innocent man a political scapegoat) *as well as* the truth he does not intend (the divine sacrifice).

It seems to me that 2 and 4 rule out the view that every statement in Scripture must be *historical* truth. And 1, 3, 5, and 6 rule out the view that inspiration is a single thing in the sense that, if present at all, it is always present in the same mode and the same degree. Therefore, I think, rules out the view that any one passage taken in isolation can be assumed to be inerrant in exactly the same sense as any other: e.g. that the numbers of O.T. Armies (which in view of the size of the country, if true, involve continu-

---

[187] 'Not I, but the Lord' (v. 10); 'I speak, not the Lord' (v. 12).

ous miracle) are statistically correct because the story of the Resurrection is historically correct. That the over-all operation of Scripture is to convey God's Word to the reader (he also needs his inspiration) who reads it in the right spirit, I fully believe. That it *also* gives true answers to all the questions (often religiously irrelevant) which he might ask, I don't. The very *kind* of truth we are often demanding was, in my opinion, not even envisaged by the ancients.

TO CHARLES MOORMAN: **from Magdalene College** (who was writing *Arthurian Triptych: Mythic Materials in Charles Williams, C. S. Lewis, and T. S. Eliot* [1960])

15 May 1959

I don't think your project at all 'presumptuous', but I do think you may be chasing after a fox that isn't there. Charles Williams certainly influenced me and I perhaps influenced him. But after that I think you would draw a blank. No one ever influenced Tolkien—you might as well try to influence a bandersnatch. We listened to his work, but could affect it only by encouragement. He has only two reactions to criticism: either he begins the whole work over again from the beginning or else takes no notice at all. Dorothy Sayers was not living in Oxford at the time and I don't think she ever in her life met Tolkien. She knew Charles Williams well, and me much later. I am sure she neither exerted nor underwent any literary influence at all. Of course it may be that, just because I was in it myself, I don't see (objectively) what was really going on. But I give my honest impression for what it is worth.

To be sure, we had a common point of view, but we had it before we met. It was the cause rather than the result of our friendship.

I hope I don't seem to be 'putting you off'. My real anxiety is lest you shd waste time on what might prove a barren field.

TO KATHLEEN RAINE (Mrs Madge): **from The Kilns**

19 June 1959

One must (and will) write poetry if one can. That one must therefore return to the place where the Muse once appeared, as if she were bound to appear there again, is quite a different proposition. The gods will not be met by appointment. They never give us their addresses. And tho' the Faculty has not been able to give you what you, reasonably, want, it does not follow that they don't want you. At any rate *postpone.* There will never be a time when you can't leave Cambridge: there could easily be one when you couldn't return.

TO 'MRS ARNOLD': **from The Kilns**

8 September 1959

No one, I presume, can imagine life in the glorified body. On this, and on the distinction (in general) between belief and imagination, I have said all I can in *Miracles.* Lor' bless us, I can picture very few of the things I believe in. I can't picture will, thought, time, atoms, astronomical distance,

New York, nor even (at this moment) my mother's face.

Your whole worry about the word *Christian* comes from ignoring the fact that words have different meanings in different contexts. The best parallel is the word *poet*. We can argue till the cows come home whether 'Pope is a poet'. On the other hand a librarian, putting 'poets' in one shelf and prose in another, after a single glance at one page of Pope, classifies him as a 'poet'.

In other words, the word has a deep, ambiguous, disputable and (for many purposes) useless sense: also a shallower, clear, useful sense. In the second sense it seems to be more useful not to classify Quakers as Christians. But this is a linguistic, not a religious question . . .

TO ROGER LANCELYN GREEN: from Magdalene College

25 November 1959

In a sense it might be said that Joy 'is' not ill at present. But the last X-ray check revealed that the cancer in the bones is awake again. This last check is the only one we approached without dread—her health seemed so complete. It is like being recaptured by the giant when you have passed every gate and are almost out of sight of his castle. Whether a second miracle will be vouchsafed us, or, if not, when the sentence will be inflicted, remains uncertain. It is quite possible she may be able to do the Greek trip next spring. Pray for us . . .

TO SIR HENRY WILLINK: **from Magdalene College**
(Sir Henry, the Master of Magdalene College, had just lost his wife.)

3 December 1959

I have learned now that while those who speak about one's miseries usually hurt one, those who keep silence hurt more. They help to increase the sense of *general* isolation which makes a sort of fringe to the sorrow itself. You know what cogent reason I have to feel *with* you: but I can feel *for* you too. I know that what you are facing must be worse than what I must shortly face myself, because your happiness has lasted so much longer and is therefore so much more inter-twined with your whole life. As Scott said in like case 'What am I to do with that daily portion of my thoughts which has for so many years been hers?'

People talk as if grief were just a feeling—as if it weren't the continually renewed shock of setting out again and again on familiar roads and being brought up short by the grim frontier post that now blocks them. I, to be sure, believe there is something beyond it: but the moment one tries to use that as a consolation (that is not its function) the belief crumbles. It is quite useless knocking at the door of Heaven for earthly comfort: it's not the sort of comfort they supply there.

You are probably very exhausted physically. Hug that and all the little indulgences to which it entitles you. I think it is tiny little things which (next to the very greatest things) help most at such a time.

I have myself twice known, after a loss, a strange excited (but utterly un-spooky) sense of the person's presence all about me. It may be a pure hallucination. But the fact that it always goes off after a few weeks proves nothing either way.

I wish I had known your wife better. But she has a bright place in my memory. It was so reassuring to the Oxford deserter to meet someone from L.[ady] M.[argaret] H.[all] and be able to talk about 'the Hippo'.[188] She will be very greatly missed—on her own account, quite apart from any sympathy with you—by every fellow of this College.

And poor Horace[189] too—'the single talent well employed'. I shall not be at the funeral. You can understand and forgive my desire, now, to spend every possible moment at home. Forgive me if I have said anything amiss in this letter. I am too much involved myself to practise any skill.

TO DR ALASTAIR FOWLER: from Magdalene College
10 December 1959

Thanks greatly. The Spenser article confirms the impression increasingly made on me while writing lectures on F.Q. last term: that of its amazing close-wovenness.[190] Damme, you can't pick up a line anywhere but it starts another line wriggling ten cantos away . . .

Sorry my OHEL is such a nuisance.[191] I only once detected a pupil offering me some one else (Elton) as his own work. I told

---

[188] Miss Lynda Greer.

[189] A kitchen porter in Magdalene.

[190] Dr Fowler, who was the Fellow of English at Brasenose College, Oxford, at this time, has edited Jack's lecture-notes on *The Faerie Queene* under the title *Spenser's Images of Life* (1967).

[191] His *English Literature in the Sixteenth Century* had become one of the critical works, along with those of Edward Dowden and Churton Collins, from which some of Dr Fowler's pupils were plagiarising.

him I was not a detective nor even a schoolmaster, nor a nurse, and that I absolutely refused to take any precaution against this puerile trick: that I'd as soon think it my business to see that he washed behind his ears or wiped his bottom . . . He went down of his own accord the next week and I never saw him again. I think you ought to make a general announcement of that sort. You must not waste your time constantly reading me and Dowden and Churton Collins as a sort of police measure. It is bad for them to think this is 'up to you'. Flay them alive if you *happen* to detect them: but don't let them feel that you are a safeguard against the effects of their own idleness.

What staggers me is how any man can prefer the galley-slave labour of transcription to the freeman's work of attempting an essay on his own . . .

TO A SCHOOLGIRL IN AMERICA: **from The Kilns**
(She had written, at her teacher's suggestion, to request advice on writing.)

14 December 1959

(1) Turn off the Radio.

(2) Read all the good books you can, and avoid nearly all magazines.

(3) Always write (and read) with the ear, not the eye. You shd hear every sentence you write as if it was being read aloud or spoken. If it does not sound nice, try again.

(4) Write about what really interests you, whether it is real things or imaginary things, and nothing else. (Notice this means that if you are interested *only* in writing you will never be a writer, because you will have nothing to write about . . .)

(5) Take great pains to be *clear*. Remember that though you start by knowing what you mean, the reader doesn't, and a single ill-chosen word may lead him to a total misunderstanding. In a story it is terribly easy just to forget that you have not told the reader something that he needs to know—the whole picture is so clear in your own mind that you forget that it isn't the same in his.

(6) When you give up a bit of work don't (unless it is hopelessly bad) throw it away. Put it in a drawer. It may come in useful later. Much of my best work, or what I think my best, is the rewriting of things begun and abandoned years earlier.

(7) Don't use a typewriter. The noise will destroy your sense of rhythm, which still needs years of training.

(8) Be sure you know the meaning (or meanings) of every word you use.

TO SOPHIA STORR (a schoolgirl): **from The Kilns**
24 December 1959

No, of course it was not unconscious. So far as I can remember it was not at first intentional either. That is, when I started *The Lion, Witch and Wardrobe* I don't think I foresaw what Aslan was going to do and suffer. I think He just insisted on behaving in His own way. This of course I did understand and the whole series became Christian.

But it is not, as some people think, an *allegory*. That is, I don't say 'Let us represent Christ as Aslan'. I say, 'Supposing there was a world like Narnia, and supposing, like ours, it needed redemption, let us imagine what sort of Incarnation and Passion and Resurrection Christ would have there.' See?

I think this is pretty obvious if you take all the seven Narnian books as a whole. In *The Magician's Nephew* Aslan creates Narnia. In *Prince Caspian* the old stories about Him are beginning to be disbelieved. At the end of the *Dawn Treader* He appears as the Lamb. His three replies to Shasta suggest the Trinity. In *The Silver Chair* the old king is raised from the dead by a drop of Aslan's blood. Finally in the *Last Battle* we have the reign of anti-Christ (the ape), the end of the world, and the Last Judgement.

TO FATHER PETER MILWARD: **from The Kilns**

Christmas Day 1959

I hope my last letter to you did not sound chilling: still less (heaven help us!) as if I were offended by criticism. I think the chief reason why I am less disposed than you for large-scale discussion by letter is the difference of our ages. In youth we conduct (at least I did) long and deep disputations through the post. It is indeed a most valuable part of our education. We put into it quite as much thought and labour as wd go to writing a book. But later, when one has become a writer of books, it is hard to keep it up. One can't fill one's leisure with the v. same activity which is one's main work. And in my case not only the mind but the *hand* needs rest. Penmanship is increasingly laborious, and the results (as you see) increasingly illegible!

If you sometimes read into my books what I did not know I had put there, neither of us need be surprised, for greater readers have doubtless done the same to far greater authors. Shakespeare wd, I suspect, read with astonishment what Goethe, Coleridge, Bradley and Wilson Knight have found in him! Perhaps a book *ought* to have more meanings than the writer intends? But then the writer will not necessarily be the best person with whom to discuss them.

You are in my daily prayers. Will you pray much for me at present? The cancer from which my wife was (as I believe, miraculously) delivered 2½ years ago, when death in a few weeks was predicted, is returning. Can one without presumption ever ask for a *second* miracle? The prophet turned back the shadow for Hezekiah once: not twice. Lazarus, raised from the dead, presently died again.

TO MRS VERA GEBBERT: from The Kilns

17 January 1960

The ghastly daily grind of unavoidable letters leaves me a hand very ill disposed to pleasanter and friendlier correspondence. It is now 9.50 A.M. and I've already been writing letters as hard as I can drive the pen across the paper for an hour and a half: and when on earth I shall get a chance to begin my own work I don't know . . . I quite realise that it wd be difficult to emulate H. B. Stowe, writing in the kitchen. But—we know what the books were like—do we know what the cooking was like? . . . I am pretty well, though always very tired.

[Joy had all her life wanted to see Greece. Before the return of her old enemy, cancer, Roger and June Lancelyn Green—who had been there on a 'Wings' tour in April 1959—offered to make arrangements for a similar visit in April 1960. The Lewises were delighted with the idea, and in September 1959 Jack told their friends which days in April would be best for them. Even the pains and the various complications of Joy's illness did not deter them. Jack and Joy were in Greece with the Lancelyn Greens during 2–14 April 1960. Roger Lancelyn Green kept a diary of their travels through Greece and it can be found in his and my *C. S. Lewis: A Biography* (1974).]

TO CHAD WALSH (who had known Jack and Joy since the late 1940s): **from The Kilns**

23 May 1960

It looked very doubtful if Joy and I would be able to do our trip to Greece, but we did. From one point of view it was madness, but neither of us regrets it. She performed prodigies of strength, limping to the top of the Acropolis and up through the Lion gate of Mycenae and all about the medieval city of Rhodes. (Rhodes is simply the Earthly Paradise.) It was as if she were divinely supported. She came back in a *nunc dimittis* frame of mind, having realised, beyond hope, her greatest, lifelong, this-worldly, desire.

There was a heavy price to pay in increased lameness and legpains: not that her exertions had or could have any effect on the course of the cancers, but that the muscles etc had been overtaxed. Since then there has been a recrudescence of the original growth in the right breast which started the whole trouble. It had to be removed last Friday—or, as she characteristically put it, she was 'made an Amazon'. This operation went through, thank God, with greater ease than we had dared to hope. By the evening of the same day she was free from all severe pain and from nausea, and cheerfully talkative. Yesterday she was able to sit up in a chair for fifteen minutes or so.

Love and greetings to you all, in which Warnie (who is fine) joins me. Thank you for your prayers.

I had some ado to prevent Joy (and myself) from relapsing into Paganism in Attica! At Daphne it was hard not to pray to Apollo the Healer. But somehow one didn't feel it wd have been very wrong—wd have only been addressing Christ *sub specie Apollinis.* We witnessed a beautiful Christian village ceremony in Rhodes and hardly felt a discrepancy. Greek priests impress one very favourable at sight—much more so than most Protestant or R.C. clergy. And the peasants all *refuse* tips.

TO DELMAR BANNER: from Magdalene College

27 May 1960

Thanks. I'm glad you liked the book [*The Four Loves*].

I quite agree with you about Homosexuals: to make the thing criminal cures nothing and only creates a blackmailer's paradise. Anyway, what business is it of the State's? But I couldn't well have had a digression on that.[192] One is fighting on two fronts. *a. For* the persecuted Homo. against snoopers and busybodies. *b.* For ordinary people *against* the widespread freemasonry of the highbrow Homos who dominate so much of the world of criticism, and won't be v. nice to you unless you are in their set . . .

---

[192] He means he couldn't have had a digression on State interference in *The Four Loves* (1960).

[Samuel Pepys had been a member of Magdalene College and his diary is the property of Magdalene. At this time the College was trying to reach a decision as to whether or not to publish the Diary in its unexpurgated entirety.]

TO SIR HENRY WILLINK: from The Kilns

17 June 1960

Francis[193] flatters me with the idea that, if there is a division as to printing those 'curious' passages in our new Pepys, my opinion might be asked for. Since I can't be sure of coming to the next meeting of the Governing Body, I have decided to let you have it in writing.

A prudential and moral problem are both involved.

The prudential one is concerned (a) with the chances of a prosecution, and (b) with the chances of disrepute and ridicule. On (a) it would be ridiculous for me to express an opinion in your presence and Mickey's.[194] As to (b), a spiteful or merely jocular journalist would certainly make us for a week or two malodorous in the public nostril. But a few weeks, or years, are nothing in the life of the College. I think it would be pusillanimous and unscholarly to delete a syllable on that score.

The moral problem comes down to the question 'Is it probable that the inclusion of these passages will lead anyone to commit an immoral act which he would not have committed if we had suppressed them?' Now of course this question

---

[193] Francis McD. C. Turner was a Fellow of Magdalene at the time.
[194] R. W. M. Dias, also a Fellow of Magdalene, was a University Lecturer in Law.

is strictly unanswerable. No one can foresee the odd results that any words may have on this or that individual. We ourselves, in youth, have been both corrupted and edified by books in which our elders could have foreseen neither edification nor corruption. But to suggest that in a society where the most potent aphrodisiacs are daily put forward by the advertisers, the newspapers, and the films, any perceptible increment of lechery will be caused by printing a few obscure and widely separated passages in a very long and expensive book, seems to me ridiculous, or even hypocritical.

A very severe moralist might argue that it is not enough to be unable to foresee harm: that we ought, before we act, to be able to foresee with certainty the absence of harm. But this, as you see, would prove too much. It is really an argument against doing, or not doing, any action whatever. For they all go on having consequences, mostly unforeseeable, to the world's end.

I am therefore in favour of printing the whole unexpurgated Pepys.

TO MRS VERA GEBBERT: from The Kilns

15 July 1960

Alas, you will never send anything along 'for the three of us' again, for my dear Joy is dead. Until within ten days of the end we hoped, although noticing her increasing weakness, that she was going to hold her own, but it was not to be.

Last week she had been complaining of muscular pains in her shoulders, but by Monday 11th seemed much better, and on Tuesday, though keeping her bed, said she felt a great improvement: on that day she was in good spirits, did her 'crossword puzzle' with me, and in the evening played a game of Scrabble. At quarter past six on Wednesday morning [13 July] my brother, who slept over her, was wakened by her screaming and ran down to her. I got the doctor, who fortunately was at home, and he arrived before seven and gave her a heavy shot. At half past one I took her into hospital in an ambulance. She was conscious for the short remainder of her life, and in very little pain thanks to drugs: and died peacefully in my company about 10.15 the same night . . .

You will understand that I have no heart to write more, but I hope that when next I send a letter it will be a less depressing one.

TO MRS VERA GEBBERT: from The Kilns

5 August 1960

I believe in the resurrection . . . but the state of the dead *till* the resurrection is unimaginable. Are they in the same *time* that we live in at all? And if not, is there any sense in asking where they are 'now'? . . .

Perhaps being maddeningly busy is the best thing for me. Anyway I am. This is one of those things which makes the tragedies of real life so *very* unlike those of the stage.

TO HERR KUNZ (in Germany): from The Kilns

16 August 1960

My *Out of the Silent Planet* has no factual basis and is a critique of our own age only as any Christian work is implicitly a critique of any age. I was trying to redeem for genuinely imaginative purposes the form popularly known in this country as 'science-fiction'—I think you call it 'future-romanz'; just as (*si parva licet componere magnis*)[195] *Hamlet* redeemed the popular revenge play.

TO MRS ANNE SCOTT: **from The Kilns**

26 August 1960

Thank you very much for your most kind and encouraging letter. You gave me great pleasure by what you said about *Till We Have Faces,* for that book, which I consider far and away the best I have written, has been my one big failure both with the critics and with the public.

My small stepson entirely agrees with your children about the present wicked misdirection of my talents, and asks 'When are you going to stop writing all this bilge and write interesting books again?'

Cookery books are not such bad reading. Have you Mrs Beeton with the original preface? It is delicious.

TO ARTHUR GREEVES: **from The Kilns**

30 August 1960

It is nice to hear from you. It might have been worse. Joy got away easier than many who die of cancer. There were a couple of hours of atrocious pain on her last morning, but the rest of the day mostly asleep, tho' rational whenever she

---

[195] 'to compare small things with great'.

was conscious. Two of her last remarks were 'You have made me happy' and 'I am at peace with God'. She died at 10 that evening. I'd seen violent death but never seen natural death before. There's really nothing to it, is there? One thing I'm very glad about is that in the Easter Vac she realised her life long dream of seeing Greece. We had a wonderful time there. And many happy moments even after that. The night before she died we had a long, quiet, nourishing, and tranquil talk.

W. is away on his Irish holiday and has, as usual, drunk himself into hospital. Douglas—the younger boy—is, as always, an absolute brick, and a very bright spot in my life. I'm quite well myself. In fact, by judicious diet and exercise, I've brought myself down from thirteen stone to just under eleven.

TO ROGER LANCELYN GREEN: **from The Kilns** (The Lancelyn Greens had invited Jack to their home, 'Poulton Hall', in Cheshire for a holiday.)

15 September 1960

Oh Hell! What a trial I am to you both! If Warnie really came home on the 23rd—and if he did not come home so drunk as to have to be put straight into a nursing home—I could and wd with delight come to you on the 24th. But neither is really at all probable. And of course I can't leave this house with no grown-up in charge. What it comes to is that you must count me out. I am *very* sorry. *Don't* make any further efforts to accommodate such an entangled man as me—it wd only for me add to the loss of a great pleasure the embarrassment of knowing I was a nuisance.

Have you seen Allan Garner's *The Wierdstone of Brisingamen*? Not bad, tho' too indebted to Tolkien. He seems to be a fairly near neighbour of yours—Aldersley, Cheshire.

Thanks, evermore thanks, and love.

TO FATHER PETER MILWARD: **from The Kilns**

26 September 1960

First, about the Grail. I think it important to keep on remembering that a question can be v. interesting without being answerable and one of my main efforts as a teacher has been to train people to say those (apparently difficult) words 'We don't know'.

We haven't even got anything that can be quite accurately called '*the* Grail legend'. We have a number of romances which introduce the Grail and are not consistent with one another. No theory as to the ultimate origin is more than speculative. The desire to make that origin either Pagan or (less commonly) heretical is clearly widespread, but I think it springs from psychological causes not from any evidence.

I do not myself doubt that it represents in a general way an imaginative and literary response to the doctrine of Transubstantiation and the visible act of the elevation. But we must be on our guard against abstraction. A story does *not* grow like a tree nor breed other stories as a mouse begets other mice. Each story is told by an individual, voluntarily, with an unique artistic purpose. Hence the real germination goes on where historical, theological, or anthropological studies can never reach it—in the mind of some man of genius, like Chretien or Wolfram. Those who have written stories themselves will come nearer to understanding it than those who have 'studied the Grail legend' all these lives.

The whole (unconscious) effort of the orthodox scholars is to remove the individual author and individual romance and substitute the picture of something diffusing itself like an infectious disease or a fashion in clothes. Hence the (really senseless) question 'What is the Grail?' The Grail is in each romance just what that romance exhibits it to be. There is no 'Grail' over and above these 'Grails'. Hence, again, the assumption that the mystery in each romance could be cleared up if we knew more about the Celtic Caldron of Plenty or the Cathari or what you will. It never occurs to the scholars that this mysteriousness may be a calculated and wholly effective literary technique.

I am entirely on the side of your Society [of Jesus] for shutting de Chardin up. The enormous boosts he is getting from scientists who are very hostile to you seem to me v. like the immense popularity of Pasternak among anti-Communists. I can't for the life of me see his merit. The cause of Man against men never needed championing *less* than now. There seems to me a dangerous (but also commonplace) tendency to Monism or even Pantheism in his thoughts. And what in Heaven's name is the sense of saying that before there was life there was 'pre-life'. If you choose to say that before you switched on the light in the cellar there was 'pre-light', of course you may. But the ordinary English word for 'pre-light' is darkness. What do you gain by such nick-names?

TO MRS VERA GEBBERT: from The Kilns

16 October 1960

I wasn't at all questioning the life after death you know: only saying that its character is for us unimaginable. The things you tell me about it are all outside my powers of conception. To say, 'They are now as they were then' and add next moment, 'unhampered of course by the body' is to me like saying, 'They are exactly the same but of course unimaginably different'. But don't let us trouble one another about it. We shall know when we are dead ourselves. The Bible seems scrupulously to avoid any *description* of the other world, or worlds, except in terms of parable or allegory . . .

TO 'MRS ARNOLD': from Magdalene College

February 1961

There are, as you know, two schools of Existentialism, one anti-religious and one religious. I know the anti-religious school only through one work—Sartre's *L'Existentialisme est un Humanisme.* I learned from it one important thing— that Sartre is an artist in French prose, has a sort of wintry grandeur which partly explains his immense influence. I couldn't see that he was a real philosopher: but he is a great rhetorician.

The religious school I know only from having heard a lecture by Gabriel Marcel and reading (in English) Martin Buber's *I and Thou.* They both say almost exactly the same thing, though I believe they reached their common position quite independently. (As a man Marcel was a perfect old dear.) And what they are saying is impressive—as a mood, an *aperçue,* a subject for a poem. But I didn't feel that it really worked out as a philosophy.

I had been classifying Tillich more as an interpreter of the Bible than as a philosopher. I dare say you are right in thinking that for some people at some moments what I call semi-Christianity may be useful. After all, the road into the city and the road out of it are usually the same road: it depends on which direction one travels in.

At the back of religious Existentialism lies Kierkegaard. They all revere him as their pioneer. Have you read him? I haven't or hardly at all.

TO DR ALASTAIR FOWLER: from Magdalene College
4 May 1961

You talk of Evolution as if it were a substance (like individual organisms) and even a rational substance or person. I had thought it was an abstract noun. So far as I know it is not impossible that in addition to God and the individual organisms there might be a sort of *daemon,* a created spirit, in the evolutionary process. But that view must surely be argued on its own merits? I mean we mustn't unconsciously and without evidence, slip into the habit of hypostatising a noun . . .

TO MRS MARGARET GRAY: from Magdalene College
9 May 1961

How right you are when you say 'Christianity is a terrible thing for a lifelong atheist to have to face'! In people like us — adult converts in the 20th century — I take this feeling to be a good symptom. By the way, you have had in most respects a tougher life than I, but there's one thing I envy you. I lost my wife last summer after a very late, very short, and intensely happy married life, but I have not been vouchsafed (and why the deuce shd I be?) a visit like yours—or certainly not except for one split second. Now about reading.

For a good ('popular') defence of our position against modern woffle, to fall back on, I know nothing better than G. K. Chesterton's *The Everlasting Man*. Harder reading, but very protective, is Edwyn Bevan's *Symbolism & Belief*. Charles Williams' *He Came Down from Heaven* doesn't suit everyone, but try it.

For meditative and devotional reading (a little bit at a time, more like sucking a lozenge than eating a slice of bread) I suggest *The Imitation of Christ* (astringent) and Traherne's *Centuries of Meditations* (joyous). Also my selection from MacDonald, *Geo MacDonald: An Anthology*. I can't read Kierkegaard myself, but some people find him helpful.

For Christian morals I suggest my wife's (Joy David-man) *Smoke on the Mountain*: Gore's *The Sermon on the Mount* and (perhaps) his *Philosophy of the Good Life*. And possibly (but with a grain of salt, for he is too puritanical) Wm Law's *Serious Call to a Devout and Holy Life*. I know the v. title makes one shudder, but we have both got a lot of shuddering to get through before we're done!

You'll want a mouth-wash for the *imagination*. I'm told that Mauriac's novels (all excellently translated, if your French is rusty) are good, tho' very severe. Dorothy Sayers' *Man Born to be King* (those broadcast plays) certainly is. So, to me, but not to everyone, are Charles Williams's fantastic novels. *Pilgrim's Progress,* if you ignore some straw-splitting dialogues on Calvinist theology and concentrate on the story, is first class.

St Augustine's *Confessions* will give you the record of an earlier adult convert, with many v. great devotional passages intermixed.

Do you read poetry? George Herbert at his best is extremely nutritious.

I don't mention the Bible because I take that for granted. A modern translation is for most purposes far more useful than [the] Authorized Version.

As regards my own books, you might (or might not) care for *Transposition, The Great Divorce,* or *The Four Loves.*

Yes—'being done good to'—grrr! I never asked even to *be.*

TO FATHER PETER MILWARD: from Magdalene College

23 May 1961

I saw nothing rude in your manner, tho' I thought you were misunderstanding me. I, you see, come to the matter from fighting on another front, against Atheists who say (I have seen it in print) 'Christians believe in a God who committed adultery with a carpenter's wife'. You used language which cd have been interpreted as an agreement with *them.* Naturally there is no disagreement between us on that point. And I wd agree that the supernatural begetting of Our Lord is the archtype, and human marriage the ectype: not the *perversion* (that wd seem to me Manichaean). All these agreements are perfectly consistent with a disagreement between us on the Immaculate Conception of Mary and your general Marian theology.

Of course when one has decided that A is the Archtype and B the ectype one has not said A = B: i.e. whichever way you work it, it remains true that Mary was not the Bride of the Holy Ghost in *the same sense* in which the words are used of ordinary marriages: whereas she was the Mother of Jesus in exactly the same sense in wh. my mother was my mother—as Gervase Mathew said.[196]

TO ROGER LANCELYN GREEN: from The Kilns

6 September 1961

It's a bit tricky. I am awaiting an operation on my prostate: but as this trouble upset my kidneys and my heart, these have to be set right before the surgeon can get to work. Meanwhile, I live on a no-protein diet, wear a catheter, sleep in a chair, and have to stay on the ground floor. I'm quite capable of having a guest, but the problem is that the date for the operation remains unfixed—it depends on how the weekly blood-tests go. This means that, for all I know, it might come just when you want to be here so I think you'd better make alternative arrangements, wh. cd be abandoned in favour of coming to The Kilns if, when the time comes, I shd be here and not in

---

[196] Father Gervase Mathew (1905–76), who was educated at Balliol College, joined the order of Dominicans in 1928 and was ordained in 1934. Most of his life was spent at Blackfriars in Oxford where he lectured for the Modern History, Theology and English Faculties. He was a member of The Inklings and such a lovable man that it is impossible to believe that anyone could have ever disliked him.

the Acland. I'd hate to miss the chance of a visit from you if it turns out to be feasible. Is this all too bothersome?

You needn't pity me too much. I am in no pain and I quite enjoy the hours of uninterrupted reading which I now get.

[Jack had neglected his own health for a long time, and now he was seriously ill. He was unable to go to Cambridge during the Michaelmas Term of 1961 and Hilary Term of 1962. However, before he returned to take up his duties at Cambridge in April 1962, he read a good deal and wrote *The Discarded Image*.]

TO 'MRS ARNOLD': from The Kilns

28 October 1961

I'm not well enough to answer your letter properly ... The nearest I can put up as a Scriptural warrant for prayers for the dead is the place in one of the Epistles about people being 'baptized for the dead'. If we can be baptised for them, then surely we can pray for them? I'd like to give you the reference, but my Concordance is upstairs and—my heart being one of the things that is wrong with me—I'm not allowed to go upstairs.

TO DOM BEDE GRIFFITHS, O.S.B.: from The Kilns

3 December 1961

Thank you for your letter of the 27 Nov. Your hand, though not yet nearly so bad as mine, deteriorates: but the bits I could read were very interesting. The difficulty about

Hinduism, and indeed about all the higher Paganisms, seems to me to be our double task of reconciling and converting. The activities are almost opposites, yet must go hand in hand. We have to hurl down false gods and also elicit the peculiar truth preserved in the worship of each. I had just heard of Vinota: but what is an *ashram* or *astram*? Like the man in *The Hunting of the Snark* you 'wholly forget that English is what I speak'!

Try to time your next letter so that it does not arrive near Christmas. Every year the merciless spate of correspondence makes this season more pestilential and less festal for me.

I forget whether you know that my wife died in July. Pray for us both. I am learning a great deal. Grief is not, as I thought, a state but a process: like a walk in a winding valley which gives you a new landscape every few miles.

All blessings. I am tired, and slightly ill, at the moment, or I wd answer your letter more as it deserves.

TO DOM BEDE GRIFFITHS, O.S.B.: from The Kilns
20 December 1961

To lose one's wife after a very short married life may, I suspect, be less miserable than after a long one. You see, I had not grown *accustomed* to happiness. It was all a 'treat'. I was like a child at a party. But perhaps earthly happiness, even of the most innocent sort, is I suspect, addictive. The whole being gets geared to it. The withdrawal must be more like lacking bread than lacking cake . . .

About Nature—you are apparently meeting, at an unusually late hour, the difficulty which I met in adolescence and which was for years my stock argument against Theism. Romantic Pantheism has in this matter led us all up the garden path. It has taught us to regard Nature as divine. But she is a creature, and surely a creature lower than ourselves. And a fallen creature—not an evil creature but a good creature corrupted, retaining many beauties but all tainted . . . The Devil cd *make* nothing but has *infected* everything. I have always gone as near Dualism as Christianity allows—and the N.T. allows one to go v. near. The Devil is the (usurping) lord of this age. It was he, not God, who 'bound this daughter of Abraham'.

Even more disturbing, as you say, is the ghastly record of Christian persecution. It had begun in Our Lord's time— 'Ye know not what spirit ye are of' (John of all people!). I think we must fully face the fact that when Christianity does not make a man v. much better, it makes him v. much worse. It is, paradoxically, dangerous to draw nearer to God. Doesn't one find in one's own experience, that every advance (if one ever has advanced) in the spiritual life opens to one the possibility of blacker sins as well as brighter virtues? Conversion may make of one who was, if no better, no worse than an animal, something like a devil. Satan was an *angel*. I wonder have any of us taken seriously enough the prohibition of casting pearls before swine? This is the point of Our Lord's remarks after the parable of the Unjust Steward. We are denied many graces that we ask for because they would be our ruin. If we can't be trusted even with the perishable wealth of this world, who will trust us with the real wealth? (The 'Lord' in this parable is of course not God but the world.) . . .

I am rather seriously ill. Prostate trouble, by the time it was diagnosed, had already damaged my kidneys, blood, and heart, so that I'm now in a vicious circle. They can't operate until my bio-chemistry gets right and it looks as if that can't get right until they operate. I am in some danger — not sentenced but on trial for my life. I know I shall have your prayers. My temptation is not to impatience. Rather, I am far too inclined to snuggle down in the enforced idleness and other privileges of an invalid.

Have you read anything by an American Trappist called Thomas Merton? I'm at present on his *No Man Is an Island*. It is the best new spiritual reading I've met for a long time.

TO 'MRS ARNOLD' (further to the letter of 28 October): **from The Kilns**

28 December 1961

I've found the passage—I Cor. XV. 29. Also I Pet. III.19–21 bears indirectly on the subject. It implies that something can be done for the dead. If so, why should we not pray for them?

Beware of the argument, 'the Church gave the Bible and therefore the Bible can never give us grounds for criticising the Church'. It is perfectly possible to accept B on the authority of A and yet regard B as a higher authority than A. It happens when I recommend a book to a pupil. I first send him to the book, but having gone to it he knows (for *I've* told him) that the author knows more about the subject than I.

TO THE REVD DR AUSTIN FARRER: from **The Kilns**

29 December 1961

I've read your book [*Love Almighty and Ills Unlimited*] with great enjoyment. You once said that you wrote with difficulty, but no one would guess it: this is full of felicities that sound as unsought as wildflowers . . .

Of course admiration is not always agreement. I stick at the diagnosis, 'Emotional reaction rather than rational conviction' . . . How do people decide what is an emotion and what is a value judgement? Not presumably just by introspection wh. will certainly be hard put to it to find a value judgement chemically pure from emotion . . . I find however that the problem of animal pain is just as tough when I concentrate on creatures I dislike as on ones I cd make pets of. Conversely, if I removed all emotion from, say my view of Hitler's treatment of Jews, I don't know how much value judgement would remain. I loathe hens. But my conscience would say the same things if I forgot to feed them as if I forgot to feed the cat . . .

TO WAYNE SCHUMAKER: from **The Kilns**

21 March 1962

Thanks for the article on *Paradise Lost*. I think I agree with all you say, especially your distinction between what is common to all the myths and what is peculiar to *Paradise Lost*. Possibly that kind of distinction should be pressed even further. Thus the child is not like the savage *simpliciter* but like a savage in close contact with and subject to civilisation: controlled, protected, corrupted and elevated by it at every turn. Again, does not a myth built into a systematic and *fully* believed theology differ, by that very fact, from a myth told by primitive man (usually in explanation of a ritual)? For I doubt whether primitives stand to their myths in a relation of full credal affirmation such as one finds in Christianity and Islam. All this had happened to the Fall story long before Milton. Indeed M's great success lies in practising the credal affirmation without losing the *quality* of myth. M *does* lose this (for me) in Books XI and XII, I'm afraid.

[Jack and T. S. Eliot had become good friends after they began meeting in 1959 as members of the 'Commission to Revise the Psalter'. The first part of the Psalter was published in 1961 and the complete work, *The Revised Psalter,* was published in 1963. Jack had also been consulted about points of translation of the New Testament section of *The New English Bible.*]

TO T. S. ELIOT: from Magdalene College

25 May 1962

You need not sympathise too much: if my condition keeps me from doing some things I like, it also excuses me from doing a good many things I don't. There are two sides to everything!

We must have a talk—I wish you'd write an essay on it—about Punishment. The modern view, by excluding the retributive element and concentrating solely on deterrence and cure, is hideously immoral. It is vile tyranny to submit a man to compulsory 'cure' or sacrifice him to the deterrence of others, unless he *deserves* it. On the other view what is there to prevent any of us being handed over to Butler's 'Straighteners' at any moment?

I'd have to know more about the Greek of that period to make a real criticism of the N.E.B. (N.T. which is the only part I've seen). Odd, the way the less the Bible is read the more it is translated.

TO JAMES E. HIGGINS: from The Kilns

31 July 1962

I shall be glad to help if I can. It is however rather a big IF, for my knowledge of children's literature is really very limited. The real expert is Roger L. Green, Poulton-Lancelyn, Bebington, Wirral, Cheshire. My own range is about exhausted by MacDonald, Tolkien, E. Nesbit, and Kenneth Grahame. The *Alice* books are, aren't they, in a totally different category, the effect being exclusively comic-nonsensical: not, in my experience, fully appreciated by children. Oh by the way, don't miss the utterly unexpected influence of Rabelais on Kingsley's *Water Babies*.

TO DOM BEDE GRIFFITHS, O.S.B.: from The Kilns

4 August 1962

By being an invalid I meant that even if the operation comes off and delivers me from the catheter and the low protein diet, I shall have to be careful about my heart—no more bathing or real walks, and as few stairs as possible. A very mild fate: especially since nature seems to remove the desire for exercise when the power declines.

Syriac too? I envy you the wide linguistic conquests you have made, though I hardly share one of the purposes for which you use it. I cannot take an interest in liturgiology. I see very well that some ought to feel it. If religion includes cult and if cult requires order it is somebody's business to be concerned with it. But not, I feel, mine! Indeed, for the laity I sometimes wonder if an interest in liturgiology is not rather a snare. Some people talk as if it were itself the Christian faith.

I am deeply interested by what emerged from that Hindu-Christian debate, but not surprised. I always thought the real difference was the rival conceptions of God. A ticklish question. For I suppose we, by affirming three Persons, implicitly say that God is not *a* Person.

I am delighted to hear that there is some chance of seeing you in England again.

TO CHRISTOPHER DERRICK: from The Kilns

10 August 1962

Yes, I jolly well have read Gombrich and give him alpha with as many plusses as you please. The writers on art have hopelessly outstripped the writers on literature in our period. Seznec, Wind, and Gombrich are a very big three indeed. I am much better: still dieted and—well, plumbered, but otherwise almost normal.

TO HENRY NOEL: **from Magdalene College** (with
reference to a theme central to *The Great Divorce*)

14 November 1962

About all I know of the 'Refrigerium' is derived from Jeremy
Taylor's sermon on 'Christ's advent to judgement' and the
quotations there given from a Roman missal printed at Paris
in 1626, and from Prudentius. See Taylor's *Whole Works,*
edit. R. Heber, London 1822, Vol. V, p. 45.

The Prudentius says, 'Often below the Styx holidays from
their punishments are kept, even by the guilty spirits . . .
Hell grows feeble with mitigated torments and the shadowy
nation, free from fires, exults in the leisure of its prison; the
rivers cease to burn with their usual sulphur'.

TO 'MRS ARNOLD': **from Magdalene College**

21 November 1962

I think I share to excess your feelings about a move. By
nature I demand from the arrangements of this world just
that permanence which God has expressly refused to give
them. It is not merely the nuisance and expense of any big
change in one's way of life that I dread, it is also the psychological uprooting and the feeling—to me or to you intensely
unwelcome—of having ended a chapter. One more portion
of oneself slipping away into the past. I would like everything
to be immemorial—to have the same old horizons, the same
garden, the same smells and sounds, always there, changeless. The old wine is to me always better. That is, I desire the
'abiding city' where I well know it is not and ought not to
be found. I suppose all these changes should prepare us for

the greater change which has drawn nearer even since I began this letter. We must 'sit light' not only to life itself but to all its phases. The useless word is 'encore'.

TO JAMES E. HIGGINS: **from The Kilns**

2 December 1962

. . . (5) I turned to fairy tales because that seemed the form which certain ideas and images in my mind seemed to demand: as a man might turn to fugues because the musical phrases in his head seemed to him to be 'good fugal subjects'.

(6) When I wrote *The Lion* I had no notion of writing the others.

(7) Writing 'juveniles' certainly modified my habits of composition. Thus (a) It imposed a strict limit on vocabulary. (b) Excluded erotic love. (c) Cut down reflective and analytical passages. (d) Led me to produce chapters of nearly equal length for convenience in reading aloud.

All these restrictions did me great good—like writing in a strict metre.

TO ARTHUR GREEVES: **from The Kilns**

3 March 1963

On July 28 W., Douglas, and I will be at the Glenmachan Towers Hotel [Belfast], and on the 29th W. will go to Eire. Can Doug and you and I go off somewhere for a week or two beginning on that date? If you don't feel up to driving us to wherever we go, I'll hire a car & driver for the journey. Wd Castlerock or Glens of Antrim be any good? Portrush only as a last resource. But we want to be pretty quick about booking three rooms (it *must* be three) and about berths for Doug & me on our return journey to England.

I saw snowdrops for the first time last week.

[As far back as 1952 Jack had started writing a book on prayer. Not much was written because it was not turning out well. It was probably during this time, while planning a holiday in Ireland, that the idea of an imaginary correspondence about prayer occurred to him. Despite the difficulty of penmanship, he thoroughly enjoyed writing *Letters to Malcolm: Chiefly on Prayer*, which was completed in May of this year. After having a typed copy sent to his publisher, Jocelyn Gibb, he was asked to write a blurb for the book. While the actual books came easily to Jack, he disliked composing what he called 'blurbology'.]

TO JOCELYN GIBB: from The Kilns

28 June 1963

I've thought and thought about the blurb but find I just can't write it—apparently I can hardly write the word either! I'd like you to make the point that the reader is merely being allowed to listen to two v. ordinary laymen discussing the practical & speculative problems of prayer as these appear to them: i.e. the author does *not* claim to be teaching.

Will it be good to say 'Some passages are controversial but this is almost an accident. The wayfaring Christian cannot quite ignore recent Anglican theology when it has been built as a barricade across the high road.'

I wouldn't stress your point about my not having given tongue v. recently. It can't *feel* like that to the public. They must get the impression that I bring out a book once a fortnight. And your denial, however true in fact, will, like the sculptor's fig-leaf, only draw attention to what it wd fain conceal.

I enclose a new passage for the last letter. This will make that letter unusually long but that's legitimate as a finale. Anyway, I like the new bit.

[The 'new bit' in the final chapter of *Letters to Malcolm* comes directly after the paragraph which ends 'There is our freedom, our chance for a little generosity, a little sportsmanship', and is a hauntingly beautiful passage about the resurrection of the body.

It is a fine thing to have on one's mind when death is made unavoidably clear. When Jack went to the Acland Nursing Home on 15 July for a blood-transfusion he had a heart attack and went into a coma. He surprised everyone by waking from it the next day—asking for his tea. By 9 August he was well enough to go home, and a few days later he resigned his Chair and Fellowship at Cambridge.]

TO SISTER PENELOPE, C.S.M.V.: **from The Kilns**

17 September 1963

What a pleasant change to get a letter which does *not* say the conventional things! I was unexpectedly revived from a long coma—and perhaps the almost continuous prayers of my friends did it—but it would have been a luxuriously easy passage and one almost (but *nella sua voluntade e nostra pace*)[197] regrets having the door shut in one's face. Ought we to honour Lazarus rather than Stephen as the protomartyr? To be brought back and have all one's dying to do *again* was rather hard.

If you die first, and if 'prison visiting' is allowed, come down and look me up in Purgatory.

It *is* all rather fun—solemn fun—isn't it?

TO THE MASTER AND FELLOWS OF MAGDALENE COLLEGE (who had elected Jack an Honorary Fellow of the College): from The Kilns

25 October 1963

The ghosts of the wicked old women in Pope 'haunt the places where their honour died'. I am more fortunate, for I shall haunt the place whence the most valued of my honours came.

I am constantly with you in imagination. If in some twilit hour anyone sees a bald and bulky spectre in the Combination Room or the garden, don't get Simon to exorcise it, for it is a harmless wraith and means nothing but good.

If I loved you all less I should think much of being thus placed ('so were I equall'd with them in renown') beside Kipling and Eliot. But the closer and more domestic bond with Magdalene makes that side of it seem unimportant.

---

[197] 'In His will is our peace.'

TO MISS JANE DOUGLASS: from **The Kilns**

31 September 1963

Thanks for your kind note. Yes, autumn is really the best of the seasons: and I'm not sure that old age isn't the best part of life. But of course, like Autumn, it doesn't *last*.

My brother's Autumn lasted, like the year's, a few weeks longer; and on that note very characteristic of his last days—peaceful acceptance, combined with enduring grief for 'mutabilitie'—I end my selection from his correspondence. —W.H.L.

INDEX